The Historic Landscape of the Mendip Hills

The Historic Landscape
of the Mendip Hills

by Elaine Jamieson

with contributions by Barry Jones,
Graham Brown, Olivia Horsfall Turner and Gary Winter

Published by Historic England, The Engine House, Fire Fly Avenue, Swindon SN2 2EH
www.HistoricEngland.org.uk

Historic England is a Government service championing England's heritage and giving expert,
constructive advice, and the English Heritage Trust is a charity caring for the National Heritage
Collection of more than 400 historic properties and their collections.

First published 2015

ISBN 978 1 84802 042 9

British Library Cataloguing in Publication data
A CIP catalogue record for this book is available from the British Library.

For more information about images from the Archive, contact Archives Services Team,
Historic England, The Engine House, Fire Fly Avenue, Swindon SN2 2EH; telephone (01793) 414600.

Brought to publication by Jess Ward, Publishing, Historic England.

Typeset in Charter 9.5/11.75 and 9.5/12.75

Edited by Merle Read
Proof read by Kim Bishop
Indexed by Ann Hudson
Page layout by Andrea Rollinson, Ledgard Jepson Ltd
Printed in Belgium by DeckersSnoeck.

Front cover: Looking north-west along the Ashen Hill barrow cemetery, Priddy. (DP158755)

*Back cover: Stream Farm and traditional farm buildings in the Old Ditch area of Westbury-sub-Mendip.
(DP069259)*

*Frontispiece: The spectacular chasm of Cheddar Gorge slices through the southern Mendip escarpment.
(NMR 24323/45)*

CONTENTS

FOREWORD

Areas of Outstanding Natural Beauty are amongst the most distinctive and best loved landscapes in the country, regarded by government as equalling National Parks in their importance.

English Heritage, and now Historic England, has a long-standing Historic Environment Accord with the National Association of AONBs which has promoted new archaeological and architectural research in many of these protected landscapes, notably the Malvern Hills, the Quantock Hills and the North Pennines. This research is aimed at providing information and analysis that will assist with the protection and management of the historic environment, as well as promoting public enjoyment of the heritage in these special places. In 2006 English Heritage embarked on a programme of archaeological and architectural survey and investigation on the Mendip Hills, an area renowned for its magnificent geological formations – caves, swallets, gorges and high plateau. Though designated for its *natural* beauty, it is our understanding of the human element – the relationship of people with the natural landscape over several millennia – which has given this area its individual character and special qualities.

Mendip is fortunate in having a thriving body of independent archaeological organisations and other devoted historians, following a tradition that goes back to the 18th century, through generations of cave explorers, to the present day. This is reflected in the existence of an active AONB Heritage Group. English Heritage was able to benefit from and work with these knowledgeable Mendip researchers and in return staff gave talks, led guided walks and ran training courses. The aims and progress of this project were warmly supported throughout by Somerset County Council and by the Mendip Hills AONB Unit. The co-operation with the AONB, has extended to this publication, which has been aided by a substantial grant from them. Historic England is delighted to acknowledge this assistance. We share a common desire to make the exciting discoveries and enhanced understanding gained through this project available in an attractive and informative manner to local communities, academic researchers and to the many visitors to Mendip.

By bringing together the wealth of new architectural and archaeo-logical survey and research undertaken by English Heritage, and synthesising existing knowledge, this book explores the archaeology and architecture of this remarkable region, from some of the earliest cave deposits in Britain, through well preserved later prehistoric and Roman earthworks, to the more subtle but nonetheless intriguing remains of medieval and post-medieval settlement and agriculture. The present work is notable for the full integration of archaeological and architectural research, making for a particularly rich account of the medieval and post-medieval periods. It would be true to say that some of the most exciting and surprising discoveries have come about as the result of research into the historic buildings of Mendip, many of which are considerably older and more interesting when examined in detail than they appear superficially. The findings of this book, and the associated archive of survey plans, reports, photographs and monument records, will provide an invaluable resource to inform the future management of the historic environment, ensuring the special qualities of this valued and unique place will be protected for years to come.

Sir Laurie Magnus
Chairman
Historic England

ACKNOWLEDGEMENTS

The fieldwork was carried out by staff from the Exeter and Swindon offices of English Heritage. Archaeological survey work was undertaken by Elaine Jamieson and Graham Brown, with contributions from Mark Bowden, David Field, Michael Fradley, Marcus Jecock, Abby Hunt, Trevor Pearson and Sharon Soutar. Thanks are due also to Phil Newman and Hazel Riley for sharing their knowledge and experience of field archaeology in south-west England. Architectural fieldwork was undertaken by Barry Jones with contributions from Allan Brodie, Nigel Fradgley, Lucy Jessop, Olivia Horsfall Turner, Rebecca Lane and Gary Winter. A large number of students and volunteers also contributed their time to the fieldwork, for which we are very grateful.

Professional ground photography was carried out by Peter Williams, James O Davies and Mike Hesketh-Roberts. Aerial photography was undertaken by Damien Grady; Kryshia Truscoe, Russell Priest and Amanda Dickson carried out the air photographic transcription. Illustrations were prepared by Deborah Cunliffe, Nigel Fradgley, Elaine Jamieson, Phil Sinton and Sharon Soutar, with reconstruction drawings produced by Allan Adams, Judith Dobie and Peter Dunn.

Mark Bowden, David Field, Rebecca Lane, Jim Leary and Rob Wilson-North all kindly commented on the draft text. Hazel Riley read the text for English Heritage. Peter Marshall advised on scientific dating and provided material for the publication. Special thanks must also go to Graham Brown for sharing his thoughts, ideas and comments, and for being a constant source of help and encouragement throughout the project.

A great number of libraries, record offices and museums were consulted during this project, and the authors would like to thank staff at the Somerset Historic Environment Record, the Somerset Studies Library, the Somerset Archives and Records Service, the Bristol Records Office, the British Library and the Historic England Archive, in particular the Historic England Library. Thanks are also given to the Wells and Mendip Museum, the University of Bristol Spelæological Society Museum and the Cheddar Museum for permission to photograph artefacts from their collections. The Somerset Museum, the Ashmolean Museum, Bristol Museum and Art Gallery, the British Museum, the Natural History Museum, the University of Bath and the Victoria Art Gallery all kindly provided photographs for inclusion in the publication.

The authors would like to give a special thanks to Sarah Jackson and staff from the AONB Service for their help and support during the project. Thanks also to Robert Croft of Somerset County Council and Vince Russett of North Somerset District Council. Many groups and individuals were generous with their time and information. Special mention must go to David Hart, Barry Lane, Pip Nabb-Osborne, Ron Penn, Lesley Ross, Albert Thompson and Steve Tofts. Thanks also to members of the Westbury Historical Society, the Blagdon Local History Society, the Charterhouse Environs Research Team and the Harptree Historical Society. The project team would like to give special thanks to Holly Nowell and all the staff at Beryl who provided a warm and comfortable haven during fieldwork.

English Heritage would also like to express thanks to all the landowners and homeowners who generously allowed access to sites and buildings, often providing invaluable information, and without whose help this project would not have been possible.

SUMMARY

The Mendip Hills, which lie to the south of Bristol, are largely formed by a gently undulating Carboniferous Limestone plateau which rises abruptly from the northern edge of the Somerset Levels and Moors. Older Devonian rocks punch through the limestone to form the highest points of the uplands and rise to more than 320m above sea level. The small irregular fields which characterise the lower escarpment slopes give way to an ordered geometric grid of stone-walled enclosures on the plateau, with grass and heather moors capping the highest hills. The spectacular cliffs of Cheddar Gorge which slice through the southern escarpment form one of the finest limestone karst features in the country and support a diverse range of insect and plant species. The unique and special qualities of the Mendip Hills landscape were recognised in 1972 when the region was designated an Area of Outstanding Natural Beauty (AONB).

There is a long and vibrant tradition of archaeological enquiry on Mendip. This ranges from antiquarian investigation undertaken in the 18th and 19th centuries to the work of independent groups and professionals in more recent years. This book presents the results of a recent interdisciplinary landscape project carried out by staff from English Heritage. The work was aimed at providing a better understanding of the historic landscape of the Mendip Hills AONB, from first exploitation by early humans through to the end of the Cold War. This targeted research included a programme of air photographic transcription, architectural survey and investigation, and detailed archaeological fieldwork focused primarily on earthwork survey. The interpretation and presentation of the project work has been greatly enhanced by a programme of ground and air photography and by new illustrative material, which includes a number of reconstruction drawings. The book attempts to set this latest research within a framework of existing knowledge, with the ideas put forward hopefully stimulating further study and informing management and conservation initiatives across the Hills. The results of this work are presented in chronological order, with the first chapter introducing the landscape and summarising a history of past research. A gazetteer lists the principal sites considered during the study, and a glossary explains the specialist terms used throughout the text.

The Mendip Hills have been fashioned over millennia and reflect episodes of past human intervention. The earliest evidence for this can be found in the region's caves, rock shelters and swallets, with these distinctive natural features proving a powerful draw to groups over long periods of time. The earliest humanly constructed monuments in the landscape are the long barrows, which were followed in the later Neolithic by the henge monuments and which represent the ceremonial structures of communities who have left little trace of settlement. Large numbers of Early Bronze Age round barrows occur across the region, crowning the hills, ridges and valley heads, and display complex phases of construction and elaboration. By the later Bronze Age permanent fields and settlement sites had developed, although the original extent of these is as yet unknown. The field systems and linear boundaries of this period were reused and adapted into the Iron Age, a phenomenon identified through detailed survey and investigation during the project of the hillforts and smaller earthwork enclosures of the region.

Many later prehistoric settlement sites continued in use into the Romano-British period. New settlement forms also developed in an era which saw the region experience an intensification of agricultural and industrial exploitation, which included the development of villa estates. In the mid-1st century AD the Roman military constructed a small fort at Charterhouse-on-Mendip, and the lead resources of the uplands were placed under Roman imperial control. The fate of the region's economy on the collapse of the Roman administration in the early 5th century is somewhat unclear, but the evidence points towards an episode of steep decline. By the later 5th and 6th centuries burial remains indicate a degree of continuity between the post-Roman population and their ancestral past. The end of the 7th century saw Somerset in the hands of the West Saxon kings who created royal and ecclesiastical centres around the foot of the Mendip escarpment.

The relative lack of evidence on Mendip for everyday life in the early medieval period is in contrast to the wealth of sites and historical information for the time after the Norman Conquest. Detailed surveys of abandoned farmsteads, shrunken settlements and relict field systems, considered in conjunction with evidence from upstanding buildings and documentary sources, have helped bring the medieval landscape more sharply into view. This was not a static place, but one which developed through time, adapting to the social, environmental and economic changes of the day. This story of adaptation and change continues into the post-medieval period, when agricultural improvements saw the remaining medieval open fields swept away and the expansive sheep walks of the uplands finally enclosed. This is also a time of transformation in the region's buildings, though one which was often firmly rooted in the past. The mineral resources of the area continued to be exploited throughout the post-medieval period, with the last lead mine closing in the early 20th century. The rural and relatively isolated nature of the Mendip landscape made it an ideal location to site a network of military installations. Survivals of these include the remains of an elaborate landscape of decoys designed to confuse and deceive enemy bombers during the Second World War, and a network of underground monitoring posts which remained in operation throughout the Cold War.

The variety of extant archaeological sites, buildings and landscapes on Mendip has enabled the construction of a complex narrative dominated by a story of adaptation and transformation. The conservation and management approaches adopted over the coming decades, informed by improved understanding, will influence how this unique and special place develops in the future, and how it will be viewed and appreciated in the years to come.

ABBREVIATIONS

AONB Area of Outstanding Natural Beauty
BL   British Library
BRO   Bristol Record Office
DHC   Devon Heritage Centre
HEA   Historic England Archive
IHR   Institute of Historical Research
NMR   National Monuments Record
NRHE National Record of the Historic Environment
SHER Somerset Historic Environment Record
SHS   Somerset Heritage Service
TNA   The National Archives
UBSS University of Bristol Spelæological Society

The Mendip Hills landscape

The natural environment

Approached from the south, the Mendip Hills rise sharply from the Somerset Levels and Moors, with the view dominated by the distinctive silhouette of Crook Peak and the 'stupendous chasm' of Cheddar Gorge (Rutter 1829, 185); *see* Figure 1.1. The natural beauty of the Mendip Hills has long been celebrated, with its most famous landmarks attracting artists, scientists, philosophers and travellers alike. The 17th-century Danish scientist and diarist Oluf Borch described the cave at Wookey Hole as 'awe-inspiring' (Shaw 1987, 65–71), with Celia Fiennes commenting that the rocks of the cavern 'shine like diamonds' (Morris 1947, 240–1). During the 18th and 19th centuries visitors were drawn to Mendip in search of the picturesque, the sublime and the romantic. George Lambert's painting *The Entrance to Cheddar Cliffs* (1755) is credited as one of the first paintings to give the English landscape a dramatic quality equal to the famous views of Italy. During their short stay on the Quantock Hills, the poets Coleridge and Wordsworth also travelled to Cheddar in search of inspiration. Their friend the Revd Richard Warner wrote of Cheddar Gorge: 'The vast abruption yawns from the summit down to the roots of the mountain, laying open to the sun a sublime and tremendous scene – precipices, rocks, and caverns, of terrifying descent, fantastic forms, and gloomy vacuity' (Woof 2002, 298–9).

Location and topography

The Mendip Hills lie to the south of Bristol, along the northern edge of the Somerset Levels and Moors (Fig 1.2). The central feature of the Mendip Hills is the gently undulating Carboniferous Limestone plateau, created

Fig 1.1
Cheddar Gorge, Somerset, by William Widgery (c 1860). (Reproduced by permission of the Victoria Art Gallery)

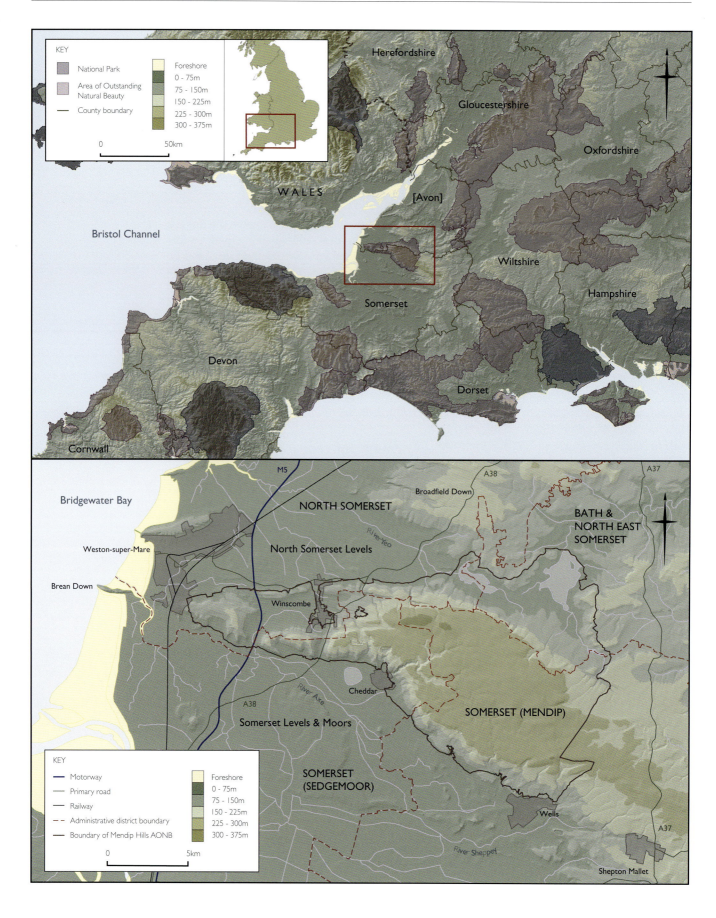

when the earth's surface was lifted, folded and eroded some 300 million years ago. Devonian rocks punch through the limestone to form the highest points of the uplands – Pen Hill, North Hill, Eaker Hill and Black Down – with the dark mass of Black Down rising to 320m above sea level. Two periclinal folds run westwards from the plateau and are cut by a number of steep-sided valleys, dividing each into a series of undulating hilltops. The northern limb between Banwell and Dolebury Warren comprises a narrow broken ridge which dips as it runs westwards. The highest point on the southern ridge is the distinctive Crook Peak, which rises to just over 185m, overshadowing the open grassland of Wavering Down and Axbridge Hill to the east. Opposing this oolitic limestone crag is the slightly lower Loxton Hill, which forms the highest point on the gently undulating western range, with the limestone ridge narrowing along Bleadon Hill towards Brean Down.

Between these two rock limbs flows the Lox-Yeo river, which turns south to join the meandering River Axe as it flows westwards to the sea (Fig 1.3). The River Axe drains much of central Mendip, including most of the caves in the Priddy area, with the river rising from the foot of the escarpment at Wookey Hole. The Cheddar Yeo also flows into the Axe Valley, rising on the Lower Limestone Shales flanking Black Down and bubbling up from beneath the ground at Cheddar. At the eastern end of the region St Andrew's Stream starts its journey at the St Andrew's Risings, a group of springs which emerge from the Triassic rocks at Wells and are fed by stream sinks on Beacon Hill. The source of the River Chew rises at Chew Head before embarking on a sinuous course northwards, filling the Chew Valley Lake reservoir and joining the River Avon at Keynsham. The Chew is fed by a number of springs and fast-flowing streams, such as the Sherbourne Spring and the Molly Brook, which start their life on the northern slopes of Mendip. The River Yeo rises at Compton Martin, with tributary streams feeding the watercourse via a network of drainage channels as it flows westwards across the North Somerset Levels. The canalised course of the River Banwell also crosses the low-lying levels, with both rivers entering the sea at Woodspring Bay.

The high plateau displays the classic features of a karst landscape, including

Fig 1.2 (opposite)
Mendip Hills AONB: location map.

Fig 1.3
Mendip Hills AONB: topography and relief.

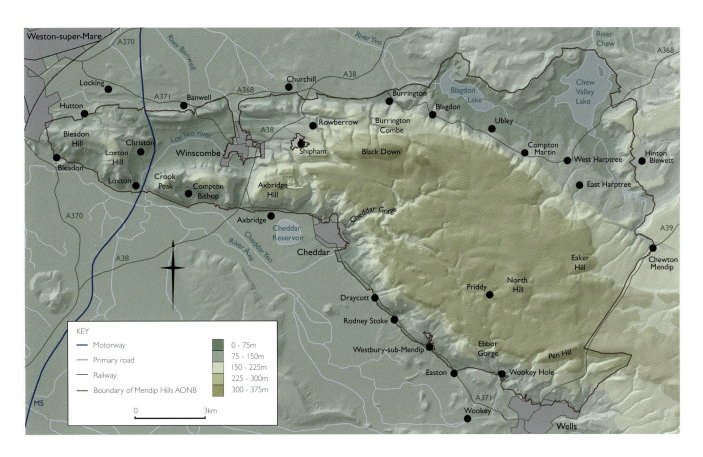

3

complex underground cave and river systems, gorges, dry valleys, swallets and fast-flowing springs. Cheddar Gorge is perhaps the finest and best-known limestone karst feature in Britain, with its dramatic cliffs supporting a diverse range of insect and plant species. Beyond its celebrated landmarks the Mendip Hills is a region of great diversity, ranging from the grass and heather moors of Burrington Ham and Black Down to the steep wooded valleys of Harptree Combe and Long Wood. The lower escarpment slopes are dominated by a patchwork of small irregular fields, mixed with a series of spring-line settlements, and connected by a network of winding roads and tracks. In contrast the uplands are largely divided by an ordered grid of geometric fields, punctuated by a scattering of small settlements and farmsteads, and interspersed with the remains of past industry. The modest landscape parks above Wells are afforded impressive views down over the cathedral city and across the Somerset Levels and Moors to Glastonbury Tor, with the Blackdown Hills and the Polden Hills beyond. Along the northern escarpment the farms and villages look out across the wide river valleys of the Yeo and the Chew towards the table-like hilltop of Broadfield Down.

The unique and special qualities of the Mendip Hills were officially recognised in 1972 when they were designated an Area of Outstanding Natural Beauty (Fig 1.4). The AONB includes the western and central region of the Mendip range, and stretches for some 27km from Bleadon in the west to Chewton Mendip in the east. The protected area covers 198sq km, of which nearly two-thirds lies within the county of Somerset, the remainder being divided between the districts of North Somerset and Bath and North East Somerset. The southern boundary of the AONB largely follows the foot of the limestone escarpment, skirting around the main areas of settlement. Along the northern escarpment the boundary again hugs the lower escarpment slopes, only deviating northwards to include the reservoirs of Blagdon and the Chew Valley Lake. Within the AONB lie many Sites of Special Scientific Interest (SSSIs) and two National Nature Reserves (NNRs), the latter lying along the southern escarpment at Ebbor Gorge and Rodney Stoke. The area contains varied and important natural habitats including limestone grassland, heather moor, ancient woodland and gorge cliffs.

Geology, soils and vegetation

The broader character of the countryside is inextricably linked to the rocks beneath. Geological formations, laid down over millions of years, represent a record of climatic change, tectonic movement and the development of life itself. The type of underlying rock dictates the form and consistence of the soils which cover them, influencing whether cattle and sheep can graze or if cereal crops can be grown. Geology can determine where springs rise and watercourses flow, shaping settlement patterns and land use. It also influences the character of vernacular architecture: when local stone is used, buildings become truly part of the landscape – hewn from it – giving the impression they sit comfortably in their own place. This is perhaps more noticeable in our modern age of stripped stone walls, as most buildings on Mendip were probably rendered or limewashed in years gone by. The lime used, however, would have been won locally from the Carboniferous Limestone beds, its colour giving the buildings of the region a more uniform appearance but one still firmly rooted in the landscape.

Fig 1.4
Fingerpost, Priddy, indicating some of the components which make Mendip a special and unique place. (DP100285)

Geology

The most ancient rocks that make up the Mendip Hills range are the tuff and volcanic conglomerates of the Silurian period, which outcrop in the extreme south-east of the region. However, in western Mendip, our area of study, the Devonian Old Red Sandstone represents the oldest geological formation, laid down some 420 to 360 million years ago (Fig 1.5). As the name suggests, these rocks are a dull purplish-red colour reflecting their origins in an arid climate. They are sedimentary rocks, formed through the accumulation of debris over long periods of time. In the Mendip area these ancient sediments were laid down by rivers, before being buried and hardened into rock. The Old Red Sandstones of the Mendip Hills – the Portishead Formation of the Late Devonian period – are largely confined to the highest hills: Black Down, Pen Hill, North Hill and Eaker Hill. A finger of Devonian sandstone

Fig 1.5
Geological map of the Mendip Hills.
(CP15/036 British Geological Survey © NERC. All rights reserved.)

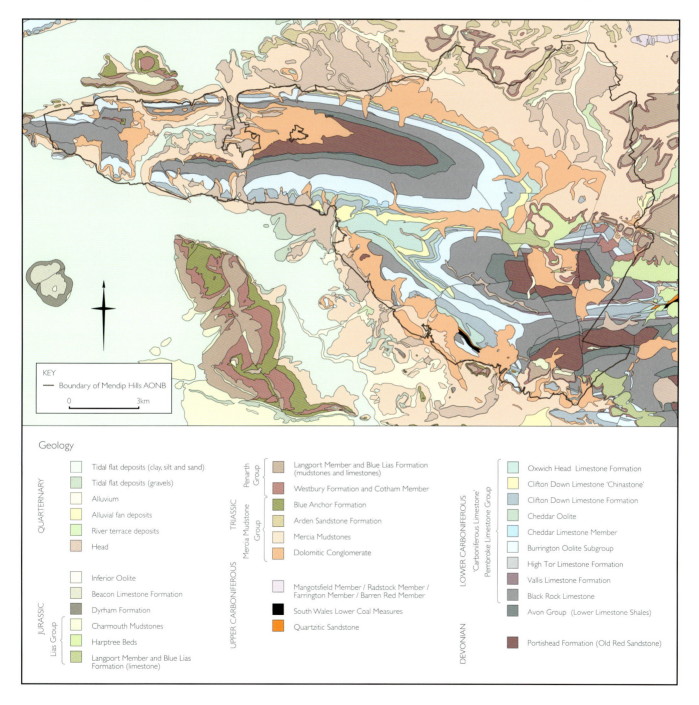

KEY

—— Boundary of Mendip Hills AONB

0   3km

Geology

QUATERNARY
- Tidal flat deposits (clay, silt and sand)
- Tidal flat deposits (gravels)
- Alluvium
- Alluvial fan deposits
- River terrace deposits
- Head

JURASSIC
- Inferior Oolite
- Beacon Limestone Formation
- Dyrham Formation

Lias Group
- Charmouth Mudstones
- Harptree Beds
- Langport Member and Blue Lias Formation (limestone)

TRIASSIC

Penarth Group
- Langport Member and Blue Lias Formation (mudstones and limestones)
- Westbury Formation and Cotham Member

Mercia Mudstone Group
- Blue Anchor Formation
- Arden Sandstone Formation
- Mercia Mudstones
- Dolomitic Conglomerate

UPPER CARBONIFEROUS
- Mangotsfield Member / Radstock Member / Farrington Member / Barren Red Member
- South Wales Lower Coal Measures
- Quartzitic Sandstone

LOWER CARBONIFEROUS

'Carboniferous Limestone' Pembroke Limestone Group
- Oxwich Head Limestone Formation
- Clifton Down Limestone 'Chinastone'
- Clifton Down Limestone Formation
- Cheddar Oolite
- Cheddar Limestone Member
- Burrington Oolite Subgroup
- High Tor Limestone Formation
- Vallis Limestone Formation
- Black Rock Limestone
- Avon Group (Lower Limestone Shales)

DEVONIAN
- Portishead Formation (Old Red Sandstone)

and conglomerate also runs westwards from Black Down, underlying Cuck Hill and Winterhead Hill, before disappearing and then reappearing in a narrow band above Winscombe Orchard.

About 360 million years ago the sea returned to Britain. The rocks that resulted from this marine transgression – known as the Carboniferous Limestone – cover more of the British Isles than any other. This formation records a time when the British Isles gloried in reefs grown under tropical sun and clear seas. Only the Carboniferous Limestone areas in Britain contain extensive cave systems, produced through the action of erosion. Water containing a weak solution of carbonic acid filters downwards through gaps in the rock, dissolving and widening the cracks until galleries of twisting fissures form. The water which rises from beneath the ground at Wookey Hole, for example, originates in upland streams, percolating down through underground passages to emerge from the ground at the foot of the hills. It is this action, undertaken over many millions of years, which has created the spectacular landscape (both above and below ground) that has drawn visitors to Mendip for centuries.

Carboniferous Limestone is the hardest of the limestone formations and makes up the bulk of the Mendip Hills range. The geological landscape we see today is largely the result of a major episode of earth movement known as the Variscan orogeny, which occurred towards the end of the Carboniferous period. The entire area was uplifted, folded and eroded, which produced a series of elongated ridges and troughs running predominantly from east to west. The oldest of the Carboniferous rocks, the Avon Group (Lower Limestone Shale), flank the Old Red Sandstone, the latter pushed upwards during the Variscan movement. The slightly curving east–west bands of limestone beds commence with the Black Rock Limestone, which ranges from dark grey to almost black in colour; the lower, more gently undulating hills of Bleadon, Loxton and Christon are dominated by this rock formation. At the top of the Black Rock Limestone a thin band of dolomitic limestone was laid down and has been mapped running westwards from Dolebury Camp, and between Wavering Down and Shiplate Slait. Next in the sequence are the grey to pale-grey limestone layers which include Burrington Oolite, Clifton Down Limestone and Cheddar Oolite (Fig 1.6). Perhaps the most recognisable example of Burrington Oolite is the 'Rock of Ages' in Burrington Combe, where Augustus Montague Toplady is reputed to have written his famous hymn while sheltering from a storm (Fig 1.7).

The final limestone formation is the Oxwich Head Limestone, which marks a stage in the area's history when the sea was reduced to tidal depth. This formation is at its most extensive on the southern side of Cheddar Gorge and stretches in a narrow band across to Ebbor Rocks. A thin intermittent band of Oxwich Head Limestone also runs along the northern escarpment, underlying Pitcher's Enclosure and Compton Wood, extending as far as the northern slopes of Dolebury Warren. The Carboniferous Limestone beds of Mendip have been quarried for centuries, with the rock extracted for use as building stone, agricultural lime and aggregate for construction projects. The growth of the aggregate industry in the post-war period has created a landscape inhabited by large quarries, their dramatic stepped appearance now competing for attention with the region's natural wonders (Fig 1.8).

Fig 1.6
Bands of Carboniferous Limestone visible in Burrington Combe. (DP163833)

Although the name 'Carboniferous' implies that the rocks of this period should contain carbon or coal, the limestone itself does not. It is the Coal Measures that follow in the geological sequence that represent the source of coal – the carbon produced from trees and other plants which grew in a vast tropical delta around 300 million years ago. These beds are predominantly confined to the north-east of the Mendip range, and were extensively worked around Radstock in the North Somerset Coalfield.

The Permian and Triassic periods saw a return to arid conditions, with the weather quickly removing the cover of Upper Carboniferous sediments from the freshly uplifted hills. Rainwater run-off caused flash floods and violent erosion to carry scree and limestone boulders down the slopes, the material spreading out like aprons around the foot of the uplands. This rock formation – the Dolomitic Conglomerate – is at its thickest where it banks up against the Carboniferous beds along the lower escarpment slopes, but also outcrops on the uplands in a band from Lower Wood across to Yoxter and Haydon Grange; it underlies the area around Rowberrow, Shipham and Sidcot, and exists in pockets to the north and east of Stockhill.

The Mercia Mudstone Group (Keuper Marls) dominates the lower slopes and main river valleys, comprising thick deposits of red-brown siltstones and mudstones. These sedimentary rocks have long been known as the 'New Red Sandstone' and were laid down some 250 to 200 million years ago. Towards the top of this

Fig 1.7
The 'Rock of Ages': a crag of Burrington Oolite located in Burrington Combe.
(DP163851)

Fig 1.8
Battscombe Quarry. Its dramatic stepped appearance now competes for attention alongside Cheddar Gorge.
(NMR 24323/43)

group are the Tea Green Marl and Grey Marl of the Blue Anchor Formation, which consist of green, greenish-grey and dark-grey siltstones and mudstones; these are largely confined to the Banwell and Wattles Hill areas. Overlying this is the Penarth Group, which includes the Westbury Formation and the Langport Member. In the Mendip region these Late Triassic rocks are found alongside the Blue Anchor beds, as well as in narrow bands above Wells, Chewton Mendip and East Harptree; on the plateau small pockets outcrop in the area surrounding Wigmoor Farm.

Marine conditions once more returned to the Mendip region in the Jurassic period (200–145 million years ago), submerging the hills beneath a shallow sea. The earliest part of this sequence, the Lias Group, mainly consists of clays and limestones and is relatively poorly represented on Mendip. There are Blue Lias outcrops on the northern side of the Hills, around Banwell and Bleadon Hill, where shallow water conditions prevailed until late Lower Lias times. It is also present in small pockets above Wells and on the plateau around the Castle of Comfort Inn, as well as in an intermittent band stretching westwards from Chewton Mendip and Ston Easton.

The silts and sands of the Upper Lias have only limited outcropping north and south of the plateau, and are overlain by the Middle Jurassic Inferior Oolite. The latter is mainly found around Doulting, where the oolitic limestone has been quarried for centuries and used in building construction. Much of Wells Cathedral was built of Doulting Stone (as were many of the area's churches), with high-status secular buildings also built from this fine-quality grey limestone (Fig 1.9). Following on from the Inferior Oolite in the geological sequence is the Harptree Beds – limestone which has silicified to form chert. These beds outcrop above East Harptree (around Pit Farm and Smitham Hill), with small pockets to the south of Wigmoor Farm and underlying the area of Priddy Circle 3.

Marine conditions continued into Cretaceous times, although a long period of structural instability and sub-aerial erosion has stripped away many of the younger rocks. During the last ice age the main ice sheets did not cover the Mendip Hills, but the fluctuating climatic conditions of the Pleistocene period were instrumental in shaping the landscape we see today. The action of freezing and thawing allowed frost-shattered rocks to be carried down to the lowlands, scouring and deepening the combes and gorges. This process also deposited gravels in the valleys, the downwash appearing as fans and terrace-like spreads on the gentle slopes surrounding the uplands. Known as 'head', these gravel deposits can be seen surrounding Langford and Churchill, in a band from Cheddar to Shute Shelve, at Winscombe and in the Chew Valley. In the period after the final withdrawal of the ice sheets, sea level rises led to the submergence of the present Severn Estuary, the Somerset Levels and Moors, and the North Somerset Levels. The estuarine surface would have been dominated by mudflats or low marsh environments, while further inland, on the floodplains of the main rivers, deposits of clay and peat accumulated.

Soils and vegetation

Despite the complex geology of the region the soil covering of Mendip is remarkably uniform, comprising mostly well-drained brown earths that are predominantly acid in nature. A

Fig 1.9
Wells Cathedral. Doulting Stone was used in its construction.
(DP082048)

detailed study of the area's soils was undertaken by the former Soil Survey of Great Britain, and published in a volume entitled *The Soils of the Mendip District of Somerset* (Findlay 1965); *see* Figure 1.10. This publication emphasised the link between soils and the parent material (the underlying geology), as well as factors such as past and present climate and vegetation cover, and human intervention. In the upland regions of Mendip, the soils mainly derive from sandstone, limestone or silty drift overlying the Carboniferous Limestone and areas of younger Triassic and Jurassic rocks. The well-drained, dark-brown silt loam of the Nordrach series is the most extensive soil on the plateau, and has been mapped stretching eastwards from Charterhouse-on-Mendip across much of the Mendip uplands. It is now dominated by swathes of improved grassland, but large areas were used for arable cultivation in the late 18th and 19th centuries when the majority of the uplands was first enclosed.

Fig 1.10
Soils map of the Mendip Hills.
(CP15/036 British Geological Survey © NERC. All rights reserved.)

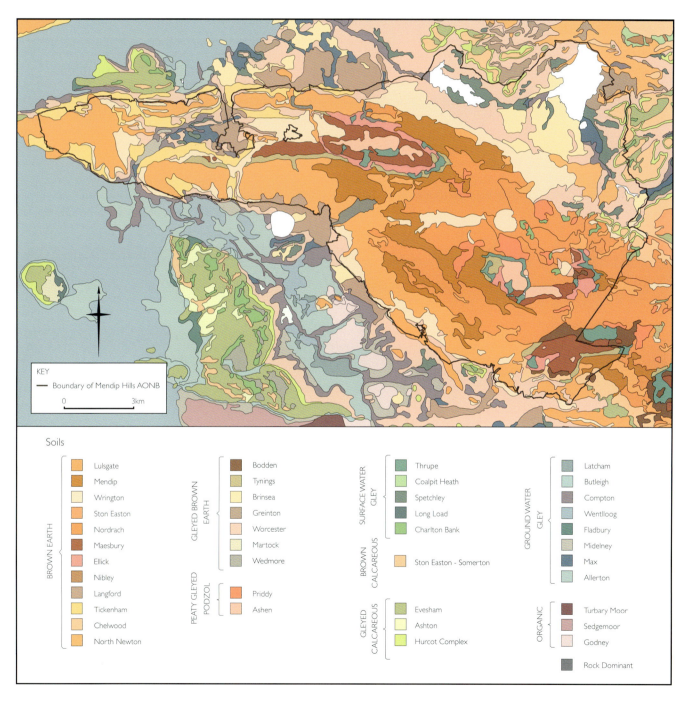

KEY
— Boundary of Mendip Hills AONB
0   3km

Soils

BROWN EARTH
Lulsgate
Mendip
Wrington
Ston Easton
Nordrach
Maesbury
Ellick
Nibley
Langford
Tickenham
Chelwood
North Newton

GLEYED BROWN EARTH
Bodden
Tynings
Brinsea
Greinton
Worcester
Martock
Wedmore

PEATY GLEYED PODZOL
Priddy
Ashen

SURFACE WATER GLEY
Thrupe
Coalpit Heath
Spetchley
Long Load
Charlton Bank

BROWN CALCAREOUS
Ston Easton - Somerton

GLEYED CALCAREOUS
Evesham
Ashton
Hurcot Complex

GROUND WATER GLEY
Latcham
Butleigh
Compton
Wentlloog
Fladbury
Midelney
Max
Allerton

ORGANIC
Turbary Moor
Sedgemoor
Godney

Rock Dominant

In locations where the Old Red Sandstone outcrops, the soils are predominantly free-draining acid brown earths of the Maesbury and Ellick series, which, on the north side of Black Down, support dense swathes of bracken. The crests of the hills are covered in poorly drained podzolised soils of the Ashen series that are moderately or strongly acidic and have been leached of plant nutrients. These areas support heather and heathland grasses, which give the high hilltops their distinctive character (Fig 1.11). Similar poorly drained podzolised soils appear in small pockets around Priddy, Ubley Warren and East Harptree Woods. These were some of the last upland areas to be improved and their very dark humous silt loam indicates the soils accumulated in a heathland environment. East Harptree Woods represents one of the three Forestry Commission plantations established in the post-war period, the largest of which, Rowberrow Warren, drapes the free-draining western slopes of Black Down.

In areas where sandstone 'head' overlies shale, rainwater moves laterally through the layers, giving rise to the poorly drained, infertile soils of the Thrupe series. These surface-water gley soils are seasonally waterlogged and support semi-natural wet heath. Small pockets of imperfectly draining gley brown earth – classified as the Tynings series – overlie the Avon Group (Lower Limestone Shales) and can be found on the north-facing slopes of Long Bottom, above Winscombe Orchard and north of Priddy.

On the Mendip escarpment and in the valleys which dissect the plateau, the soils are generally shallower on limestone or Dolomitic Conglomerate. Along the southern escarpment slopes the Lulsgate series predominates. These thin, dark reddish-brown soils also stretch along the narrow northern ridge from Burrington Ham to Banwell Hill, and dominate the western range above Bleadon and Loxton. These areas now comprise improved pasture, rich calcareous grassland and pockets of ancient woodland (comprising lime, ash, hazel and oak), but archaeological evidence indicates they also supported episodes of arable cultivation. On the sheltered north-facing slopes the shallower limestone and conglomerate

Fig 1.11
Black Down. The poorly drained soils on the crest of the hill support heather and heathland grasses. (NMR 24330/10)

Fig 1.12
The southern escarpment. Its thin soils now support areas of improved pasture and pockets of ancient woodland, with the earthwork remains of strip fields (top right) evidence of former arable cultivation. (DP099813)

soils sustain areas of ash–hazel woodland and mixed plantations, often confined to the steep escarpment slopes (Fig 1.12).

In the dry valleys and at the upland margins where soil depth is very variable, profiles typical of both the plateau and the slopes appear side by side. These have been categorised as the Mendip complex and can be found on Piney Sleight and Blagdon Hill, as well as in a narrow band stretching from Hunters Lodge to Cheddar Head. On the lower escarpment slopes the red soils associated with Dolomitic Conglomerate – the Wrington series – give the areas around Christon, Shipham, Blagdon and Compton Martin a distinctive character. These shallow red-brown soils also stretch in a thin intermittent band along the southern escarpment, and can be found in pockets on the uplands around Yoxter Farm and Eaker Hill.

In the lowlands the majority of the soil cover is derived from Triassic sediments, mainly Keuper Marl, with others from 'head' deposits of Cretaceous times. The soils which developed over the marl are imperfectly drained and are predominantly represented by the Worcester series. These fertile clay and silt soils can be found along the edge of the main river valleys and cover the lower ground around Wells, Westbury-sub-Mendip and Rodney Stoke, with a narrow band continuing westwards from Cheddar. To the north the Worcester series occupies the pasture slopes above East Harptree and Litton, and stretches in a band from Compton Martin to Blagdon. At the western end of the range, on the more moderate lower slopes, lies a band of deep, reddish-brown loam characterised as the Tickenham series; this can be found at Bleadon, Hutton, Yarborough and Barton, as well as in a thin band stretching from Banwell to Upper Langford.

Areas of gravelly 'head', represented by the very gentle slopes at the foot of the escarpment, are composed of freely draining loamy soils of the Langford series. These are predominantly located at the base of the main gorges and combes, at Cheddar, Churchill and Burrington, but are also found at Winscombe, Draycott, Wookey and Wells. The soils around Chewton Mendip and Ston Easton derive from the Lower Lias limestones of the Jurassic period, and are characterised as the Ston Easton/Somerton series. These dark greyish-brown clay soils also cover the Lias Tablelands to the north, around Hinton Blewett and Burledge Hill.

The alluvium of the main river valleys and the Levels and Moors is underlain by Keuper Marls, which gives rise to fine-textured reddish-brown soils, deposited by successive flood episodes. Riverine clay alluvium and gravel and clay alluvium, characterised as the Compton series and the Max series, are found along the main river courses. Narrow bands are also associated with tributary streams, such as at the Langford Brook, and have been mapped at the foot of the hills around Hutton and Elborough. Where the clay alluvium overlies peat at the margins of the moors (as happens to the east of Christon and along the southern escarpment around Rodney Stoke), drainage is poor, and these areas of pasture often include rushes, sedges and tufted hair-grass.

A history of research

Antiquarian investigation

The earliest references to archaeological monuments on the Mendip Hills can be found in medieval documents relating to grants of land. In the 12th century the perambulation of the bounds of Witham Priory's holding at Charterhouse-on-Mendip recorded Stow Barrow and Stonebarrow, two of the largest barrows on the Mendip plateau. However, it is through the work of antiquaries and diarists that we gain our earliest view of the historic landscape. For example, the antiquarian and natural historian William Worcester visited Mendip in the 15th century, documenting the landscape and buildings he encountered. He wrote an evocative description of the cave system at Wookey Hole, which he explored by reed light, 'at the entrance of which is the image of a man, called the porter, of whom leave must be asked to enter the hall of Woky' (cited in Collinson 1791, 419).

In the mid-16th century John Leland visited the Mendip Hills; his diaries provide a brief insight into the landscape he encountered as he journeyed from Chewton Mendip 'by hilly ground' to Wells. He also visited Cheddar and Axbridge before travelling along the northern escarpment from East Harptree to Banwell, observing sites such as the 'olde meane maner place' at Ubley with its 'castelle like' gatehouse and park. The fate of Richmont Castle was also documented by Leland, as was the much-repeated legend or popular saying about the hillfort at Dolebury that 'If Dolbyri dyggyd ware, Of golde shuld be the share' (Toulmin Smith 1964, 85). Several other diarists wrote of their experiences of Mendip in the 16th and 17th centuries, including William Camden, Oluf Borch and Celia Fiennes, all of whom were drawn to the area by the much celebrated natural phenomenon of Wookey Hole.

The scholar and country gentleman John Strachey (1671–1743) of Sutton Court (near Chew Magna) is perhaps best known through his published works as a pioneering geologist. Strachey was also a keen observer and recorder of the landscape, and produced the first large-scale map of Somerset in 1736. His ambition was to publish a physical and historical description of the county of Somerset to be entitled *Somersetshire Illustrated*, though sadly this work was never completed. That said, the Strachey manuscript collection gives us some of the earliest written descriptions of archaeological monuments on the Mendip Hills, including those of Burledge or 'Bowditch' Hillfort and Burrington Camp. His account of the latter reads: 'on the rampart behind two ditches on the Ham is a camp or entrenchment of 150 paces square said to be British but rather Saxon because it is reported to be in opposition to Dolbery or Danesbury in Churchil'. The description is accompanied by a small sketch-plan showing three concentric rectangles with entrances on three sides (Williams 1987, 61). As an accomplished geologist, Strachey also visited many of the area's underground cave systems, including those at Cheddar Gorge, Burrington Combe and around Churchill, and enlivened his accounts with tales of local folklore.

During the 1780s John Collinson and Edmund Rack were collecting material for their *History and Antiquities of the County of Somerset* (Collinson 1791). Collinson's account includes detailed descriptions of some of the area's ancient monuments, and relates anecdotal evidence of archaeological finds. Dolebury Camp, for example, he records as being 'fortified with a double vallum', the hillfort taking the form of 'a parallelogram, open at each end'. He also noted that within the enclosure 'Roman and Saxon coins have frequently been found … as have also spear-heads, pieces of swords, and other war-like weapons' (ibid, III, 579). Dolebury Camp also featured in the work of John Rutter, author of *Delineations of the North Western Division of the County of Somerset, and of Its Antediluvian Bone Caverns* (1829), which includes what would appear to be the earliest depiction of the hillfort and its interior (Rutter 1829, 114). A second plan of Dolebury, made by Philip Crocker, appears in the *History and Antiquities of Somersetshire*, published by William Phelps in 1836. Phelps, the vicar of Bicknoller between 1811 and 1854, misinterpreted the two pillow mounds at the eastern end of the fort as 'long barrows, under which were deposited the remains of some departed chieftains', even though the site apparently still functioned as a rabbit warren at that time (Phelps 1836, 99).

The work of Rutter and Phelps also reflects the intense interest in the region's caves in the early 19th century, the antediluvian significance of which, according to Rutter, drew visitors more than the rock formations themselves (Rutter 1829, 295). The Mendip caves, and the bones and fossils found within them, were considered sites of scientific and religious interest from the 17th century onwards. The discovery and investigation of human and animal bones by scholars such as John Beaumont (c 1640–1731), a physician and natural philosopher who lived in Ston Easton, contributed to the debate concerning early man and were promoted as evidence of the biblical Flood. Interest in the caves of Mendip accelerated through the 18th and 19th centuries, with William Beard (1772–1868), a farmer's son from Banwell, perhaps one of the best known of the bone collectors. Beard's excavating career began with his work at the Banwell Bone Cave, which, with the help of two miners, he discovered in 1824. The Bishop of Bath and Wells, George Henry Law, went on to create a visitor attraction at the site, using the Pleistocene fauna to promote the triumph of Christianity over paganism.

Beard's diaries indicate that he and the Revd David Williams (1792–1850), the rector of Bleadon, also collected material from Burrington Combe. The discovery of Aveline's Hole in 1797 (famously by two young men pursuing a rabbit in the gorge) generated a huge amount of antiquarian interest, and Williams was responsible for publishing accounts of both Aveline's Hole and Goatchurch Cavern (Williams 1829). The Revd William Buckland (1794–1856) also wrote of the discoveries at Aveline's Hole (Buckland 1822), though it remains uncertain whether he ever personally visited the cave (Boycott and Wilson 2011, 214). Later in the century the well-known cave excavator William Boyd Dawkins (1837–1929) led work at Hyaena Den (Wookey Hole) and Aveline's Hole, and named the cavern at Burrington after his mentor and friend William Talbot Aveline (Boyd Dawkins 1865).

The most notable antiquary at work in the early 19th century on Mendip was the Revd John Skinner (1772–1839). Rector of Camerton from 1800 to 1839, Skinner dedicated much of his spare time to investigating and recording archaeological sites and monuments. His work was never published, but his extensive journals – which include enlightening sketches of the people he encountered, the monuments he visited and the landscape which surrounded him – were bequeathed after his death to the British Museum and are now held in the British Library. As well as documenting the Mendip landscape and its upstanding archaeology, Skinner was also responsible for undertaking a large number of excavations, employing local people (often farm labourers or miners) to carry out the work. He is perhaps best known for his barrow investigations, particularly in the Priddy area: he excavated the Ashen Hill cemetery in September 1815 and opened a further 15 barrows over three days in August of the following year (BL Add MS 33648, fols 123–7, 160). Skinner also undertook work at Charterhouse-on-Mendip alongside his friend and near neighbour Sir Richard Colt Hoare. It was the latter who was the first to realise the scale of earthwork survival in the area, noting squares, circles and irregularities on the ground, and both he and Skinner produced the first sketches of the upstanding archaeology (BL Add MS 33653; Hoare 1821, 42); *see* Figure 1.13.

The work of Skinner was clearly well known by his contemporaries. In 1874 the Revd H M Scarth (1814–1890) published an account

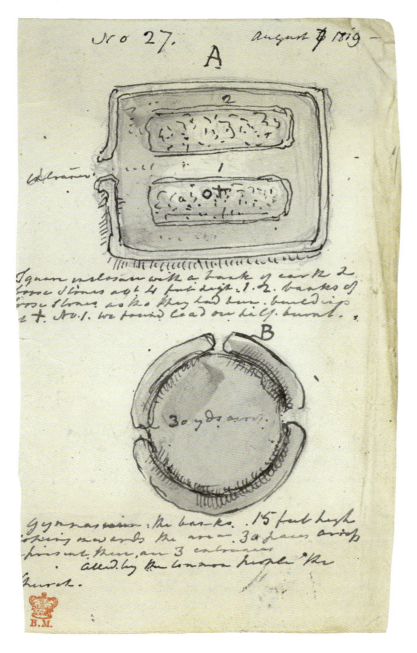

Fig 1.13
Sketch produced by the
Revd John Skinner showing
some of the upstanding
earthworks at
Charterhouse-on-Mendip.
(Add MS 33653, folio 215
© The British Library
Board)

These early antiquaries at best documented the archaeology they encountered, but there were few systematic attempts to accurately record the upstanding remains. Possibly one of the first metrically accurate surveys can be attributed to C W Dymond, a civil engineer, who produced a remarkably detailed plan (for the time) of Dolebury Camp in 1872 (Dymond 1883); *see* Figure 1.14. He also wrote a comprehensive description of the earthworks, providing valuable information, such as recording wall faces within the main northern rampart which he likened to those seen at Worlebury Hillfort, a site he had excavated two years previously (1883, 108–9; 1902).

Modern research

The caves and rock shelters of Mendip continued to be a focus for research during the early part of the 20th century. Herbert Balch (1869–1958) was a pioneer of cave exploration and undertook numerous arch-aeological excavations in Ebbor Gorge, Cheddar Gorge and Wookey Hole. He worked at Hyaena Den (first investigated by Boyd Dawkins), Badger Hole and the Great Cave of Wookey Hole, where he demonstrated an episode of extended occupation from the later prehistoric through to the Romano-British period (Balch 1914). Balch was one of the early members of the Wells Natural History and Archaeology Society (WNHAS), and having founded Wells Museum in 1894, he remained its honorary curator for the following 60 years. He was elected a Fellow of the Society of Antiquaries in 1926, and he published extensively, including *Mendip: Cheddar, Its Gorge and Caves* (1935) and *Mendip: Its Swallets, Caves and Rock Shelters* (1937).

A contemporary of Balch was A T Wicks (1880–1960), a master at Monkton Combe School, who is probably best known for his study of Mendip barrows. Wicks undertook this research on behalf of the WNHAS and the Mendip Nature Research Committee, adopting a field-based approach and building on the work carried out by Skinner a century earlier. This systematic study by Wicks and his collea-gues, which included cartographic research, produced a threefold increase in the number of known barrows on Mendip, which stood at around 226 by 1924 (Grinsell 1971, 77). The early 20th century also saw the archaeologist Harold St George Gray (1872–1963), a member

of Skinner's barrow excavations at Priddy in 1859, and Skinner's observations at Aveline's Hole clearly inspired later published accounts (Boycott and Wilson 2011). The initial discov-eries made by Skinner and Hoare were uncovered amid the fervour for agricultural improvement in a period which also saw the reworking of old mining waste, which revealed more archaeological material and drew anti-quaries and collectors alike. These included Mr Waldron of the Cardiff Naturalists' Society, who published an account of the finds made at Charterhouse-on-Mendip during mining oper-ations in the later 19th century (Waldron 1875).

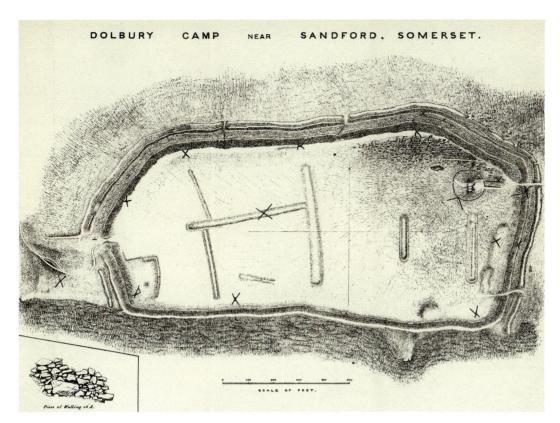

Fig 1.14
Survey of Dolebury Camp
undertaken by C W Dymond
in 1872.
(Dymond 1883, opp 104)

of the Somerset Archaeological and Natural History Society (SANHS), direct excavations on the purported amphitheatre site at Charterhouse-on-Mendip. As part of this work Gray produced a contour survey of the monument but conceded that the excavations, carried out in June and July, were not 'altogether satisfactory' on account of the 'persistent wet and stormy weather' (Gray 1909, 124).

The amphitheatre site was later excavated by the University of Bristol Spelæological Society (UBSS), probably one of the most prolific of the amateur groups at work on the hills in the early 20th century. The society was founded in 1919, a reincarnation of the Bristol Spelæological Research Society established seven years previously; the members initially travelled to Mendip from Bristol by bicycle. Their first major archaeological excavation was carried out at Aveline's Hole, and was quickly followed by work at Read's Cavern and Rowberrow Cavern. One of the early members was Edgar Kingsley Tratman (1899–1978), then a dental student, who brought a meticulous and scientific approach to excavation, and went on to become president of the society in 1948. Tratman published around 200 articles

relating to archaeology, with some of his major excavations including Hyaena Den, Sun Hole and Picken's Hole. The efforts of Tratman and the UBSS were not confined to subterranean archaeology, however: excavation was undertaken at sites including the Priddy Circles, the Tyning's Farm barrow group and Gorsey Bigbury. The latter was excavated under the misconception that the monument was a disc barrow; the work of the UBSS confirmed the site's status as a Neolithic henge monument (Fig 1.15).

Tyning's Farm formed part of a wider programme of barrow excavation initiated by the UBSS in the 1920s. This project included the investigation of a number of monuments in the Burrington area, as well as some emergency recording of sites threatened by demolition elsewhere. The comprehensive work of Dr H Taylor at Tyning's Farm revealed the range of construction techniques, burial practices and grave goods found within a single barrow cemetery, highlighting the complex and diverse nature of these prehistoric monuments. The barrows of Mendip were also included in a major thematic study undertaken by Leslie Grinsell (1907–1995), forming part of his county inventories. Grinsell was a pioneer of field archaeology, and visited and surveyed almost every barrow he included in the inventory. He also drew upon the work of A T Wicks, the UBSS and the Revd Skinner, publishing his work on the barrows of north and east Somerset in 1971. Grinsell became Keeper of Archaeology at Bristol's City Museum in 1952, and contributed to the volumes *Prehistoric Sites in the Mendip, South Cotswold and Bristol Region* (1966) and *The Mendip Hills in Prehistoric and Roman Times* (1970).

The mid-20th century saw the formation of a number of new archaeological societies in the Mendip area. The Axbridge Caving Group and Archaeological Society (ACGAS), formed in 1951, developed from the Axbridge Caving Group and had a remit to investigate the western end of the Mendip range. Perhaps one of its highest-profile excavations was at Winthill, where evidence for Romano-British occupation was uncovered, including a spectacular mid-4th-century glass bowl (Chapman 1955; Hunt 1961b). In 1976 the society split into the Axbridge Caving Group and the Axbridge Archaeological and Local History Society (AALHS), both of which remain active to this day. The site at Winthill was also the focus of several seasons of excavation by the

Banwell Society of Archaeology, established in 1958. The society cut its teeth at Banwell Camp, uncovering material which dated the first phase of enclosure to the Early Iron Age (Hunt 1961a). Members also worked on development projects, such as Oldmixon and the M5 motorway, excavating a group of storage pits at Dibble's Farm, Christon, and producing evidence for Early Iron Age occupation. A study of the wider landscape at Christon was undertaken by R L Clarke, the work forming the basis for a series of articles published in *Search: Journal of the Banwell Society of Archaeology* (1969–73). Clarke identified the 'Celtic' fields on Flagstaff Hill and would appear to have been the first to recognise Christon as a 'shrunken' medieval settlement.

Members of the ACGAS excavated the Roman villa site at Star, and worked under the direction of Philip Rahtz (1921–2011) on the vicarage site at Cheddar (Hirst and Rahtz 1973). This work followed on from Rahtz's excavations at the Saxon and later medieval royal palace at Cheddar, where he uncovered a sequence of timber halls, ancillary buildings and ditched enclosures (Rahtz 1979). Rahtz began his career alongside Ernest Greenfield working for the Ministry of Public Buildings

Fig 1.15
Members of the UBSS in the rock-cut ditch of the henge monument during the excavations at Gorsey Bigbury in the 1930s. (Photographer unknown. From the collection of the University of Bristol Spelæological Society, with permission)

and Works, recording archaeology ahead of the construction of the Chew Valley reservoir. The excavation was often carried out in difficult conditions, and Rahtz published this extensive body of work in a volume entitled *Excavations at Chew Valley Lake, Somerset* (Rahtz and Greenfield 1977). Development-led excavations were also undertaken at Wells Cathedral, on behalf of the Committee for Rescue Archaeology in Avon, Gloucestershire and Somerset (CRAAGS). This joint rescue and research programme uncovered a complex stratigraphic sequence, revealing evidence for the cathedral's early development alongside the remains of a Middle Saxon cemetery (Rodwell 2001). A wholly research-focused excavation was undertaken by the University of Exeter at Charterhouse-on-Mendip between 1993 and 1995; this work concentrated on the area of the Roman fort and adjacent mining remains, revealing evidence for industrial activity dating from the later prehistoric and Romano-British periods (Todd 2007). More recently the University of Worcester carried out a small-scale excavation and palaeo-environmental assessment at Priddy Circle 1 (Lewis and Mullin 2011). The same site was also the focus of an archaeological evaluation by English Heritage in 2013, carried out to inform a programme of archaeological mitigation work (Leary and Pelling 2013).

An archaeological survey of the area of the Mendip Hills AONB, funded by English Heritage and Somerset County Council, was undertaken between 1986 and 1988 by Peter Ellis, the results of which were published in a thematic study, *Mendip Hills: An Archaeological Survey of the Area of Outstanding Natural Beauty* (1992). This project combined a programme of aerial photographic transcription and fieldwork, with sites visited on the ground subject to a written and photographic record augmented by sketch-plans. The project resulted in the discovery of over 400 previously unrecorded archaeological sites, illustrating the potential for new discoveries within the study area. English Heritage also funded a programme of urban surveys, undertaken by Somerset County Council between 1994 and 1998, aimed at assessing urban archaeology as part of the Monument Protection Programme; this work included the towns of Cheddar, Wells and Axbridge and the former port of Rackley.

In 1989 the Royal Commission on the Historical Monuments of England undertook an analytical earthwork survey of an area known as Ramspits, above Westbury-sub-Mendip. This fieldwork project recorded in detail a group of deserted farmsteads and their associated enclosures, trackways and field system, highlighting a sequence of occupation and abandonment stretching from the medieval period through to the 18th century (Pattison 1991). The Mendip Hills have also been the focus of a number of student research projects, some of which have led to publications, such as *Monuments, Ritual and Regionality: The Neolithic of Northern Somerset* (Lewis 2005). The English Heritage Historic Landscape Characterisation Project has been completed for the Mendip Hills area.

The Somerset Aggregates Levy Sustainability Fund (SALSF) and the Mendip Hills AONB funded an aerial photographic and lidar (light detection and ranging) survey of the Mendip Hills. The aim of the project was to enhance the archaeological record of the aggregate mineral-producing areas in the county, and the work resulted in the publication of *Mendip from the Air: A Changing Landscape* (2007). The SALSF also funded the Somerset Aggregates Lithic Assessment (SALA), commissioned in 2007 by English Heritage. The aim of this project was to provide an assessment of the extent, date and character of lithic collections, and incorporated assemblages from the Mendip Hills plateau. They included those recovered by Mrs A Everton (a member of the AALHS) and Mr B Hack, one of the most prolific of the region's collectors, who amassed over 8,000 lithic objects from across the hills (Firth and Faxon 2008).

The long-standing tradition of archaeological research by local groups and individuals continues on Mendip. The Charterhouse Environs Research Team (CHERT), a community archaeology group, is involved in a programme of earthwork survey, geophysical survey and excavation across the central region of the AONB. The Westbury Society, the Blagdon Local History Society and the Harptree History Society are actively engaged in researching and publishing information on the archaeology and history of their respective parishes. Preliminary work on the Winscombe Project, a multidisciplinary study looking at the development of the Winscombe area, has also begun under the auspices of the Winscombe and Sandford Local History and Archaeological Society (Aston *et al* 2011, 167–9).

Panel 1.1 Antiquarian investigation: the Revd John Skinner and the Ashen Hill barrows

Fig P1.1.1
Aerial photograph showing Ashen Hill barrow cemetery.
(NMR 24328/19)

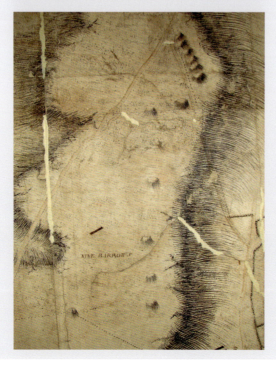

Fig P1.1.2
Extract from Rocque's map of 1740 showing Priddy Nine Barrows and Ashen Hill barrow cemetery (top right).
(SHS DD/WG/MAP/1, reproduced with permission of Somerset Archive and Local Studies)

The Ashen Hill barrows dominate the skyline above Priddy and form one of the largest linear barrow cemeteries on the plateau (Fig P1.1.1). Along the ridge to the south stretch the Priddy Nine Barrows, with the Priddy Circles marching across the lower-lying ground to the north. The Ashen Hill barrows have been recognised for hundreds of years, having evidently formed prominent markers in the landscape. Perhaps their earliest depiction is on an estate map of Chewton Mendip produced by the surveyor and cartographer John Rocque in 1740 (SHS DD/WG/MAP/1). Rocque's map shows six mounds in the Ashen Hill group and eight in the Priddy Nine Barrows group, the mounds appearing like hairy tufts floating amid the open common of the uplands (Fig P1.1.2).

In the early 19th century the Ashen Hill barrows caught the attention of the antiquary the Revd John Skinner. He wrongly identified the group as the Priddy Nine Barrows, suggesting barrow no. 9 had been dug up and the material carried away to be used in the construction of a new enclosure wall. However, his notes and plans clearly show that the eight barrows he opened in September 1815 represented the Ashen Hill barrow cemetery (BL Add MS 33648, fols 123–7, 133–9). Skinner numbered the barrows from east to west and gave directions to four labourers to begin digging a shaft through the centre of each mound, and to stop when they reached a cist or charcoal (Fig P1.1.3).

When Skinner arrived on site the following week, the labourers had dug down 8ft (2.4m) through barrow no. 2 and discovered a small, stone-lined cist covered by a flat stone. The cist contained cremated human bone accompanied by five amber beads, one 'somewhat in the shape of a heart', and a bronze knife and rivet. Not far from the cist lay a small clay cup (about 10cm long and 7.5cm wide) embossed with 'projecting knobs' (BL Add MS 33648, fol 123) (Fig P1.1.4). The cist had been covered by loose stones to the height of about 1m then enlarged with earth by a further 1.4m, which clearly indicates two phases of mound construction. In contrast, barrow no. 3 was constructed entirely of loose stones, some as much as 200lb in weight, causing 'considerable alarm to the men, as the stones were in constant danger of

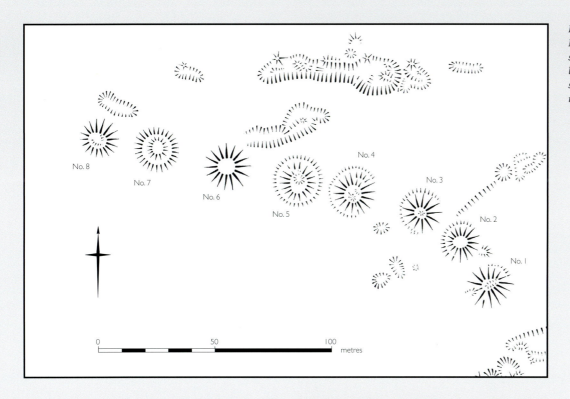

Fig P1.1.3
Modern earthwork survey of Ashen Hill barrow cemetery showing Skinner's numbering system.

falling in upon them' (BL Add MS 33648, fol 124). The excavators discovered two burial deposits within this mound: the primary burial within a stone cist and the secondary cremation in a pit high up in the mound and sealed by a flat stone.

As work continued, the range of materials employed in construction, and the complex phasing within each barrow, became more apparent. The excavation at barrow no. 1 showed it was almost entirely composed of earth, which made it light work for the weary labourers. The mound contained three burial deposits, all located at different depths; the primary deposit was associated with an inverted urn placed within a small cist. Barrows no. 4, no. 6 and no. 7 were all shown by Skinner to have been constructed in at least two phases – having originated as low stone cairns and subsequently been enlarged by the addition of an earthen mound. Only barrow no. 4 was found to contain a cist, within which had been placed burnt bones and a bronze riveted knife (about 13cm long and 2.5cm wide). Barrow no. 6 contained a large urn and considerable quantities of burnt bone and charcoal, with

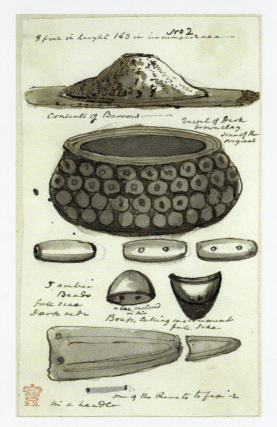

Fig P1.1.4
Sketch by the Revd John Skinner showing grave goods from barrow no. 2. (Add MS 33648, folio 135r, © The British Library Board)

mound no. 7 overlying a heap of burnt bone and charcoal, accompanied by part of a bronze knife. The final barrows to be opened in the group were no. 5 and no. 8, both of which were never excavated fully, and without any record of barrow no. 5 being made. At the bottom of barrow no. 8 a small quantity of burnt bone was discovered, although Skinner remained unconvinced that it was the primary interment (BL Add MS 33648, fol 127).

The work Skinner undertook at Ashen Hill and elsewhere on Mendip, although limited in scope and primitive in execution, demonstrates the complex nature of barrow monuments. His work illustrates both the diversity in mound construction and the range of deposits found within them. The different phases of construction identified by Skinner can also be directly related to the subtle changes in profile recorded through modern earthwork survey (*see* Fig P1.1.3). His work therefore gives us an insight into what lies beneath, helping to demonstrate that the form of these barrows represents the culmination of a complex sequence of actions, and highlighting their potential for further research.

The English Heritage Mendip Hills AONB Project

The English Heritage Mendip Hills AONB Project was initiated in 2006 as a response to the need for a programme of new archaeological and architectural survey work, and a requirement to appraise and evaluate past archaeological research. The beauty and accessibility of the Mendip Hills AONB has resulted in ever-increasing visitor numbers, which generate pressure on the fragile archaeological and built environment. This pressure has been augmented by growth in the aggregate industry and changes in agricultural practices, which affect long-established patterns of land use and create a conflict between those wishing to exploit the natural resources of the area and those wishing to conserve the landscape, archaeology and built heritage. To allow the successful monitoring of landscape change, and to inform the sustainable management and conservation of the historic landscape, a sound knowledge base is required.

The archaeological and architectural fieldwork which forms the core of this publication was undertaken by the Archaeological Survey and Investigation and the Architectural Investigation teams of English Heritage (now the combined Assessment team), between 2006 and 2009 (Jamieson 2006). The background information for the survey work was gathered from the relevant Historic Environment Records (HER) and the English Heritage National Record of the Historic Environment (NRHE), supplemented with data produced by the National Mapping Programme (NMP). The whole of the Mendip Hills AONB was considered during the archaeological and architectural fieldwork, as were many of the settlements which lie along its bounds. A north–south transect crossing from Westbury-sub-Mendip to East Harptree was selected for more detailed architectural investigation.

A wide range of earthwork sites from all periods were investigated and recorded, with a focus on previously poorly understood monument classes and landscape areas. All the major prehistoric monuments in the region were assessed, including known field systems, settlement sites and ritual monuments, with the HER and NRHE data used to identify barrow monuments worthy of further assessment. Representative examples of Neolithic and Bronze Age barrows were surveyed at 1:200 or 1:500. All the upstanding hillforts and prehistoric enclosures were investigated and surveyed at 1:500 or 1:1000, depending on the size and complexity. This work was undertaken using a total station theodolite or Global Navigation Satellite System (GNSS) survey equipment, supplemented by traditional survey methods (Fig 1.16). Other sites, areas and monument types were also the focus of large-scale surveys, with the main sites discussed in the text listed in Appendix 1. Architectural investigation and recording looked at a wide range of building types – including farms, vernacular buildings in general, churches, manor houses and industrial sites. This work involved the rapid assessment of specific geographic areas and building types, as well as the detailed investigation, survey and recording of individual buildings (Fig 1.17).

The NMP is a project managed by the English Heritage Aerial Investigation and Mapping team, and aims to map the archaeology of England as seen from the air. The NMP work for the Mendip Hills AONB has been jointly funded by English Heritage, the Mendip Hills AONB and Somerset County Council through the Somerset Aggregate Levy Sustainability Fund. The archaeology of the whole of the study area was transcribed at 1:10 000 using NMP standards developed by English Heritage. The Mendip Hills AONB was the first NMP project to use both aerial photographs and lidar data during the mapping phase. The lidar survey was commissioned by the Mendip Hills AONB and flown by the Cambridge University Unit for Landscape Modelling during 2005 and 2006. The transcription was carried out by contractors from Somerset County Council and Gloucestershire County Council Archaeological Service, who together created 405 new NRHE records and updated a further 465. Information gathered during this work has proved crucial in quantifying the extent of mining activity across the region, as well as highlighting more transient features such as First and Second World War military installations. The results of this project have been published in the form of two English Heritage reports: *The Aggregate Landscape of Somerset: Predicting the Archaeological Resource: Archaeological Aerial Survey in the Central Mendip Hills* (Truscoe 2008) and *Archaeological Aerial Survey in the Northern Mendip Hills: A Highlight Report for the National Mapping Programme* (Priest and Dickson 2009).

English Heritage also carried out several seasons of air photographic reconnaissance over the Mendip Hills AONB. A large number of new oblique aerial photographs have been taken during the course of the project, with images capturing archaeological sites, settlements and farmsteads, as well as illustrating the wider Mendip landscape. A programme of ground photography was also undertaken, with sites such as farm buildings, manor houses, churches, industrial complexes, Second World War bunkers and prehistoric monuments recorded. Finally, a key aspect of the project was to provide a training programme for local community groups and individuals. This involved all aspects of landscape investigation ranging from non-

intrusive methods, such as building recording, geophysical and earthwork survey, through to archaeological excavation. The basic records of the archaeological and architectural survey work, and the aerial photographic transcription, are available for consultation at the Historic England Archive (Swindon), as are the archive plans, photographs and site reports.

Fig 1.16
Surveying Longbottom Camp, Shipham.
(Elaine Jamieson)

Fig 1.17
Surveying Manor Farm, Charterhouse-on-Mendip.
(DP044430)

2

The Palaeolithic and Mesolithic

Palaeolithic bones and fossils recovered from the caves of Mendip – representing the remains of animals such as spotted hyaena, woolly rhinoceros, bear and lion – have captured the imagination of scholars for centuries (Fig 2.1). For example, in the early 19th century at Uphill Quarry the Revd David Williams uncovered bones which he recorded as 'belonging to animals of a country and climate differing from our own' (Rutter 1829, 79). This is because the Palaeolithic is characterised by varied and changing climatic conditions experienced over extended periods of time. It also represents an era of complex human physical evolution. The people who inhabited Britain during this time are thought to have been highly mobile groups who utilised natural features such as caves and river valleys as they travelled through the landscape, possibly following traditional migratory patterns in a similar way

to the animals they hunted. The stone and flint tools they made and used represent some of the earliest and most durable evidence for human activity. Small but significant changes in material culture provide us with an insight into how the lifestyle of these early humans developed, and how they interacted with and understood the world they inhabited.

In the period after the last ice sheets receded, temperature and sea-level rise resulted in an expansion of natural habitats, which increased the range of foodstuffs available to the communities living in the region. The Mesolithic period can be viewed as a time of very gradual transition which witnessed a move from the hunter-gatherer lifestyle of the Palaeolithic towards the farming communities of the Neolithic. As in earlier periods, the highly adaptable family groups who utilised the resources of Mendip are still mainly visible

Fig 2.1
The skull of a huge form of brown bear found in Banwell Bone Cave.
(© Somerset County Council Museums Service)

through the flint and stone tools they left behind; these are usually found as small surface scatters and often intermixed with material from later periods. Burial remains deposited in caves and swallets also help bring them more clearly into view, revealing information about their physical appearance, dietary habits and cultural beliefs.

The Palaeolithic landscape (to *c* 10,000 cal BC)

The Lower Palaeolithic

Lower Palaeolithic deposits, probably of MIS 15 age, have been found along the Mendip escarpment above Westbury-sub-Mendip. These Pleistocene layers were first uncovered by workmen at Westbury Quarry in 1969 in what appears to be the remains of a large collapsed cave system. The main chamber of the cave was formed within the Carboniferous Limestone of the Clifton Down Group and contained a considerable depth of deposits, with the exposed cross section measuring around 100m long and 30m high. The cave was positioned high on the southern escarpment, on the very edge of the plateau, with commanding views out over the upper Axe Valley and the Somerset Levels and Moors. The upper layers held abundant bones, included those of mammals such as bear, wolf, lion, wild horse, extinct 'European jaguar' and wild dog, along with the remains of small vertebrates and birds (Bishop 1974, 301–18). This bone assemblage may have accumulated through the process of natural deposition, or it could have been brought to site by animals using the cave as a lair.

The degraded nature of the lithic assemblage at Westbury Quarry has meant that until relatively recently evidence for human occupation was regarded as highly speculative. Cook's detailed analysis of the material concluded that it had more affinity with naturally modified flint than with flint shaped by hominids (1999, 211–74). However, the discovery of flint, not a naturally occurring material on Mendip, raises questions as to how it found its way into the cave at Westbury-sub-Mendip. The nearest sources for flint are on the western side of Salisbury Plain, although chert – a silicified form of limestone similar to flint – can be found in the region's

Jurassic layers. The recent recognition of butchery marks on a deer bone from the main chamber of Westbury Cave (Macphail and Goldberg 1999) supports the argument for human intervention, and represents the earliest evidence for hominid activity on Mendip. The material from Westbury-sub-Mendip therefore suggests that over half a million years ago early humans were visiting Mendip to hunt and butcher animals.

The fauna from Westbury Quarry has been used as an indicator of environmental conditions and to map episodes of climatic change (Andrews and Stringer 1999). The long Cromerian sequence contains evidence for two episodes of fully temperate conditions separated by a period of significant climatic deterioration. The faunal assemblage suggests that during the first warm temperate episode the landscape would have comprised broad-leaved deciduous woodland and supported mammals such as red deer, roe deer and wild horse. This period was followed by cooler, drier conditions which created a more open landscape of boreal forest and steppe/tundra habitats – consisting of broad-leaved woodland, dwarf shrubs, sedges and grassland. A second temperate period followed that saw a return to more wooded and warmer conditions, with the evidence suggesting a climate more comparable to southern Europe than to southern England today. Following this the climate then cooled dramatically, which led to cyclical periglacial activity, suggesting a prolonged period of devegetation and erosion of the Mendip soil cover; species such as tundra vole, Norwegian lemming, Arctic lemming and reindeer are all present in the faunal record for this period.

The Middle Palaeolithic

The Anglian was the first in a series of great glacial events that defined a period of prolonged climatic instability. It is against this background of fluctuating climatic conditions that early human occupation has to be considered. In Britain there is a clear divide between the earlier and later Middle Palaeolithic, marked by a period when the region was abandoned by hominids. When this period of human absence began is at present unclear, but it may have started around 180,000 years ago when the region's climate moved from an interglacial into a glacial stage (MIS 9 to MIS 8). At present, secure evidence for human occupation does not reappear in the archaeological record until around 60,000 years ago (Jacobi and Currant 2011).

Early Middle Palaeolithic

The climate during the Last Interglacial (MIS 5e, often referred to as the Ipswichian Interglacial) was considerably warmer than today. During this period significant rises in sea levels caused the extensive plain beneath what is now the southern North Sea to be submerged, and areas of south-eastern Britain were lost to the sea. The present Severn Estuary, the Somerset Levels and Moors, and the North Somerset Levels were submerged under these rising tides. The estuarine margin of the Somerset Levels and Moors would have been dominated by mudflats, while further inland on the floodplains of the main rivers low marsh environments developed (Allen 2001, 17). The higher ground of Mendip would have been characterised by dry grassland and deciduous forest, comprising oak, maple, ash and hazel. Evidence for this last interglacial stage has been found at Milton Hill Quarry, near Wells, where the bones of hippopotamus, spotted hyaena, straight-tusked elephant, fallow deer and bison (Fig 2.2) have been recovered (Balch 1948, 142–3). Milton Hill would have been located on the edge of the Palaeolithic marsh-lands, allowing easy access to the resources it

provided; the rich faunal assemblage probably washed into the cave from above through fissures in the rock (Fig 2.3). Although Balch believed that there was evidence for hominids at Milton Hill, no supporting evidence has been found (Jacobi and Currant 2011, 47).

From around 117,000 years ago there was a gradual deterioration in climatic conditions, characterised by a series of stadial and interstadial oscillations. These temperature fluctuations resulted in a number of expansions and contractions in the European ice sheets which led to a succession of sea-level changes. A recent re-evaluation of the material from the Banwell Bone Cave has concluded that the bones (which include those of bison, reindeer, wolf and brown bear) date from the last of these interstadial or high sea-level events (MIS 5a), and represent mammals from the preceding cooler stadial period that were trapped in Britain when the low land beyond south-east England was submerged and Britain became an island (Jacobi and Currant 2011).

An assemblage containing similar faunal remains has also been uncovered at Brean Down (Currant *et al* 2006). The deposits, stacked against the cliff face, contain faunal remains higher in the sequence which included the bones of mammoth, wild horse, reindeer, Arctic fox, lemming and hare (ApSimon *et al* 1961). Jacobi and Currant have suggested that the reappearance of species such as wild horse

Fig 2.2
Bison horn cores from Upper Milton Quarry, now in Wells and Mendip Museum. (DP158761)

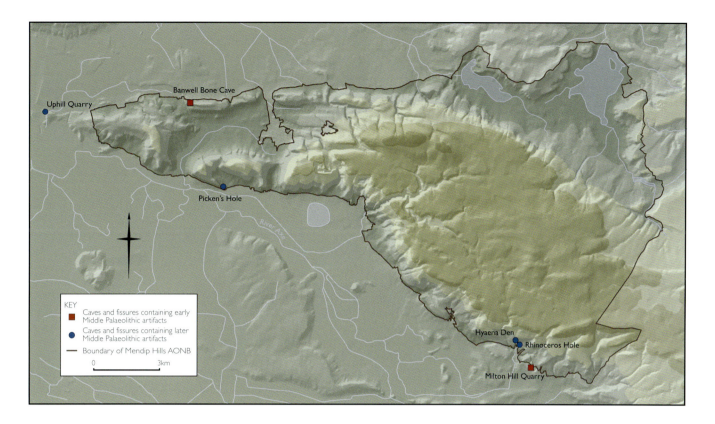

and mammoth in the faunal record reflects a reduction in sea levels and the restoration of dry land between the British Isles and continental Europe (2011, 49). The higher deposits have therefore been attributed to the onset of the last glacial stage (MIS 4), around 71,000 years ago, which saw an expansion of the Scandinavian ice sheets and a return to very cold conditions. Although ice probably covered northern Britain, southern regions would have remained largely ice-free at this time. Temperatures in the south would have dipped to Arctic levels in the winter months and the area would have been characterised by open tundra vegetation (Barton 1997).

Later Middle Palaeolithic

The start of the later Middle Palaeolithic period is characterised by a sharply oscillating climate, when short cooling periods were interspersed with milder climatic episodes (MIS 3). The cool, dry conditions created a landscape on Mendip dominated by rich, arid grasslands with the possibility of a few stunted trees and shrubs in the sheltered gorges (Tratman *et al* 1971). This environment supported animals such as mammoth, woolly rhinoceros, bear, spotted hyaena, lion and wild horse. The migration of these animals into

Britain coincided with the return of Neanderthal man (*Homo neanderthalensis*), who brought new ways of making flint tools, generally characterised by flakes (used as cutting edges or retouched tools) and specific hand-axe forms, including *bout coupé* hand-axes. Later Middle Palaeolithic sites in Britain are widely dispersed across the landscape, but tend to cluster in river valleys either as open-air sites or within caves. They contain small accumulations of tools and waste and are generally interpreted as low-density sites occupied for short periods of time.

On Mendip, later Middle Palaeolithic artefacts have been found within caves at Hyaena Den, Rhinoceros Hole and Picken's Hole, with material also discovered further west at Uphill Quarry. Hyaena Den, in Wookey Hole ravine, was discovered accidentally in 1852 by workmen cutting a new leat for the paper mill. It was first excavated in 1859 under the direction of William Boyd Dawkins, who reported the cavern as being 'filled with debris up to the very roof' (Dawkins 1863, 201). Within this debris Dawkins found a bone layer containing Pleistocene fauna (the assemblage dominated by spotted hyaena, wild horse and woolly rhinoceros) and concluded that the most likely method of introduction for the

Fig 2.3
The distribution of caves and fissures containing early and later Middle Palaeolithic artefacts across the Mendip Hills.

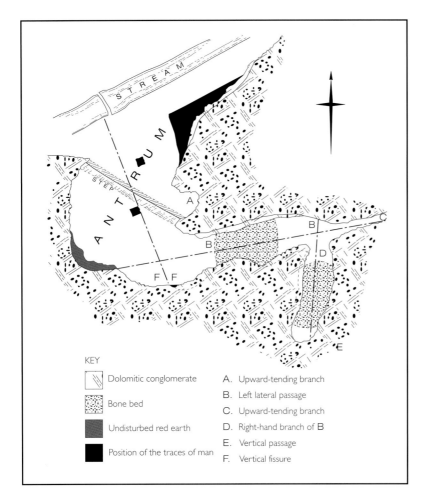

KEY

Dolomitic conglomerate	A.	Upward-tending branch
Bone bed	B.	Left lateral passage
	C.	Upward-tending branch
Undisturbed red earth	D.	Right-hand branch of B
Position of the traces of man	E.	Vertical passage
	F.	Vertical fissure

Fig 2.4
Hyaena Den: plan of the
cave showing the location
of the flint artefacts found
by Dawkins.
(After Dawkins 1863, fig 1)

material was by hyaenas using the cave as a lair. Dawkins also found three distinct groupings of human-made implements within the entrance chamber of the cave, including scraper fragments, flakes of both chert and flint, and eight small flint and chert hand-axes (Fig 2.4).

Several episodes of excavation were also undertaken at Hyaena Den in the later 19th century by Herbert Balch, who identified a series of hearths within the cave (Balch 1914, 168). In the late 1960s members of the UBSS carried out work at this site, and their efforts primarily illustrate how comprehensively it had been excavated by Dawkins (Tratman *et al* 1971). In the early 1990s an area across the cave entrance and along part of its south wall was subject to further investigation (Hawkes and Jacobi 1993). Perhaps surprisingly this work revealed undisturbed sediments on the north and south sides of the cave, within which debris from flint and chert working was found. These sediments also produced a small number of bones and teeth dating to *c* 50,000–45,000 cal BC, suggesting a later Middle Palaeolithic

date for the fauna and associated stone artefacts (Jacobi and Currant 2011, 53). The site of Hyaena Den may therefore be interpreted as a hunting camp, where early humans sheltered from the elements, lit fires, worked stone tools and butchered animals.

A further cave, Rhinoceros Hole, lies adjacent to Hyaena Den, on the east side of Wookey Hole ravine. The site was first investigated by Balch in the early 19th century and comprehensively excavated in 1970 by the UBSS (Balch 1914; Hawkins and Tratman 1977). The cave produced a similar faunal assemblage to Hyaena Den – dominated by brown bear, spotted hyaena and woolly rhinoceros – suggesting it also functioned as an animal lair. Human activity was represented by six flint artefacts – a small *bout coupé* hand-axe, hand-axe-trimming flakes and a retouched blade – all found low in the cave sequence (Proctor *et al* 1996, 246). The assemblage is chronologically similar to that from Hyaena Den, indicating the cave may have been used by the same Neanderthal group when they visited the ravine.

Another Mendip site to reveal probable evidence for human activity from MIS 3 is Picken's Hole, near Compton Bishop. This small cave was excavated by E K Tratman in the 1960s (Tratman 1964) and was found to contain a layer of fauna almost identical to that from the Wookey Hole caves. The deposit also produced the bones of red deer, giant Irish deer, reindeer, mammoth and Arctic fox, along with two human teeth. A number of stone artefacts, principally formed from chert, were also uncovered from the same layer and included two hammer-stones, core fragments, waste flakes and thermally fractured pieces (ApSimon 1986, 55–6). The choice of Picken's Hole, Rhinoceros Hole and Hyaena Den as temporary stopover sites for hunting groups may relate to the natural topography of the surrounding area. Jacobi has suggested the box-like form of Wookey Hole ravine, for example, would have made it ideal for trapping game as well as providing easy access onto higher ground (2000, 46). The same could be said for Picken's Hole, the cave being located on a ridge overlooking an enclosed valley, with these narrow basins leading off the broader Axe Valley where large herds of wild game would have roamed.

Further westwards, beyond the bounds of the AONB, are the cave and rock fissures at

Uphill Quarry which were first investigated by the Revd David Williams in the early 19th century. The assemblage from Uphill Quarry represents two separate deposition events, dating from the later Middle Palaeolithic and the early Upper Palaeolithic, with the earliest humanly modified artefacts including three hand-axes, a retouched scraper, chert flakes and a bifacial knife or side-scraper. Jacobi and Currant have suggested that this material may have filtered down to the cave from a hilltop camp by way of fissures in the rock (2011, 54). The high ground along the Mendip escarpment would have allowed spectacular panoramic views out over the Severn/Bristol Channel and the Axe Valley. Neanderthal hunting parties may have been drawn to these elevated areas as they would have provided a wider prospect of the landscape, and permitted the movement of game to be monitored from afar.

The Upper Palaeolithic

Around 30,000 years ago, Neanderthals, who had coexisted with anatomically modern humans in Europe for around 10,000 years, disappeared from the archaeological record. The modern human population who replaced them (*Homo sapiens sapiens*) have been linked to a cultural industry distinctively different from the earlier Mousterian tradition. This was characterised by improved methods of working stone, including the development of new forms of stone tools, and the introduction of ornaments and artefacts manufactured from bone, antler, shell and ivory. This increasingly sophisticated range of material culture was accompanied by changes in social, cultural and ritual behaviour, including the development of new hunting methods and the introduction of elaborate burial practices. The innovative developments from this time were progressive, however, evolving over thousands of years, and are marked by distinctive industrial traditions that can be grouped by changing artefact typology.

Early Upper Palaeolithic

The early Upper Palaeolithic is defined as the period before Britain experienced its last glacial event (towards the end of MIS 3). This was a time of sharply fluctuating temperatures which saw periodic cooling events interspersed with warmer episodes. Britain's position on the extreme edge of the inhabited Palaeolithic

world made it particularly susceptible to human abandonment during episodes of climatic deterioration. The cool, dry conditions of the milder intervals encouraged the development of a mammoth-steppe environment, with the landscape of Mendip supporting animals including wild horse, spotted hyaena and mammoth.

The earliest Upper Palaeolithic technologies to be found on Mendip are characterised by hafted weapon-heads termed 'leaf-points' and 'blade-points' (Jacobi and Currant 2011, 55). These flint tools are considered to be too large to represent arrowheads and were most likely spear tips used for hunting large animals across the open grasslands. Evidence for this form of stone technology has been found at three cave sites within the Mendip Hills AONB – Soldier's Hole, Badger Hole and Hyaena Den – as well as at Uphill Quarry to the west (Fig 2.5).

Investigations at Soldier's Hole, on the south-eastern side of Cheddar Gorge, were first undertaken by Herbert Balch and continued by R F Parry between 1928 and 1929 (Balch 1928; Parry 1931). The cave entrance is located about 46m above the floor of the gorge and gives access to a single chamber 8.5m wide and 8.2m long (Campbell 1977, 42–3). Within the cave Parry identified a small collection of early Upper Palaeolithic artefacts comprising seven flint tools sealed beneath a layer of later Upper Palaeolithic material. This assemblage (Fig 2.6) included fully bifacial leaf-points, flint and chert blades, and a bone or antler point (Parry 1931, 51).

Badger Hole, on the eastern side of Wookey Hole ravine, has also produced Upper Palaeolithic material. This site was excavated intermittently between 1938 and 1953 under the direction of Herbert Balch, although the results of his work were never fully published. Badger Hole was later investigated by McBurney (in 1958) and then by Campbell (in 1968), with both excavations highlighting the extent of later human and animal disturbance (McBurney 1961; Campbell 1977). A small group of early Upper Palaeolithic artefacts was found within the cave, including four blade-points, retouched pieces and broken blades (Jacobi and Currant 2011, 57); *see* Figure 2.7. A premolar of a wild horse, excavated by Balch from an undisturbed context and associated with one of the blade-points, has been radiocarbon dated to 39,640–37,720 cal BC (Jacobi *et al* 2006, 567–8; Jacobi and Currant 2011, 59). Taken in conjunction with evidence from elsewhere, this

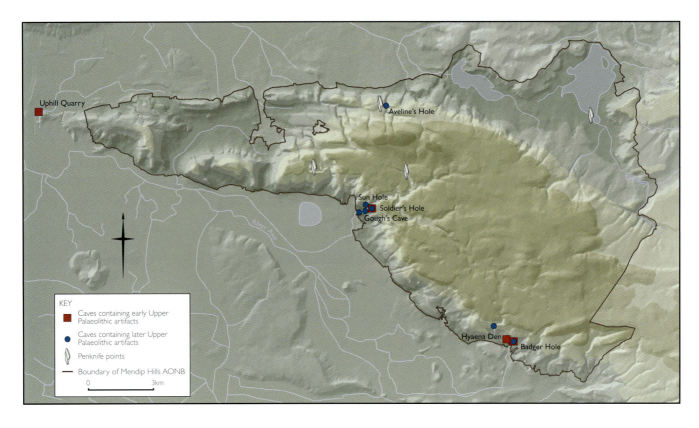

Fig 2.5
The distribution of early
and later Upper Palaeolithic
artefacts across the
Mendip Hills.

would suggest technologies with blade-points can be placed at the very beginning of the Upper Palaeolithic, and it may be possible to place other Mendip sites within the same time frame.

Two blade-points have also been recorded from the nearby Hyaena Den (Tratman *et al* 1971, 261–2), and what would appear to be four fragments of blade-points from Uphill Quarry were illustrated by Garrod (1926). A bone or antler lozenge-shaped point has also been recognised from among the faunal

assemblage at Uphill Quarry and identified as an Aurignacian artefact (Jacobi and Pettitt 2000). Towards the back of Hyaena Den a further antler or bone point was discovered in the late 19th century; these tools were possibly used to tip a composite throwing spear or short dart. The two radiocarbon measurements are statistically indistinguishable, which means they could be of the same actual age: they date to 34,240–33,100 cal BC (OxA-13716) and 34,210–32,830 cal BC (OxA-13803). It is conceivable that these

Fig 2.6
Early Upper Palaeolithic
flint assemblage from
Soldier's Hole, now in
the Museum of Prehistory,
Cheddar.
(DP158768, reproduced by
permission of the Museum
of Prehistory, Cheddar)

Fig 2.7
Early Upper Palaeolithic
flint assemblage from
Badger Hole, now in Wells
and Mendip Museum.
(DP158756, reproduced by
permission of Wells and
Mendip Museum)

sites may have been used by the same group of anatomically modern humans making their way down the Axe Valley during a seasonal hunting expedition (Jacobi and Currant 2011, 61).

Later Upper Palaeolithic

By around 18,000 years ago ice sheets once again covered much of northern Britain, creating an almost barren polar desert. During this period, known as the Last Glacial Maximum (MIS 2), only the hardiest tundra species survived in southern Britain and humans would appear to have once more retreated into Europe. The end of this cold stage is marked by a series of climatic oscillations, the first of which is termed the Late Glacial Interstadial. This period saw a rapid rise in temperatures which reached their peak around 13,000 years ago. During the latter stages of this interstadial, wooded conditions once more became established. The woodland was dominated by birch and inhabited by animals such as mammoth, wild horse, red deer, wild cattle and brown bear (Barton 1997, 38).

It was during the first part of the Late Glacial Interstadial that evidence for human occupation is once again found on Mendip. Later Upper Palaeolithic material has been identified at sites including Gough's Cave, Aveline's Hole, Badger Hole, Soldier's Hole and Sun Hole. The most informative of these cave sites are possibly Gough's Cave and Aveline's Hole, both of which have produced large quantities of later Upper Palaeolithic material. Aveline's Hole, in Burrington Combe, attracted a great deal of antiquarian interest after its discovery in the late 18th century, but it was not until the 1860s that William Boyd Dawkins carried out the first systematic excavations at the site. Several seasons of investigation were also undertaken by the Bristol Spelæological Research Society and the UBSS in the early 20th century, and this work produced evidence for later Upper Palaeolithic and the early Mesolithic activity in the cave (Dawkins 1864; Davies 1921, 1922, 1923, 1925).

Evidence of human presence at Aveline's Hole was primarily represented by stone and antler artefacts, with perhaps the most striking being a bilaterally barbed point made from red deer antler (Davies 1921, 69). This hunting tool was unfortunately destroyed by bombing during the Second World War; however, images and casts survive and the weapon clearly represents the point of an arrow, dart

Fig 2.8
Bilaterally barbed point
from Aveline's Hole
(scale 1:1).

or spear (Fig 2.8). Stone tools were primarily represented by various forms of backed blades, with a noticeable absence of hide-working implements such as scrapers or burins. This low artefact diversity has been interpreted as evidence for short periods of specialist occupation at the site, with only a limited number of tasks undertaken in the cave such as tool maintenance and initial animal butchery (Jacobi 2005, 275–7). The cave is positioned on the eastern side of Burrington Combe, towards the floor of the steep-sided ravine, and must have represented a relatively cold and dark space. It is possible the cave was briefly used by a hunting party as it moved through the landscape, with the combe forming one of the main access routes onto the higher ground.

Gough's Cave

Gough's Cave, on the south-east side of Cheddar Gorge, was discovered in the last decade of the 19th century by Richard Cox Gough, who opened it to the public as a show cave in May 1899. In 1903 a nearly complete human skeleton, representing a young adult male, was found in the cave by workmen and subsequently exhibited as the 'Cheddar Man'. The skeleton was initially thought to be contemporary with the later Upper Palaeolithic material but was subsequently shown to be early Mesolithic in date (Barker *et al* 1971, 157–

88). Gough's Cave was systematically excavated by Parry between 1927 and 1931 and has been subjected to numerous investigations since, including by cave staff and by a joint team from the University of Lancaster and the British Museum (Natural History) (Parry 1931; Donovan 1955; Currant *et al* 1989). Parry's initial excavations produced well over 7,000 artefacts made of stone, antler, bone and ivory, the variety of which has led to the site's interpretation as a 'base camp' for the exploration of Mendip (Campbell 1977, 162–3). Gough's Cave was probably in use for at most a couple of hundred years around 13,000 cal BC (Jacobi and Currant 2011, 64).

The assemblage of later Upper Palaeolithic stone tools from Gough's Cave includes backed and truncated blades, burins, piercers and end-scrapers (Fig 2.9), with many of the flint and chert implements displaying evidence of retouching (Jacobi 2004). A high proportion of the backed blades show signs of damage, which would suggest they formed the tips of spears or arrows used during hunting. Cut-marks on many of the bones show that flint and chert tools were also used in butchery – for skinning, dismembering, filleting and tendon removal – primarily on the carcasses of wild horse and red deer. Tendons and ligaments may have been used to make snares, nooses or nets for trapping small game; sinew could also be

Fig 2.9
Gough's Cave assemblage
of flint tools, now in the
Museum of Prehistory,
Cheddar.
(DP158769, reproduced by
permission of the Museum of
Prehisory, Cheddar)

used in the production of composite bows or as thread for the manufacture of clothing (Parkin *et al* 1986, 319–28).

A number of well-made bone, ivory and antler tools were also recovered from the cave, including *bâtons percés'* made from reindeer antler, bone awls or piercers, and the shank of a small bone needle (Fig 2.10). The piercers had been formed by pointing the tibiae of mountain hare, and debris from the manufacture of needles indicates they were made from cores of swan bone. Slender 'rods' manufactured from mammoth ivory were also uncovered in the cave. These implements supported a pair of opposed bevels at one end for hafting and are thought to represent weapon heads used during hunting (Currant *et al* 1989, 133). The material and form of these implements suggest that, as well as hunting large mammals, activities also included the trapping of small game and fowling, the latter possibly undertaken along the Axe Valley. The range of tools indicates the inhabitants of the cave were also engaged in working hide and in the manufacture or mending of clothing.

Although mammoth is recorded from elsewhere in Britain at this time, it is unclear whether it formed part of the local fauna; the raw material for the ivory rods therefore may have been sourced from outside the region (Charles 1989, 407). Good flint for tool production was evidently brought to Mendip from at least 70km away and may suggest a relatively wide territorial range (Jacobi 2004, 12). Amber pebbles were also found in the cave, with their nearest available source identified along the east coast of England. It has been suggested that at least one piece of amber from Gough's Cave may have originated in the Baltic region (Charles 1989, 401), the material possibly having been brought to Mendip through exchange.

The cave has also produced artefacts with deliberate linear marks or 'notations'. These include an engraved stone, found by Parry, which had a number of lines inscribed transversely across it with a single horizontal line running the length of the pebble. Parry also uncovered a bone awl or piercer with inscribed horizontal lines grouped in blocks of four or five along its length (Parry 1931, 48–9). During a systematic examination of animal bones from the cave, a decorated segment of a rib bone with a series of grouped incisions was also discovered (*see* Fig 2.10), with a collection

of small mammoth ivory objects bearing similar markings found during the 1986–7 excavations (Hawkes *et al* 1970, 138; Charles 1989). Whether these marks were functional or purely decorative is a matter of debate; some of these objects may have functioned as aids for measuring, represented calendars or message sticks, or been used in gaming (Jacobi and Currant 2011, 69).

Gough's Cave has also produced human remains dating from the later Upper Palaeolithic. Analysis of these bones has shown them to represent a minimum of five physically modern-looking individuals – a young child around three years old, two adolescents, an

Fig 2.10
Gough's Cave assemblage of bone and antler tools, including three bâtons percés, a bone awl or piercer (top right) and a decorated segment of rib bone (top left). (© Natural History Museum/The Trustees of the Natural History Museum, London)

adult and an older adult (Humphrey and Stringer 2002, 164–7). The remains also display evidence for cut-marks produced by stone tools, with the human and animal remains similarly treated, which suggests a common butchery practice. The cut-marks have been interpreted as indicators of disarticulation and excarnation, with the shattering of marrow-containing bones put forward as evidence for cannibalism (Andrews and Fernández-Jalvo 2003).

More recently, the treatment of the skulls, including the systematic removal of the facial bones, has been interpreted as evidence for the manufacture of skull-cups – used as containers or drinking-cups. Three skull-cups, manufactured from the remains of two adults and a young child, have been identified among the human remains (Fig 2.11). Age determinations on two of the cranial vaults of 13,120–12,310 cal BC (OxA-17848) and 13,220–12,730 cal BC (OxA-17849) make them the oldest dated examples of skull-cups in the archaeological record, and the only example from the British Isles (Bello *et al* 2011). In contrast to the somewhat elaborate inhumations of the earlier Aurignacian tradition, the evidence from Gough's Cave indicates a radically different approach to the treatment of the dead in the period after the Last Glacial Maximum.

At the time that Gough's Cave was occupied, summer temperatures are thought to have been higher than they are today, although climatic deterioration had begun before the cave was finally abandoned. When these early

Fig 2.11
Gough's Cave skull-cup. (© Natural History Museum/The Trustees of the Natural History Museum, London)

hunter-gatherers visited Mendip the region would have supported a diverse and varied landscape. Bare ground and moorland probably covered the higher plateau, giving way to scrub then deciduous woodland on the low slopes and in the sheltered combes, with the surrounding lowlands carpeted in grassland (Jacobi 2004, 75). The apparent concentration of material in the caves of Cheddar Gorge may be related to the natural qualities of the area, such as its sheltered location, proximity to a range of habitats and easy access to water, all of which would have made it an attractive location for a hunting camp (Fig 2.12).

As the climate slowly deteriorated and the environment changed, human activity in the region would also appear to have declined. The technology of this period is characterised by straight-backed and curved-backed flint blades and points – known as 'penknife points'. Penknife points with secure provenance have been recovered from four sites in the area – Callow Hill, Long Wood, Aveline's Hole and Herriott's Bridge. Interestingly, only one assemblage is from a cave context, which some have suggested may reflect a shift towards the occupation of open sites rather than natural shelters in the latter part of the Late Glacial Interstadial (Jacobi 2004, 80). An alternative view could be that the distribution of these artefacts is simply a consequence of survival, with evidence for human activity at open sites generally more difficult to detect and more vulnerable to degradation over time than in caves or rock shelters. It may be that this factor has served to condition our view of Palaeolithic life. Many cave sites must have represented cold, dark space, which brings into question their desirability as habitation sites and forces us to consider if they are truly representative of human activity in the region.

The Mesolithic landscape (c 10,000–4000 cal BC)

The Late Glacial Interstadial was followed by a cold cycle – the Loch Lomond Stadial – which started around 11,000 years ago and lasted for nearly a millennium. This brought a return to dry, tundra-like conditions, and during the coldest part of this cold cycle it would appear the region was abandoned by humans. Towards the end of the Loch Lomond Stadial hunter-gatherer communities once more returned to Britain. A period of rapid warming followed

Fig 2.12
Cheddar Gorge. Its natural qualities would have made it an attractive location for a hunting camp.
(NMR 24323/25)

which saw temperatures rise as much as 5–7°C over a few decades, reaching at least those of the present day. This period of warming resulted in rapid sea-level rises, which led to the submergence of the Severn Estuary and the Somerset Levels and Moors. By the early Mesolithic the most extensive intertidal zone would have comprised either mudflats or low saltmarsh, characterised by soft mud, sparse vegetation and deep tidal creeks (Haslett *et al* 2001, 49). In contrast the uplands of Mendip would have supported boreal forest containing relatively open birch–pine woodland intermixed with areas of grassland (Schulting 2005, 240). As sediments were laid down and relative sea-level rises slowed during the later Mesolithic, areas of mid- and then high saltmarsh expanded and the first freshwater reed swamps developed (Haslett *et al* 2001, 50). The uplands would have supported deciduous woodland of varying density – comprising alder, hazel and oak – punctuated by grey limestone crags, rocky gorges and natural clearings.

Although there is a good range of evidence to indicate Mesolithic hunter-gatherers were utilising the varied resources of the Mendip region, habitation sites are rare in the South-West (and in Britain as a whole). However,

evidence for possible Mesolithic structures was identified at Lower Pitts Farm, Priddy, where two 'Mesolithic huts' were discovered and excavated as part of the Priddy Plateau Project (Taylor 2001, 260); *see* Figure 2.13. The structures sat side by side and were constructed over a shallow depression, with the small turf-built huts measuring approximately 3.5m in diameter and displaying evidence of burning. Three possible hearths were identified externally but only a small quantity of Mesolithic flint was found associated with the structures. The site was interpreted by Taylor as a late Mesolithic hunting camp, although the radiocarbon results put forward suggest an early Neolithic date (2001, 268). The true nature of this site remains unclear.

The main evidence for Mesolithic communities on Mendip derives from the stone and flint implements recovered, in particular certain diagnostic pieces known as microliths. The distribution of these tools across the landscape suggests hunter-gatherer communities were active over much of the Mendip plateau by the late Mesolithic. There are a small number of early Mesolithic flints recorded from the region, but these are not common and do not indicate extensive exploitation of the uplands. Translating distributions of lithic

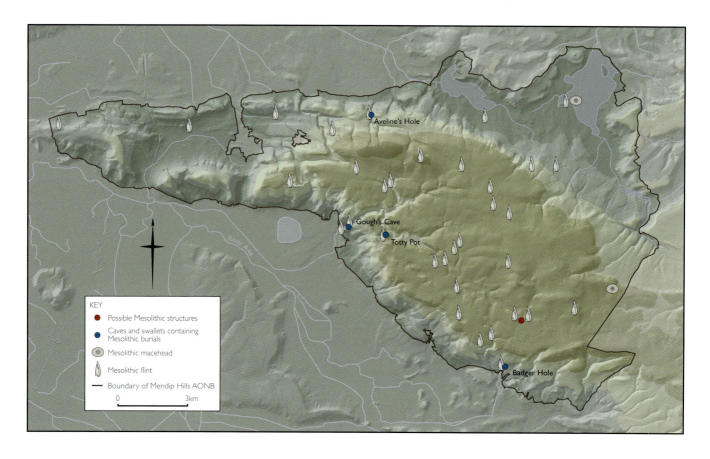

KEY

● Possible Mesolithic structures

● Caves and swallets containing Mesolithic burials

◎ Mesolithic macehead

◇ Mesolithic flint

— Boundary of Mendip Hills AONB

0   3km

Fig 2.13
The distribution of Mesolithic settlement, burials and artefacts across the Mendip Hills.

scatters into general patterns of movement is difficult. Assemblages of flint implements often have no clear provenance, with many attributed to specific collectors who rarely recorded the location and nature of their finds in detail. The distribution patterns of lithic finds are therefore a very blunt tool for interpreting patterns of Mesolithic exploitation. At their simplest level they do suggest human activity increased across the high plateau into the later Mesolithic, with habitation possibly clustering along the main access routes onto and through the uplands.

As in earlier periods, lithic scatters can be interpreted as locations where groups set up their base camps or hunting camps, or reflect more general areas of landscape exploitation. Flint implements can also be seen as indicative of past human practice, with tools representing evidence for specific tasks. The small later Mesolithic flint assemblage recovered from above Ebbor Gorge, for example, contains tools including retouched blades and scrapers. This site has been interpreted as a short-stay or specialist camp, possibly representing a location where animal hides were processed (Lewis 1998, 146–7). Small lithic scatters may therefore represent locations where rela-

tively transient activities took place, signifying areas where tools were manufactured, animals processed, seasonal foodstuffs harvested or fuel gathered.

Sites where larger quantities of Mesolithic flints have been recovered may be considered as more representative of areas of seasonal or specialist occupation. The flint collected from around Fernhill Farm, for example, represents more than the signature of a mobile hunting party travelling through the landscape. The assemblage comprises nearly 300 flint blades, microliths, scrapers, blade cores and waste flakes. The size and diversity of the artefact collection suggests a site with a more prolonged period of use, possibly representative of cyclical activity. Locations visited over many generations could develop into meaningful places through the repetition of social practice, possibly stimulated by inherent environmental factors. For example, it has been suggested that the large assemblage of late Mesolithic flints recovered from around Charterhouse-on-Mendip reflects the area's status as a 'special place', with people possibly drawn to the region by the distinctive qualities of its abundant mineral deposits (Lewis 2011, 107–10).

Caves and swallets

The concept of a special or meaningful place may also have extended to other components of the landscape. For example, the early Mesolithic use of caves on Mendip would appear to have been almost exclusively for burial. Human bones dating from the late 9th millennium BC have been recovered from Aveline's Hole, Gough's Cave and Badger Hole. The famous 'Cheddar Man' from Gough's Cave is the most complete surviving early Mesolithic skeleton in Europe, and the child's skull recovered from Badger Hole may represent one of the earliest known Mesolithic burials in the country. It is possible that caves were considered strange places – passages into the underworld – and as such were associated with myths, legends and the ancestors. Upper Palaeolithic tools and calcium-encrusted animal bones would have been visible within Gough's Cave and Aveline's Hole when Mesolithic groups entered; the material may have served to reinforce the cave's connection with distant ancestors and the mythical past. The caves are located along some of the main routeways up onto the high plateau, routes which would have

been used repeatedly in what was a period of high mobility (Fig 2.14). The deliberate placement of ancestors in these locations may reflect their continuing role in society, with the caves possibly forming fixed points in the landscape which anchored the past with the present and set patterns of social movement.

Aveline's Hole

The 50 or more individuals recorded from Aveline's Hole render the cave a rare example of an early Mesolithic cemetery (Fig 2.15). Radiocarbon dating has shown that the human bones from the cave were deposited within about a century either side of 8300 cal BC, suggesting the remains represent a single phase of burial activity (Schulting 2005, 227–8). This short date-span may also indicate the site was used by the same early Mesolithic group over a number of generations, with all members of society represented in the bone assemblage. Evidence of a slightly later date for human bone (8200–7590 BC), along with what may be two late Mesolithic microliths, could suggest the site continued to be used after the main burial event, which possibly signifies the cave's enduring status as a special or venerated space.

Fig 2.14
Burrington Combe. The burials placed within Aveline's Hole (centre right) were located along a main routeway up onto the high plateau.
(NMR 24819/21)

Fig 2.15
Aveline's Hole, Burrington
Combe. The cave is a rare
example of an early
Mesolithic cemetery.
(DP163832)

Disturbance by early antiquaries, including the removal of skeletal remains, makes interpretation of the evidence from Aveline's Hole problematic. Incomplete and conflicting accounts also hamper our understanding, particularly in relation to how the bodies were treated after death (although their position on the floor towards the left-hand side of the cave seems secure). Some early 19th-century accounts state that when discovered the bones had the appearance of having been 'thrown down carelessly', with others describing 'near 50 perfect skeletons lying parallel to each other' (Boycott and Wilson 2010, 14–19). It is therefore difficult from these accounts to ascertain whether the bodies were complete or disarticulated when found. However, a re-examination of the surviving bone assemblage has revealed the presence of small hand and foot bones which favours the theory that the cave contained entire, articulated skeletons, rather than secondary, disarticulated burials where small bones of the extremities are generally not present (Schulting 2005, 188).

Excavations undertaken by the UBSS in the early 20th century recovered around 20 individuals from Aveline's Hole, including a double inhumation that was placed in a cut in the cave floor. The bones of this double burial were stained with ochre, and perforated animal-tooth beads were found with the bodies. In addition, 18 intact red deer teeth were uncovered scattered among the bones, and seven ammonites were found near the head of one of the individuals. It is unclear if the double inhumation is contemporary with the bodies placed on the cave floor (the cave has produced evidence for later Upper Palaeolithic occupation), but if this is the case, then the evidence would suggest different models of mortuary treatment were being employed by the same group at this site.

The surviving bones from Aveline's Hole have recently been subjected to a new programme of scientific investigation (Schulting 2005). This has included stable carbon and nitrogen isotope analysis aimed at investigating the dietary habits of the early Mesolithic group. This work has shown that marine protein did not form a significant part of the community's diet, unlike animal protein, which was well represented. This would indicate a 'terrestrial' diet, and may suggest the group's territorial range did not extend to the coast. However, perforated winkle shells were extremely common finds at Aveline's Hole, and the lack of marine protein in the diet could simply imply that these early Mesolithic people did not exploit the resources of the Severn Estuary to any significant extent (Schulting 2005, 223).

Evidence for a terrestrial diet during the Mesolithic has also been demonstrated by isotope work undertaken on human bones from Totty Pot, a swallet hole located approximately 1km south-east of Cheddar Gorge. This site is again positioned overlooking one of the main routes through the uplands, with human bone recovered from the swallet recently dated to 7460–7080 cal BC (OxA-16457) and 7460–7040 cal BC (BM-2973) (Schulting et al 2010). The deposition of human material down swallets and vertical shafts may relate to the concept of transition from one place to the next, or define the separation of certain individuals from the living community (Conneller 2006). The remains at Totty Pot date from nearly a millennium after the bodies were placed in the cave sites at Burrington Combe and Cheddar Gorge, and were found in a location later used by a Neolithic group to dispose of their dead.

3

The Neolithic and Early Bronze Age

The Neolithic and Early Bronze Age communities of Mendip are perhaps most evident through the monuments they created – the barrows, enclosures, henges and megalithic monuments – many of which continue to form an important component of the countryside four to five millennia later. These sites often reveal a direct relationship with the landscape itself, from the eye-catching burial mounds strung along the skyline, to the less prominent standing stones of the river valleys (Fig 3.1). They demonstrate the increasing importance of time and place, in a period when we see a shift from a hunter-gatherer existence to one reliant to varying degrees on domesticated livestock and cereal cultivation. This is also a time of substantial evolution in material culture, with the introduction of pottery to Britain and the development of a more sophisticated range of ground stone and flint tools.

By the second half of the 3rd millennium BC the first evidence for metalworking – copper and, later, bronze – appears in the form of ornamental objects, tools and weapons. These technological developments were accompanied by changes in social structure, with a move away from the importance of the community towards a society focused more on the individual. Round barrows are the dominant monument from this period and were often initially constructed to contain the remains of a single individual, sometimes associated with grave goods. This period also saw the introduction of new artefact forms, such as

Fig 3.1
Looking west across the Mendip plateau, with the Ashen Hill and North Hill barrow cemeteries in the foreground.
(NMR 24328/10)

decorated Beaker pots, flint daggers and barbed-and-tanged arrowheads, reflecting an increasingly sophisticated society. The settlement evidence for these social groups is elusive, however, and is largely confined to stone and flint artefacts found scattered across the landscape, possibly reflecting the temporary or transitory nature of these prehistoric sites.

The Neolithic landscape (4000–2200 BC)

In the early Neolithic the Mendip Hills would have been covered in a blanket of deciduous woodland, punctuated by rocky gorges and small natural clearings. The forest canopy, formed by oak, alder, birch and elm, probably extended from the valley floors right up onto the hilltops and supported an under-storey of hazel (Macklin *et al* 1985, 49). As the Neolithic period progressed, the number of open areas increased as trees were cleared to allow small-scale cereal and stock farming. The ritual monuments of the period were also set within clearings, possibly linked to the wider community by a network of paths and tracks. The people who worked and maintained these clearings were represented by small mobile groups who took advantage of the gaps in the forest canopy, through either arable cultivation or the exploitation of natural resources. The territorial range of these groups may have been relatively extensive, with stable isotope analysis suggesting that some individuals may have travelled between Mendip and Dorset, some 60km to the south-east (Green 2000, 79).

Environmental evidence indicates that pockets of arable cultivation existed along the Mendip river valleys by the early Neolithic (Macklin *et al* 1985, 49). The main arable crops grown in these lower-lying areas would have been wheat or barley, sown once a year and possibly forming short-lived episodes of tillage. By the middle or late Neolithic at least some relatively large areas of open grassland had developed in the upland zone (Lewis and Mullin 2011, 150), although evidence for land use elsewhere is limited, and largely confined to deposits found in the caves and swallets. The animal bones collected from these sites suggest that domesticated cattle and pigs predominated, with sheep or goats comparatively rare, which points towards a landscape of relatively limited open grazing. The areas of woodland harboured animals such as deer, wolf, badger, boar and aurochs, the latter again implying the continuation of extensive tree cover.

The southern escarpment of the Mendip Hills rises steeply from the low-lying Somerset Levels and Moors, an area exploited by Neolithic communities from the middle of the 4th millennium onwards. At that time the Levels and Moors comprised a series of sand islands, supporting trees and sedges, separated by shallow areas of open water forming reed swamp. Communication routes between these islands were established using a network of raised wooden footpaths, the oldest of which, the Sweet Track, has been dated to *c* 3800 BC. The construction of this track marked a period of woodland clearance when dry areas were opened up for farming, an episode which lasted for about 400 years (Coles and Coles 1986). The early Neolithic saw a reduction in the area of swamp, and these regions eventually developed into fen woodland comprising large coppice stands of willow, birch and alder. By the end of the Neolithic period changing climatic conditions had caused a gradual transformation of this lowland landscape. Increased rainfall resulted in the Levels and Moors flooding once more, allowing areas of raised bog to develop, overwhelming the fen woodland and ultimately leading to its destruction (Hibbert 1978).

Stone, flint and wood artefacts were found associated with almost all of the excavated trackways across the Levels and Moors, including the remains of several yew bows and leaf-shaped arrowheads, some still attached to their hazel shafts. Flint and stone axes were found alongside the Sweet Track, including a jadeitite axe originating from the Alpine foothills which was discovered partly sealed beneath one of the trackway's collapsed timbers (Coles and Coles 1986). This artefact forms part of a small cluster of Alpine axes recovered from northern Somerset, which includes an example from Quantoxhead, on the northern edge of the Quantock Hills. A jadeitite axe fragment was also discovered on the southern Mendip escarpment at Ebbor and was probably brought to the area from France, the raw material having originated in the Italian Alps (Grinsell 1970, 12; Sheridan *et al* 2010). These exotic items almost certainly represent the deliberate deposition of a valued ceremonial object and indicate long-distance contacts across Europe.

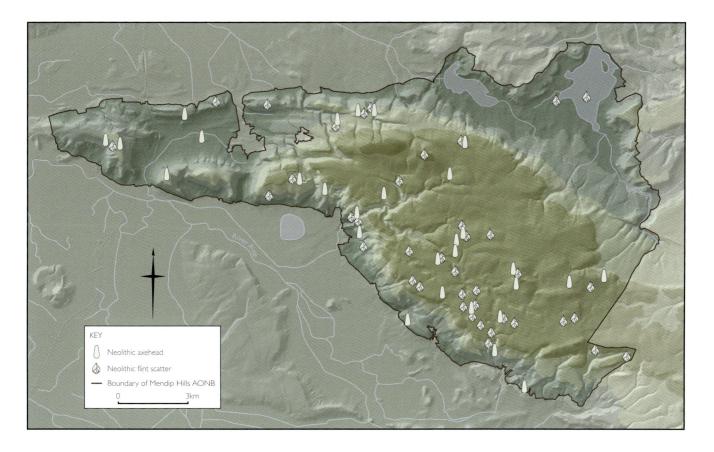

Finds of stone and flint tools form the largest body of evidence for Neolithic activity on the Mendip plateau. These artefacts can be interpreted as representing permanent settlement, favoured locales or more general areas of landscape utilisation. Flint and stone axes represent one of the key artefact types and can be seen distributed across the region, though largely confined to the limestone uplands (Fig 3.2). A large proportion of these artefacts are broken or fragmentary and many are chance finds, such as the ground flint axe found in Rowberrow Plantation during the construction of a forestry road. Others have been discovered through excavation: for example, the green-stone axe from Bridged Pot Hole (Fig 3.3) and the ground flint axe from Soldier's Hole. Perhaps one of the most intriguing finds comes from Brimble Pit Swallet, where a pristine ground greenstone axe was recovered during a speleological investigation, lying approximately 10m below the ground surface (Lewis 2000).

The greenstone and flint from which these tools were made could not have been sourced locally – the greenstone probably came from Cornwall and the flint from Wessex or Devon (Fig 3.4). The distribution pattern of stone and flint axes, which have a wide range of practical applications, can be viewed as representing more general landscape exploitation rather than specific settlement patterns. Casual finds of leaf-shaped and transverse arrowheads can be interpreted in a similar way, as they are generally thought to represent losses sustained during hunting expeditions or in warfare. The axes found in the caves and swallets, however, would suggest that at least some of these artefacts may have been deliberately placed in nooks and niches, possibly defining areas of ritual, cultural or spiritual significance.

Fig 3.2
The distribution of Neolithic stone and flint tools across the Mendip Hills AONB.

Fig 3.3
Greenstone axe from Bridged Pot Hole, now in Wells and Mendip Museum. (DP158759, reproduced by permission of Wells and Mendip Museum)

Fig 3.4
Ground flint axe from
Charterhouse-on-Mendip,
now in Wells and
Mendip Museum.
(DP158758, reproduced by
permission of Wells and
Mendip Museum)

As noted from the Mesolithic period, interpreting patterns of settlement from distributions of lithic scatters is difficult as they often represent the presence of individual collectors or specific research projects as much as prehistoric communities. At their simplest these scatters tell us that Neolithic groups were active across Mendip during the 4th and 3rd millennia BC. The lithic evidence hints at a concentration of activity towards the southern escarpment of the hills, possibly reflecting movement between the low-lying areas of the Levels and Moors and the Mendip plateau.

There is some evidence to suggest that, by the late Neolithic, groups had begun to settle the upland areas and were farming small arable plots. On the southern slopes of Priddy Hill approximately 600 flints were collected after the area was ploughed prior to cultivation in the 1980s. These finds included scrapers, gravers, knives, two leaf-shaped and transverse arrowheads, retouched flakes and a large quantity of waste trimmings. A range of other material was also collected, including saddle querns, the tip of a ground flint chisel, fragments of two greenstone axes, a large chert chopper and a polissoir, used for grinding axe-heads (Hack 1987, 58–62). The bulk of the finds are thought to be indicative of a late Neolithic domestic site, and the saddle querns indicate that cereal crops were being processed close by, suggesting arable cultivation in the immediate vicinity. The cultivated area may not have been extensive, however, and the quantity of flint scrapers in the artefact assemblage – used for butchery, bone working and the preparation of hides – indicates a continuing emphasis on pastoral activities.

Although flint and stone artefacts are relatively widespread across the region, direct evidence for Neolithic domestic structures is very rare in Somerset, as it is in most regions of Britain. Excavations undertaken prior to the construction of the Chew Valley Lake revealed the remains of a possible Neolithic timber structure within Chew Park (Rahtz and Greenfield 1977). The remains took the form of a series of postholes interpreted as defining a 'house', measuring 3.6m by 3m, with an entrance on its southern side. The only dating evidence from these cut features was a fragment of Western Neolithic pottery, although a leaf-shaped arrowhead, a flint end-scraper and a hammer-stone were recorded from within the structure itself, suggesting an early Neolithic date. A number of other pits and postholes were identified in the immediate vicinity, including an oval pit, 0.3m deep, which contained pottery, flint flakes, calcined bone, charcoal and hazelnut shells. The pottery from this pit was undecorated and represented the bases and rims of round-bottomed bowls of Western Neolithic type, roughly contemporary with the 'house' site.

A shallow oval pit, no more than 0.5m across, was also found at Ben Bridge and contained charcoal, burnt gravel, flint flakes and sherds of Grooved Ware pottery (Rahtz and Greenfield 1977, 85). The digging of pits is a phenomenon common to the late Neolithic, but the size and form of these features make it unlikely they originated as storage pits. They are frequently associated with burning, which has led some to suggest that they represent hearths. Their contents are not always fired, however, and are often diverse for domestic rubbish, sometimes including human bone possibly indicative of grave deposits.

Early Neolithic ceremonial monuments

Long barrows

Linear mounds are a distinctive feature of early Neolithic northern Europe, with their architectural form possibly reflecting that of earlier longhouses and replicating the processes involved in their abandonment and decay (Bradley 1998). In the British Isles long mounds began to appear around the beginning of the 4th millennium BC, and have clear regional distributions focused on Wessex, Sussex, Lincolnshire and Yorkshire, although this may reflect the survival of extant monuments. Concentrations of linear mounds can also be found in Wales and Scotland, where they come in a range of forms including the distinctive horned long cairn. In Britain these monuments ranged in size from *c* 20m to over 125m in

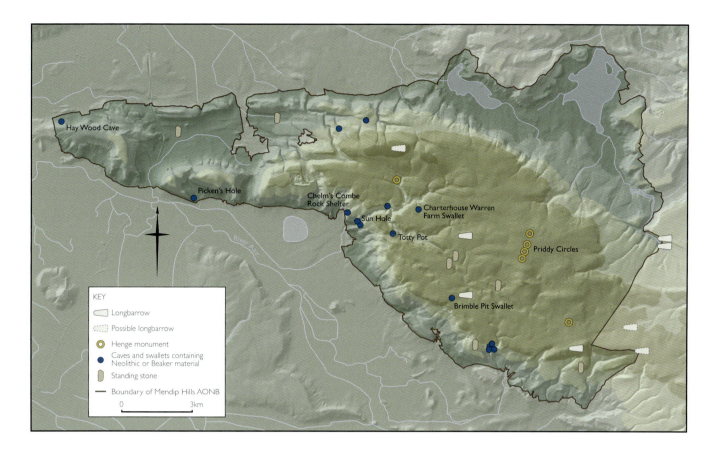

length, and were constructed in a range of architectural styles, forming a series of cells or single or multiple chambers covered by earthen or stone mounds.

Long barrows form the earliest humanly constructed monuments within the Mendip Hills AONB. There are, however, just three such sites identified as upstanding earthworks – Pen Hill, Priddy Hill and Priddy Long Barrow – all of which are confined to the eastern half of the area (Fig 3.5). There is a fourth site, located on Beacon Batch, which may also represent the degraded remains of a Neolithic long mound. The feature comprises a U-shaped stony bank, which stands a maximum of 0.3m high, enclosing an area of loose stones, consolidated cairn material and larger boulders (Fig 3.6). The monument sits on the southern slopes of Beacon Batch, just below the summit, and in 1819 was visited by the Revd John Skinner, who noted that the barrow at that time was being quarried away for walling material (BL Add MS 33653, fol 43). Tratman also visited the site and described it much as it appears today (Tratman 1926), including the three large stones in the south-west corner which may represent the remains of a small cist or stone kerb.

A further four sites are known from just outside the AONB's eastern boundary, between Chewton Mendip and Green Ore, of which only two survive as earthwork features – Mountain Ground and Barrow House Farm. At Green Ore the long barrow was levelled by ploughing in

Fig 3.5
The distribution of Neolithic monuments and caves across the Mendip Hills AONB.

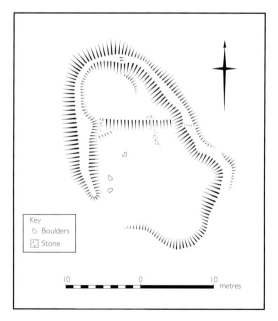

Fig 3.6
Beacon Batch: earthwork plan of possible long barrow.

the post-war period and is now only visible on early aerial photographs; Haydon Drove long barrow was lost to development in the later 20th century but was visited by Grinsell in 1963, when he recorded it as a ploughed-down linear mound (Grinsell 1971, 87). The relatively recent destruction of these monuments could imply that the distribution of long barrows we see today may have more to do with modern agricultural practices than with variations in Neolithic land use. With that said, the relatively few long barrows within the region, and their grouping towards its eastern end, undoubtedly reflect a far more complex pattern of activity.

Physical characteristics

The Mendip long barrows form a small group which vary in size from 21m to 60m in length. They are largely trapezoidal in shape, ranging from 10m to 28m in width, although the majority fall within the range of 10m to 18m. The Pen Hill long barrow is one of the best-preserved examples in the area, and has a wider eastern end and a sinusoidal northern side, tapering and dropping in height towards the west. There is a series of undulations along the ridge of the monument, making it slightly bulbous towards the centre, with its swollen east end possibly covering a mortuary chamber (Fig 3.7).

The height of the Mendip long barrows varies quite radically from 0.3m to 3m, but this again may be partly attributed to later land use. There are traces of a flanking ditch along the northern side of the Pen Hill long barrow, but to the south the ditch may have been covered by slippage from the mound or damaged during the construction of a concrete anchor point for the Pen Hill mast. When Grinsell (1971) visited the site it sat within open heath, and the monument's associated side ditches were more clearly defined; he recorded them as not running parallel to the mound but widening towards the south-west. There is no evidence of side ditches associated with any of the other extant mounds, but their location, predominantly within enclosed farmland, would suggest the ditches may have been infilled.

Immediately to the east of the Pen Hill long barrow is a round barrow, separated from the linear mound by a narrow trackway. The co-location of such monuments is not uncommon and numerous examples of such pairings have been recorded elsewhere, such as Milston Firs long barrow on Salisbury Plain and Lake Barrow 41 near Stonehenge (McOmish et al 2002, 47; Bowden et al 2012, 10). This phenomenon is repeated on Mendip at Mountain Ground, where the long barrow forms part of a later barrow cemetery comprising four round

Fig 3.7
Earthwork plans of long barrows: (a) Priddy Long Barrow and (b) Pen Hill.

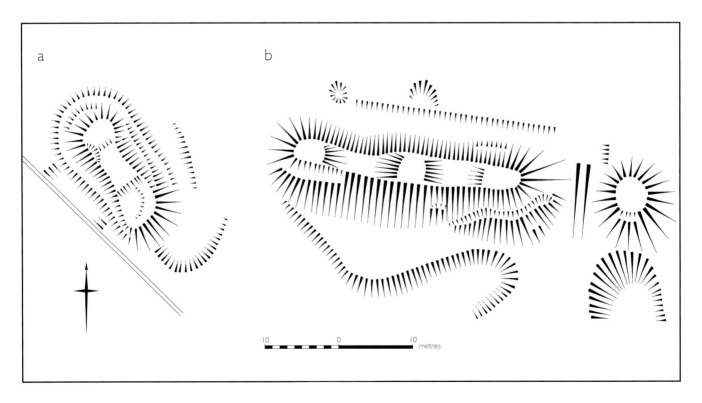

barrows, one located at either end of the long mound. The mortuary monument on Beacon Batch is also closely associated with a later barrow cemetery. This is a common occurrence, with other examples including Winterbourne Stoke Crossroads 1, where the long barrow forms part of an extensive barrow cemetery (Bax *et al* 2010, 45).

The relationship between long barrows and later monuments may indicate the dominance of such features in the landscape, or may raise the possibility that at least some of these round mounds may be early features. Earthen round barrows or 'rotunda' were constructed in a number of regions during the early Neolithic, with some covering stone or wooden structures and others defining open spaces. Regional groupings have been recorded in areas including the Peak District, Dorset, Wiltshire, Yorkshire, Scotland and the Cotswolds. Some round mounds have been clearly shown to pre-date Neolithic long mounds (though probably only by a short period of time) with others identified encased within them (Darvill 2010, 130–5). Although on Mendip no Neolithic round mounds have been identified to date, features such as the undulating nature of the Pen Hill long barrow and the co-location of linear and round mounds may hint at a more complex monument tradition than previously appreciated.

Priddy Long Barrow

Priddy Long Barrow (Fig 3.8), lying roughly 1.2km west of the village of Priddy, was visited in 1925 by Tratman, who recorded the monument as trapezoidal in shape and noted 'the tips of the two uprights of the entrance passage at the south corner' (Tratman 1926, 286). His observations led to the monument's excavation by the UBSS in 1928, and this work has given us our only glimpse at what lies beneath these enigmatic mounds (Phillips and Taylor 1972). The excavations revealed a complex series of activities and practices at the site, the earliest of which pre-date the creation of the mound. The initial phase of activity was represented by a pit, centrally positioned in relation to the mound, which may have originally contained a timber post or a standing stone. The upright was later removed and the pit infilled with stone, and a cremation burial placed on top marks the position of the former post or stone. Two hearths were also identified which pre-dated the mound, one of which contained

fragments of human bone and had been covered by a rough stone cist.

The core of the barrow comprised a platform or pavement of horizontally laid stones, some 12.8m long by 7.3m wide, over which a cairn had been constructed, making it similar in form to some Wiltshire long barrows. Evidence from the Wiltshire examples suggests that in certain cases these pavements may have functioned as excarnation platforms – areas where bodies of the dead were left exposed to the elements (McOmish *et al* 2002, 30–1). The overlying cairn comprised large stones at its eastern end and predominantly smaller stones and earth to the west, bounded by an irregular kerb; the cairn material was combined with fragments of both burnt and unburnt human bone and a selection of flint tools. The diversity in cairn material may represent separate phases of activity or may relate to specific processes, such as the sealing of a timber mortuary chamber. At the end of the monument's active life a capping of small stones and earth was placed over the central core, which sealed and extended the mound to create the long barrow we see today (Phillips and Taylor 1972, 31–6).

Siting and distribution

Although most of the Mendip long barrows are orientated roughly east–west, and therefore possibly aligned on the rising or setting sun, this is not exclusively the case. Priddy Long Barrow is orientated north-west to south-east, with its wider end to the south-east. The long

Fig 3.8
Priddy Long Barrow: looking west over the grass-covered stony mound. (NMR 26591/19)

barrow sits above the lip of a natural basin and follows the contour of the slope – making the monument appear more impressive on the downslope side. The Pen Hill long barrow also utilises the natural slope in this way, positioned below the summit on the southern side of the hill, its location creating a false-crest effect. It may be that these monuments were intended to be viewed from below or from a specific vantage point created to provide maximum impact. If we consider the wooded nature of the early Neolithic landscape, it is possible that carefully constructed vistas were cut through the trees to manipulate both the observer's experience of the monument and their access to it. The barrows themselves may have sat within clearings, possibly resembling pockets of light within the dark woodland, their false-crest position restricting views from the site and adding to the atmosphere of the space.

It is also possible that the topographic setting of sites may relate to the adoption or referencing of significant landscape features (Jones 2005). Components of the landscape – such as rivers, hills, caves and rock outcrops – may have been perceived in specific ways by Neolithic communities and would have carried their own explicit meanings. Priddy Long Barrow sits above a steep-sided natural amphi-

theatre which forms part of the southern side of the Cheddar Valley. This geographic feature may have formed a natural clearing with its own distinctive qualities in the Neolithic, possibly a space where dispersed groups came together to honour ancestors or to generate and reproduce social networks.

Water may also have played a significant part in ritual activity, with springs evoking connotations of birth, life and regeneration. On the northern side of the hills, Mountain Ground and Barrow House Farm long barrows occupy ridges on either side of the headwater of the River Chew, the latter orientated with its north-western end towards the spring. These spring sites may have been perceived as providing a connection between the monuments and the wider landscape, implying a sense of movement or transition from one place to the next. The Pen Hill long barrow is situated above the head of a steep-sided valley named Walcombe where several springs issue and flow south-west before disappearing back into the earth. The Haydon Drove monument is positioned in a similar location, with the water from both these sites re-emerging at the foot of the escarpment to feed the River Sheppey. The action of water disappearing below ground has clear parallels with death and loss, and these sites were perhaps viewed as gateways to the underworld.

Cheddar Gorge cuts a deep scar through the southern escarpment of the Mendip Hills, and the distribution of monuments and artefact scatters along its route imply a concentration of activity in this area during the Neolithic (Fig 3.9). The Priddy Hill long barrow is located above the northern flank of the Cheddar Valley and, with its position on the summit of the hill, commands two northern branches of the main route. Priddy Long Barrow lies to the south and again has a clear relationship with the Cheddar Valley. The Longwood Valley also forms a northern branch of Cheddar Gorge and is overlooked by the mortuary monument on Beacon Batch. Valley floors may have formed relatively open areas providing easier access through the landscape. The location of these features may reflect an attempt by mobile groups to define rights of access to particular areas or resources using carefully constructed and positioned monuments.

The control of access and the referencing of landscape features may only be part of the picture. There is evidence to suggest that the position of monuments may have been more

Fig 3.9
The distribution of Neolithic long barrows, stone and flint tools, and caves across the central plateau.

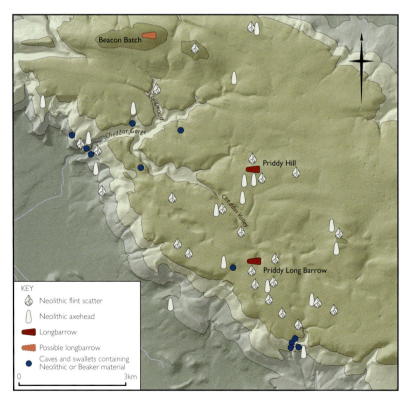

KEY

⬦ Neolithic flint scatter

◓ Neolithic axehead

▬ Longbarrow

▬ Possible longbarrow

● Caves and swallets containing Neolithic or Beaker material

0   3km

intimately related to the history and associations of specific places (Pollard 2005). That at least some of the region's Neolithic monuments were constructed in places of existing significance is illustrated by the archaeological evidence. Pre-monument activity at the site of Priddy Long Barrow is demonstrated in the form of a pit and hearths, the alignment of which was reflected in the construction of the later mound. The incorporation of elements of pre-existing features into the structure, and the referencing of their location (such as the cremation over the pit at Priddy Long Barrow), creates links to the past through the monument's physical construction. Evidence for a long sequence of landscape utilisation is also apparent through material culture, with Mesolithic flints discovered in close proximity to the Priddy Hill long barrow and from the mound itself at Priddy Long Barrow (D Field, pers comm). The construction of these monuments therefore appears to represent the perpetuation of activity at a site with existing significance using culturally charged material, possibly reflecting an attempt to draw upon the past associations of that specific place.

Caves, rock shelters and swallets

Some of the caves and rock shelters of Mendip, the Peak District, Derbyshire and Wales have also been interpreted as Neolithic ceremonial sites. These subterranean spaces, generally found in limestone areas, were predominantly used for burial or ritual deposition. Activity at cave sites often extended over a prolonged period of time, with these spaces possibly being perceived in a different way to the above-ground ceremonial monuments. On Mendip a concentration of cave sites utilised during the Neolithic has been identified around Cheddar Gorge and Ebbor Gorge, although it is conceivable that many more sites elsewhere have gone unrecognised or unrecorded. As mentioned, these gorges would have formed the main routes up from the lowlands onto the high plateau and may have been seen as 'gateways' into the upland zones. The unique texture of the natural landscape would also have added to the special character of the area.

Many of the caves of Mendip are multi-period and have suffered from later animal or human disturbance destroying stratigraphy and making interpretation of the archaeological material difficult. However, radiocarbon

results from four caves – Chelm's Combe Rock Shelter, Hay Wood Cave, Picken's Hole and Totty Pot – indicate that these sites were in use during the early Neolithic. The earliest phase of Neolithic activity at Totty Pot swallet has been dated to 3630–3370 cal BC, and forms part of what was evidently a long-lived tradition of deposition at the site (Schulting et al 2010, 81). At Chelm's Combe Rock Shelter, pottery, flint and the remains of four individuals were excavated prior to the site's destruction by quarrying. The human bone was primarily concentrated in two layers, dated through pottery to the Neolithic and Beaker periods. The skull of a middle-aged man was found associated with round-bottomed bowls (Fig 3.10), bone implements and flint scrapers, with bone from the site producing a radiocarbon determination of 3630–3365 cal BC (Balch 1926; Schulting et al 2010, 86).

Investigations at Hay Wood Cave, towards the north-western tip of the region, were undertaken by the Axbridge Caving Group between 1957 and 1971. The excavation was confined to the entrance and overhang of the cave, where animal bones, flints, pottery and the remains of 28 individuals of all ages, both male and female, were discovered. The majority of the flint artefacts were thought to be Mesolithic or Neolithic, with radiocarbon results from a sample of human bone returning a date of 3795–3385 cal BC (Schulting et al

Fig 3.10
Neolithic round-bottomed bowl from Chelm's Combe Rock Shelter, now in Wells and Mendip Museum. (DP158762, reproduced by permission of Wells and Mendip Museum)

2010, 85). The burials would appear to signify at least three phases of activity, the earliest represented by three complete bodies placed at the southern end of the cave. The second phase involved placing mixed bones from incomplete or partially decomposed bodies on top of the initial burials, before covering the whole lot with a mound of rocks and earth. Finally, a very fragmentary group of human bones was inserted into the northern end of the mound followed by more bones tipped onto the side and then covered over (Everton and Everton 1972, 19).

Recent research into radiocarbon dates for human bones from British caves has shown an apparent concentration of activity from the early Neolithic onwards (Aldhouse-Green *et al* 1996). This increase in the use of caves as mortuary sites occurs at about the same time as chambered tombs and long barrows are created in the landscape, possibly indicating a change in how social groups processed some of their dead. It has been suggested that caves may have been viewed as a natural alternative to chambered tombs, with the space within them used in a similar way (Lewis 2005, 125). However, it is now widely accepted that long barrows were only used for a relatively short period of time, in contrast to some of the cave sites, which continued in use throughout the Neolithic. Undoubtedly the story is more complex, but there is certainly a degree of similarity between the mortuary processes employed at Hay Wood Cave and the earthen long barrow at Priddy, for example.

Middle and late Neolithic ceremonial monuments

Henge monuments

By the early 3rd millennium BC the construction of henge monuments had become relatively widespread across Britain, with the greatest density found in the south and east of the country. By the middle of the millennium some were constructed on a scale previously unseen, with many forming elements of larger ceremonial complexes. Henge monuments can range in size from the henge enclosures of Marden and Durrington Walls which measure over 500m in diameter, to more modest monuments, such as Wormy Hillock in Donside, the interior of which measures only

6m across. The enclosures often underwent several phases of activity, with the initial construction sometimes incorporating a circle of timber posts in the interior. These internal features may have been used to manipulate movement within the space, helping to define and perpetuate ritual within the enclosure. Some enclosures have a formal approach, possibly constructed to create a carefully contrived view of the interior and control people's experience of the site. Henge monuments are characteristically associated with carefully placed deposits of artefacts and animal bones, sometimes attributed to ceremonial feasting. Human cremations are also frequently found as secondary deposits in their internal ditches, or associated with postholes in their interior, but do not define the initial use of the monument.

Gorsey Bigbury and Hunters Lodge

Two of Mendip's henge monuments are very similar in form – Gorsey Bigbury and Hunters Lodge – and can be defined as Class I henges (Fig 3.11). A third possible Class I henge has been suggested at Charterhouse-on-Mendip, where a substantial earthwork enclosure, identified as a Romano-British amphitheatre, may have been remodelled from an earlier monument (Fradley 2009, 53). The site was excavated by Gray (1909), who demonstrated at least two phases to the construction of the earthwork, with the interior lowered, the external ditch cut and the west entrance created after the construction of the original core. The monument is located overlooking the Blackmoor Valley and adjacent to former springs. It is slightly oval in form, measuring about 52m in diameter, and originally had a single entrance on its eastern side.

Both Gorsey Bigbury and Hunters Lodge are located within the upland zone, an unusual setting for monuments of this type, which are generally associated with valley-floor locations; the enclosures measure 47m and 51m in diameter respectively. At Hunters Lodge the low earthworks form an almost circular enclosure comprising a ditch with external bank defining a platform with a small mound at its centre. The ditch circuit is not complete and there is a causeway on the north-north-west side mirrored by a gap in the bank. A narrow berm separates the ditch and outer bank; the bank now stands no more than 0.3m high and apparently comprises spoil from the ditch. The monument was first observed under thick vegetation in 1926 but was not investigated until the area was under the plough in 1954. At that time Tratman (1958) recorded the bank as standing 0.9m high and the ditch 0.6m deep; he suggested the central mound had the appearance of a recent stone heap. When the monument was visited by Grinsell in 1963 the field was laid to grass but the monument stood only 0.3m high and was categorised by him as a possible henge or disc barrow (Grinsell 1971). A recent geophysical survey has identified the location of two pits towards the centre of the monument, as well as hinting at the possibility of an external ditch (Lewis 2005, 75–7).

The Gorsey Bigbury henge is very similar in form to Hunters Lodge, although it is better preserved as its archaeological significance was recognised much earlier. The site was visited in 1819 by the Revd John Skinner, who described it as a 'religious circle' and commented that 'the banks were upwards of six feet high, sloping inwards … considerably lowered last year, when preparing the ground for a potato crop' (BL Add MS 33653, fol 178). When Tratman visited the site in 1926 he interpreted the earthworks as a disc barrow. Under this misconception the site was extensively excavated by the UBSS, and the work confirmed the monument's status as a Neolithic henge: *see* Panel 3.1 (Jones 1935, 1938). The monument is now in a pasture field and comprises a ditch and outer bank separated by traces of a berm, with the ditch a maximum of 0.6m deep and the bank up to 0.5m high. The internal platform measures 18m in diameter (slightly larger than Hunters Lodge) and has a low mound at its centre; the space is accessed via a causeway on the north side.

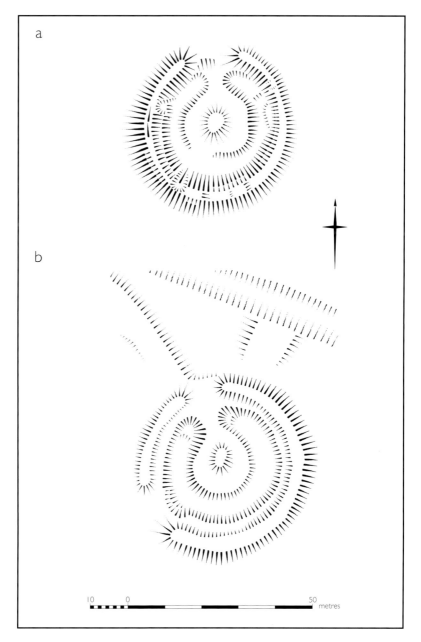

The Priddy Circles

The Priddy Circles are four enclosures located towards the centre of the Mendip plateau, forming a linear arrangement running north-north-east, all of which are defined by a bank and outer ditch. They are strikingly circular in form, demonstrating a precise degree of planning and control over their construction, and each would appear to have a single entrance. The enclosures have all been affected to varying degrees by agricultural improvement, with the best-preserved sections of bank and ditch standing around 0.9m high and 0.4m deep. Detailed survey work has shown that

the southern circle, Priddy Circle 1, displays evidence for a slight counterscarp bank associated with the ditch (Fig 3.12). The enclosures range in size from 154m to 168m in internal diameter, the biggest being represented by the northernmost, Priddy Circle 4, which is slightly misaligned and apparently incomplete. There is approximately 57m between each of the three southern circles, with around 357m between Priddy Circle 3 and Priddy Circle 4. This has led to the suggestion that there may have been a monument in the intervening gap which has now been lost. However, there is no archaeological evidence

Fig 3.11
Earthwork plans of henge monuments: (a) Gorsey Bigbury and (b) Hunters Lodge.

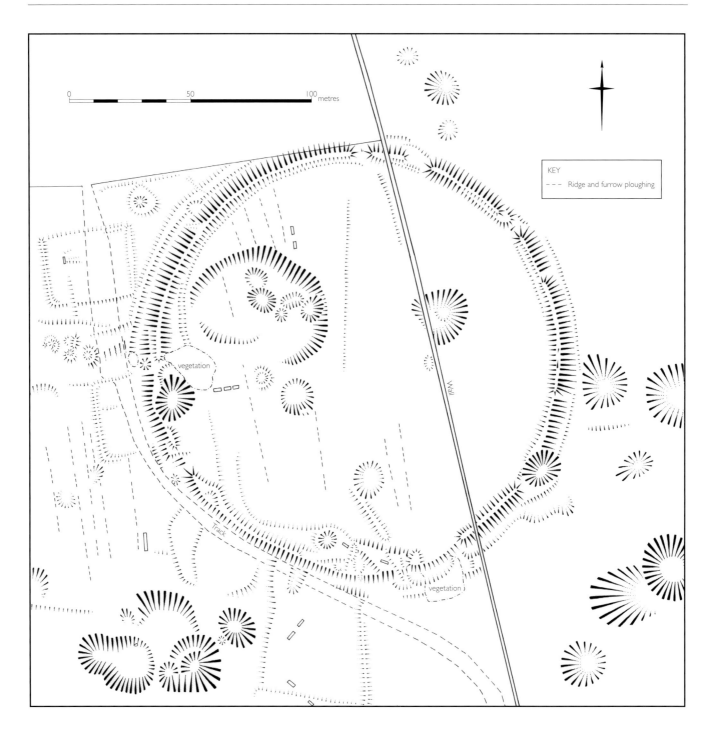

Fig 3.12
Priddy Circle 1. The
earthwork plan shows
the counterscarp bank
associated with the north-
western quadrant, and the
slight remains of earthwork
banks to the south and
west of the enclosure.

to support this, and the space (now cut by a Roman road) may have performed a different function or possibly represented an area which held pre-existing spiritual significance.

Excavations undertaken at Priddy Circle 1 by the UBSS revealed a range of methods, materials and activities related to the construction of the enclosure bank (Taylor and Tratman 1957; Tratman 1967). The initial act of construction was represented by a very shallow

marking-out trench, no more than 0.15m wide, which defined the space. Two concentric rings of posts were then erected within the circle, spaced approximately 2m apart, with timber stakes placed in between to form parallel timber revetments. Stones were then packed against the inner faces of these structures forming two rough walls about 0.45m wide and 0.6m high. The gap between the walls was then filled with stones from the surrounding area, and finally the whole was capped with earth from the outer ditch. This created a structure standing approximately 1.5m high.

The work also revealed that although the northern and western sides of the circuit were defined in stone, the eastern quadrant was made of low walls of turf. The different treatment of this section of bank may suggest a separate phase of construction, or signify a deliberate attempt to distinguish it from the rest of the circuit. To add to this, recent excavation work has revealed a more complex story, identifying a turf-with-stone section of bank within the eastern and southern quadrants (Fig 3.13). This new research has also revealed that the posts were removed before the earth capping was applied, which implies the timber uprights were taken away before the ditch was cut (Lewis and Mullin 2011, 157–9; Leary and Pelling 2013, 16–19). This may have been a functional necessity, the posts having reached the end of their natural life, or may represent a deliberate statement related to the changing nature of the monument.

Excavations across a gap in the north-east circuit revealed a causeway and ditch terminal, confirming its status as an original entrance. The eastern side of the entrance represents the start of the turf wall, with three pits uncovered on either side of the gap interpreted as stone holes pre-dating the enclosure walls.

These stones were later removed and the pits backfilled. Two fallen stones were recorded at the ditch terminal on the west side of the causeway and are thought to be contemporary with the enclosure (Taylor and Tratman 1957, 7–17; Tratman 1967, 97–125). Radiocarbon dating of charcoal recovered from the primary ditch fill of Priddy Circle 1 returned a result which suggested the ditch was cut before 2870 cal BC (Lewis and Mullin 2011, 155). However, during more recent excavations a fragment of a probable late Neolithic transverse arrowhead was recovered sitting on top of a layer low down in the bank make-up. Recorded as coming from a layer of recent disturbance, it is thought the implement originated from the bank and had been displaced during modern demolition (Leary and Pelling 2013, 16). Further work is therefore required if a secure date for the construction of Priddy Circle 1 is to be ascertained.

What is also unclear is the time span between each construction event. For example, we do not know how soon after the posts were erected the infilling occurred, a process which would have transformed the monument from a relatively open space to one closed from view. The creation of a ditch, and the concealment of the turf and stone walls, would also have altered the outward appearance of the monument considerably. This may imply a change in the

Fig 3.13
Priddy Circle 1: photograph of section through bank in south-eastern quadrant, facing east.
(Jim Leary)

monument's use or people's view of the space. The ditch, for example, may have been perceived as having a magical or religious function, and not simply as a source of material for the bank. The different phases of construction could in themselves have held ritual and spiritual significance, the understanding of which may have changed through time.

The construction sequence of the four enclosures is also at present poorly understood. It is unclear whether the complex originated from a single episode of monumental construction or a series of separate events undertaken over a prolonged period of time. The regularity in form and spacing of circles

Fig 3.14
The Priddy Circles: aerial photograph looking south over the enclosure complex with the 'incomplete' Priddy Circle 4 in the foreground. The earthwork remains of a Roman road can be seen passing between circles 3 and 4.
(NMR 24327/47)

1 to 3 could hint at a contemporary phase of construction. The form and position of Priddy Circle 4 (Fig 3.14), however, may suggest it was constructed at a slightly different time or performed a separate function. It is clear that the enclosures we see today represent the culmination of a complex sequence of actions, but how the developments recorded at Priddy Circle 1 relate to the other enclosures is now unclear. For example, is the 'incomplete' nature of Priddy Circle 4 simply a result of the monument's development ending earlier in the construction sequence, or a deliberate architectural statement related to a specific purpose or activity? Clearly there are many questions which at present remain unanswered.

Internally there is little evidence to suggest how the monuments were originally used. The earthwork remains of later ploughing, quarrying and archaeological trenches are the only features visible in the interior of Priddy Circle 1, apart from several depressions formed by sinkholes or swallets. These natural hollows pepper the free-draining limestone plateau, adding to the unique texture of the landscape, and possibly formed part of the draw to this area for early communities.

Siting and distribution

There is a clear distribution of henge monuments on Mendip focused towards the eastern half of the region and confined to the upland zone. Although located on the plateau, the henge monuments do not occupy the highest ground. For example, Gorsey Bigbury is situated on a promontory on the western side of the Longwood Valley (Fig 3.15), and Hunters Lodge is located on a saddle at the head of the Cheddar Valley. The positioning of these monuments may again be related to movement through the landscape, with the sites arguably occupying strategically important locations in this regard. These were communal monuments where people came at important times of the year to participate in seasonal festivals, reinforce social networks, and celebrate both life and death. Routes to these sites would have played an important role in their use – groups would have needed to know how to get there – and a close association with clear topographic features (such as main valley systems) would have assisted with this. The importance of the surrounding topography has also been highlighted by Bradley (1998, 2000), who suggests a possible correlation between the

siting of monuments and the overall configuration of the wider landscape. There is also
evidence to suggest that these monuments
were constructed on sites that had been used
before (for example, the Mesolithic flints found
at Gorsey Bigbury and Priddy Circle 1), possibly
indicating an existing understanding of that
specific place.

Gorsey Bigbury is sited above the confluence
of two streams, with its entrance referencing
the northern watercourse and possibly allowing
direct access to it. The earthwork remains of
a dried-up stream-bed were also recorded
immediately north of Hunters Lodge, with the
entrance once again orientated towards it.
In an upland limestone area the significance
of water, and the ritual and spiritual meanings
associated with it, would have been even
greater than in regions where water was abundant. As groups moved through the landscape
they would have focused on areas where
water could be obtained for both themselves
and their livestock. Through perpetuation,
these locales would have accrued sacred
significance far beyond the practical need for

this vital resource. These upland springs and
watercourses also influence the environment
of the lowland landscape, and in a period of
changing environmental conditions this may
have strengthened the perceived significance of
these areas. Other natural elements – such as
swallets, caves, mineral deposits and prominent
hills – would all have played their part in adding
to the distinctive properties of the wider
landscape, a landscape imbued in the Neolithic
with sacred and spiritual meaning.

Caves, rock shelters and swallets

A number of swallets on Mendip have been
shown to contain deliberately placed Neolithic
deposits. Recent scientific analysis of the partial
remains of three individuals (an adult and two
young children) from Totty Pot swallet, for
example, returned dates of 3355–2930 cal BC
(Schulting *et al* 2010, 81). Human remains and
cultural material uncovered from Charterhouse
Warren Farm Swallet, south of Velvet Bottom,
indicate these natural depressions continued
to function as ceremonial sites into the later

Neolithic. The lower deposits within the shaft contained disarticulated human bone, Grooved Ware and Beaker pottery, a bone pin, an antler spatula and a selection of flint implements, including a dagger. Despite the material being separated into four distinct horizons, radiocarbon dating has shown that the human bone layers were deposited in a relatively short time frame, returning a date of 2460–1995 cal BC. The material from the site has been interpreted as deliberate deposition, with the artefacts placed down the shaft rather than thrown or washed down over time (Audsley *et al* 1988; Levitan and Smart 1989, 394; Stanton 1989, 395–9).

Another site which has produced late Neolithic material is Brimble Pit Swallet, located towards the edge of the southern escarpment above Westbury-sub-Mendip. When excavated the swallet was found to comprise two entrance shafts, with the southern shaft containing 200 worked pieces of flint, human bones, animal bones and 42 pottery sherds representing two Grooved Ware vessels (Lewis 2000). The large amount of cultural material from these sites is in stark contrast to the unaccompanied human remains placed in Totty Pot swallet in the early and middle Neolithic. This disparity may represent a change in ritual practices or reflect the cultural developments of the age.

Caves also continued to be utilised by communities during the late Neolithic. At Sun Hole, in Cheddar Gorge, a large hearth was discovered towards the mouth of the cave containing fragments of Grooved Ware and Beaker pottery, bone implements and flint artefacts. Human bones, representing two adults and two children, were also discovered, the majority uncovered near the cave's east wall (Tratman and Henderson 1928). Burial deposits are often found at or close to cave entrances, perhaps indicating that Neolithic groups were reluctant to venture too far into caves, possibly viewing them as passageways to the afterlife. Caves also represent confined spaces and are often located in relatively inaccessible locations, heightening people's perception of them as special and exclusive places. Elsewhere, caves have been widely interpreted as providing an interface with the supernatural world and are central to origin myths. It is evident that particular caves were chosen because of their location, form or past associations, with a range of mortuary

processes employed at different caves. Evidence from Irish examples indicates that, although some caves were used as the primary focus for burial, others were used for excarnation and were therefore temporary or transitory places which represented only part of a complex mortuary ritual (Dowd 2008, 312–15).

Standing stones

Stone circles are largely confined to the north and west of Britain, with an especially rich concentration in Devon, Cumbria, Scotland and the Peak District. Stone circles come in a variety of sizes, ranging from around 10m in diameter to the Great Circle at Stanton Drew, north of Mendip, which measures over 112m across. At Stanton Drew the complex comprises three stone circles and two stone avenues, as well as a setting of three upright stones known as the 'Cove'. Recent geophysical investigation within the Great Circle has shown it was once a much more complex monument. A highly elaborate pattern of buried pits arranged in nine concentric rings was revealed within the circle of stones, with further pits also found towards the centre of the circle. The pits almost certainly held upright timber posts and were located no more than one metre apart. The survey also revealed that the Great Circle itself originally sat within a large ditched enclosure with a broad entrance to the north-east (David *et al* 2004).

Within the Mendip Hills AONB there are no impressive megalithic monuments such as the stone circles and stone rows of Dartmoor or the more modest stone settings of Exmoor. There were, however, 16 recumbent stones recorded within two adjacent fields in the area of Cheddar Head, to the north-west of Priddy. These limestone slabs, ranging from 2.5m to 0.7m in length and between 1.5m and 0.2m wide, led Hack to suggest they may represent the 'male' and 'female' types identified with prehistoric stone circles and alignments (1985, 4–7). A quantity of Neolithic and Early Bronze Age implements have been recorded from the immediate area but it is now impossible to tell if these stones represent the remains of a contemporary monument. Another possible megalithic monument was identified during evaluation work prior to the construction of a pipeline in a field north of Star, close to the site of a Roman villa. This took the form of a semicircle of stones, defined by five blocks forming an east-facing arc 3m wide – the three larger stones composed of blocks placed on their sides. It is suggested that the feature may have been a kerb around a (removed) standing stone or a stone setting (SHER 12789).

There are a number of monoliths within the region which may date from the late Neolithic or Early Bronze Age. Perhaps the most striking of these is the Yarborough Stone, which occupies a valley-floor location to the north of the Lox-Yeo river. The monument is composed of local Dolomitic Conglomerate, 0.4m thick, and stands an imposing 2.3m high (Fig 3.16). The monument has commanding views both eastwards up the Lox-Yeo Valley and south-westwards, past Crook Peak out to the Levels and Moors. Its location is also close to the confluence of the Lox-Yeo river and a smaller tributary which flowed down from the north-west; the tributary has now been diverted by the construction of the M5 motorway.

A second fine monolith, the Wimblestone, can be found approximately 4km to the east, near Star (Fig 3.17). The stone is located adjacent to a field boundary on the southern side of the Towerhead Brook, and takes the form of a triangular slab of local stone standing a maximum of 1.75m high. A possible barrow was identified by Grinsell (1971) immediately adjacent to the stone, and it was suggested that the monument may have once formed part of a megalithic tomb. According to folklore, the stone is said to walk about between midnight and dawn, exposing a heap of gold beneath (Dobson 1931, 57).

There are also a number of smaller isolated stones on the high plateau. One such stone is located close to the eastern boundary of the churchyard surrounding St Laurence's church at Priddy. The stone stands just over 0.5m high and is located on the south-eastern slopes of Green Hill overlooking Solomon Combe, where a series of springs rise before quickly disappearing to continue their journey underground. A second stone lies close to a field corner on the southern slopes of Prior's Hill, a spur of land to the south of Pen Hill. The stone stands no more than 0.7m high and is positioned overlooking Biddle Combe, which carries a stream south-westwards feeding the springs at Wells. The Deer Leap Stones, two quartzite pillars, are located within a pasture field above Hope Wood, near Ebbor Gorge (Fig 3.18). These paired stones were once located adjacent to a boundary bank which was

Fig 3.16
Yarborough Stone. This lichen-covered conglomerate slab stands an imposing 2.3m high.
(DP100279)

Fig 3.17
Wimblestone. This triangular slab now stands adjacent to a field boundary.
(Elaine Jamieson)

removed in the 1960s (Tratman 1968), the earthwork remains of which can still be seen snaking through the field. The original southern stone was evidently destroyed at this time, but subsequently replaced and the northern stone re-erected (Stanton 1981, 63). The existing

Fig 3.18
Deer Leap Stones. This pair
of stones was once encased
within a boundary bank;
one of the original uprights
was destroyed and
subsequently replaced.
(Elaine Jamieson)

earthfast stones are approximately 1m high and 15.6m distant and are located on a natural spur overlooking the Levels and Moors.

It is impossible to tell if these monuments are prehistoric in origin or if they represent later boundary markers or animal rubbing stones. They can, however, be compared to the small single and paired stones found on the uplands of Exmoor, both in size and landscape position. The Exmoor examples form part of a tradition for low stone monuments which also includes the more complex stone settings. A correlation between such monuments and the headwaters of valleys has been noted on Exmoor (Riley and Wilson-North 2001, 24) and is apparent on Mendip, with many of the monuments occupying sites on spurs overlooking minor tributaries. The stones on Green Hill and Prior's Hill are in close proximity to small barrow cemeteries, with a possible barrow also recorded adjacent to the Wimblestone. The association of standing stones with cairns or barrows is widespread. On Exmoor the stone

setting on Kittuch Hill comprises a linear group of eight stones aligned on a cairn (Jamieson 2001, 21); the embellished round cairns of Dartmoor incorporate a circle of spaced upright stones which define the perimeter of a flat-topped cairn.

The distinctive recumbent stone settings of north-east Scotland are perhaps a more elaborate form, generally incorporating a ring cairn encircled by monoliths graded in height, with a large horizontal boulder (the recumbent) on the southern side. Recent excavations have shown that the stone circle was a secondary phase of these monuments, with the primary cairn returning radiocarbon dates of between 2600 and 2400 BC (Bradley 2002, 843). In Wales, standing stones have been found incorporated into barrows, sometimes pre-dating the construction of the mound, and could be completely hidden or left projecting through the top of the monument (Williams 1988, 32). How these monoliths were used on Mendip is as yet unclear.

Panel 3.1 Gorsey Bigbury

Gorsey Bigbury clearly demonstrates the multifaceted nature of henge monuments, revealing a range of complex actions which significantly changed how the monument was used and perceived through time. Following initial construction, a number of ritual and ceremonial activities were undertaken at the site. These involved changes in the monument's form, the deposition of human remains and artefacts, the later redistribution of bones, and a final deposition of cultural material. The evidence indicates the monument formed the focus of ceremonial and spiritual activity over a period of several hundred years, spanning the late Neolithic and Early Bronze Age.

Located on a promontory on the western side of the Longwood Valley, near Charterhouse-on-Mendip, Gorsey Bigbury was excavated by the UBSS between 1931 and 1935, and then again in 1965 (Jones 1935, 1938; ApSimon 1951; Tratman 1966). The initial excavations exposed the entire area of the central platform but failed to reveal any post-built structure, indicating the bank and ditch formed the earliest episode of monumental construction. The irregular rock-cut ditch ranged from 3.6m to 6.3m in width, and was at its deepest towards the north-west, where it was cut 2.4m below the rock surface (Fig P3.1.1). The causeway across the ditch was of undisturbed rock (Jones 1938, 3–56). Sections through the bank revealed it comprised a low earthen mound overlain by limestone rubble, indicating it was constructed using material excavated from the ditch. The area of the entrance was excavated in 1965, and revealed two pits asymmetrically located on either side of the causeway. These were interpreted as postholes related to the initial phase of the monument, the uprights having been later removed and the pits infilled (Tratman 1966, 25–9).

The initial excavations revealed the remains of a crouched male burial within a rough stone cist in the north-west segment of the ditch, some 3m west of the causeway. The cist comprised rough boulders and stones, with the base formed by two flat slabs laid on the bottom of the ditch. The burial was accompanied by grave goods – four bone needles, a bone scoop, a Beaker sherd, a flint knife (placed by the

head) and a barbed-and-tanged arrowhead (placed by the knee). A substantial part of this skeleton along with that of an adult female was recovered from the overlying fill of the ditch, which indicates the burial had been disturbed. Two individuals, a young woman and a child approximately five years old, were also identified from within the ditch on the opposing side of the causeway. It has been suggested that these may all have originated from the cist burial, and that the redistribution of bones represents a separate phase of activity at the site (ApSimon *et al* 1976, 155–83).

The north-east, east and south-west segments of the ditch produced large quantities of cultural material, including Beaker pottery, flint, burnt daub and animal bones. The finds were separated from the ditch bottom by a layer of yellow clay silt, which indicates they represented a secondary phase of activity. In two places a platform of closely packed stones had been laid on the clay prior to deposition. The next layer was composed of a charcoal band, over which more charcoal,

Fig P3.1.1
Gorsey Bigbury. The henge monument is now under pasture and comprises a ditch and outer bank, separated by traces of a berm, with a low mound at the centre of the internal platform. (NMR 24823/21)

Fig P3.1.2
Assemblage of flint
arrowheads and Beaker
pottery from Gorsey
Bigbury, including a
leaf-shaped arrowhead
(top left) and two barbed-
and-tanged arrowheads
of different form. The
selection of pottery
demonstrates the wide
range of decoration.
(DP164508, reproduced
by permission of the
University of Bristol
Spelæological Society)

earth and stones (interspersed with pottery, flint and bone) had been placed. The excavated finds included some 2,000 worked flints and an equal number of waste flakes. The assemblage predominantly comprised small convex scrapers, but a quantity of arrowheads, including barbed-and-tanged and various triangular forms, were also recovered. The pottery assemblage represents around 120 vessels, which included comb-decorated fine wares and rusticated coarse wares of late Beaker date (Figs P3.1.2 and P3.1.3).

Radiocarbon analysis of charcoal and bone from the site returned dates which suggest two main episodes of activity centred around 2250 BC and 2000 BC. The story is undoubtedly more complex, however, with the archaeological evidence suggesting a number of phases of monument development and ritual deposition. The latest phase of activity has been interpreted as a final act of site 'closure', with the deposition of culturally charged material possibly representing a tangible shift in how people perceived and interacted with the monument (Lewis 2005, 81).

Fig P3.1.3
Reconstructed Beaker vessel
from Gorsey Bigbury.
(DP164509, reproduced by
permission of the University
of Bristol Spelæological
Society)

The Early Bronze Age landscape (2200–1500 BC)

By the end of the 3rd millennium BC the first metal objects had reached Britain – weapons, tools and ornaments made from copper and copper alloys. Some of the earliest metal artefacts, copper and bronze axes, daggers and spears, were never used or sharpened and primarily functioned as status symbols to be carried and displayed. The axe is again one of the key artefact types and occurs in a variety of forms, which gives it a central role in the construction of typologies and sequences (Barber 2003, 155). The earliest form was the flat axe, thought to represent a direct copy of stone and flint implements, a bronze example of which was recovered from a cleft of stone at Deer Leap Quarry, near Wookey Hole, in 1913 (Dobson 1931, 81–2). A flat axe was also found in Slitter Cave, Cheddar, with a bronze flanged axe – possibly dating from the end of the Early Bronze Age – recovered from a ledge within a natural cavern in Burrington Combe.

Axes are most commonly deposited as single items or in hoards – collections of items buried underground – and would have represented valuable objects to the individuals or groups who left them. Metal artefacts can also be found deposited within round barrows, although copper and bronze grave goods are relatively rare. On Mendip, bronze knives or daggers were found associated with three primary cremations within the Ashen Hill barrow cemetery (BL Add MS 33648, fols 123–7). In the late 18th century 'some brazen spear heads, and other weapons, to the amount of a dozen or more' were found by a labourer within the mound material of Westbury Beacon; the artefacts were sold for two gallons of cider and subsequently melted down (BL Add MS 33655, fol 298; 33677, fol 84). Spearheads or daggers are the most common metal artefact found in grave deposits although other metal objects have also been uncovered on Mendip, such as the bronze lozenge-shaped awl found below an inverted cremation urn in the Tyning's Farm east barrow (Read 1924, 145). Metal objects may have been deposited at these sites because they carried inherent meaning, linked to the life or death of the individual, possibly reflecting the social status of the deceased or the aspirations of the living.

The introduction of metal artefacts to the British Isles coincided with the appearance of a new style of pottery – finely made and decorated Beakers. These tall, open-mouthed vessels were in circulation in Britain from about 2500 BC to 1700 BC and were used for domestic as well as funerary purposes (*see* Fig P3.1.3). The form of this pottery has led to their interpretation as drinking vessels, with more specialised types such as 'pigmy cups', a uniquely funerary object, thought to have contained incense. As we have seen, large quantities of Beaker pottery were found within the ditch fill at Gorsey Bigbury henge, the material dated to around 2000 BC, with stylistically similar pottery also recovered from Bos Swallet, Burrington (ApSimon *et al* 1976, 180). Detailed examination of Beaker vessels from these sites has shown that the pottery was made locally, possibly on a site-by-site basis, rather than imported from a central production area (Russell and Williams 1998, 138). The Beaker pottery and animal bones from Gorsey Bigbury have been interpreted as evidence for settlement, with the occurrence of burnt daub in the artefact assemblage thought to indicate house structures close by (ApSimon *et al* 1976, 181). It is unclear whether this location represents an area of permanent settlement or a transitory site used on a cyclical basis. It is possible the material represents 'special' deposition connected to the ritual or spiritual use of the site (Lewis 2005, 83).

At Bos Swallet, sherds of Beaker pottery (representing 20 vessels), flint implements and burnt sheep bones were discovered along with a hearth, burnt stones and a series of pits, one of which was thought to have contained a water-holding tank or cistern. Bos Swallet has been interpreted as an occupation and 'boiling' site – an area where water was heated using fired stones. Boiling sites are rare in south-west England, but have been recorded from the West Midlands, Hampshire, Wiltshire, Gloucestershire and the New Forest. They can also be found in Scotland, Ireland and Wales and are often termed 'burnt mounds' – usually represented by a kidney-shaped bank of stones and often located close to a source of water. Although the function of these sites is somewhat enigmatic, it is generally thought they represent areas where cooking took place, though the suggestion they represent saunas or sweat-houses has also been put forward (Buckley 1990; Hodder and Barfield 1991; Smith 1999).

It has been suggested that Bos Swallet was chosen as it was sheltered and had a water supply, with the site possibly used seasonally by a small group or community who utilised the uplands as summer grazing for their flocks (ApSimon 1997, 43–82). The animal bone in the assemblage strengthens the suggestion that the site was used as an eating area, with the high proportion of sheep bones indicating that, although cattle and pigs continued to pre-dominate, certain areas of Mendip had been cleared for pasture. This site is located close to a substantial flat cemetery and barrow group from where Beaker pottery has been recovered. Swallets evidently had a continuing draw for people during the Early Bronze Age, with Beaker deposits found at sites including Charterhouse Warren Farm, possibly suggesting the evidence from Bos Swallet represents more than mundane domestic activity.

Evidence from Bos Swallet and elsewhere indicates that by the Early Bronze Age the Mendip Hills may have supported a more varied and diverse natural environment. Pollen analysis of sediment samples taken from a round barrow on Beacon Hill, for example, indicates that deciduous woodland – comprising oak, elm and alder – existed at the time the monument was constructed. This forest canopy supported an under-storey of hazel and was punctuated by more open areas of woodland colonised by birch. Birch may also have defined the woodland margins, bordering substantial clearings of open, well-drained heath or grassland (Woodland 2008).

The proliferation of mortuary monuments witnessed at this time suggests an increasing number of clearings were being created – focused on hilltops, ridges and valley heads. Some of these monuments were constructed from turf, which hints at relatively large areas of open grassland in their immediate vicinity. In addition, the secondary use of later Neolithic ceremonial monuments (such as Gorsey Bigbury) shows that these areas continued to be maintained, attracting new burial monuments and leading to increasingly larger clearings. That people were also farming the land is attested to by a quern rubber from an Early Bronze Age burial site in Chew Park and a barley grain impression on a Beaker vessel from Gorsey Bigbury (Rahtz and Greenfield 1977, 29; Helbaek 1952, 226). Vegetation was therefore cleared locally at least, for both farming and ceremonial purposes, but how extensive these endeavours were is at present unclear.

The communities of Early Bronze Age Mendip would have continued to comprise groups of forest farmers who travelled freely across the landscape. The settlements these communities occupied are elusive, however. As with the earlier periods, finds of stone and flint tools can be interpreted as reflecting locations of permanent or transient settlement, or more general areas of landscape exploit-ation. The distribution pattern of lithic finds indicates that Early Bronze Age communities were active across the region, utilising the same areas as their Mesolithic and Neolithic ancestors, although the evidence suggests a possible decline in occupation levels (Fig 3.19). Along the southern escarpment a substantial quantity of prehistoric flint has been collected, representing human activity stretching from the Mesolithic through to the Early Bronze Age. At the head of Ebbor Gorge an assemblage of late Neolithic/Early Bronze Age flint has been interpreted as representing a Beaker settlement of the late 3rd millennium BC (Lewis 1998, 141–7).

Early Bronze Age ceremonial monuments

The late Neolithic and Early Bronze Age saw changes in society, beliefs and customs which are most evident in the landscape by the way these communities treated their dead. Inhumation burials have been found placed in the ditch terminals of Neolithic henge monuments, occasionally associated with a range of grave goods including Beaker vessels. Around 2000 BC cremation became the pre-dominant burial ritual and cremated remains were deposited in containers in the ground, sometimes within enclosed cemeteries and often marked by a round mound. This is the period when large numbers of round barrows and cairns were first built across Britain, sometimes in large linear or clustered ceme-teries, but more often as single monuments dispersed across the landscape (Fig 3.20).

There are over 30,000 round barrows or cairns recorded in the British Isles but there must have been many more visible during the Early Bronze Age (Parker Pearson 1993, 81). These monuments come in a wide variety of sizes and forms, ranging from the large disc-barrows of southern England, upwards of 40m in diameter, to small satellite cairns measuring

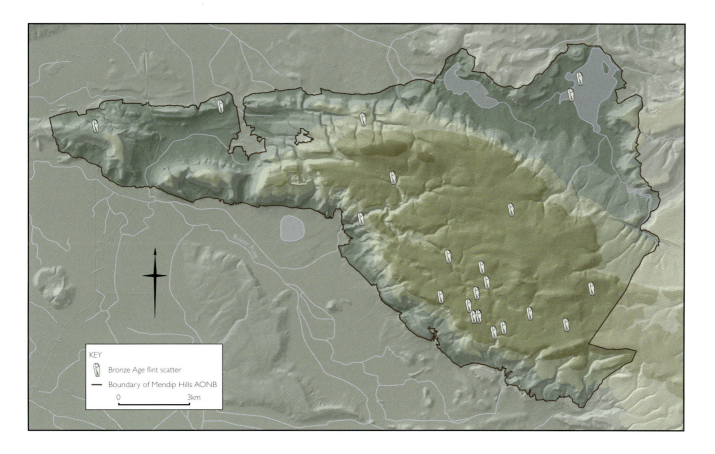

KEY

🜚 Bronze Age flint scatter

— Boundary of Mendip Hills AONB

0   3km

less than 5m across. By the Early Bronze Age burials had become more individualistic, with barrows often comprising the remains of a single individual accompanied by a range of personal belongings. These could include flint or metal tools, ornamental objects and pottery vessels, such as highly decorated Beakers. Barrow burials sometimes contained exotic items which must have been carried a considerable distance before being deposited, such as jet and amber beads. After 2000 BC Food Vessels and Collared Urns were used as grave goods, often as holders for cremated ashes; unlike Beakers, they were a specifically British form of pottery not found on the continent. New monuments continued to be constructed throughout the Early Bronze Age, with some existing mounds selected for progressive elaboration and enlargement. This could involve the addition of new mound material, often associated with the insertion of secondary cremations, sometimes deposited within an urn, a stone-lined cist or a simple pit.

Not all graves were marked by a round mound at this time. Flat cemeteries have been recorded across Britain but by nature are much harder than barrows to detect in the landscape.

On Mendip, flat cemeteries have been identified on Black Down and in Chew Park. Upwards of 50 pits containing cremation burials were discovered while a small cemetery of round barrows was excavated on the northern slopes of Black Down. In Chew Park a roughly circular

Fig 3.19
Map showing the distribution of Bronze Age flint tools across the Mendip Hills AONB.

Fig 3.20
Tyning's Farm barrow group. These barrows survive as islands of green amid a sea of arable cultivation. (NMR 26594/22)

pit, approximately 1m in diameter, was found to contain the cremated remains of a man, probably in his mid-thirties. He was buried with over 80 sherds of pottery and a range of flint and stone artefacts, including a pristine barbed-and-tanged arrowhead and an axe fragment from the axe quarry of Great Langdale, Cumbria. The pottery represented no fewer than eight Beaker vessels, both fine and coarse wares, including Bell Beakers, a Beaker bowl and a Beaker cup (Rahtz and Greenfield 1977, 29). There was no evidence to suggest the grave had been marked by any kind of mound, but it is possible such sites had other forms of above-ground elaboration, such as posts, timber structures or encircling banks.

Caves and swallets also continued to be utilised at the beginning of the Early Bronze Age, often perpetuating sites which were used for ritual deposition during the Neolithic period. Beaker pottery has been found associated with human remains at numerous Mendip cave sites, including Chelm's Combe Rock Shelter, Sun Hole and Charterhouse Warren Farm Swallet. At Beaker Shelter, in Ebbor Gorge, the remains of four individuals were found associated with large Beaker sherds

and a floor of limestone flagstones, with the burials dating from the very beginning of the Early Bronze Age.

Round barrows and cairns

Almost 300 barrows and cairns have been recorded within the Mendip Hills AONB, the majority of which are located on the high plateau (Fig 3.21). It is likely that more barrows existed, others having been levelled completely. Several new barrows were identified during the course of recent survey work, including a rather ploughed-down but well-defined barrow about 100m to the east of the well-known Ashen Lane barrow group in Priddy. The monument was possibly previously overlooked as people were drawn to its larger and more striking neighbours. At least five barrows on Bleadon Hill were demolished around 1819 when the area was being enclosed and improved; one was excavated prior to destruction and an urn containing charcoal, flints and burnt bone was discovered (BL Add MS 33654, fol 157; 33655, fol 116).

Barrows undoubtedly existed in the lower-lying regions but have been swept away by later

Fig 3.21
The distribution of barrows and cairns across the Mendip Hills AONB.

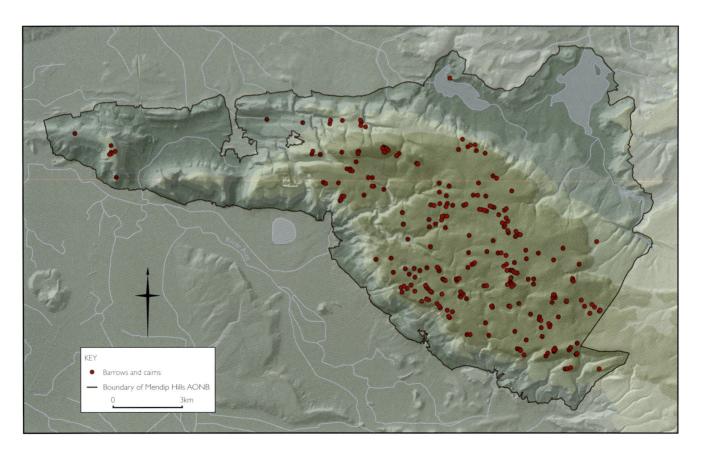

KEY
● Barrows and cairns
— Boundary of Mendip Hills AONB
0   3km

development, with field names or cropmarks often the only clue to their former location. Of the upstanding barrows, a large number have been damaged through the actions of agricultural improvement or the activities of enthusiastic antiquaries. The extensive areas of mining which cover Mendip have also had an effect on the survival of Bronze Age mounds, with a number of barrows either completely or partially destroyed (Fig 3.22). With that said, however, barrows and cairns form the largest group of prehistoric monuments on Mendip. Some of the most striking examples can be seen on the tops of hills or following ridgelines, with many more sited on the lower slopes or on saddles of land at the head of valleys. They can sit in isolation or form part of a small group or larger cemetery; sometimes they are located close to long barrows, henge monuments or standing stones.

It is not unusual on Mendip to see later enclosure walls running alongside or even over Bronze Age barrows. Round barrows have been used as route and boundary markers for many centuries. There is evidence to suggest that when constructing the Roman road to Charterhouse-on-Mendip, the surveyors may have used Bronze Age burial monuments to guide their route. Medieval charters contain a limited number of possible references to barrows, but the 12th-century perambulation of the bounds of Witham Priory's land at Charterhouse provides the earliest written record for barrows on Mendip. A number of barrows can be found on the boundaries of parishes, such as Bristol Barrow in Chewton Mendip, and many were used when defining fields associated with parliamentary enclosure. The prominent location of barrows and cairns has also led to their exploitation as fire beacons, a use often attested to by their name – Beacon Batch and Westbury Beacon, for example.

Antiquarian investigation

Barrows attracted the attention of antiquarian investigators, many of whom were little more than treasure hunters looking for urns, bones and grave goods. Large numbers of the barrows and cairns on Mendip show signs of having been opened at some point in the past – as is often evident in the form of a large hole dug into their centre – in many cases without any record of what was discovered. As we have seen, Bronze Age burial mounds were one of the many archaeological monuments to catch

the attention of the Revd John Skinner, who commented that many of the barrows and cairns on Mendip had been plundered prior to his investigations. After opening a cairn on Beacon Batch, he concluded 'it is probable it had been previously opened, as some of the tumuli adjoining evidently had been' (BL Add MS 33656, fol 40).

Skinner worked on Mendip in the first few decades of the 19th century, during a period of enormous agricultural change, when large areas of the former common wastes were being enclosed and improved for the first time in well over a millennium. It was during this period

Fig 3.22
An aerial photograph showing the close association between the Hunters Lodge henge monument (centre foreground) and the Hunters Lodge disc/bell barrow, which has been partly destroyed by mining activities. (NMR 24332/16)

that Bishop Law, a Fellow of the Society of Antiquaries, encouraged Skinner to open some of the burial mounds located on episcopal land in search of artefacts for his private collection. The bishop accompanied Skinner to North Hill in 1826, at which time they opened three barrows within the Bronze Age cemetery – the only grave goods encountered were two blue cylindrical beads. The same day the party also opened a barrow in a group to the north, near the Castle of Comfort Inn, but found little to excite the bishop (BL Add MS 33691, fols 279–82).

In the early 20th century the UBSS initiated a programme of barrow excavation, the results of which appeared in a series of reports published in the society's journal (Read 1923, 1924; Taylor 1926, 1933, 1951). This work included the investigation of a number of monuments in the Burrington area, as well as some emergency recording of sites threatened by demolition elsewhere on Mendip. Perhaps its most accomplished piece of work was the extensive excavations at the Tyning's Farm barrow group, carried out between 1924 and 1933. The society excavated all five barrows in this small nucleated cemetery, with the work highlighting the complex range of processes adopted by Early Bronze Age communities in the treatment of their dead. Activities included the setting of fires, the deposition of artefacts and the insertion of cremated remains in a range of containers – cists, pits or pottery vessels. The residue of these ritual and funerary processes was subsequently sealed under a mound of earth or stone, with the mound material itself also charged with cultural debris such as flint, pottery and bone. In some cases this was not the final act at the site: secondary burials and deposits were inserted into the mounds at a later date, signifying the contin-uing ritual and spiritual significance of these monuments to Early Bronze Age communities.

During the 1920s the UBSS also embarked on a regional archaeological survey which included visiting, recording and indexing all field monuments – a large proportion of which were round barrows. A similar field-based approach was adopted by A T Wicks, who studied the barrows of Mendip for the Mendip Nature Research Committee of the Wells Archaeological and Natural History Society during the early 20th century. The information gathered from these previous bodies of work was brought together by L V Grinsell and

included in his extensive study of Somerset barrows, his paper on the monuments of north and east Somerset (Grinsell 1971, 44–137).

Physical characteristics

At their simplest, barrows and cairns are circular mounds constructed from loose stone, a mixture of earth and stone, or turf. The barrows and cairns of Mendip form a relatively diverse group, ranging in size from around 6m to 40m in diameter and standing anything from 0.2m to 3m in height. The monuments were clearly designed to present a range of profiles, with some piled high with earth and stone and others much flatter, lower structures. In his gazetteer of Somerset barrows Grinsell (1971) divides the monuments into three main categories – round barrows, bell barrows and disc barrows. In reality the story is far more complex, with round barrows encompassing a wide range of forms including bowl barrows, stone cairns, ring cairns and platform cairns/embanked platform cairns (*see* Glossary). Even within these classes there are subgroups: bowl barrows are clearly represented by two main forms – those which stand around 1.7m high and lower, flat-topped mounds which are about 1m in height. The majority of the nine bell barrows identified by Grinsell within the region can largely be discounted, as few display the characteristics of true bell barrows. In reality these classifications only relate to the surface remains, which are often the final phase in a lengthy process of monument construction. As a result, various classes of structure may be incorporated within the architecture of another monument, forming part of its developing physical history.

Some Mendip barrows contained cists – small chambers defined by boulders or slabs of stone. These features could be constructed above ground level or sunk beneath the soil with their top left flush with the surface, and could be sealed by a cap of stone, timber or turf. Cists sometimes formed an element of secondary burials, and could contain human bone, charcoal or grave goods. They vary in size, sometimes defining an area of no more than 0.4m by 0.3m, and could be rectangular or oval in form (Fig 3.23). These chambers were usually covered by barrow material and are generally only known from excavated or dismantled monuments. Excavated evidence has shown that not all barrows contain cists, however, with burials often placed in a simple pit (sometimes defined by a ring of boulders), deposited either within a container or in a loose pile placed on a slab of stone, or directly onto the ground.

A barrow near Pool Farm, West Harptree, was excavated in 1930 and found to contain the cremated remains of an adult and a child. They had been placed within a large stone-lined cist, measuring 1.65m by 1.35m, with a paved floor and a capstone. The south-western slab of the cist was later found to bear carvings representing 7 foot- and 10 cup-marks, an unusual discovery. The cremated remains had been placed centrally against the carved side of the cist (possibly within a bag or pouch) and have been radiocarbon dated to 1920–1735 cal BC. It has been suggested that the combination of small and large footprints on the slab (Fig 3.24) may reflect the adult and child in the burial (Horne 1931; Grinsell 1957; Pitts 1978; Coles *et al* 2002). Footprints are indicative of movement, however, and this very specific form of rock art may have been a device to aid with the journey to the spirit world.

On Mendip less than 10 per cent of barrows display evidence for an encircling ditch, although more may have existed than is now apparent. Some ditches possibly silted up over time as material from the mound slumped, or were infilled through the process of later cultivation. At the western end of Pen Hill, for example, a low round barrow was defined by an encircling ditch which is now only visible as a slight depression around its northern and eastern sides. Where ditches are present they may represent the earliest phase

of construction, possibly used to demarcate a specific space and define access to its interior. That some ditches appear to be interrupted or segmented (such as Westbury Beacon and Lord's Lot barrow) may imply that access to the interior formed a key consideration during construction. The Tyning's Farm south barrow began life as a ditched enclosure with a low, internal bank, the interior accessed by way of a causeway on the south-western side. Within the enclosure was a series of pits and hearths representing ritual or 'token' deposition and the lighting of fires, activities which predated the directly funerary function of the

Fig 3.23
Cist B of the Tyning's Farm north barrow. Note the pigmy cups (top right). (Reproduced by permission of the University of Bristol Spelæological Society)

Fig 3.24
The Pool Farm cist slab bearing carvings representing 7 foot- and 10 cup-marks. (Reproduced with the kind permission of Bristol Museums, Galleries and Archives)

area (Taylor 1951, 131–62). Ditches could therefore be constructed to provide a focus for ritual events, manifested in the deposition or burial of objects, with the structure possibly designed to keep spirits in or out.

That ditches were not simply constructed as sources of cairn material is evident by the sheer size of some of the Mendip barrows. On Stockhill an impressive bowl barrow stands 2.1m high and is surrounded by a shallow ditch – clearly inadequate for providing all the earth and stone required to construct the mound. If the ditch was insufficiently large, or a barrow had no outer ditch, where did the material for the mound come from? On Exmoor, stone quarries specifically used for mound material have been identified in close proximity to barrow groups on Dunkery Beacon and Robin and Joaney How (Riley and Wilson-North 2001, 37). Much of Mendip is peppered with pits and depressions, features which are almost impossible to date, but some undoubtedly represent the source of material for the barrows and cairns. It is also possible that earth and loose stone was simply gathered from surrounding fields, or deliberately carried to the area from significant locations, possibly where stone was abundant, as in the rocky gorges and combes (Lewis 2007, 79).

Some barrows were constructed of turf stripped from the surrounding area, an action which may in itself have held significant religious or spiritual meaning. In 1925 a large round barrow located on the northern slopes of Ashen Hill was excavated prior to its destruction, which revealed that the bulk of the barrow was constructed of turfs arranged in concentric layers. The soil adhering to the turfs was predominantly red, clayey sand deriving from the area immediately adjacent to the monument (though not from directly beneath it), with some turfs comprising grey and yellow soil, evidently brought from further afield (Taylor 1926, 213–15; Soil Series 1in map, 280 Wells). A barrow within Beacon Hill Wood was constructed from layers of turf, some of which displayed evidence of having been burnt (Leach 2007). It is possible the turf was lifted from an area where ritual activities had taken place – the pyre site, perhaps – with the inherent meaning of the material transferred to the barrow through its reuse in the fabric of the monument.

The turf, earth or stone of a barrow mound could sometimes be retained by a kerb – a wall of large boulders or upright stones positioned around the base of the monument. Where these kerbs did exist they have often been obscured by material slumped from the barrow as it eroded over time, with their tops sometimes left visible, poking through the turf. Blocks of stone which may represent kerbstones were noted on Beacon Batch and North Hill, although it is probable many more barrows had retaining kerbs than the records suggest. The west and central barrows at Tyning's Farm were both bounded by stone slabs or blocks which may have functioned as retaining kerbs. The central barrow was defined by a wall of Old Red Sandstone boulders, surmounted by a coping of long blocks and faced with large upright limestone slabs (Taylor 1951, 120). A barrow to the north of Rodney Stoke airfield (Grinsell's Cheddar 20) revealed two phases of stone revetment, the second a renewal of the kerb after the mound had slumped over it (Lewis and Mullin 2001).

Ring ditches, ring cairns and embanked platform cairns

Although relatively rare, across the region there have been recorded a number of ring ditches, ring cairns and platform/embanked platform cairns. The latter take the form of low flat-topped mounds of stone or earth, sometimes topped by a low encircling bank; ring cairns are represented by small embanked enclosures formed by earth and stone, with ring ditches often defining a relatively small space accessed by a narrow causeway. Some of these monuments have funerary remains associated with them, while others display little or no evidence of burials. Excavated evidence has also shown that in some cases these monuments formed the first phase of mound construction. A barrow excavated on the northern slopes of Ashen Hill, for example, evidently began life as a ring cairn but was subsequently mounded over with turf (Taylor 1926, 213–15). Three of the round barrows in the Tyning's Farm barrow group were also shown to have developed from enclosed spaces defined by causewayed rock-cut ditches and internal banks (Taylor 1951, 120). At the Tyning's Farm south barrow, the pits and fires constructed within the interior of the space were left exposed long enough to become overgrown by vegetation (ibid, 147).

A ring cairn was recently discovered on Stockhill within an area of intensive mining.

The monument is 21m in diameter and comprises an encircling bank, a maximum of 0.3m high, with a low mound towards its centre. A second probable ring cairn has been identified within the barrow group on Beacon Batch, previously recorded as a disc barrow (Fig 3.25). The monument comprises a pear-shaped enclosure, a maximum of 31m in diameter, defined by a spread bank with a small stony mound located off-centre. It is possible the outer bank was formed by stone robbing of a more substantial barrow, but the size and consistency of the bank suggests it is more likely to represent a ring cairn or cairn enclosure.

A group of monuments – two ring cairns (with central mounds) and a low embanked platform cairn – were excavated on the lower slopes of Black Down in 1923 (Read 1923, 1924). These monuments ranged in size from 11m to 16m in diameter, with a fourth unexcavated site in this group taking the form of an embanked platform cairn standing a maximum of 0.5m high. These monuments form part of an extensive flat cemetery, with the mounds at each site sealing a single cist or burial pit. A series of other features was also identified underlying the mound material; one site contained a substantial hearth within which coarse pottery, charcoal, flints and burnt human bone had been deposited. Evidence for burning and ritual deposition was also recorded beneath the embanked platform cairn where a stone-capped trench, containing charcoal, burnt bone and flint implements, was discovered towards the centre of the mound. The sealing of these ritual and funerary deposits under a mound did not always form the final act at these sites, however; two subsequent phases of mound enlargement were recorded at one ring cairn and related to the insertion of an urn containing a secondary cremation.

Jones (2005) has argued that most Cornish barrow sites were initially enclosed in some way, with the funerary deposits often

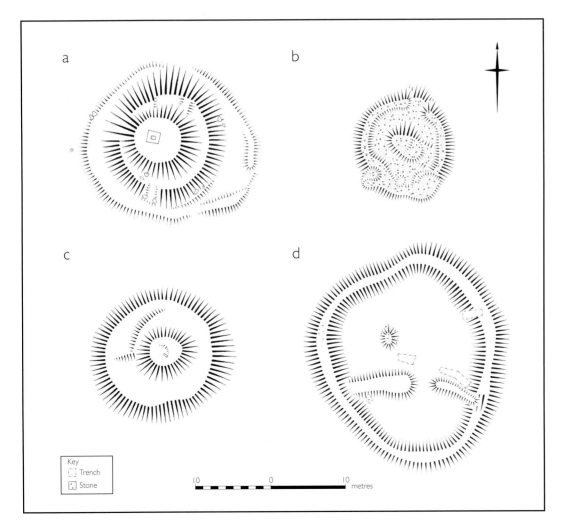

a

b

c

d

Key
Trench
Stone

10   0   10
metres

Fig 3.25
Earthwork plans of ring cairns, embanked platform cairns and multiphase barrows: (a, c, d) Beacon Batch and (b) Burrington.

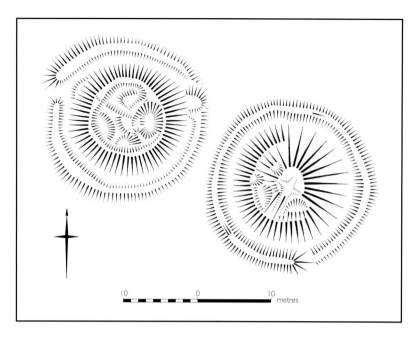

Fig 3.26
North Hill barrow cemetery: an embanked platform cairn and a bowl barrow sitting side by side and displaying different development histories.

sites. Recent excavations suggest they date from around the period *c* 2000–1500 cal BC (Garwood 2007, 34), with Beaker vessels recovered from some of the Mendip monuments indicative of a date at the beginning of this period.

Monument elaboration and secondary interments

Many Mendip monuments demonstrate two or sometimes three phases of elaboration, usually visible as subtle changes in the profile of the mound. In some cases the form of these barrows represents the culmination of a complex sequence of actions, with the different classes of barrow representing monuments which came to an end at different points in that sequence. A good example of this can be seen on North Hill, where two monuments sit side by side but clearly have contrasting development histories (Fig 3.26). One barrow takes the form of an embanked platform cairn, standing 0.8m high, surrounded by a ditch and outer bank. Its neighbour to the south-east is a bowl barrow, about 2m in height, again with a ditch and outer bank. The upstanding remains clearly show that the higher mound comprises two phases – represented by a break in slope visible around its western half – indicating the monument originated as a much lower mound, very similar to its neighbour. The addition of mound material to a monument can often correspond with the insertion of a secondary cremation, possibly reflecting a desire to mark the additional burial event. The Revd John Skinner dug into two of the larger monuments in the North Hill group and recorded evidence of secondary cremations, one located within an oval cist defined by six stones (BL Add MS 33691, fol 281).

Evidence for multiphase monuments can be seen within numerous barrow cemeteries, such as Beacon Batch, Ashen Lane and Ashen Hill (Fig 3.27). Two-thirds of the barrows on Ashen Hill show clear evidence for secondary activity, visible as breaks in slope or narrow berms, with half originating as low platform cairns/ embanked platform cairns, standing between 0.2m and 0.7m high. These platform cairns possibly indicate a development from 'open' monument to 'closed' monument – from a structure with relatively little visual impact to one which dominates the skyline. One barrow clearly displays at least three phases of

representing one of the later actions in the sequence of development. The funerary deposits were quickly covered by a mound in some cases, but in others burials appear to have remaining exposed for a period of time. Recent excavation at Longstone Edge, Derbyshire, has shown that burial cists could sometimes remain largely uncovered for a number of years (Last 2007, 162–3). The process of monument development could therefore span a considerable length of time and possibly include significant periods of inactivity. The continuing development of these monuments indicates their importance as focal points for ritual and spiritual activity, and highlights the complex nature of how these sites were used and reused over time.

The mounding-over of these structures (by stone, turf or earth) may be viewed as an act of closure – a technique employed to seal the deposits from future disturbance. It is evident, however, that some monuments remained active after this process, with secondary burials inserted into the mounds at Black Down and Tyning's Farm, for example. That relatively few ring ditches, ring cairns and embanked platform cairns have been recorded from Mendip may reflect the ephemeral nature of such sites, with low earth or stone banks easily lost to agricultural improvements (the Black Down monuments sit within an area of unenclosed heath). The lack of modern archaeological excavations in the area has also restricted our understanding of such

enlargement, but many more undoubtedly represent multiple phases of activity. Evidence from Skinner's excavations (*see* Panel 1.1) indicates that different material was used in the construction of these monuments: the primary mound was constructed of stone, with earth predominantly used for the secondary phase of enlargement (BL Add MS 33648, fols 125–7). The story is undoubtedly more complex than this, with each stone or earth component possibly representing more than one phase of activity.

It has been argued that multiphase monuments are not indicative of the wider range of Early Bronze Age funerary monuments (Garwood 2007, 34). In reality, evidence for multiple phases may simply have gone unnoticed or unrecognised in the past, with a lack of detailed survey work and modern barrow excavations hindering our understanding of such sites. Bradley's comments that surface observation cannot distinguish between mounds that were built in one operation and those that grew incrementally (Bradley 2007, 177) is misguided. Detailed

survey on Mendip and elsewhere (Salisbury Plain and Stonehenge, for example) has shown that a significant number of monuments display clear signs of later elaboration in their upstanding remains (eg McOmish *et al* 2002, 38). When these episodes of elaboration and enlargement were undertaken on Mendip is more problematic, however; our understanding is hampered by the lack of modern barrow excavations and scientific dating evidence.

Not all secondary interments were accompanied by substantial amounts of new barrow material. Evidence for cremated remains being inserted into existing barrow mounds has been demonstrated at Tyning's Farm, where urns were placed at the top of existing monuments with minimal mound enlargement. The secondary burials at the Tyning's Farm north barrow – represented by two upright finger-printed Biconical Urns – may have been related to the stone capping of the earthen mound, with the material doing relatively little to change the profile of the barrow but changing its character considerably (Taylor 1951, 130). At Beacon Hill Wood an urn

Fig 3.27
Ashen Hill barrow cemetery.
Two-thirds of the barrows
show clear evidence for
secondary activity visible
as breaks in slope or
narrow berms.
(DP158754)

containing the cremated remains of a young woman was found inserted into an earlier barrow, the vessel having been placed in a pit dug into the top of the monument and then backfilled with stone; the cremated bone from this site was radiocarbon dated to around 1600 cal BC (Leach 2007; SHER 28132).

Why some burial events were marked by substantial monument elaboration when others were not is intriguing. It may be more relevant, however, to consider why some monuments continued to attract funerary episodes long after other sites were abandoned. This may be a reflection of the continuing importance of place and the draw of certain areas, monuments or individuals over a prolonged period of time.

Barrow cemeteries

On Mendip there are both linear and nucleated barrow cemeteries, some forming tight groups and others more scattered distributions. There are few very large linear groups, although the cemeteries on Ashen Hill and North Hill (Priddy Nine Barrows) are noteworthy exceptions. Many cemeteries comprise no more than four to six barrows. Some of the tight linear cemeteries have barrows positioned 10m to 50m apart, with the more loosely scattered groups, such as the large cemetery focused on Westbury Beacon, containing barrows up to 350m apart. The

linear groups tend to follow topographic features – hilltops, ridges and spurs – occupying crest positions and often commanding extensive views out over the wider landscape (Fig 3.28). In contrast, the compact nucleated cemeteries, such as Beacon Batch, Stockhill and Pen Hill, occupy both the summit and slopes of hills and are predominantly inward-facing, looking across the plateau or down over specific landscape features. Some groups, such as Tyning's Farm and Yoxter Farm, occupy valley-head positions, possibly sited to respect natural springs and watercourses. The presence of water may also have influenced the positioning of the Beacon Batch, Ashen Hill, North Hill and Pen Hill cemeteries, which populate areas of Old Red Sandstone outcrop, where water rises and flows downhill before disappearing below ground when limestone is reached. The underlying geology of Mendip may have influenced the location of monuments in other ways, with the distinct characteristics of the area reflected in the cave and swallet formations and the natural mineral deposits, all of which would have held specific meaning for Early Bronze Age communities.

Some cemeteries contain a range of barrow types, while others have a more restricted repertoire. On North Hill there are large ditched and un-ditched bowl barrows, a ditched and embanked platform cairn and smaller, possibly later, satellite cairns (Fig 3.29). Smaller cemeteries may comprise a single 'fancy'-type

Fig 3.28
North Hill barrow cemetery. The impressive mounds of this linear cemetery punctuate the skyline. (DP158739)

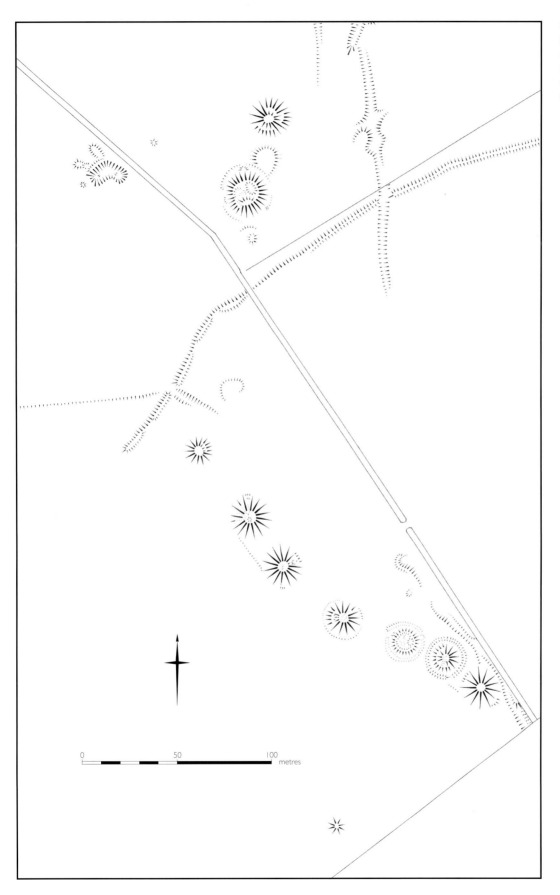

Fig 3.29
North Hill barrow cemetery: earthwork plan showing that this large linear cemetery contains a range of barrow types.

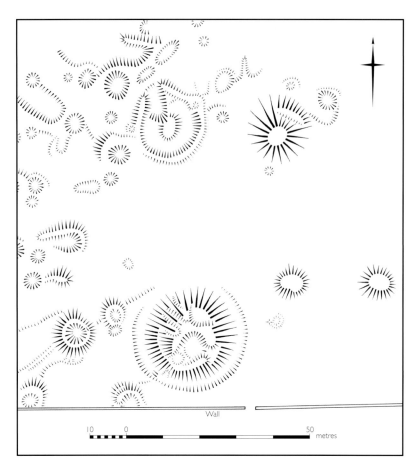

Wall

10 0   50
                                            metres

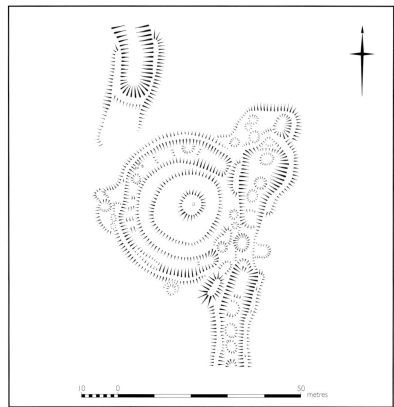

10 0   50
                                            metres

barrow, such as the Westbury Beacon bell barrow, or the large multiphase platform cairn in the Four Barrows group. Ring cairns are often recognised as forming a part of such cemeteries. This has been illustrated on the Quantock Hills where ring cairns/embanked platform cairns form an integral part of the Black Hill and Wills Neck barrow cemeteries, perhaps suggesting a deliberate pairing of different monument forms (Riley 2006, 38–41). The examples from Mendip demonstrate similar groupings, with ring cairns/embanked platform cairns possibly representing a specific element of the ritual processes related to ritual burning or sacred deposition (Fig 3.30). Alternatively, some may simply signify sites which for some reason experienced a shorter active life than their neighbouring monuments, failing to develop into larger, more imposing barrows.

Perhaps one of the largest and most impressive barrows on Mendip is the Hunters Lodge disc/bell barrow, which forms part of a loose linear cemetery (Fig 3.31). The barrow measures 40m in diameter, and has an encircling ditch and outer bank. The ditch defines an internal platform surmounted by a low mound on which there is a second, smaller mound slightly off-centre, with the mounds standing no more than 1.2m high. This series of mounds indicates a sequence of elaboration, possibly representing the reuse of the site over many generations, and makes the monument difficult to characterise definitively. As the only monument of this type within the region, its close relationship with the earlier henge site (300m to its south) must be considered significant, as the area obviously continued as a focus for ritual activity from the late Neolithic onwards.

There are also a number of paired barrows (Eastwater Farm, for example) and conjoined bowl barrows, such as the Longwood and Bristol barrows. The latter monuments take the form of elongated mounds, sometimes narrowing towards their centre, of which there are five recorded within the area. At Longwood geophysical survey has shown that the mound material overlies two adjacent ring ditches, both with apparently opposing causeways (Lewis 2003, 11). Recent excavation of a conjoined barrow at Chilcompton has shown it to comprise two round mounds, with the individual monuments probably constructed in relatively quick succession, both barrows being defined by a kerb of water-worn stones (J Lewis, pers comm). The close pairing of monuments in this way may reflect the importance of a specific area or the primary burial placed upon it. This notion is strengthened at Chilcompton, where only the primary mound was reused for secondary cremation burials.

Within some barrow cemeteries there is clear evidence of monument elaboration, while others appear to represent a group of monuments with a single construction episode. Perhaps one of the most striking examples of this is the Ashen Lane barrow group, which occupies a south-facing spur or promontory overlooking the Cheddar Valley. In this linear group of six the three northernmost barrows overlap and may represent a conjoined barrow with a series of subsequent elaborations (Fig 3.32). The other three barrows in this group are again almost touching, which implies there was either a great desire to place monuments or burials on this exact spot, or space for these activities was severely restricted. A series of small linear barrow cemeteries cluster along this section of the Cheddar Valley and their close relationship, especially when compared to other groups on Mendip, would suggest this location may have held particular significance for Bronze Age communities.

Priddy Long Barrow is also located in this region, with flint artefacts dating from the Mesolithic onwards recovered from the surrounding area, suggesting a long sequence of landscape utilisation. The relationship between individual barrows and barrow cemeteries and earlier monuments has been touched upon before. Almost without exception there would appear to be a close correlation between the position of barrow groups and earlier ceremonial sites. Perhaps one of the clearest examples of this can be seen at Priddy Circle 4, where the remains of at least three barrows are visible within the Neolithic enclosure. This may relate to the developing function of such monuments or reflect the continuing importance of place – possibly used as a device for connecting social groups with their ancestral past.

Within some of the larger barrow cemeteries there would appear to be small subgroups and individual sites. On Beacon Batch there is a linear arrangement of three closely spaced barrows, all of similar size and height, which represent a small subgroup within the larger nucleated cemetery; another group of three

can be seen within a cluster of seven barrows on the northern slopes of Pen Hill. These combinations may represent specific family groups or reflect construction episodes, with the barrows possibly forming the primary monuments and a focus for later activity. Even though today many monuments in barrow groups appear superficially similar – often surviving as grass-covered mounds – distinctive differences between monuments have been highlighted by the excavations at Tyning's Farm and Ashen Hill. This work has shown the range of materials which could be employed in mound construction within a single cemetery, as well as the variety of ritual and burial deposits found within them. The distinctive texture of mound material, be that stone, earth or turf, may have held a significant place in ritual and funerary activities, possibly as important as the form of the monuments themselves.

Smaller outlying cairns, often occupying false-crest positions, can form part of major

Fig 3.30 (opposite top) Stockhill barrow cemetery. A ring cairn forms part of this small clustered cemetery, which sits on the edge of 'gruffy' ground.

Fig 3.31 (opposite bottom) Hunters Lodge disc/bell barrow, one of the largest barrows in the region.

Fig 3.32 Ashen Lane barrow cemetery. The three northernmost barrows in this tightly packed cemetery overlap, perhaps indicating the importance of this particular place.

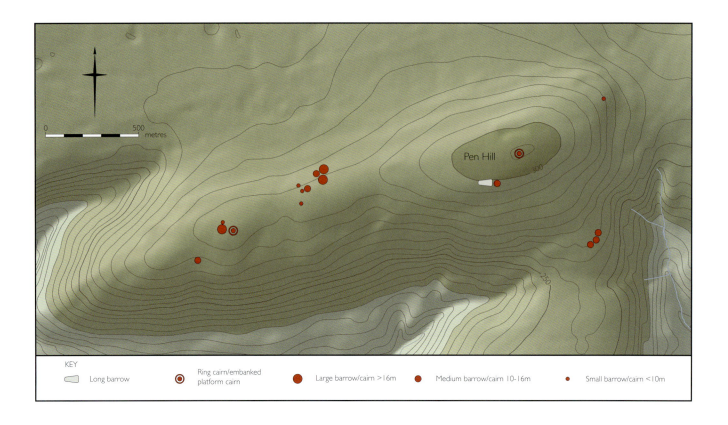

KEY

- Long barrow
- ⊚ Ring cairn/embanked platform cairn
- ● Large barrow/cairn >16m
- ● Medium barrow/cairn 10-16m
- · Small barrow/cairn <10m

Fig 3.33
Pen Hill barrow cemetery. Smaller outlying cairns form part of this major barrow group.

barrow groups; examples are visible on Pen Hill (Fig 3.33), Beacon Batch, Ashen Hill and North Hill. These satellite cairns are sometimes not visible from the main barrows in the cemetery, positioned on small terraces or bluffs, possibly located to be seen from below. Within other (generally smaller) barrow groups there is usually a high degree of intervisibility between the monuments, and indeed out over the wider landscape. The prominence of some of these monuments in the landscape today does not necessarily reflect their physical presence during the Early Bronze Age, however. As discussed, many of these barrows were

initially formed by the construction of low platforms or banks which would not have drawn the eye in the same way as the larger bowl barrows. The landscape may also have been more wooded, which would have inhibited lines of sight and shielded monuments from view. The elaboration of monuments may reflect a changing perception of visible presence, a greater desire to dominate the surrounding landscape. This may have been influenced by the changing environment, as trees were cleared to accommodate growing areas of enclosed farmland – a process which accelerated into the later prehistoric period.

4

The later prehistoric period

While the landscape of the earlier periods is dominated by ritual and ceremonial monuments, the later prehistoric gives us our first clear evidence for settlement and agriculture. By the Late Bronze Age large areas of woodland were being cleared to make way for blocks of planned fields, the sheer magnitude of which suggests a drive to order and control the landscape. The considerable task of reclaiming and dividing these areas would have been undertaken by small communities or family units living in single or groups of roundhouses, sometimes enclosed within ditches and banks and sometimes unenclosed. The increasing importance of land division is evident through the linear ditch systems which were created in the later Bronze Age. This period also witnessed the development of ever more sophisticated forms of metal weapons, tools and ornamental objects, often representing prestigious items used for exchange. Some of these objects were deposited in the ground, either singly or in hoards, possibly as a reflection of their religious and symbolic functions as well as their economic value.

The early 1st millennium BC saw new metalworking technology introduced to Britain, with tools made from the more widely available ore – iron. The introduction of this new technology may have been driven by economic uncertainties, climatic deterioration and social change. This period saw the continental exchange system decline and large quantities of bronze removed from circulation. Cultural and social changes are perhaps most visible in the landscape through the creation of the first hillforts – sited on prominent positions and dominating the surrounding area (Fig 4.1).

Fig 4.1
Dolebury Hillfort: aerial photograph showing the hillfort and wider landscape. (NMR 24819/40)

The worsening climate may have led to a shorter growing season, limiting the range of crops that could be cultivated and possibly leading to a reordering of existing land divisions. By the Middle Iron Age a probable rise in population numbers and an improving climate facilitated a growth in productivity, as reflected in the development of an increasingly broad range of material culture.

The Middle to Late Bronze Age landscape (1500–750 BC)

Around the middle of the 2nd millennium BC the seasonal sites of earlier generations would have begun to develop into areas of more permanent settlement. What started as small-scale clearance in the Neolithic and Early Bronze Age became a more comprehensive reordering of the landscape. Along the river valleys and spring lines, small enclosed or unenclosed settlements surrounded by blocks of arable fields and enclosed pasture developed. How extensive this changing pattern of human land use was across Mendip, or how it developed over time, is as yet unclear. In

contrast to other upland areas of the South-West, such as Dartmoor and Exmoor, there is little surviving evidence for middle or later Bronze Age settlement within the Mendip Hills AONB. There are several factors which may have contributed to this, not least the wholesale enclosure and improvement of the commons during the late 18th and 19th centuries. It is also possible, but perhaps less likely, that the upland areas of Mendip remained largely unenclosed during the prehistoric periods, utilised primarily for seasonal pasture. Continuity of settlement may also have played its part, with spring-line locations favoured as settlement loci over millennia. This continuity was demonstrated at Bleadon, where Bronze Age pottery was found alongside evidence for Middle Iron Age activity, which itself lay within an area of medieval and later occupation (Young 2008).

At the western end of Mendip the remains of two Middle Bronze Age roundhouses (sitting side by side) were discovered eroding out of the cliff face at Brean Down. The larger of the two structures was roughly circular, with the external wall possibly constructed from close-set posts, planks or wattlework, combined

Fig 4.2
The distribution of Middle and Late Bronze Age metalwork across the Mendip Hills AONB.

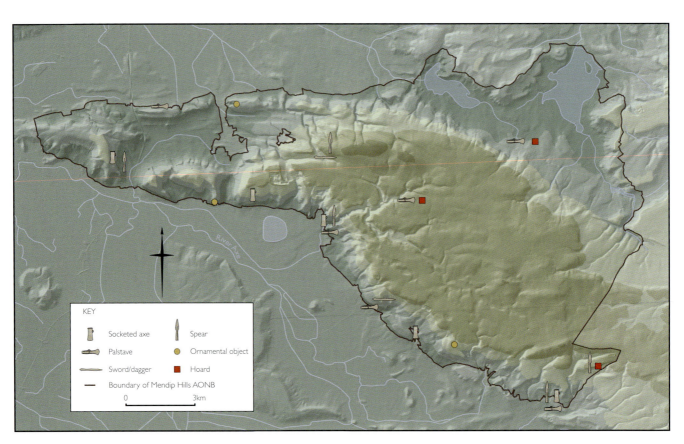

KEY

- Socketed axe
- Palstave
- Sword/dagger
- Boundary of Mendip Hills AONB
- Spear
- Ornamental object
- Hoard

0   3km

with a stone retaining wall. The house had a cobbled entrance facing south-east and a central hearth, around which evidence for cooking activities, cloth making and salt extraction were discovered (Bell 1990, 37–57). Unlike Dartmoor, where massive granite slabs were often used as building materials, Bronze Age buildings on Mendip may have been constructed of timber, or a combination of stone and timber as seen elsewhere (Exmoor, for example). Even in areas where stone was freely available, timber structures have been recorded surviving as slots or 'ring-grooves' cut into the ground, or patterns of postholes and packing stones (Fleming 1988, 78). At best, the remains of such structures may survive as terraced platforms or cropmarks in arable fields, but are more likely to leave no visible trace today.

Perhaps one of the most striking finds from Brean Down was two linked gold bracelets, found eroding out of the cliff (Bell 1990, 6). Indeed, the majority of evidence for middle and later Bronze Age activity on Mendip comes in the form of metalwork (Fig 4.2). Finds of bronze and gold objects have been made across the region, the majority confined to the fringes of the uplands. The most common objects recorded are bronze spears, daggers (Fig 4.3) and palstaves (a type of axe). The majority of these items represent chance finds of single objects, such as the bronze looped palstave discovered in the village of Rodney Stoke and presented to the Somerset Museum in the 1860s (Fig 4.4). Ornamental objects have also been uncovered, including a plain gold bracelet or arm-ring found just outside the entrance to a cave in Hope Wood, Easton. The bracelet had trumpet-shaped ends and was Late Bronze Age in date – the discovery gave 'Bracelet Cave' its name (Haldane 1969, 99–101). Metal artefacts could be placed in the ground, thrown into rivers or streams, or left within caves; some objects were whole when deposited, and others were deliberately broken.

Metalwork dating from the Middle and Late Bronze Age was also deposited in hoards, thousands of which have been found across the British Isles. These hoards could be represented by only a few objects, or comprise hundreds of pieces of metalwork in a range of forms including weapons, tools, ornamental objects and scrap or broken metal. The artefacts were sometimes deposited together within a box, bag or pottery vessel, or could be scattered

across a much wider area. Hoards have been classified into a variety of types defined by the range of artefacts included in the collection. A 'founders' hoard' was the term given to collections of scrap metal and metal ingots; a 'merchants' hoard' was represented by new or unused weapons or tools; a 'personal hoard' could contain weapons, tools and ornamental objects. The terms reflect the belief during the 19th and 20th centuries that these artefacts had been deposited in the ground by artisans and individuals for safekeeping, but never retrieved. Now it is thought more likely that many represent votive offerings deliberately placed in the ground, possibly left in a special place and dedicated to the supernatural (Bradley 1990).

Many such hoards were discovered during the 19th and early 20th centuries; their contents were poorly recorded and the artefacts often subsumed into private collections. For example, a hoard of a dozen bronze objects was found while a drain was being dug at Park Mead, Compton Martin, in 1905. Little is known about the contents of the hoard other than it included a bronze palstave which was donated to Bristol Museum. More recently, a hoard of bronze artefacts was discovered on the southern slopes of Horrington Hill, above West Horrington. Two bronze spearheads – one complete and one broken – were retrieved from the bank of a

Fig 4.3
A bronze dagger/knife discovered in 1935 at Rowberrow Warren, Shipham.
(© Somerset County Council Museums Service)

Fig 4.4
A bronze looped palstave discovered in the village of Rodney Stoke.
(© Somerset County Council Museums Service)

rough track near the summit of the hill in 1973 (Fig 4.5), and fragments of a third spearhead were found near the same spot a few years later; these presumably formed part of the same Middle Bronze Age hoard. In 1998 a metal-detecting survey was undertaken across the hill and a fourth spearhead and a bronze flanged axe were also uncovered, again on the southern slopes of the hill. Why such valuable items were deposited on Horrington Hill may never be known, but the association between a potentially defensible location and the consumption of weapons is striking.

One of the most spectacular hoards from Mendip was found in November 2005, when a metal detectorist located a collection of twisted and distorted gold artefacts in the parish of Priddy. The hoard comprised 19 pieces of gold, probably representing 17 objects, and is one of the largest finds of Bronze Age gold in south-west England (Fig 4.6). Two bronze palstaves were also uncovered which probably formed part of the hoard (mixed hoards of gold and bronze are not unknown from the Middle Bronze Age). The deposit was found within topsoil towards the bottom of a south-facing slope, but had probably been moved from its original place of deposition through the action of the plough (Minnitt and Payne 2012). A third palstave was recovered not far from the hoard, which may again have formed part of the original deposit (W Small, pers comm).

The Iron Age landscape (750 BC – AD 43)

Evidence for new metalworking technology first appears in Britain soon after the beginning of the 1st millennium BC in the form of objects and tools made from iron. This technological development was viewed by early archaeologists as a definitive change in British society and has been used to define the beginning of the shortest period of British prehistory – the Iron Age. The transition is now thought to have been a more gradual one, however, taking several centuries to complete, with bronze

Fig 4.5
A bronze spearhead recovered from Horrington Hill. It forms part of a Middle Bronze Age hoard now in Wells and Mendip Museum. (DP158760, reproduced by permission of Wells and Mendip Museum)

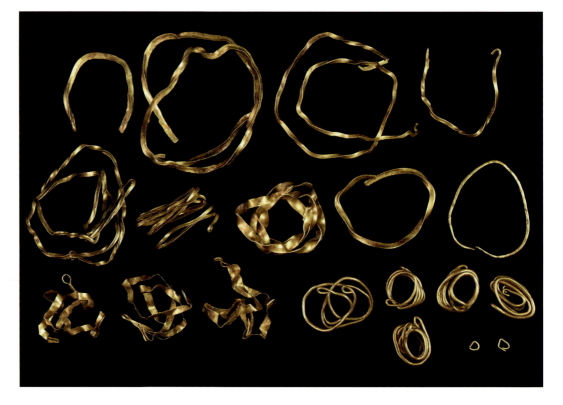

Fig 4.6
Priddy hoard. The collection of gold comprised five torcs, two penannular bar bracelets, three double and hooked ribbon bracelets, five double and hooked bar bracelets, and two small D-shaped penannular bars. (© Somerset County Council Museums Service)

continuing to be worked and a steady rise in the range of artefacts made from iron. The use of this new metal was initially confined to prestigious items but gradually spread to weapons and specialist tools, then finally to ordinary tools and ornamental objects.

Perhaps one of the most impressive assemblages of iron objects from the Mendip region comes from the cave excavations at Wookey Hole, where numerous metal artefacts were revealed, including iron currency bars, daggers, arrowheads, knives, sickles and saws (Balch 1914). Bone, wood, stone and antler implements were also found, accompanied by pottery vessels and shale ornaments. A tin and lead ingot was uncovered in the cave, which suggests that tin was being imported from Cornwall, with the lead undoubtedly sourced locally from the reserves in the Mendip uplands. The assemblage indicates that a range of craft and industrial activities were being undertaken – such as spinning, weaving, metalworking and pottery manufacture – with more mundane activities represented by food-storage vessels and domestic waste (Fig 4.7). The utilisation of Wookey Hole was probably contemporary with the 'lake villages' of Meare and Glastonbury, which were occupied in the Middle and Late Iron Age.

During the construction of the M5 motorway, a series of Iron Age pits was discovered at Dibble's Farm, Christon. Pits are a common feature of both defended and undefended sites of this period. At Worlebury Hillfort, for example, 93 pits were identified and found to contain pottery vessels, bone, wood and antler tools, metal and glass ornaments, human burials and grain (Evans 1985; Barrett *et al* 2000). Around 65 rock-cut pits and 25 postholes were revealed at Christon, with the larger pits interpreted as grain storage pits. When no longer needed for storing grain, the pits at Christon had been reused for refuse disposal and contained a range of material, including pottery, animal bones, quernstones, weaving weights, a bronze-working crucible and iron slag. The pottery suggests that the site was occupied continuously from the end of the Early Iron Age through to the Middle Iron Age. The artefacts discarded within these pits again represent both domestic and industrial activities, revealing a community employed not only in agricultural production, but also in cloth making and metalworking, both bronze and iron (Morris 1988, 23–81).

Evidence for metalworking during this period has been found at sites across Mendip, including Burledge Hillfort, where pieces of iron slag with burnt clay adhering to them were tentatively interpreted as evidence for an iron-smelting furnace (Rahtz and Greenfield 1977, 170). Iron slag and iron waste were also found at Rowberrow Cavern, with a furnace complete with blowhole from Chelm's Combe Shelter dated through pottery to the Early Iron Age (Taylor 1923, 43; Balch 1926, 98). Saye's Hole revealed evidence for possible Late Iron Age metalworking in the form of slag and small iron and bronze artefacts (Barton *et al* 1987). Whether there is a true correlation between cave sites and specialist metalworking activities is unclear, as there is evidence to suggest small-scale metalworking was being undertaken at a number of settlement sites across the region. It has been suggested by Bryant that Chelm's Combe Shelter and Rowberrow Cavern may have been selected as smelting sites during the Early Iron Age because of their relative inaccessibility and perceived mystical qualities (2011, 139–57).

At the western end of the Mendip Hills a series of storage pits was also excavated at Whitegate Farm, on the edge of Bleadon; the pits have been radiocarbon dated to the later Middle Iron Age (around 380–175 cal BC). Here a total of 10 pits was uncovered (2 of

Fig 4.7
Iron Age bone combs discovered during the cave excavations at Wookey Hole, now in Wells and Mendip Museum.
(DP158763, reproduced by permission of Wells and Mendip Museum)

which represented the recutting of an earlier pit), all of which were circular or oval in plan, with several lined using limestone slabs. A range of material was found within the fill of these pits – mixed soils, limestone rubble, animal bones and pottery – and two of the sites were reused as graves (Fig 4.8). These crouched inhumations represented the remains of two individuals, a woman who was buried with a penannular brooch, and a man (who may have been accompanied by a pottery vessel), and were radiocarbon dated to 210 cal BC – 1 cal AD and 400 cal BC – 70 cal AD respectively (Young 2008, 31–81).

The reuse of storage pits for burial is again mirrored at Christon, where human remains representing 21 individuals – male and female, young and old – were also found within the pits. Personal artefacts were associated with 5 of the individuals, which allowed the remains to be clearly identified as burials. The recovery of grave goods with human burials in Iron Age pits is relatively rare outside Yorkshire. The range of burial items at both these sites appears to be restricted to one item per person – one bronze brooch or hook, one iron spiral armlet, one boar's tusk pendant or one pottery vessel (Morris 1988; Young 2008). As mentioned above, human burials were also found in pits within Worlebury Hillfort, some of which were accompanied by iron weapons, possibly indicating a tradition for grave goods in the Mendip region (Evans 1985, 14).

The reuse of grain storage pits for human burial may have held symbolic meaning linked to life, death and regeneration, a process visible in the cycle of nature and connected to the function of the pits themselves. Redundant storage pits were not the only features reused for burial, however, as human remains from Charterhouse Warren Farm Swallet have been radiocarbon dated to 360–5 cal BC, indicating that natural features could also be utilised in a similar way (Levitan and Smart 1989, 393). Ritual or symbolic deposition within pits was also extended to animal bones and groups of pottery or metal artefacts, usually placed at the bottom or low down in pit fills. At Bleadon an overall pattern of selected deposition was identified which indicates that different animal species were sorted and deposited in specific pits or pit groups. Sheep were placed at the western side of the site and were predominantly associated with pottery finds; cattle, dog and horse were largely concentrated to the east and may have been deposited following a defined hierarchy (Young 2008, 74–5). The bronze-working crucible from Christon could also represent ritual deposition, with metalworking (a technique involving the transformation of matter from one state into another) viewed as a magical process by many societies.

The artefacts from Bleadon and Christon also give us an insight into how the wider landscape was utilised at this time. The animal bone assemblages from both sites indicate that sheep were the most widespread species, although domesticated cattle, pig and horse were also recorded. The age data from the sheep bones at Bleadon is in many ways comparable with the evidence from Christon, and suggests significant natural losses of foetal and newborn lambs – indicating the animal remains in the pits were deposited between spring and late autumn. There would also appear to have been a deliberate policy of culling lambs in their first and early second years of life, possibly a method for retaining flock sizes and reducing numbers of livestock for overwintering (Young 2008, 51–2). The culling of lambs in the autumn may also be related to the cycle of ritual and seasonal festivals, fulfilling the demand for fresh and tender meat that these communal events generated.

The animal bone evidence suggests that flocks may have been kept on or close to the settlement during the winter months and into the spring lambing season, then moved to open grazing during the summer. This would fit well with a mixed farming regime where sheep and

Fig 4.8
Bleadon: illustration of two pits containing crouched inhumations excavated at Whitegate Farm. (After Young 2008, fig 11)

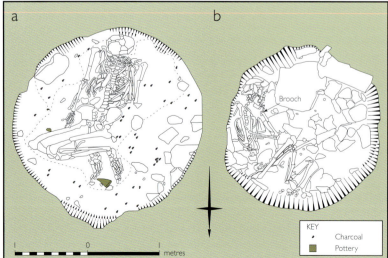

KEY
• Charcoal
▪ Pottery

cattle not only provided hides, wool and meat, but also fertilised the land. That arable farming formed part of the economy of these settlements is attested to by the function of the pits themselves. Cereal grains representing *Triticum* sp. (wheat), *Hordeum* sp. (barley) and *Avena* sp. (oats) were identified in small quantities from Bleadon, samples of which were dated to the Middle Iron Age (Young 2008, 57–60). Quernstones from Christon indicate grain was milled by hand for flour, with bread probably baked in small ovens constructed of wattle and daub. Barley may have been used to make beer, with surplus grain and waste products providing winter fodder for livestock.

Although both these sites indicated domestic activity close by, neither revealed direct evidence for settlement. Most family groups in this period lived in small hamlets or individual farmsteads, comprising a selection of domestic and agricultural buildings, storage pits and enclosed paddocks or yards. Investigations in Chew Park revealed evidence for Iron Age occupation and agriculture, including the remains of two roundhouses – one overlying the other. These roundhouses were defined by intersecting ditches, their entrances marked by breaks in the south-eastern side, enclosing areas of about 9.5m and 11m in diameter (Rahtz and Greenfield 1977). These ditches may have held a series of close-set timber posts or planks harvested from the surrounding woodland; the houses were probably thatched with reeds from the Levels and Moors. It has been noted that a high proportion of such structures have an east- or south-east-facing entrance, possibly orientated to shield the interior from the worst of the weather, or positioned to allow the spring or autumn sunrise to flood the house with light (Smith *et al* 2001). Architectural form, and the social use of space within buildings, has also been linked to cosmological beliefs (Oswald 1997, 87–95).

Later prehistoric field systems and settlements

Field systems

The earliest visible evidence in the landscape for Mendip's prehistoric farmers can be seen in the remains of the fields they created and cultivated. These have primarily been identified from aerial photographs, scattered across the survey area, with the densest pocket of survival located along the southern slopes of Bleadon Hill (Fig 4.9). The fragmentary remains of ancient fields have also been identified along the northern escarpment of the main plateau, stretching east from Dolebury Hillfort and out across Burrington Ham. On the upper slopes of the southern escarpment fragments of early fields have been recorded above Ebbor Gorge and Bradley Cross, and on the steep-sided Shute Shelve Hill, near Winscombe. There is little evidence for early field systems across the high plateau; fragments of fields which

Fig 4.9
Bleadon Hill: aerial photograph showing the remnants of ancient fields fossilised within an area of pasture.
(NMR 24822/36)

may be prehistoric in origin were identified at Charterhouse-on-Mendip and on the southern slopes of Stockhill. Regions apparently devoid of field systems may indicate areas of managed woodland or open pasture, or reflect different forms of landholding or tenure. The remnants of early field systems are primarily located on the former commons and areas of marginal land, such as steep-sided valleys and combes, where attempts at improvement were relatively late and short-lived. Some of the field systems that were recorded from early aerial photographs have degraded significantly through time, due to the more intensive farming methods of the 20th century. The fields above Bradley Cross and on the slopes of Shute Shelve Hill are good examples of this, both systems now being barely visible in improved pasture.

The evidence from Mendip points towards a prehistoric landscape of relatively extensive and organised blocks of fields, connected by drove-ways and tracks, much of which has now been masked by later activity. Elements of field systems undoubtedly survive within areas of woodland where they cannot be detected using aerial photography and are difficult to distinguish on the ground. The large expanses of medieval strip fields along the escarpment slopes almost certainly conceal evidence for an earlier phase of enclosure, and may incorporate elements of it within them. That earlier field layouts continued in use over a prolonged period of time is evident on the lower slopes of Bleadon Hill. Here prehistoric fields can be seen fossilised in the modern field pattern, surviving in areas of former medieval common, and demonstrate that in some cases the earlier field divisions formed the framework for later land allotments (Fig 4.10). This was not universally the case, however, as some later fields appear to pay little regard to relict systems. On Flagstaff Hill, strip fields can be seen to overlie the remains of a prehistoric field system, the long narrow strips cutting at right angles across the smaller, subrectangular fields, with the faint remnants of their boundaries evident on the treads of the strips.

Physical characteristics

The majority of field systems in the region would appear to be 'cohesive' or 'coaxial' in plan, comprising small square or rectangular paddocks, enclosed within embanked or lyncheted boundaries, forming a linear, grid-like pattern. Individual blocks of fields display a common symmetry of layout, with a general preference for boundaries running up the hillside. There are inevitably exceptions to this, where, due to topography, some blocks were laid out along the contour of the slope – as seen around Pitcher's Enclosure. The axial geometry of the blocks is generally adhered to regardless of the underlying topography, which suggests they represent a planned episode of enclosure carried out in a single undertaking or in a series of closely spaced actions. The axial layout of the field system on Dolebury Warren is repeated to the west on Lyncombe Hill, which indicates both systems formed a coherent block and were created in a relatively open landscape. In contrast, the fields on Flagstaff Hill run at right angles to the system on Bleadon Hill to its west, indicating they were laid out in a separate episode – perhaps at a different time or by a separate group.

The setting out of these field systems represents a considerable undertaking, with the larger systems undoubtedly denoting the work of a community or band of individuals working together. On Dolebury Warren the coaxial field system covers just under 30ha

Fig 4.10

Bleadon Hill: map showing relict field boundaries recorded from aerial photographs and their relationship to the 19th-century field pattern.

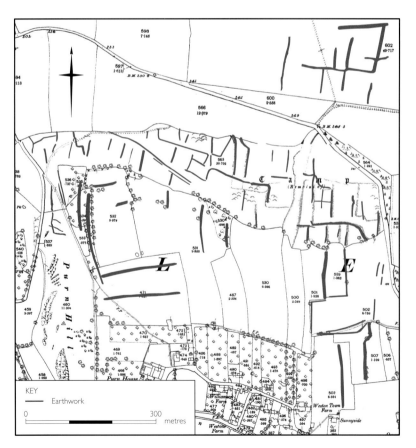

KEY

— Earthwork

0   300
                metres

and is remarkably regular, with the main boundaries spaced at intervals of 32m to 34m apart, indicating that a considerable degree of organisation and planning went into its layout and construction. Areas where this planning is not adhered to may represent a separate phase of construction, the reuse of pre-existing boundaries or a later modification of the original fields. On Dolebury Warren the fields become smaller towards the south-western corner of the system and lie on a slightly different alignment, following the contours of the slope. Evidence for settlement is confined to this region and could suggest that this area formed the earliest phase of enclosure (Fig 4.11).

Although most field systems appear to be divided into rectilinear enclosures, when examined more closely there is a wide degree of variability in both shape and size. On Flagstaff Hill, for example, the fields are predominantly subrectangular in form, with those on the northern slopes of the hill notably smaller and squarer than those to the south (Fig 4.12). Some of the smaller fields are no more than 30m by 15m but clearly represent later subdivisions of once larger fields. By contrast, the fields on the southern slopes are around 88m by 35m and are generally more elongated in form. The main elements of the fields are defined by spread scarps or lynchets which stand 1.2–3.5m high, with the better-defined boundaries possibly representing areas where agriculture was more extensive and long-lived or the terrain more challenging. The location and aspect of a site may also have determined the form and function of individual fields, with fields on steep north-facing slopes unlikely to have been extensively used for arable cultivation. The majority of the surviving prehistoric field systems are confined to south- or south-east-facing slopes, indicating that their location was carefully chosen to maximise arable production. It is doubtful that any fields were permanently under the plough, however; a mixed farming regime would have been employed, with fields left fallow or under pasture on a cyclical basis.

The fields are now largely defined by lynchets but may originally have been marked out by a sturdy fence, hedge, ditch or line of boulders. When Skinner visited the western end of Mendip in November 1819 he was struck by the square, stone-built enclosures that covered the southern slopes of Bleadon Hill.

He stated that these enclosures extended from Shiplate Combe to Uphill Common Field, an area nearly 2 miles in length. Skinner also visited Littleton Hill, which he said was 'covered with lines of enclosures similar to those on Bleadon Hill, to which it adjoins'. While Skinner's party was on the hill they came across a group of men who were dismantling one of the enclosure walls and removing the stone. Skinner took this opportunity to examine the construction of the wall, noting that it was 'evidently formed without cement, large stones being placed on the surface of the soil by way of foundations, and smaller stones piled upon them'; he recorded that some of the banks stood over 2m in height (BL Add MS 3654, fols 115, 153). This evidence would suggest the fields were formally laid out, their boundaries initially defined by a line of large stones. The lack of clearance cairns also implies that smaller stones were moved to the boundaries of fields, either by hand or by the action of the plough, and accumulated over time to create the strongly marked boundaries that Skinner encountered.

Dating evidence

The dating of field systems is notoriously difficult, and there is no fixed chronology for the fields on Mendip. That they continued to be used over a prolonged period of time is evident through the subdivision and reworking of their boundaries – visible as breaks of slope and ledges on their scarp faces. A relative chronology for the field systems may be ascertained through studying their relationship with other more securely dated features. There is a distinct correlation between areas of relict field systems and known prehistoric settlement. Evidence for Early and Middle Iron Age occupation and agriculture has been identified at Bleadon and Christon, with both sites adjoining large blocks of prehistoric fields. The small hilltop enclosure of Tinker's Batch also sits close by and is surrounded by relict prehistoric fields. The field systems on Dolebury Warren and Lyncombe Hill are located adjacent to Dolebury Hillfort and the now levelled Dinghurst Camp, with the small enclosed settlement on Burrington Ham sitting side by side with the remains of early fields.

Perhaps one of the most compelling pieces of dating evidence, however, can be seen at Pitcher's Enclosure. Here, a small cluster of Iron Age roundhouses sits at the northern end of a

Fig 4.11
Dolebury Warren:
earthwork plan of
prehistoric fields, with
settlement remains visible
towards the south-west
corner of the system.

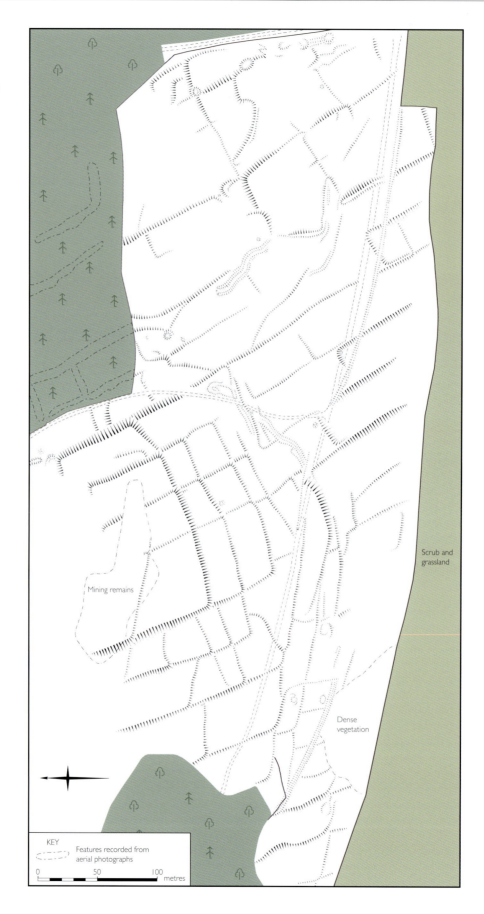

Scrub and
grassland

Mining remains

Dense
vegetation

KEY

Features recorded from
aerial photographs

0   50   100
metres

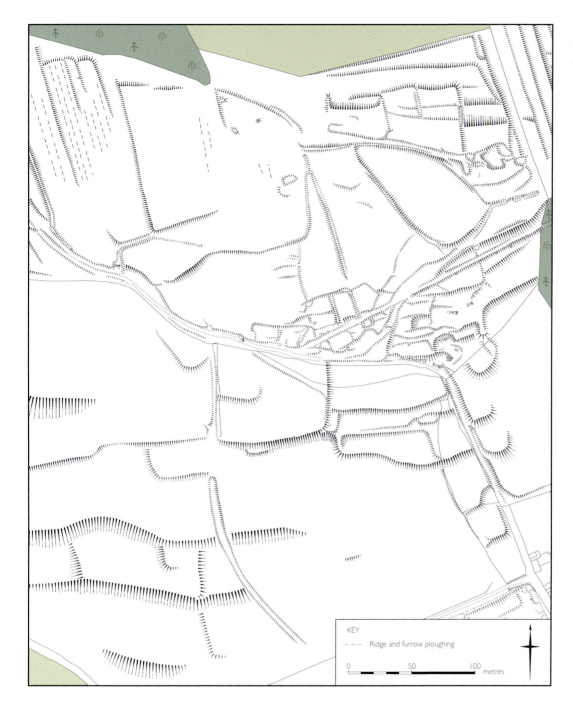

Fig 4.12
Flagstaff Hill: earthwork
plan of field system.

KEY

- - -   Ridge and furrow ploughing

0   50   100
                                              metres

U-shaped enclosure. Beyond the settlement lie the fragmentary remains of a prehistoric field system, the lyncheted boundaries of which can be seen to underlie the enclosure and were even utilised in its construction. The field boundaries within the enclosure bank are slight and less well defined than those beyond – standing little more than 0.3m high – indicating the outer fields continued in use after the enclosure was constructed. The crude pottery recovered from the interior of the enclosure suggests that the

settlement is of Early Iron Age date (Powlesland 2009, 43).

The fragmentary remains of a possible prehistoric field system were also recorded at Banwell Camp. A series of slight, parallel linear scarps extend approximately east–west within the main ramparts of the fort. The field system would appear to pre-date the earliest phase of the fort, which has been dated through excavation to the Early Iron Age (Hunt 1961a). Neolithic and Bronze Age flints have also been recovered from within the enclosure, which indicates earlier activity (if not necessarily occupation). The evidence from these sites suggests that the initial setting out of the field systems on Mendip could have been as early as the Late Bronze Age or Early Iron Age. Evidence from elsewhere, such as Dartmoor, Salisbury Plain and the Marlborough Downs, has shown that some upland coaxial field systems originated in the Middle Bronze Age (Fleming 1988; McOmish *et al* 2002; McOmish 2005). A similar pattern has been revealed in lowland areas of southern Britain where two separate phases of coaxial construction have been identified – the first related to the Bronze Age and the second to the Late Iron Age and Romano-British periods (Yates 2007, 60). In Somerset, recent work at Shepton Mallet has identified fields and land divisions dating from the later Bronze Age (Leach 2009).

Settlements

The most enduring symbols of later prehistoric occupation and settlement are the hillforts. Clearly these monuments only reflect one part of the settlement history, however, with many more enclosed and unenclosed settlements populating the area at this time. The natural caves and rock shelters of the region were also utilised in the later prehistoric period, some on a sporadic or short-term basis and others over a prolonged period of time. Unenclosed roundhouses are perhaps the most elusive form of prehistoric settlement, with buildings generally represented by no more than a low bank or small circular platform, both of which are easily lost to later activity. The remains of two such buildings were identified within the

field system on Dolebury Warren, surviving as terraced platforms large enough to hold structures around 6m in diameter (Fig 4.13). The survival of these building stances can undoubtedly be attributed to their topographic position, on a relatively steep south-facing scarp where subsequent agricultural improvement was minimal. A similar example can be seen above Draycott where a small terraced platform, around 4.8m in diameter, survives nestled below an area of limestone outcropping.

In areas where prehistoric settlement has been lost to later agriculture, its former location is sometimes visible through crop- or soil-marks in areas of arable production. Unenclosed settlement may be visible as clusters of pits, postholes or ring ditches, sometimes associated with field banks and enclosures. It is the recognition of such settlement complexes from aerial photographs that has helped change our perception of occupation density in the later prehistoric period. The cropmark sites discovered along the southern escarpment of the Quantock Hills, for example, clearly illustrate the number of settlements lost to later agriculture in comparison to those which survive as upstanding monuments (Riley 2006, 68–70). In other instances, targeted geophysical survey and fieldwalking may be used to locate former occupation sites.

At the western end of Wattles Hill, aerial photography has revealed a complex of three ditched enclosures or paddocks associated with a series of field boundaries and settlement remains, including pits and postholes (Fig 4.14). At least five ring ditches, probably representing roundhouses, form part of the complex, one of which is tucked into the corner of the western enclosure. A second ring ditch is clearly overlain by the enclosure boundary, which suggests a sequence of occupation and settlement development. A further group of three roundhouses was located to the west, outside the enclosure complex, which may represent a separate phase of unenclosed settlement (Truscoe 2008, 24).

A number of circular and rectilinear enclosures have also been identified through aerial photography, most of which are defined by a single ditch. The enclosures range in size from 33m to 70m in internal diameter and are found on both hillside and valley-bottom locations. An enclosure was recorded to the north of Ramspits, sitting within an area of parliamentary enclosure at about

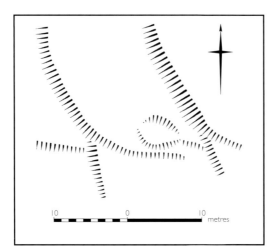

Fig 4.13
Dolebury Warren:
earthwork plan of
building platform.

260m above Ordnance Datum (OD). This subcircular ditched enclosure has a maximum internal diameter of about 68m and displays evidence for a short entrance passageway through its southern side (Fig 4.15). Along the northern fringe of the plateau a slightly smaller curvilinear enclosure was identified, towards the western end of Windmill Hill, near Churchill, with the enclosure displaying a simple gap entrance to the west (Priest and Dickson 2009, 24). Below the southern slopes of Wattles Hill the cropmark remains of two subcircular enclosures were identified, at about 50m OD, close to the spring line. The larger enclosure measures approximately 70m in internal diameter with the smaller enclosure about 50m across (Fig 4.16). The enclosures both show evidence for an elongated entrance flanked by side ditches, the passageway of the larger southern enclosure a maximum of 15m long (Truscoe 2008, 24). The features lie approximately 55m apart and have opposing entranceways, which may suggest they are contemporary.

A group of three rectilinear enclosures was recorded within the Lox-Yeo Valley, two of which survive as cropmarks, with the third a spread earthwork bank and ditch measuring 46m by 36m internally (Fig 4.17). These sites are all near or adjacent to the Lox-Yeo river, sitting on the clayey river alluvium of the flood plain. A double-ditched rectilinear enclosure was also identified adjacent to a tributary of the Yeo river, near Havyatt Farm, measuring 66m by 48m internally (Priest and Dickson 2009, 33–4). It is unclear when these sites date from, but rectilinear enclosures form a recognisable category of later Iron Age and Romano-British settlement in the South-West. For example, a series of rectilinear enclosures excavated at Toulton, on the southern side of the Quantock Hills, produced dates ranging from the Iron Age through to the 3rd and 4th centuries AD (Riley 2006, 71). It is possible that the Mendip enclosures are more recent in date, however, with their potential functions ranging from stock enclosures to medieval moated sites; only further investigation will provide a clear chronological framework.

Earthwork enclosures

In contrast to the impressive ramparts and skyline locations of the hillforts, a series of more humble earthwork enclosures – sited in less prominent positions and defined by more

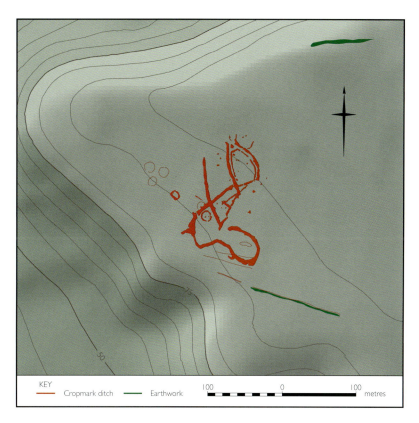

KEY
— Cropmark ditch   — Earthwork

Fig 4.14
Wattles Hill: aerial photographic transcription of settlement.

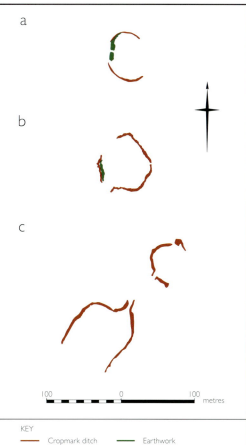

KEY
— Cropmark ditch   — Earthwork

Fig 4.15
Circular enclosures recorded from aerial photographs:
(a) Windmill Hill,
(b) Ramspits and
(c) south of Wattles Hill.

Fig 4.16
Aerial photograph showing
cropmark evidence of
enclosures located south
of Wattles Hill.
(NMR 15519/9)

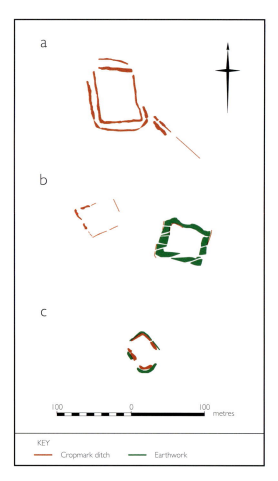

100   0   100
metres

KEY
— Cropmark ditch   — Earthwork

Fig 4.17
Rectilinear enclosures
recorded from aerial
photographs:
(a) Havyatt Farm and
(b, c) Lox-Yeo Valley.

modest ramparts – are visible across the Mendip region. These earthwork enclosures form a relatively diverse group, ranging from simple rectilinear enclosures to multiphase monuments. There are a total of seven prehistoric enclosures surviving as earthworks within the Mendip Hills AONB (Fig 4.18), the majority less than 1ha in extent; the exception is Pitcher's Enclosure, which defines an area of more than 3.4ha. These enclosures are mainly found on the northern and western fringes of the hills, with the exception of the Charterhouse Green enclosure which lies at the heart of the uplands. Indeed, there would appear to be a concentration of monuments towards the north-western end of the main limestone plateau, in the area around Black Down, although this may be a consequence of subsequent land use rather than a true representation of Iron Age activity (as hinted at by the cropmark evidence). The earthwork enclosures are mainly located in areas of former common, sited between 175m and 275m OD, often surviving where enclosure and improvement was late or non-intensive.

A number of the Mendip sites fall into the hill-slope category of enclosure, a form of monument common in the South-West, particularly Cornwall and south-western Wales, but

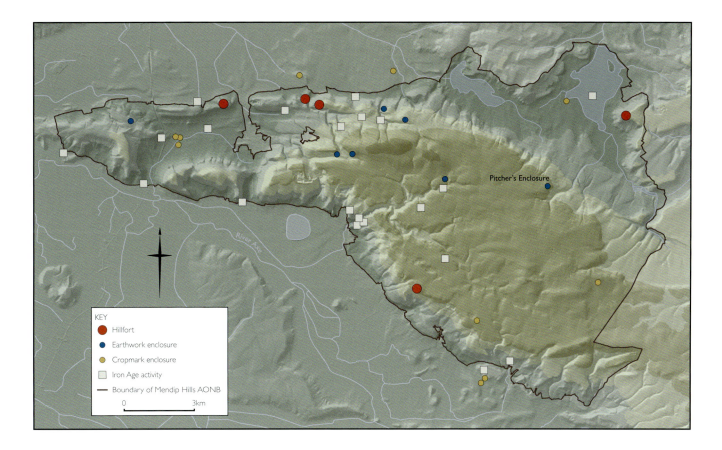

KEY
● Hillfort
● Earthwork enclosure
● Cropmark enclosure
▢ Iron Age activity
— Boundary of Mendip Hills AONB
0   3km

which have also been recorded from across much of the British Isles. They are essentially characterised by an area of ground defined by a relatively substantial stone or earthen bank, the interior accessed by a simple gap entrance. Earthwork and cropmark evidence has revealed that some Mendip sites display more complex entranceways, however, in the form of elongated passageways defined by a ditch or bank. At Pitcher's Enclosure, for example, the bank turns outwards to create a funnel-shaped approach, a feature also visible at the cropmark sites near Wattles Hill and Ramspits (*see* p 85). These short passageways might have been created for defensive purposes or to make the entrance more impressive – possibly accommodating a sequence of timber gates. The contrived approaches set these sites apart from the hill-slope enclosures of Cornwall, Exmoor and the Quantock Hills, possibly indicating different social or economic influences, or highlighting varying dates and functions.

It is unclear whether any of these small enclosures were intended as defensive works, as few occupy strategic positions. The majority of the enclosures are located on open hillsides or gently sloping spurs, which suggests defence

was not a key consideration. The only exception to this is Burrington Camp, which is positioned on the edge of a rocky gorge, but again its siting may not be wholly related to defensive needs (Fig 4.19). This variation in monument location may imply that enclosures had a variety of functions, some requiring stout defences and others not, perhaps representing monuments of varying date and purpose. Where some enclosures are defined by substantial banks and ditches, in excess of 2m in height, others are bounded by more modest earthworks, often no more than a low bank or simple ditch. Pitcher's Enclosure and West Twin, for example, display no evidence for an outer ditch, making it less apparent where the material for the bank was obtained. It is possible that the quarry ditches at these sites were later infilled, particularly in the case of Pitcher's Enclosure, where the earthworks were lowered considerably in the 1960s.

The ramparts themselves could have been surmounted by a timber palisade of close-set posts or wattlework, a substantial hedge or a drystone wall. The clearest indication we have for the form of rampart construction comes from Burrington Camp, which was excavated

Fig 4.18
The distribution of hillforts, enclosures and Iron Age activity across the Mendip Hills AONB.

Fig 4.19
Aerial photograph showing
Burrington Camp positioned
on the edge of the gorge.
(NMR 24819/12)

by the UBSS in 1948 and again in 1960 (Tratman 1963). This work showed that the earth and stone bank along the eastern side of the enclosure was of dump construction – created from material excavated from the ditches – with a berm or level area separating the bank and ditch top. The outer ditch was flat-bottomed and cut into the natural limestone, with stone from the cutting piled onto the outer face of the bank; the stone revetment would have undoubtedly added to the impregnable appearance of the barrier. The excavations also demonstrated that the enclosure ditches had silted significantly, with the outer ditch *c* 1.8m deeper when originally constructed: the prehistoric earthworks there-fore would have formed a formidable obstacle well over 4m high.

Although most of the enclosures are of simple univallate (*see* Glossary) construction, some sites have a more complex form. The hilltop enclosure of Tinker's Batch, located on Elborough Hill, for example, is defined by a near vertical rock face along its southern side, with the northern and eastern boundary formed by a double scarp and internal quarry ditch. When Tratman visited the site in 1935 the western extent of the enclosure comprised a double bank and outer ditch, with a gap towards the southern end interpreted as the location of a possible entrance (Tratman 1935, 256–8). In the years following his visit the western defences of the fort were largely levelled, with material from the outer bank used to infill the ditch. The enclosure is now barely visible, with only the northern ramparts (which are shrouded in dense scrub) surviving to any significant height. It is adjacent to a substantial block of prehistoric field system, suggesting that the site may have formed the focus of a productive agricultural landscape.

Other sites display evidence for a more complex development history, such as Burrington Camp, which has two clear phases of construction. The primary phase took the form of an L-shaped ditch and bank which cut off a small spur, utilising the natural topography to create a monument which had an affinity with a promontory fort (Fig 4.20). The interior was most probably accessed

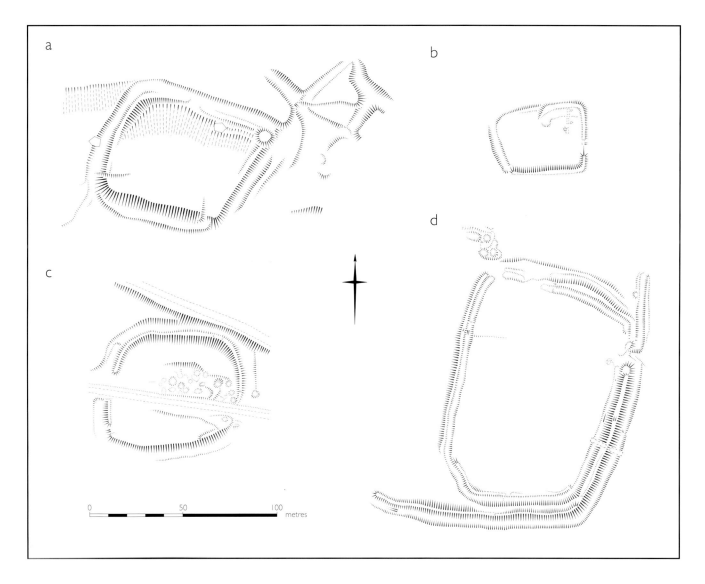

0   50   100 metres

from the east, around the northern end of the linear earthwork, where the ditch displays a short section of outer bank. The second phase of construction defined a complete circuit. An inner quarry ditch was dug and the material used to enlarge the original rampart on the south and east sides, with a low inner bank also created on the southern side. On the north and west sides the material from the quarry ditch was thrown outwards to form an outer bank, with a short section of outer ditch also created along the northern side. This second phase of activity created a subrectangular enclosure defining an area of approximately 0.8ha, with an entrance cut through the original L-shaped bank and ditch on the eastern side to allow access to the interior.

The creation of an internal quarry ditch to obtain material to enlarge the rampart as opposed to enlarging the outer ditch may have been undertaken for practical reasons. It would have been much easier to excavate earthen material from the interior than to extend the rock-cut outer ditch. The construction of an outer ditch along the northern boundary of the enclosure may reflect this side's greater vulnerability, or could be related to its close proximity to the entrance and indicate a greater desire for display. The remodelling of the enclosure and enlargement of its defences could be related to a change in the use or status of the site, or possibly a phase of reoccupation after a period of abandonment. The form of the L-shaped bank and ditch, and its simple dump construction, may indicate a construction date as early as the later Bronze Age – the monument may have been abandoned then reused in the Early to Middle Iron Age.

Fig 4.20
Earthwork plans of enclosures: (a) Longbottom Camp, (b) West Twin, (c) Rowberrow Camp and (d) Burrington Camp.

Several episodes of construction are also evident at Charterhouse-on-Mendip, culminating in the construction of a small Roman fort in the 1st century AD (*see* Fig 5.2). The site is positioned on a gently sloping tongue of land overlooking the Blackmoor Valley, at about 250m OD. The earliest phase of construction took the form of a curving linear ditch which cut off the spur to the east, creating a promontory enclosure. As with Burrington Camp, the next phase probably defined a complete circuit, although the eastern and southern sides of the enclosure have largely been lost to later activity. The surviving earthworks enclose an area of at least 1ha, defined by a bank and outer ditch; excavations revealed that the bank was constructed of clay with an external rock-cut ditch (Todd 1993, 63). Where the initial ditch was reused along the western side a counterscarp bank was created, which suggests part of the ditch may have been recut and increased in size during the second phase of construction. An entrance is also visible along this side, defined by a break in the bank approximately 8m wide.

The recovery of Neronian pottery from the lower ditch fills of the enclosure led a previous commentator to attribute this second phase of remodelling to the 1st century AD (Todd 1993, 63). The multiple construction phases identified suggest, however, that the site had earlier origins, almost certainly dating from the 1st millennium BC. Indeed, the second phase of enclosure may also be late prehistoric in date, with the site maintained until its acquisition by the Roman military forces – hence the fill of Neronian pottery. If this interpretation is correct, it would further confirm earlier theories of extensive later prehistoric activity in the Charterhouse-on-Mendip area, almost certainly linked to the importance of mineral exploitation, given its prime location over-looking the Blackmoor and Velvet Bottom valleys. We know from sites such as Wookey Hole Cave that, as well as forming a component of alloys, lead was used for everyday objects in the Iron Age, such as spindle whorls (Balch 1914). The creation of such an enclosure and the investment of time and resource in its construction demonstrate the importance of control over mineral production in the later prehistoric period.

Three of the earthwork enclosures show clear evidence for settlement in their interior, with the remainder almost completely devoid of internal features. At Burrington Camp a total of 15 trial pits were dug in the interior of the enclosure and 'not a single ancient object was found' (Tratman 1963, 21). The rectilinear enclosure of West Twin, the smallest extant hill-slope enclosure recorded on Mendip at just over 0.14ha in area, does, however, contain evidence for settlement. The enclosure sits on a spur between the East Twin and West Twin brooks on the northern side of Black Down, and has spectacular views straight down Burrington Combe and out over the Yeo Valley towards Broadfield Down. The enclosure sits at about 275m OD and is defined by an outer bank on three sides and a shallow ditch along its western extent. A simple gap through the eastern bank marks the entrance. A levelled terrace and building platform are tucked into the north-eastern corner of the enclosure, defining the site of a former structure about 5m in diameter. Aerial photography has also identified some linear features in the area surrounding the enclosure which may represent the residue of former fields (Truscoe 2008, 25). That the field system does not appear to be well developed and has a north-facing aspect could suggest that this enclosure represents a pastoral or seasonal settlement – perhaps used by a shep-herd tending a flock in the summer months.

Evidence for late prehistoric settlement can also be seen within Pitcher's Enclosure, the largest enclosure in this category and perhaps the most unusual. It consists of a curvilinear U-shaped bank enclosing a gently sloping spur. The bank is predominantly low and spread, with the enclosure's straight south-eastern side defined by a simple scarp – almost certainly the result of reusing elements of a pre-existing field system (Fig 4.21). At the north-eastern end of the enclosure is a group of roundhouses, several of which were almost completely levelled by agricultural improvements in the 1960s. Early aerial photographs do, however, show the roundhouses prior to demolition, where they can be seen to comprise both well-defined individual buildings and conjoined structures (Fig 4.22). The surviving roundhouses are marked by low stony banks, a maximum of 3m in width, and range in size from 13m to 6m externally. The best-preserved house unusually has an entrance to the north connected to which is a short section of bank – possibly the remains of an entrance porch constructed to shelter the interior from the worst of the Mendip weather.

Fig 4.21 (opposite) Pitcher's Enclosure: earthwork plan.

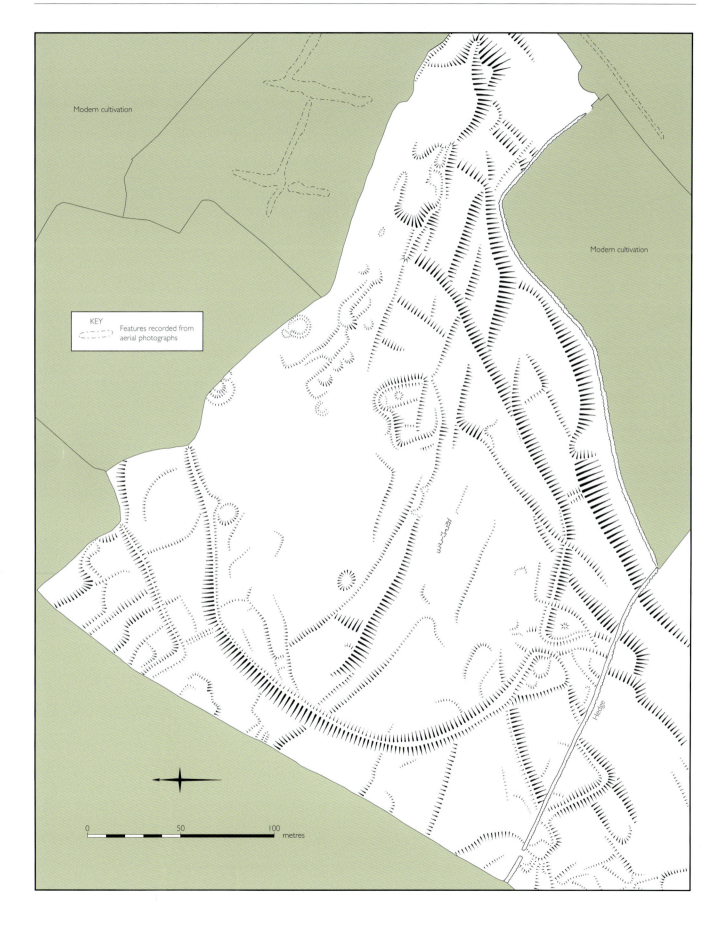

KEY

Features recorded from
aerial photographs

Modern cultivation

Modern cultivation

Hedge

0   50   100
metres

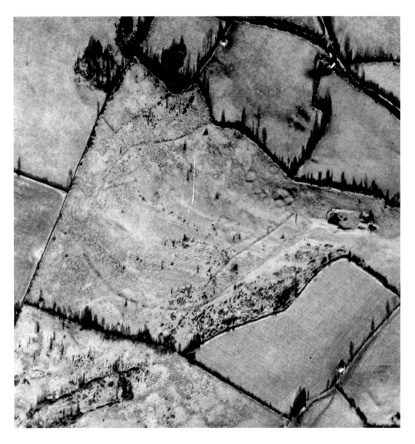

Fig 4.22
Pitcher's Enclosure: aerial photograph showing the roundhouses (centre right) prior to demolition. (RAF 3G TUD UK 25 PTIII 5290, Historic England [RAF photography])

prehistoric settlement. Some of the buildings would appear to lie beyond the bounds of the enclosure and may suggest the bank was created to enclose an originally 'open' scarp-edge settlement, possibly for defensive purposes or to corral livestock. The creation of this enclosing bank may again represent a period of social or economic change within the region. U-shaped 'enclosures' from this period have been identified elsewhere, Brigmerston Down on Salisbury Plain, for example (McOmish *et al* 2002, 71–2), and illustrate the complex and diverse range of monument within this class.

Settlement evidence was also recorded within an enclosure at the eastern end of Burrington Ham (Fig 4.23). The complex, which occupies the summit of the ridge, comprises a subrectangular enclosure just under 0.6ha in area, defined by a low stony bank with a possible entrance to the east and a more modest access at the north-western corner. Within the enclosed area the remains of three possible roundhouses were identified, the buildings all approximately 11m in external diameter. The best-preserved roundhouse is tucked into the south-western corner of the enclosure and survives as a level platform surmounted by the remains of a stone wall, with an entrance gap through its eastern side. The other building stances are less well defined, surviving as low circular platforms, which may have supported less substantial structures with walls constructed of timber posts, planks or

As mentioned above, the enclosure bank was constructed over terraced and embanked fields, making the fields within its circuit redundant. There is no evidence for a boundary along the north-eastern circuit, and the existing modern field boundary cuts through elements of the

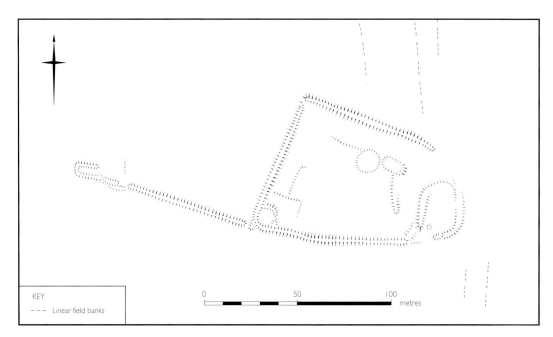

Fig 4.23
Burrington Ham: earthwork plan of enclosed settlement.

KEY
- - - Linear field banks

0   50   100
metres

wattle and daub. The different construction methods could represent separate phases of occupation, or a hierarchical sequence of prehistoric buildings. The enclosure displays evidence of having been subdivided internally, with all the houses associated with small yards or garden plots, possibly originally defined by timber or wattlework fences. A length of bank runs westwards from the enclosure and a series of linear field banks has been identified to the north and east. The latter lie on a different alignment to the settlement remains and may represent a separate phase of land use; a fossilised field bank within the enclosure suggests the fields pre-date the closed settlement, although they may have continued in use during the life of the enclosure.

The hill-slope enclosures of Longbottom Camp and Rowberrow Camp (or Roman Camp) are located within 600m of each other at the confluence of two valleys – Long Bottom and Rowberrow Bottom (Fig 4.24). Longbottom Camp survives as a smoothed earthwork within a pasture field on a gentle south-facing slope, at about 200m OD. The subrectangular enclosure is defined by a ditch and spread earthwork bank on three sides and by a steep scarp to the south, defining an area of about 0.37ha. Evidence suggests the enclosure may have been modified or reused; the straighter, eastern side of the enclosure possibly formed part of later settlement remains. Alternatively, the enclosure may itself have reused elements of an earlier field system in its construction, as happened at

Pitcher's Enclosure. The interior was accessed through a gap towards the centre of the northern rampart, but there is no evidence that the enclosure contained buildings.

Rowberrow Camp is better defined, standing within an area of former plantation at about 235m OD. The enclosure is subrectangular with distinctly rounded corners, defining an area of 0.35ha. The enclosure is formed by a ditch and bank around three sides, with a substantial scarp forming its southern boundary. The original entrance to the enclosure was placed roughly centrally along its western side, above which the ground rises sharply. The steep nature of the slope on which the enclosure lies would almost certainly have limited occupation to the southern half of the site. Unfortunately this area has suffered substantial damage through mining activity and the construction of a forestry track which bisects the enclosure, with any evidence for original occupation possibly destroyed.

The close proximity and strategic location of the sites may indicate the deliberate pairing of these monuments. Long Bottom and Rowberrow Bottom are two of the main routes up onto the western side of the Mendip massif, allowing access from both the southern and northern sides of the hills. Access from the north would also have been overlooked by Dolebury Hillfort and Dinghurst Camp, which highlights the strategic importance of this thoroughfare. This major topographic junction was evidently significant for millennia, with

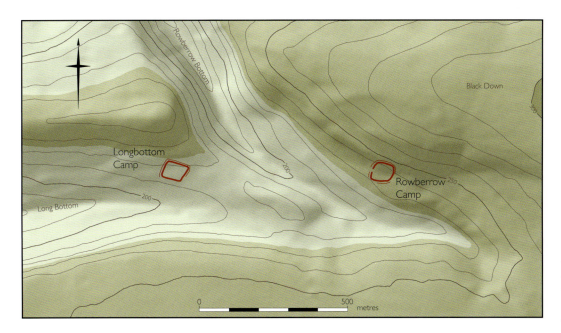

Fig 4.24
Longbottom Camp and Rowberrow Camp: map showing the topographic position of the enclosures.

groups of Bronze Age barrows overlooking it from Tyning's Farm and Cuck Hill.

The morphological similarity between these two enclosures raises questions about their relationship, not least whether the sites were contemporary. The lack of evidence for activity in their interior makes it difficult to ascribe a function to them, and subsequently to ascertain a relationship between the two monuments. Such sites are often interpreted as enclosed farmsteads, the focus for a family group or small community – these separate enclosures possibly represent the holdings of different social groups or an expansion of a family unit. The topographic setting of the sites may reflect an element of control over access through the landscape, or define distinct territorial areas. In

many ways it may simply be the survival of these two monuments that makes them exceptional. The settlement features on the southern side of Wattles Hill were also recorded in close proximity to one another, and sites such as these possibly represent the vestiges of what was once a densely populated landscape.

Hillforts

By far the most imposing monuments in the Mendip landscape are its hillforts, which can be seen ringing the uplands – located in commanding positions and dominating the surrounding landscape (Fig 4.25). Hillforts are found across Britain, with marked concentrations in southern, western and north-eastern England, as well as Wales and Scotland. They are usually defined by massive earth or stone banks with external ditches, sometimes forming a single ring of defence and sometimes a series of concentric banks and ditches. There is, however, great disparity between both the strength of hillfort defences and the extent of the area they enclose. Some of the great Somerset forts, such as Cadbury Castle, have massive ramparts comprising multiple banks and ditches enclosing a relatively small area, with others defining a huge area, such as Ham Hill. In contrast, the smaller forts of the South-West, such as Cow Castle and Mounsey Castle on Exmoor, have far less impressive earthworks, with a single rampart often defining an area of no more than 1ha to 2ha and possibly reflecting different cultural and social traditions.

When these monuments were constructed, and for what purpose, is not entirely clear. Hillforts are largely considered a phenomenon of the 1st millennium BC, with most early forts thought to date from around the 6th or 5th centuries BC. There is evidence, however, that some hillforts have earlier origins, dating from the Late Bronze Age, with others defining areas which have been utilised by communities over millennia. For example, finds of Neolithic and Bronze Age stone and metal artefacts have been recovered from Banwell Camp and Dolebury Hillfort, and many other sites have revealed evidence of earlier use. How long these forts were occupied may again have varied from site to site, with some experiencing periods of abandonment and recolonisation and others occupied for only a short period of time.

Although hillforts represent enclosed and defended places, they may have served a variety of functions, ranging from areas of communal

Fig 4.25
Aerial photograph looking east from Banwell Camp towards Sandford Hill, with the 'Churchill Gap' and Dolebury Camp beyond. (NMR 24820/18)

settlement to ritual or ceremonial centres. Hillforts have been interpreted by some as representing central places, the focus of power and control within a community or territory, occupied and run by a secular or religious elite (Cunliffe 2003). That some forts were the focus for extensive settlement has been demonstrated at sites such as Danebury and Midsummer Hill (Cunliffe 2003; Bowden 2005, 22–4). In contrast, other forts show little indication of settlement within their interior, and possibly functioned on a more cultural or symbolic level. These sites may have been used on a seasonal basis, as the focus of a transhumant pattern of life, centred on cultural, spiritual or agricultural needs (Bowden 2005, 24–5). Gatherings held within these enclosures would have been used to enforce social, political or economic relationships, strengthening community bonds built and maintained over generations. How individual hillforts functioned may also have changed through time, their internal and external layouts altering in response to changing cultural needs. Some sites possibly developed from seasonal meeting places into areas of permanent settlement or locations of refuge during periods of unrest (I Brown 2008).

As well as fulfilling practical and defensive needs, the ramparts themselves may have held symbolic meaning, linked to prestige, power and social inclusion (Bowden and McOmish 1987, 76–84). This is often evident at the entrance to a site where enlarged ramparts, and sometime complex entrance ways, may have been as much about display and control as security and defence. In some cases the size of ramparts increases the closer to the entrance they are, indicating the greatest construction effort was concentrated where it was most likely to be seen. These major engineering projects could only have been undertaken by groups of people or communities working together, people with a common goal and shared identity – be that through kinship, culture or place. The ramparts may have been erected over many years; some display evidence of 'gang working', where the ramparts were constructed in separate sections by teams of people, possibly over several seasons. The ramparts and ditches were also maintained and refurbished, a process which could continue over many generations and may again have held symbolic significance.

There are four extant hillforts within the area of the AONB – Banwell Camp, Dolebury Camp, Burledge Hillfort and Westbury Camp. A fifth site, Dinghurst Camp, has also been put forward as a hillfort (Tratman 1927). The monument was described by Phelps in 1836 as 'surrounded by a vallum with double agger and fosse' and mapped by the Ordnance Survey in 1885 as a sinuous bank, about 150m long, running around the eastern and northern sides of Churchill Batch (Phelps 1836, 100). Quarrying activities have now almost completely removed any trace of this enclosure, which makes further interpretation impossible.

The majority of the upstanding hillforts of Mendip lie between 85m and 150m OD, with the exception of Westbury Camp, which is located high on the southern escarpment at 260m OD. The forts occupy both hilltop and spur locations and range in size from 2ha to over 9ha in extent. When looking at the distribution of hillforts, there would appear to be a marked concentration of sites along the northern escarpment of the hills. This distribution pattern is in part a result of the bounds of the study area, with Maesbury Castle lying just outside the eastern boundary of the region and helping to redress the southern imbalance. That said, the distribution of the hillforts (and hill-slope enclosures) remains striking, and displays a distinct correlation with the main river valleys and access routes around and through the landscape. This raises questions about both the role and use of the Mendip forts, and indeed their relationship to one another. With only limited excavation evidence none of the hillforts can be securely dated, and whether they are strictly contemporary is at present unknown.

Dolebury Camp is the largest hillfort in the study area at just over 9ha in extent (Fig 4.26). It lies at the western end of Dolebury Warren, a limestone ridge forming part of the northern escarpment of the Hills, rising to around 180m OD. Dolebury Camp overlooks the 'Churchill Gap', one of the main access routes up onto the western end of the high plateau, and affords spectacular views out over the Yeo Valley and the North Somerset Levels and Moors. In the early 19th century the site was inevitably visited by Skinner and in 1872 was surveyed by C W Dymond, who produced a remarkably accurate and detailed plan of the site for the time (see Fig 1.14). There are no recorded excavations within the fort apart from a casual examination in the centre, which was reported by Dymond (1883, 109), and a trench dug in 1904 when

Fig 4.26
Dolebury Camp: aerial
photograph of the
hillfort looking east.
(NMR 24819/36)

some pottery, animal bone and a whetstone were recovered (Allcroft 1908, 693–4). A bronze spearhead and some Bronze Age pottery which are thought to have come from Dolebury Camp possibly hint at an earlier period of activity.

Dolebury Camp is partly univallate on the south side where the natural slope is particularly steep, but mainly bivallate (*see* Glossary), though the outer ditch is slight along the northern side (Fig 4.27). The impressive stone and earth banks are largely grass-covered, with the exception of some sections of the main rampart where areas of bare scree-like stone are visible, particularly to the north. Dymond noted wall faces within the main rampart at several points around the northern part of the circuit; he likened the style of masonry to that seen at Worlebury, which he had excavated two years previously, and found the rampart to be constructed from a series of drystone revetments (1883, 108–9; 1902). No evidence for faced masonry could be traced during the recent earthwork survey (Bowden 2009, 5). Within the hillfort and immediately behind the rampart are internal quarry scoops, which

presumably result from winning material for the original rampart construction, or possibly a later heightening of it. These scoops are particularly substantial to the south-east but also extend around the north-west and part of the north and east sides. Apart from these quarry scoops there are no internal features which can be confidently dated to the prehistoric period. This is possibly a result of the fort's later use as an enclosed rabbit warren (*see* Chapter 7).

The impressive entrance at the west end of the hillfort is the only original access to the site. The main rampart terminals flanking the entrance were subtly enlarged to enhance their visual impact. Although other commentators have suggested a more elaborate configuration at the entrance, including inturned ramparts and 'outworks' (Hollinrake and Hollinrake 1986, 7), no evidence for these was identified. The 'outworks' at the entrance appear to be the combination of natural features and a later hollow-way; this interpretation was postulated by Dymond, who quite explicitly stated, 'There neither is, nor, evidently, ever was any such outwork' (1883, 106). The original approach to

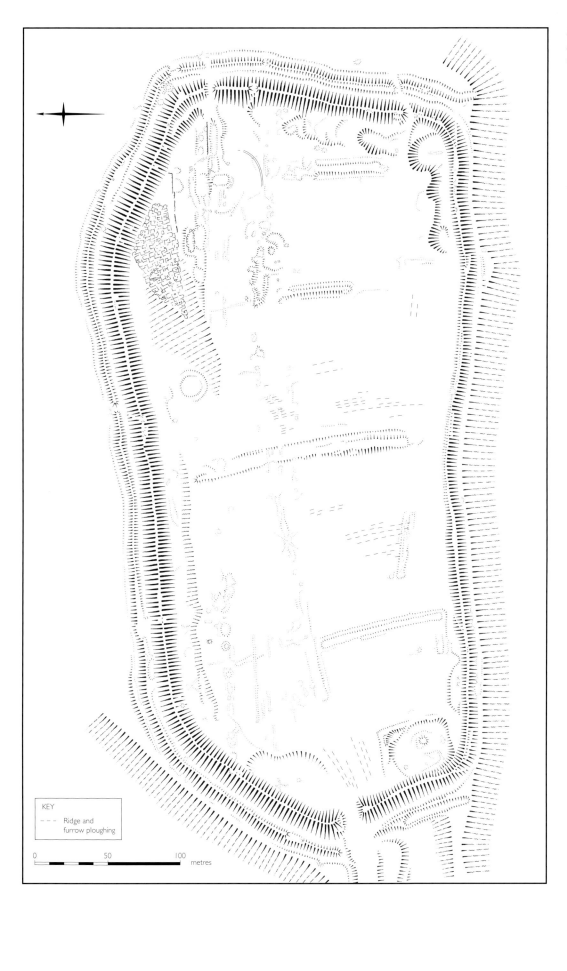

Fig 4.27
Dolebury Camp:
earthwork plan.

KEY

– – – Ridge and
furrow ploughing

0   50   100
metres

the fort presumably would have been from the west by way of a steep natural gully leading up from the lower ground – again indicating that the 'Churchill Gap' represented a main thoroughfare. On approaching the fort the visitor was confronted by formidable stone defences standing upwards of 5m in height and would have been forced to turn left and then right to gain the entrance, which was probably barred by a stout timber gate.

The west-facing entrance is atypical, as most hillforts of this size in southern Britain have two entrances, east and west, and where only one entrance is present it almost invariably faces east. The distinctive form of the eastern rampart, and the lack of an apparent original entrance along this side, may indicate that these earthworks pre-date the hillfort – possibly being remodelled from a cross-ridge dyke constructed during the later Bronze Age (the bronze spearhead was recovered from the ditch along this side of the fort). The breach towards the northern end of the eastern rampart could therefore have been created in antiquity, and possibly represents an east-facing entrance

created during the main phase of fort construction (Bowden 2009, 13). An east-facing entrance would have allowed access out over Dolebury Warren, where evidence for agricultural activity may be contemporary with the life of the fort.

Another enclosure which may have developed from earlier origins is Burledge Hillfort, which occupies a spur-end position overlooking the Chew and Yeo valleys (Fig 4.28). It is north of the main Mendip plateau and is well sited to dominate the surrounding landscape. The hillfort is defined by a subrectangular enclosure with a linear 'outwork' lying approximately 40m to the east. The outwork comprises a substantial stony bank and a broad outer ditch, the former standing over 4m high in places and the latter up to 2m deep. The earthwork would appear to be linked to the hillfort by a scarp along its northern side, though this is almost certainly the result of later quarrying. The bank and ditch are carefully positioned to cut off the western spur of the hill and may represent an earlier cross-ridge dyke or perhaps define an

Fig 4.28
Burledge Hillfort: aerial photograph showing the ramparts of the hillfort shrouded in trees (centre foreground), with the earthwork remains of the field system (centre right) on the slopes below and a possible cross-ridge dyke (centre top).
(NMR 24817/03)

earlier promontory fort. The bank and ditch have a gap towards their southern end which, although heavily disturbed, represents an original entrance. A second linear feature lies 0.5km to the east of the hillfort, and is now defined by a substantial grass-covered lynchet (Fig 4.29). The much degraded earthwork clearly originated as a large bank, over 500m long, which cuts off Burledge Hill from the ridge to its east. This feature may therefore represent another prehistoric cross-ridge dyke, possibly functioning as a land division, and could date from the Late Bronze Age or Early Iron Age.

The main ramparts of Burledge Hillfort enclose an area of just under 3ha and are bivallate on the northern and southern sides, with a single stone and earth rampart to the east (Fig 4.30). At the western end the rampart stands an impressive 5m in height and has a central gap forming an imposing entranceway. Here the earthworks turn inwards to create a short, deep entrance approximately 7m wide, leading up into the interior of the fort. The northern and eastern side of the fort have suffered heavily from later quarrying activities; the north section of the eastern rampart has

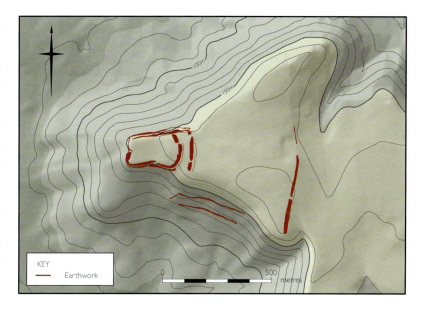

also been considerably lowered as a result of agricultural improvements. A track leading up from the entrance punches through this section of rampart, but does not represent an original eastern access. A further break in the rampart about 35m to the south is also later, as is the track that cuts through the southern side of the

Fig 4.29
Burledge Hillfort: map showing the topographic position of the hillfort and associated linear features.

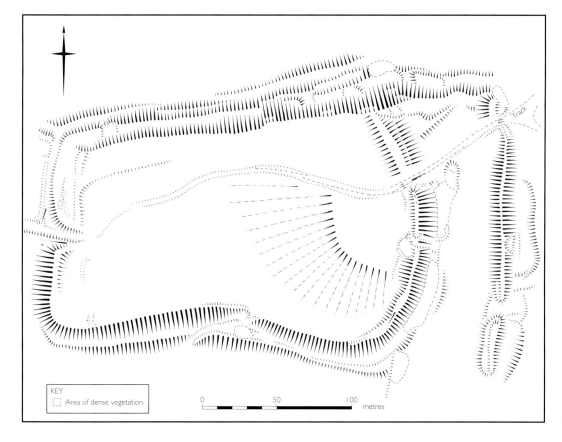

KEY
☐ Area of dense vegetation

0   50   100
              metres

Fig 4.30
Burledge Hillfort: earthwork plan.

fort. This hillfort, possibly like Dolebury, would therefore appear to have only a single western entrance, one which is still approached by a well-defined track. The lack of an original eastern entrance to complement the break in the outwork raises questions about the relationship between these two features, and may strengthen the suggestion they represent two separate phases of construction and use.

The ground within Burledge Hillfort slopes downwards from east to west, falling around 10m, and there are no earthwork features in the interior to indicate prehistoric activity. Two linear banks towards the western end of the fort represent the remains of later field boundaries. Some 26 test pits, approximately 1.2m square, were excavated within the interior of the hillfort by members of the UBSS, predominantly in the southern half of the site (Crook and Tratman 1954). Evidence for prehistoric activity was largely confined to the south-western corner of the fort where postholes, pits, gullies and ditches were revealed. Artefacts uncovered from the pits included Iron Age pottery, a rubbing stone, iron

slag, animal bones and part of an iron brooch. The pits also revealed evidence for a stone inner face to the rampart along the southern and western sides of the hillfort (Rahtz and Greenfield 1977, 170).

That several separate phases of construction could be incorporated into a single hillfort is possibly best demonstrated at Banwell Camp. The ramparts of this hillfort are now largely hidden by trees and occupy a limestone outcrop dividing the Lox-Yeo Valley from the North Somerset Levels and Moors (Fig 4.31). The domed hilltop of Banwell Plain rises to just over 95m OD and was evidently the focus for a range of activities stretching over many centuries. The main occupation evidence at the site is defined by at least two episodes of hillfort construction, but these do not represent the earliest periods of activity. Slight traces of prehistoric fields pre-dating both forts have been recorded from within the interior; these predominantly lie within the western half of the site and take the form of spread linear scarps standing a maximum of 0.3m high (Fig 4.32). Elements of the field system were

Fig 4.31
Banwell Camp: aerial photograph showing earthwork remains within the interior of the hillfort. (NMR 24820/10)

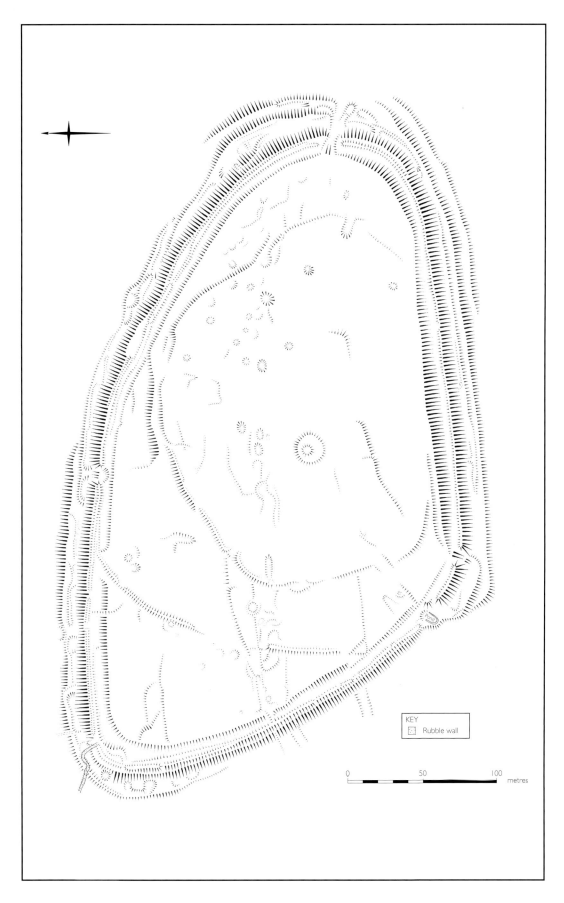

*Fig 4.32
Banwell Camp:
earthwork plan.*

KEY

Rubble wall

0   50   100
                         metres

almost certainly abandoned when the hill was enclosed by the first phase of rampart construction. Excavations undertaken on the summit in 1958 revealed a sealed soil layer containing scatters of pottery, bone, teeth and flint (Hunt 1961a, 15). The flints were identified as Neolithic or Bronze Age in date and complement a series of flints previously retrieved from the area which included leaf-shaped arrowheads.

The first enclosure phase defined an area of about 3.4ha, marked by a low scarp, though the southern rampart was largely destroyed by the construction of the later fort (Fig 4.33). The surviving rampart is segmented, formed by individual sections of low bank or scarp, some with gaps between and others constructed slightly offline. A small excavation was undertaken across the western section of this rampart in 1959 and demonstrated that the earth and stone bank originally had a shallow outer ditch (Hunt 1961a). Two postholes uncovered beneath the main earthwork were interpreted by the excavators as the remains of a timber 'stockade'. This evidence could suggest the perimeter of the enclosure was largely defined by a timber palisade or box rampart, formed from upright posts linked by timber planks or wattlework, behind which a quantity of stone and earth was packed. The segmented nature of the earthworks could suggest the enclosure was constructed by separate gangs of labourers working on discrete sections of rampart, possibly representing the efforts of individual family units or kinship groups. Alternatively, the segments may represent separate phases of construction, with the enclosure possibly incorporating elements of the earlier field system.

A second linear bank was constructed to the north-west of this timber enclosure and may be an outwork or annex related to it. Alternatively, it could pre-date the initial enclosure, although there is no direct relationship between the two features to substantiate this. The linear earthwork would appear to be earlier than the secondary phase of fort, as the inner quarry ditch along the fort's northern side terminates either side of the bank. There is no evidence to suggest this bank continued round the contour of the hill to form a separate phase of enclosure, and its purpose and precise date must remain obscure.

The later phase of Banwell Camp is effectively a contour fort, defined by two earth and stone banks separated by a ditch along all but the western circuit, where only a single rampart is evident. The ramparts enclose an area of around 7.5ha and have been extensively robbed for stone, particularly along their northern side. Knight, quoting from Rutter, records: 'within memory of persons living in his time, many cartloads of freestone had been taken from the spot' (1902, 407). The internal quarry ditch mentioned above extends around the entire circuit and would have supplied material for the original rampart construction, or for any later enlargements. The fort has a single original entrance to the east, where a further line of defences was added to create an entrance passageway approximately 30m long. A deep hollow-way ascends the hill from the north-east and probably represents the original approach. On climbing the hill a visitor would have been rewarded by the most impressive view of the fort, defined by a section of triple ramparts, possibly surmounted by a timber palisade or stone wall. To enter the fort the visitor would have had to turn sharp right into the entrance passageway, probably passing through a series

Fig 4.33
Banwell Camp: phase plans.

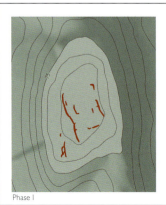

Phase I

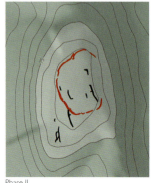

Phase II

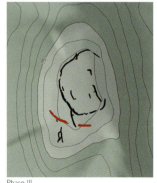

Phase III

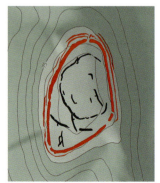

Phase IV

of timber gates, before winning the interior.

In the interior a range of artefacts was recovered from the ditch and rampart of the first phase of fort, including pottery, flints, quern fragments and yellow ochre. The Banwell Ochre Caves lie on the north side of the hill and were mined during the early 20th century; a series of pits across the centre of the hill may represent trial pits related to this period of exploitation. Ochre was also prized during the Iron Age, possibly having ritual or sacred associations (a lump of ochre was found in the mouth of an individual buried in a pit in Worlebury Hillfort), and may have imbued this area with particular significance. The pottery recovered at Banwell Camp possibly suggests an Early Iron Age date for the first phase of rampart construction. A quantity of iron slag and fragments of clay furnace-lining were also found just behind this rampart, indicating industrial activity was undertaken within the enclosure. Just outside the inner rampart a pit was found to contain sherds of pottery, quern fragments, a rubbing stone, flints and animal bones; the pit was sealed with rubble and a complete saddle quern of Old Red Sandstone had been placed on top (Hunt 1961a, 17–23). In the western half of the fort a rectangular platform which was interpreted as a 'hut site' was excavated. A series of postholes, ditches and low walls were associated with this platform, but it is unclear what they represent (Hunt 1962, 11–19). Industrial, agricultural and domestic activities were therefore undertaken within the fort, but how these relate to the different phases of fort construction remains unclear.

Where some sites have complex development histories, others would appear to represent a single construction episode. Westbury Camp (or Stoke Camp) is a subrectangular hillfort located within an area of enclosed limestone grassland (Fig 4.34). The earth and stone ramparts of the fort enclose approximately 2.5ha and sit on a slight spur on the southern Mendip escarpment. The fort is defined by relatively modest ramparts, with an outer ditch and bank along two sides and a single bank or scarp defining the remainder of the circuit (Fig 4.35). The fort has a simple gap entrance to the east, where the main rampart thickens and turns inwards slightly to form an opening about 3.6m wide. The northern half of the interior is relatively level, falling only slightly from north-east to south-west, before dropping

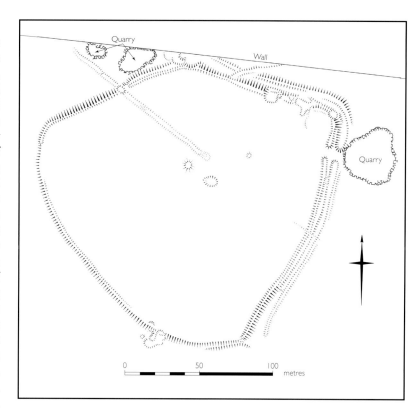

appreciably to the south-west. A slight curvilinear scarp in the interior may define a building platform, approximately 12m in diameter, which is tucked into the north-eastern corner of the fort. The lack of occupation evidence elsewhere in the hillfort may reflect later land use, as several episodes of enclosure and improvement are evident, including the construction of a limekiln into the southern rampart.

The northern and eastern approaches to Westbury Camp are over relatively level ground, making these the least defendable sides of the hillfort. The construction of an outer ditch and bank beyond the northern and eastern ramparts may have served to strengthen the enclosure's defences on these vulnerable sides. We must be cautious, however, in attributing a purely defensive explanation to the form of hillforts. Westbury Camp was most easily approached from the north and east, with the entrance located towards the northern end of the east side. The construction of an outer ditch and bank along these sides could have served to make the enclosure appear more impressive, conveying a message of strength and power to approaching visitors (Fig 4.36).

There are several factors which suggest that Westbury Camp may date from the earliest

Fig 4.34
Westbury Camp: earthwork plan.

Fig 4.35
Westbury Camp: surveying the relatively modest earth and stone ramparts of the hillfort.
(Elaine Jamieson)

Fig 4.36
Westbury Camp: reconstruction drawing showing how the east entrance may have appeared to approaching visitors.

period of hillfort construction, such as the simple univallate form of the enclosure and the modest size of the ramparts. The simple gap entrance to the hillfort is also suggestive of an early date, as entrances had a tendency to become more elaborate and complex as the Iron Age progressed. The existence of a berm, and the relative narrowness of the bank (*c* 4.7m), may indicate a box rampart construction (*see* Glossary). This form of construction would suggest a date of no later than the 6th century BC for the creation of the fort, with the possibility that the site may even pre-date the conventional beginning of the Iron Age.

The modest size of the rampart may also be indicative of early abandonment. Sites such as Cadbury Castle have shown that hillfort ramparts were frequently remodelled and enlarged in the mid- to late Iron Age, often undergoing several phases of alterations and rebuilding (Barrett *et al* 2000). Initial timber-framed construction was often followed by glacis or dump construction where successive dumps of soil created a continuous slope from rampart top to ditch bottom; the existence of a berm at Westbury Camp suggests this form of construction was never employed. Cunliffe (1993) noted the abandonment of early enclosures in Wessex by the middle of the 1st millennium BC, and suggested that the phenomenon must be viewed as a major threshold in the socio-economic development of the area.

5

The Romano-British and early
medieval periods

The arrival of the Roman fleet off the south coast of Britain in the late summer of AD 43 was the first act in a succession of military campaigns which would bring much of Britain under Roman imperial control. Although Roman culture and patronage had influenced southern British society since at least the time of Caesar (100–44 BC), the impact of the Claudian invasion on much of the country would have been profound. In the years following the conquest, the adoption of Roman culture is visible in the archaeological record through the use of new forms of pottery, ornamental objects and metalwork. In more Romanised areas some pre-conquest round-houses were gradually abandoned in favour of rectilinear timber or stone-built structures. The Romano-British period also brought an intensification of agricultural production and the development of new settlement forms, reflecting fundamental changes in the industrial and agricultural economy of the region.

The subsequent departure of the Roman administration in the 5th century AD, and the social and economic changes which followed, had a marked effect on the British landscape. Long-established trade networks ceased to function, the production and distribution of pottery and metalwork began to fail, and coinage stopped circulating. Building materials also changed, with timber largely replacing stone and mortar. The loss of these key classes of archaeological evidence has left us with a population on Mendip which at first appears elusive; however, burial remains indicate a degree of continuity between the post-Roman population and their ancestral past. By the end of the 7th century AD Somerset was a territory of the West Saxon kings, and our clearest picture of Anglo-Saxon life comes from the great royal and ecclesiastical centres they created. The 10th and 11th centuries saw a gradual change in the nature of landholding,

with the developing system of local lordship ultimately shaping elements of later social and religious life.

The Romano-British period (AD 43–400)

The Claudian invasion

At the time of the Claudian invasion Britain was divided into a series of tribal groupings, with the South-West comprising three tribal areas controlled by the Dumnonii, the Durotriges and the Dobunni. The Mendip Hills lay towards the southern boundary of Dobunni territory, which stretched up into Gloucestershire, with the Durotriges controlling the Somerset Levels and Moors as well as much of Dorset and Wiltshire. Although the tribes of the South-West clearly presented some resistance to the invading army, they proved no match for the professional forces of Rome. Whether through warfare, treaties or bribes, the subjugation of the native tribes was achieved by AD 47 and Somerset lay under military control.

To support the Roman campaign the Fosse Way was constructed, linking forts both along its line and to the west, ultimately running from the legionary fortress at Exeter (established around AD 55) right up into Lincolnshire. This important route was largely in place by the middle of the 1st century AD and possibly defined the edge of the original frontier zone. The road allowed the rapid movement of soldiers, supplies and communications, with the forts positioned along its length used to garrison troops and enforce military rule.

How much unrest the Roman military had to contend with in Somerset in the years immediately following the invasion is unclear. At Cadbury Castle, for example, the main timber gates of the fort were destroyed by fire on two occasions; the second incident was followed by a period of Roman military occupation and dated to around the middle of the 1st century AD (Barrett *et al* 2000). At Ham Hill, finds of armour, spears and ballista bolt heads indicate a similar date for military occupation. The creation of a fort at Ilchester has also been attributed to this period, with its construction interpreted as a possible response to the wider instability of that time (Leach 2001b, 25). Ultimately the military campaign in the South-West was successful, however, and II Augusta had left its legionary base at Exeter by around AD 66. The Roman military presence at Ilchester ended soon after, with the withdrawal suggesting a period of relative stability within the region (Leach 2001b).

The conquering army was quick to identify the mineral-rich areas of the South-West, and by the mid-1st century AD a small fort had been established at Charterhouse-on-Mendip (Fig 5.1). A lead ingot (or pig) stamped with Claudius's title for the year AD 49 was found at Wookey Hole in 1544 (Gough 1967, 20) and demonstrates that lead (and probably silver) was being exported from the frontier-zone mines on Mendip within a few years of the invasion. The military occupation at Charterhouse-on-Mendip would appear to represent the reappropriation of a late prehistoric enclosure (*see* Chapter 4), demonstrating a direct transference of power and control from the native population to the incoming Roman authorities (Fradley 2009, 54–5). Within the existing enclosure a roughly square fort was constructed, defining an area of around 0.3ha, with an entrance located centrally along its southern side (Fig 5.2). During excavation a high proportion of imported pottery was recovered from the

Fig 5.1
Charterhouse-on-Mendip:
aerial photograph showing
the slight earthwork
remains of the Roman fort.
(NMR 1460/420)

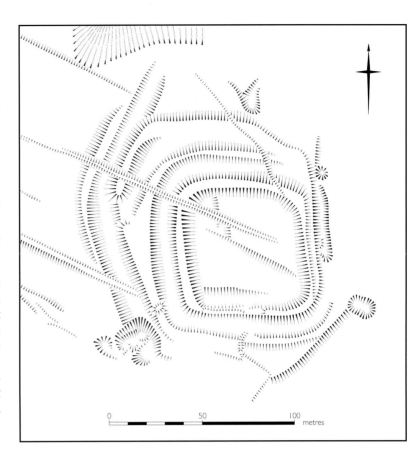

site (much of it related to eating and especially drinking), with the material attributed to the specific preferences of Roman troops and suggesting a period of military occupation between AD 50 and 75 (Todd 2007, 41 and 65).

A Roman road linked the small fort at Charterhouse-on-Mendip to Old Sarum and Southampton Water, crossing the Fosse Way on Beacon Hill. Sections of this high-level route can still be traced across the Mendip plateau, passing close to the Roman mining complexes at Green Ore and Priddy, before terminating on the eastern side of the Blackmoor Valley; the road was recorded on a map of 1570 when it was named 'Sheptons brode wey' (SHS DD/X/NW). A further Roman road, Stratford Lane, has also been identified running north across the plateau, defining the line of the parish boundary between Compton Bishop and West Harptree, before dropping down into the Chew Valley and passing close to the villa site in Chew Park (Rahtz and Greenfield 1977). Undoubtedly existing minor roads or trackways would have continued in use, supplementing the new military network and linking small settlements to their hinterland and beyond.

The post-conquest landscape

At the time of the conquest Mendip was already a productive agricultural landscape, defined by large blocks of arable fields, pasture and managed woodland – comprising oak, ash and hazel (Rahtz and Greenfield 1977). Dispersed among these were small enclosed and unenclosed settlements, many of which continued largely unchanged into the post-conquest period. It is this continuity that is striking, with the initial adoption of Roman culture often only visible through the use of new forms of pottery and ornamental objects. In more Romanised areas some settlements experienced structural and architectural alterations, possibly reflecting the status or aspirations of their occupants. At Hole Ground, Wookey Hole, for example, excavations revealed a Late Iron Age roundhouse which had been superseded by a sequence of Romano-British buildings, representing a period of continuous occupation from the later prehistoric through to the 4th century AD (Ashworth and Crampton 1963).

Much of the evidence for Romano-British activity on Mendip is in the form of pottery, coins and metalwork, examples of which have

been recorded from across the region (Fig 5.3). Perhaps one of the most significant finds to be discovered in recent years was a solid bronze Roman figurine of Capricorn, dating from the 1st or 2nd century AD (Fig 5.4). Figurines of Capricorn are rare, and this example is without parallel due to its quality and size – it measures 21cm in length and weighs 900g. The object was discovered at Burrington, not far from the lead mines at Charterhouse-on-Mendip, and may be associated with II Augusta, as Capricorn was the emblem of the legion.

With the exception of the mining areas on the plateau, finds of Romano-British artefacts are largely confined to the lower, more productive agricultural areas to the west and along the northern and southern escarpments. At Chewton Mendip, for example, close to the parish church, the Revd John Skinner recorded the discovery of Roman pottery and metalwork which included a 4th century AD bronze coin of Constantine (BL Add MS 33655, fol 291; 33663, fol 122). Towards the western end of the hills, during the construction of a railway tunnel through Shute Shelve, near Winscombe, workmen uncovered Romano-

Fig 5.2
Charterhouse-on-Mendip: earthwork plan of the Roman fort.

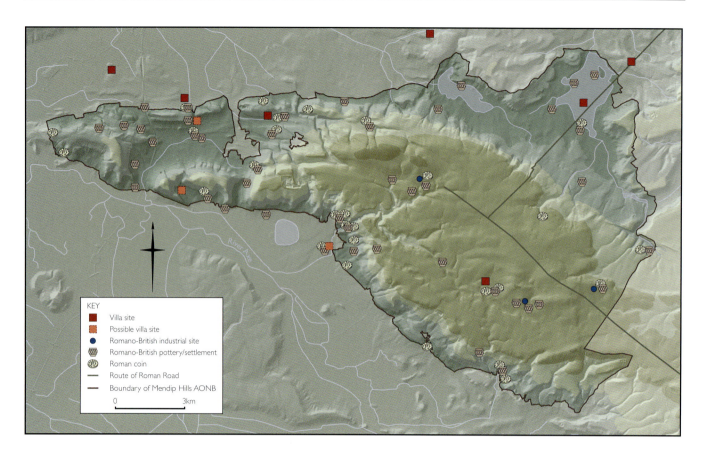

Fig 5.3

The distribution of Romano-British villas, industrial sites, pottery finds and coins across the Mendip Hills AONB.

Fig 5.4

A solid bronze Roman figurine of Capricorn found at Burrington and dating from the 1st or 2nd century AD.

(© Somerset County Council Museums Service)

British skeletons, brooches, lead and the remains of a furnace. Roman pottery, including Samian and later wares, was discovered close by, possibly indicating the location of a contemporary settlement (SHER 10462, 10056). Less than 1km to the north, near Hale Combe, finds of pottery, coins and quernstones suggest the location of another small Romano-British community. The caves of Mendip have also produced evidence for Romano-British activity, with pottery, metalwork and coins from Gough's Old Cave and Long Hole, Cheddar, suggesting these sites were utilised in the 3rd and 4th centuries AD (Branigan and Dearne 1991, 29).

The variation in scale and morphology of the Romano-British settlements of Mendip indicate a society with a broad spectrum of social conditions. Settlements ranged from the lower-status timber buildings identified at Herriott's Bridge to the more opulent stone-built villa at Banwell complete with mosaic pavements and heated bathhouse. There were also slightly less well-off or lesser villas such as Chew Park and Locking, which may be interpreted as little more than large farmsteads with social aspirations. Nucleated and linear settlements have also been identified, focused along roads or 'streets', such as those at Charterhouse-on-Mendip and North Hill, Priddy. That more examples of this form of settlement existed in the region has been demonstrated at sites such as Cheddar, where excavations revealed elements of an early 2nd century AD roadside settlement (Hirst and Rahtz 1973, 77). To the east the Fosse Way attracted new linear settlements, with a small Roman town springing up either side of the road near Shepton Mallet in the later years of the 1st century AD (Leach 2001a). The growth of this form of settlement may be viewed as one of the most conspicuous developments of the period, with their formation possibly the consequence of a changing industrial and agricultural economy.

An intensification of agricultural production in the region by the end of the 1st century AD is suggested by the creation of planned ditch-systems at Herriott's Bridge and around the Roman villa in Chew Park. Here areas of marginal land on the floodplain of the River Chew were drained to facilitate both agricultural production and domestic occupation (Rahtz and Greenfield 1977). Undoubtedly the existing blocks of prehistoric fields on the escarpment slopes continued to be used, modified and extended during this period, with scatters of Roman pottery in the fields above Christon indicative of land improvement and arable production (Clarke 1969). The ditch systems of the Chew Valley may be viewed as relatively small-scale improvement, however, and it is not until the 3rd century AD that there was investment in large-scale operations. It is in this period that the intertidal marshes around Brent Knoll, the Axe Valley and the North Somerset Levels were reclaimed. This was achieved through the creation of a series of sea banks and ditched field systems, and once reclaimed these areas were quickly settled and used for arable production, hay meadows and rough pasture. The drainage of these areas would have been a costly process, however, and how it was funded is unclear. Rippon suggests that the reclamation of the North Somerset Levels may have been undertaken in a piecemeal fashion, with separate areas of marsh embanked and reclaimed by individual villa estates (2006, 80).

With the reclamation of the intertidal marshes, it is probably fair to say that the landscape of the Mendip region was more extensively exploited during the Romano-British period than in any of the preceding centuries. Working the land became easier with improved plough technology, and surplus crops were treated in drying ovens before being stored in timber granaries. The predominant crop was wheat, both spelt and emmer, which was supplemented by barley, oats and horse-beans. Along the river valleys it was a mixed farming regime centred on beef production and sheep rearing, although pigs, horses and dogs were also kept (Rahtz and Greenfield 1977). A similar picture has emerged from the reclaimed marshland, where it has been suggested that the cultivation of hay meadows

indicates a significant pastoral dimension to the agricultural economy by the second half of the 3rd century AD (Rippon 2006, 73). The transition from a mutton-based diet to one focused more on beef was evidently swift in the vicinity of the small fort at Charterhouse-on-Mendip, with cattle contributing to over 80 per cent of the diet by AD 50–65, possibly the result of the influx of Roman military personnel. The upland areas of Mendip would have been used as open grazing for cattle, sheep and pigs, with the comparatively high proportion of pigs recorded at Charterhouse-on-Mendip attributed to the continuingly wooded nature of the upland landscape (Todd 2007, 57).

Villa settlement

Our idea of Romano-British rural settlement is largely epitomised by the villa – a complex of domestic and agricultural buildings usually forming the centre of a country estate. The agriculturally rich areas of Somerset supported one of the largest concentrations of villas in Britain, predominantly focused on the Roman towns of Ilchester and Bath. The growth of these villa estates may have been fuelled in the post-conquest period by the development of new markets and an increased demand from a growing urban and military population. The villas of Mendip are relatively modest in comparison to some of the large and sophisticated villa complexes associated with the larger Roman towns, such as Keynsham and Low Ham. Within the area of the Mendip Hills AONB there have been three villa sites identified through excavation – Star, Priddy and Chew Park – with a further two possible sites at Winthill and Compton Bishop. Just beyond the boundary of the survey area, villa sites have been recorded at Banwell, Lye Hole, Golds Cross and Locking, with a further villa postulated at Cheddar on the basis of the discovery of 3rd-century AD wall plaster (Hirst and Rahtz 1973, 78).

These villa-based estates are largely located along the main river valleys and fen edges, often occupying the same general location as medieval and modern villages. The proposed villa at Priddy is in some ways an exception to this, located high on the limestone plateau. The site may be interpreted in spatial terms as an estate centre for upland settlement, although its proximity to the mining areas of Mendip could indicate a more complex economic function. Excavations undertaken at the site in 1964 revealed traces of stone walling and coloured wall plaster, roofing and hypocaust tiles, Samian and coarse-ware pottery, oyster shells, glass, bone pins and metalwork – including silver and bronze coins dating from the 1st to the 3rd century AD (Barlow 1967, 7–11). More recent geophysical survey in the area has revealed a sequence of ditched enclosures surrounding the building complex, as well as a possible compound to the east (Thompson 2010a). The archaeological evidence points towards a relatively opulent Romano-British development, possibly the centre of an upland agricultural or industrial estate, although its precise form and extent are as yet unclear.

Excavation at Winthill, on the north side of the Lox-Yeo Valley, has also produced evidence for Romano-British occupation (Chapman 1955; Hunt 1961b; Tabrett 1969). A relatively small stone building was uncovered in a field to the east of Winthill Farm and dated to the 4th century AD, with several other Romano-British features including pits, structures and a stone-built enclosure revealed in fields to the south-east (R Broomhead, pers comm). An infant burial was uncovered beneath the floor of the building, a common element at Romano-

British sites of this period. The interpretation of this as a villa site is largely based on some high-status finds recovered during excavation, including a mid-4th-century AD glass bowl, believed to have been made in Cologne. The bowl has a hunting scene engraved on the outer surface with a Latin and Greek inscription ('Long life to you; drink, and good health') indicating it was intended as a drinking bowl (Fig 5.5). The building uncovered was not opulent, however, and Winthill's villa status has yet to be confirmed.

In contrast to later prehistoric dwellings, villa buildings were often ostentatious with painted plasterwork, mosaic floors and heated bathhouses. At Banwell the remains of a Roman bathhouse were uncovered on the northern side of the town, close to the western bank of the River Banwell. Excavations in 1968 revealed the almost complete plan of a 3rd- to 4th-century AD bathhouse, which comprised a hot room with plunge pool, a warm room with an apsidal eastern end and a cold room. The warm and cold rooms were paved with mosaic floors of red, white and blue tesserae. The warm room was heated by hot air passing through limestone rubble under the floor, with the hot room raised on a hypocaust system through which heat from the adjacent furnace passed. The main villa buildings were arranged around an open area to the south and were linked to the bathhouse by a paved room or corridor. Test pitting in the region of the villa complex indicated that it too had mosaic pavements (Rye 1968).

A small bathhouse was also recorded as part of the villa complex at Locking and comprised a hot room with plunge pool and a warm room, both of which had painted plasterwork but no mosaic floors. The bath block was constructed around AD 300 but had been dismantled by the mid-4th century AD (Linington and Rogers 1957). Locking may represent a lower-status or tenanted villa, possibly subservient to its neighbour at Banwell. Many of these smaller villas developed from less ostentatious pre-conquest farmsteads, demonstrating continuity in landholding and the downward spread of wealth. At Locking, a Late Iron Age roundhouse (possibly positioned within a ditched enclosure) was the earliest evidence for occupation at the site (Linington and Rogers 1957). At Star, Iron Age pottery, a clay-lined storage pit, metalworking debris and a possible hearth have been interpreted as pre-conquest

Fig 5.5
Mid-4th-century AD glass bowl from Winthill, with a hunting scene engraved on the outer surface.
(© Ashmolean Museum, University of Oxford)

occupation (Barton 1964), with the villa at Chew Park constructed next to the remains of a late prehistoric roundhouse which had evidently continued in use into the Romano-British period (Rahtz and Greenfield 1977).

Continuity of settlement is a recurring theme, with evidence for numerous phases of construction and building modification evident throughout the Romano-British period. At Chew Park and Locking the earliest Romanised structures took the form of rectangular timber buildings. Two phases of timber building were recorded at Locking, dated to the 2nd and mid-3rd century AD; the second phase was interpreted as a barn and had been constructed with a rammed stone floor. The timber building at Chew Park was late 1st century AD in date and comprised a rectangular post-built structure defining an internal area of around 11.4m by 4.5m. The main posts were set approximately 2.4m apart and may have been infilled by wattle and daub, with the whole structure covered by reed thatch. This building possibly represents a timber granary and evidently continued in use for a considerable period of time, with some of the posts replaced on more than one occasion (Rahtz and Greenfield 1977, 37–8).

The timber buildings at both these sites were superseded by small stone-built villa complexes sometime in the late 3rd or early 4th century AD. At Locking several stone buildings were constructed around at least two sides of a central courtyard and accompanied by the small bathhouse mentioned above. The villa building in Chew Park was of corridor type with projecting wings, orientated to face south-east, and had a rear service corridor. Only two rooms on the north-eastern side of the building produced evidence of wall plaster and these were interpreted as the principal living quarters, although there was no evidence for underfloor heating. The remains of three ovens were revealed within the larger central area but the excavators were unclear whether this zone was originally roofed or formed an open courtyard. A quantity of roof tile was recovered from the site, which suggests that at least the principal rooms were covered in tile, with the walls constructed from mortared limestone blocks. A limekiln dated to the late 3rd century AD was identified east of the villa building and may have been used to supply lime during construction. The upstanding remains of the building evidently survived into the

12th century, when it was comprehensively robbed, and the stone burnt on site in a series of medieval limekilns (Rahtz and Greenfield 1977).

In contrast to Chew Park and Locking, the earliest Romano-British building phase at Star (dated to the late 1st or early 2nd century AD) was of stone construction – which possibly suggests it formed part of a higher-status complex. The site's proximity to one of the mineral-rich areas of the region may again suggest that the villa formed the centre of a more diverse estate economy. The building complex at Star was located north of Pyle Well, the source of the Towerhead Brook, and was excavated in 1959, when several phases of villa structure were revealed. The 1st-century building was not fully excavated but evidently comprised a large southern room (around 9m²) with a slightly later cobbled courtyard to the north enclosed by corridors. To the west a further room revealed evidence of a mosaic floor of grey limestone tesserae. The structure comprised limestone columns and had glazed windows, and the building was roofed with tile; it was abandoned in the 3rd century AD, sometime prior to its demolition.

The second phase of villa construction began shortly after AD 321 and was followed by a series of closely spaced alterations and enlargements. The initial structure formed at least three rooms with an external corridor to the west, and was probably single storey with a stone tile roof. Two of the rooms had decorated wall plaster, one comprising a broad red dado above which a border of interlocking black, yellow and red rings had been painted on a white ground. Towards the end of the building's life two of its rooms were destroyed by fire, possibly as a result of using one of the internal ovens as a corn-dryer. The third room continued to be occupied until the building finally went out of use sometime after AD 353, at which time the roof was systematically stripped of its tiles and timber (Barton 1964, 45–93).

Recent earthwork and geophysical survey at Star has revealed the site to be more complex than previously thought. The new survey work has identified a second range of buildings, approximately 30m to the east of the excavated site, probably arranged along the opposing side of a central courtyard. This newly identified structure would appear to represent a corridor-type building, approximately 55m in length, comprising up to five rooms. The work has also demonstrated that both these buildings sat within a rectilinear enclosure, with a possible bathhouse located centrally along its southern side (SHER 17859, 18719). Which phase of construction this second range of buildings relates to is at present unclear, but the corridor arrangement suggests it is more likely to be associated with the rebuilding of the early 4th century AD.

Investment in villa buildings reached its zenith during the late 3rd and early 4th centuries AD. At Chew Park, Locking and Star this outlay represented the aggrandisement of existing farmsteads and could be interpreted as a sign of growing rural wealth. In many cases this increased prosperity was relatively short-lived, however, with most villa complexes apparently abandoned by their owners during the second half of the 4th century AD. Where villa buildings continued to be occupied, there is some evidence to suggest that their use or status may have changed. At Chew Park the coin evidence indicates that the villa building was abandoned sometime after AD 361, possibly following a period of decline (Rahtz and Greenfield 1977, 64). At Star the final phase of activity within the villa buildings was interpreted as 'squatter-type' occupation, suggested by the temporary nature of the settlement evidence (Barton 1964, 66). The handmade pottery associated with this phase of habitation indicates fine imported wares were no longer accessible, which possibly indicates a later occupation date than the coin evidence suggests. This pattern of villa decline is repeated throughout Somerset, and can be viewed as symptomatic of the changing fortunes of these rural estates in a period of growing instability and shifting market conditions (Leach 2001b, 117).

The decline of the vibrant market economy which sustained the region during the first centuries of Roman rule would have affected all members of society. The wealth and security of many landowners would have come under threat with growing social and political instability. The large number of 4th-century AD coin hoards recorded from Somerset has been attributed to this changing economic climate, as precious metal ceased to be imported and the value of coinage soared (Costen 1992, 52). Over half of the Romano-British coin hoards recorded from across Mendip can be dated to the latter years of the 4th century AD. At Chelm's Combe a gold coin of Valentinanus II (dated to AD 375–92) was placed in the ground along with a hoard of 1,000 bronze coins – their date of deposition is comparable to that of the East Harptree silver hoard (see below). A hoard of 860 bronze coins was uncovered in the village of Star during modern construction work; the assemblage was minted between AD 248 and 355 (SHER 15266). The date of the coins would suggest they were deposited in the ground around the same time the nearby Star villa site was being abandoned by its wealthy owner.

Romano-British mining

The mineral resources of Mendip were undoubtedly the focus of Roman imperial interest and a key priority for the invading army. The rapid appropriation of the lead mines at Charterhouse-on-Mendip suggests prior knowledge of the area's mineral wealth and hints at earlier mining in the region. The construction of the small Roman fort demonstrates the importance of control over mineral production, with the investment required to link it to the main road network reflecting the region's economic significance to the wider Roman Empire. Other areas of Somerset were also targeted for their natural resources in the post-conquest period, with iron extracted from the Blackdown Hills and Exmoor by the 1st and 2nd centuries AD (Julleff 2000, 3–4). The small deposits of iron ore on Mendip may also have been exploited during this period, with evidence for iron smelting uncovered at Green Ore (adjacent to lead-processing debris) and dated to the 1st and 2nd centuries AD. This processing site was located on a ridge overlooking the Tor Hole Valley, and comprised a series of rough working-floors associated with Roman pottery, pieces of lead and iron, and a large amount of iron slag and clinker (Ashworth 1970, 6–7). Iron-smelting furnaces, workshops and quantities of iron slag have also been uncovered from Roman contexts at other sites, such as Chew Park and Cheddar (Rahtz and Greenfield 1977, 44; Hirst and Rahtz 1973, 77).

Evidence for Roman lead mining on Mendip has been found at Charterhouse-on-Mendip, Green Ore and St Cuthbert's lead-works near Priddy. Roman settlement remains found close to the former lead workings on Old Down, near Star, could suggest this site was also worked in the Romano-British period (Knight

1915, 102). At Green Ore four lead ingots dating from Vespasian's reign (AD 69–79) were discovered in a pit in 1956 (Palmer and Ashworth 1958, 52–88), with a fifth lead ingot uncovered close by in 1992 and dated to the same period (SHER 23209). These ingots were stamped 'BRIT EX ARG VEB', meaning 'British [lead] from the Veb… lead-silver works' (Fig 5.6). It has been suggested that 'Veb' may be an abbreviation of Vebriacum, possibly the Roman name for Charterhouse-on-Mendip or perhaps for the whole imperial estate (Campbell *et al* 1970, 29; Leach 2001b, 72). The name 'Ischalis' (noted by Ptolemy) has also been associated with the settlement at Charterhouse-on-Mendip (Millet 1990, 155), although others see it as derived from a river name and more convincingly linked to a port on the River Axe, possibly at Cheddar (Leach 2001b, 72).

Lead ingots from the mines of Mendip were exported around Britain and have been found in Bristol, Gloucestershire, Hampshire and London. Two ingots dating from the reign of Vespasian were discovered at Clausentum, a Roman port on the River Itchen, which may suggest that the metal was transported overland to the south-coast harbours before being exported to the continent (Todd 2007, 68). A lead ingot from the Mendip region, cast during the reign of the Emperor Nero (AD 54–68), was found at Saint-Valery-sur-Somme in France and bears the stamp of the Second Legion. Mendip lead therefore reached the continent relatively rapidly after the invasion, with the mark of II Augusta indicating the mines were run under military supervision. The mineral rights were subsequently leased to individuals and companies, and a lead ingot dated to AD 60 was stamped with the name Gaius Nipus Ascanius, a Mendip official who later appeared as the lessee of the Flintshire mines. The latest dateable Mendip lead ingot was previously thought to have been cast around AD 164–9, although an example found in Normandy and dated

to AD 197–211 may have come from Mendip (Campbell *et al* 1970, 28–9). However, a much smaller and cruder example has more recently been identified from Fosse Lane, inscribed 'MINNIVS' (possibly the name of the producer), which indicates that lead continued to be mined and exported well into the 4th century AD (Leach 2001a, 249).

Silver was also an important mineral to the Roman administration, as bullion was used to pay its soldiers and officials. Several of the Mendip ingots are stamped 'from the lead-silver works', which suggests that this precious metal was won from the area's argentiferous lead deposits. Quantities of litharge – waste material from silver extraction by cupellation – identified at Green Ore and North Hill (near St Cuthbert's lead-works) indicate that the lead was separated from the molten metal before it was reheated on a flat cupel or hearth to release the silver (Ashworth 1970, 15). The concentration of Roman silver coin hoards in the region has been cited by Todd as evidence for a locally available source for the metal, one which continued until the later years of Roman rule (2007, 72–4). One of the largest silver hoards from Mendip was discovered in East Harptree, where around 1,500 silver coins dating from the 4th century AD were found in a pewter jug, along with 3 silver medallions, 5 silver ingots and a silver ring.

Extraction remains

The early origin of many of the Mendip mines was first recognised largely through the reworking of the sites in the 19th century. The smelted ore left behind by the early miners was deemed to contain sufficient quantities of lead to make it profitable to smelt over again, the sifting process being cheaper than sinking new shafts. In 1820 the Revd John Skinner recorded meeting miners smelting ore near the Wells road, not far from Chewton Mendip, the metal being procured from heaps of rubbish left by

Fig 5.6
A lead ingot found at Green Ore and dating from the reign of Vespasian, now in Wells and Mendip Museum. (DP158766, reproduced by permission of Wells and Mendip Museum)

the 'old miners' (BL Add MS 33656, fol 25). The lead mines at Charterhouse-on-Mendip, Green Ore and St Cuthbert's all continued to be worked throughout the medieval and post-medieval periods, with extensive reworking during the 19th century. In the Blackmoor Valley, while digging through the refuse from earlier workings, the 19th-century miners uncovered a range of artefacts, including Romano-British brooches, metal ornaments, Samian and coarse-ware pottery, glass, coins and several ingots of lead (Waldron 1875, 2); pottery from the 'lead workings' collected by Mr A C Pass in 1867–76 has been attributed to the 1st and 2nd centuries AD (Todd 2003, 185–6). At Charterhouse-on-Mendip the area known as 'Town Field' was also stripped of surface peat and turf in search of profitable ore. Here the miners found quantities of slag and charcoal, as well as the foundations of stone buildings and smelting furnaces, including a small sandstone furnace with lead and charcoal still adhering to the inside (Waldron 1875, 3).

As well as revealing evidence for early mining activity on Mendip, the later reworking of these sites was also responsible for conceal-ing or destroying it. The field remains for mineral extraction on Mendip come in a variety of forms including pits or shafts, linear rakes and extensive open works. This range of extraction techniques represents separate periods of mining, with the same ore bodies often exploited over many centuries. That 'the ancient people usually dug trenches straight forwards' was pointed out to Skinner by miners reworking the waste deposits at Charterhouse-on-Mendip (BL Add MS 33653, fol 178). That some linear rakes do indeed represent Romano-British extraction remains has been demonstrated by Todd (2007), who examined a narrow mining cut or rake on the western slopes of the Blackmoor Valley (Fig 5.7). A series of trenches excavated along the line of the rake all produced evidence for early Roman activity in the form of South Gaulish Samian, flagons and fine-ware pottery, the material contemporary with the period of 1st-century AD military occupation at the fort (ibid, 15).

The work showed that in some sections the rake was no more than a narrow groove 0.3m wide, with the deposits excavated to a depth of up to 2m. No evidence for fire-setting was

Fig 5.7
Aerial photograph showing pits and rakes on the western side of the Blackmoor Valley, below the Roman fort.
(NMR 24331/8)

observed in the rake and no pick-marks were seen on the rock faces, which suggests that the ore (or galena) was easily extracted. This form of mining would appear to represent a relatively quick method for winning ore-bodies located close to the surface, making mineral extraction on Mendip cheaper and easier than at the imperial-controlled deep mines of north-western Spain. Lead ore was not the only mineral won from the Mendip mines, however; there is evidence to suggest haematite was also mined using the same extraction techniques (Todd 2007, 16).

Industrial settlement and processing sites

Industrial settlements and processing sites associated with the main ore-extraction areas on Mendip have previously been recognised, but their precise form and extent was less clear. Occupation and mineral processing have been recorded from Charterhouse-on-Mendip, Green Ore and North Hill, near St Cuthbert's lead-works (Fradley 2009; Ashworth 1970; Williams 1999). Quantities of ore were also transported further afield before being processed, with lead and furnace remains discovered at Shute Shelve and Herriott's Bridge, the evidence being indicative of small-scale industrial activity (Rahtz and Greenfield 1977, 78).

Undoubtedly the bulk of the material was processed at or near the point of extraction, with the known processing sites on the Mendip plateau all located on south- or south-east-facing slopes, possibly reoccupying areas of earlier settlement. They also lie on or adjoining areas of Old Red Sandstone out-cropping, where water for domestic use and washing ore was freely available. At Green Ore a series of rough floors and possible timber structures were revealed to the north of Vespasian Farm. Associated with these were quantities of lead- and iron-processing debris, ditches and postholes, Samian and coarse-ware pottery, lead weights and rivets, beads, rotary hand querns, bronze artefacts and a late 2nd-century AD coin. The evidence suggests the site was predominantly occupied during the 1st and 2nd centuries AD, but New Forest ware pottery recovered from the area during fieldwalking indicates the site experienced a second period of occupation, probably in the later 3rd or 4th century AD (Ashworth 1970).

On the sheltered slopes of North Hill, overlooking St Cuthbert's lead-works, a series of compounds, trackways and ditches are visible as cropmarks and slight earthworks on aerial photographs (Truscoe 2008, 25). This complex had previously been mapped by R G J Williamson (1999), and an excavation undertaken within one of the compounds revealed evidence for a small structure, mineral-processing waste and Romano-British coarse-ware pottery (Mason 1953, 1–4). Ploughing to the north and west of the excavated area revealed black circular patches (about 10m in diameter) which were found to contain Roman pottery, tile, lead and slag (Hawkes 1968, 20). More recently, geophysical survey in the area has revealed evidence for pits, hearths, trackways, compounds and industrial features – including possible furnace remains. Sherds of Samian and black-burnished ware pottery have been recovered from across the site, the former dating from the 1st to the 3rd centuries AD (Thompson 2010b) (Fig 5.8).

The settlement on North Hill covers an area of at least 12ha, but may originally have been more extensive, with aerial photographic evidence suggesting it possibly extended further eastwards. It comprises a number of compounds set along a network of trackways forming a relatively regular grid. These tracks fed outwards, giving access to the mining areas

Fig 5.8
North Hill: settlement and processing site recorded from aerial photographs and geophysical survey.

KEY
—— Cropmark ditch   —— Earthwork   ----- Geophysical anomaly

KEY

- - - Ridge and furrow ploughing

⌁⌁⌁ Features recorded from aerial photographs

100   0   100
                              metres

of Stockhill and possibly westwards to the villa site at Priddy. The regular layout of the compounds suggests the settlement may have taken its form from underlying fields. Coaxial fields were noted on the slopes of Stockhill to the east in 1946 prior to afforestation, and elements of the system were subsequently recorded from aerial photographs on the lower slopes of the hill (SHER 23249, 19129). That the field system clearly follows the same axial geometry as the North Hill compounds is a strong indication that the settlement has pre-Roman antecedents, a phenomenon recognised at many of the Romano-British villages on Salisbury Plain (McOmish *et al* 2002, 88–91).

Charterhouse-on-Mendip

By far the largest and best-preserved Romano-British industrial settlement on Mendip is at Charterhouse-on-Mendip. The main settlement remains cover an area of at least 27ha and are located on the sheltered south-east-facing slopes of Black Down, overlooking the small fort and mineral-rich valleys of Blackmoor and Velvet Bottom (Fig 5.9). The earthworks at Charterhouse-on-Mendip again represent a compact unenclosed settlement laid out along a network of trackways or 'streets', some of which were originally flanked by small drainage ditches (Boon 1950, 203). The settlement form appears to have been adapted to follow the natural topography, extending little above the 290m contour, and incorporated a number of water sources including wells and natural springs. The complex also comprised a small amphitheatre, located above the main area of settlement and possibly remodelled from an earlier prehistoric feature, and may be related to the period of military occupation at the fort (Fig 5.10).

The most clearly defined earthworks lie at the western side of the site where a series of embanked terraced compounds are located within a relatively regular grid of 'streets' (Fig 5.11). These compounds are accessed through a series of short trackways and may originally have been surrounded by a fence, wall or hedging. The units are subrectangular in form, up to 75m² in area, and contain a series of platforms and terraces, representing former buildings, gardens and enclosed yards. The majority of the compounds contain a number of building platforms, ranging in size from 5m to 20m in length. Some of these structures show evidence for internal subdivision and others are

clearly grouped together around a central yard (Fradley 2009, 56).

Over 65 probable building platforms were recorded across the site, although they may not all be contemporary. The settlement undoubtedly contained many more structures in the Romano-British period, their form and location now lost to later development and cultivation. Investigations undertaken in the area during the 19th century revealed stone building foundations along with roof tiles, window glass, flue tiles and mortared floors. Associated with these structures were roofing nails, iron hinges, glass vessels, brooches, lead weights, and large quantities of Samian and coarse-ware pottery (BL Add MS 33655, fol 292). Excavations undertaken towards the western end of the site in the 1960s indicated that the settlement was occupied throughout the 1st to the 4th centuries AD, with the pattern and form of buildings changing through time. This work identified a sequence of structures built from limestone, sandstone and timber, all of which were associated with large quantities of charcoal and metalworking debris (Budge *et al* 1974, 330–3).

The subtle variations in settlement form may reflect the different requirements of the specialist metallurgical processes undertaken at the site. The smelting of ore, the cupellation of silver from lead and the manufacture of metal artefacts could all have been carried

Fig 5.9 (opposite) Charterhouse-on-Mendip: earthwork plan of settlement, showing fort (bottom right) and amphitheatre (top left).

Fig 5.10 Charterhouse-on-Mendip: oblique aerial photograph of the amphitheatre. (NMR 24331/25)

and tracks that spread outwards from the settlement.

It is the scale of the settlement at Charterhouse-on-Mendip which sets it apart from Romano-British lead-mining areas elsewhere in Britain. In Shropshire, Flintshire, Derbyshire and the Yorkshire Dales there is little evidence for mining settlements connected to the known extraction areas. The true extent of the settlement at Charterhouse-on-Mendip is still unclear, but it may have covered as much as 36ha, making it comparable with the Fosse Lane roadside settlement and the largest villages on Salisbury Plain (Leach 2001a; McOmish *et al* 2002, 88–100). The contemporary population would have included slaves, miners and their families, artisans and skilled professionals – including soldiers, engineers and mining officials – representing a vibrant and diverse community. That some occupants possessed a degree of wealth is suggested by the hoard of 900 coins buried in the late 3rd century AD, as well as finds of gemstones, brooches, figurines and a bronze 'mask'. Inscribed stone fragments could represent the vestiges of tombstones connected to the military presence at the fort, and a number of cinerary urns and a cist grave containing an inhumation burial have also been recorded from the site (Scarth 1874, 190; Waldron 1875, 3; VCH 1906, 337; Gough 1967, 33). Cremation urns found to the north-east of the settlement may define the outer limit of occupation, with the burials possibly placed alongside one of the main approaches to the settlement (Stanton 1944, 148).

Religion and burial

In the Romano-British period natural features such as hilltops, rivers and springs were favoured as locations for shrines and temples, sometimes perpetuating earlier centres for religion and sacred ritual. At that time buildings, springs, caves, trees and specific places could all be venerated in divine form and regarded as the home of a spirit, a concept which would have been familiar to Britain's pre-conquest inhabitants. Spiritual beliefs would have played a significant role in the day-to-day lives of the agricultural and industrial communities scattered across Mendip. A small household shrine or *lararium* may have been placed in the corner of a room or in a dedicated space within a larger villa building; altars and

Fig 5.11
Charterhouse-on-Mendip. Clearly defined settlement earthworks are visible in the foreground, with the amphitheatre beyond. (NMR 24331/30)

out by skilled metalworkers and artisans in workshops within the settlement. Many of these processes required heat and therefore fuel, and the large quantities of charcoal recovered from across the area suggest managed woodland formed a significant part of the wider landscape. The area immediately surrounding the mining settlement may have comprised a combination of coppiced woodland and open grazing, with livestock possibly corralled close to the settlement in enclosed paddocks. The lack of evidence for cultivation would imply agricultural produce was imported from the more fertile regions surrounding the plateau, transported along the network of roads other votive goods could have been set up in the open air – on roadsides, next to streams or close to temple sites.

Romano-British temples are sometimes found in or near prehistoric monuments, such as the temple at Brean Down on the western tip of Mendip, which was positioned close to a Bronze Age barrow cemetery and small Iron Age hillfort. The Romano-Celtic temple was formed by a cella – a central tower-like structure – surrounded by a concentric ambulatory, attached to which were flanking chambers (ApSimon 1965). The building would have been considered as home to a deity, with a representation of the god or goddess stored within the cella. Another temple associated with a later prehistoric hillfort was discovered at Henley Wood, near Cadbury Congresbury, north of Mendip. Here a sequence of temple buildings culminated in a Romano-Celtic temple with a square central cella surround by an ambulatory (Leach and Watts 1996). The construction of this form of temple building reached its zenith in the early 4th century AD, possibly as a result of local patronage. At this time estate owners were also investing in ever-grander villa buildings, which suggests a period of general economic wealth and stability.

Other possible sites for hilltop temples in the Mendip region have been suggested at Worlebury and Brent Knoll (Leach 2001b). Roman coins, pottery and three bronzes of the 3rd and 4th centuries AD from the interior of Dolebury Hillfort also point towards Romano-British activity, perhaps associated with a temple or shrine. Knight recorded that Roman remains were also identified within Banwell Camp, but no further evidence has come to light (Knight 1902, 407). The association of prehistoric forts with hilltop temples may be an indication of the perceived former social, ritual or political importance of these enclosures in the pre-Roman period. The veneration of these sites could also demonstrate their significance to Roman society, with their reuse possibly creating a connection between the native Romano-British population and their ancestral past.

Somerset is relatively rich in rural hilltop temples – such as Pagans Hill and Lamyatt Beacon – but other natural features also formed the focus of ritual activity. Perhaps one of the best known of these is the temple of Sulis Minerva, constructed next to the sacred spring at Bath. On Mendip the springs at Wells and

Banwell may have been venerated in a similar way, although not necessarily furnished with a temple building. Shrines could have been set up close to the pools, with votive offerings deposited in the water. A Claudian coin and some Roman domestic objects were found in Banwell Pond when it was drained in 1923. Evidence for Romano-British activity has also been identified close to St Andrew's Well in Wells, including a possible late Roman mausoleum (Rodwell 2001). The source of the River Axe at Wookey Hole, and the head of the River Chew at Chewton Mendip, may also have attracted spiritual or ritual activity (as was the case during the prehistoric period). Deep within the cave system at Wookey Hole, where the river wells up out of the rock, a number of Romano-British burials were uncovered, accompanied by ornamental objects, pottery, latch-lifters and coins. Some of the bodies were placed in the cave fully clothed, wearing rings, bracelets and boots, and their deposition has been dated to around the late 3rd century AD (Hawkes et al 1978).

In the earlier centuries of the Romano-British period a large proportion of burials took the form of cremations. Evidence for this type of interment is relatively rare, however, and is often represented by chance finds such as the cremation urns from the 1st and 2nd century AD recovered from Charterhouse-on-Mendip (see above). Cremation burials could be placed in the ground singly or in cemeteries, often positioned on the outskirts of settlement or along roadside approaches; some were deposited in vessels or containers and others were simply placed in pits. The small cremation cemetery excavated at Ben Bridge comprised three subrectangular enclosures which surrounded four cremation burials, and the remains were deposited in pits roughly centrally within the enclosures. The enclosure ditches may have carried foundations for some form of timber structure or low wall, with the complex probably dating from the 2nd or 3rd century AD (Rahtz and Greenfield 1977, 85–8).

By the 3rd century AD inhumation burials had become the dominant form, although there is evidence that cremation continued to be practised into the 4th century AD (Leach 2001a, 286). Romano-British inhumation burials have been discovered at numerous sites across Mendip, including Wookey Hole, Herriot's Bridge, Chelm's Combe, Cheddar and Shute Shelve (Fig 5.12). Roman remains were

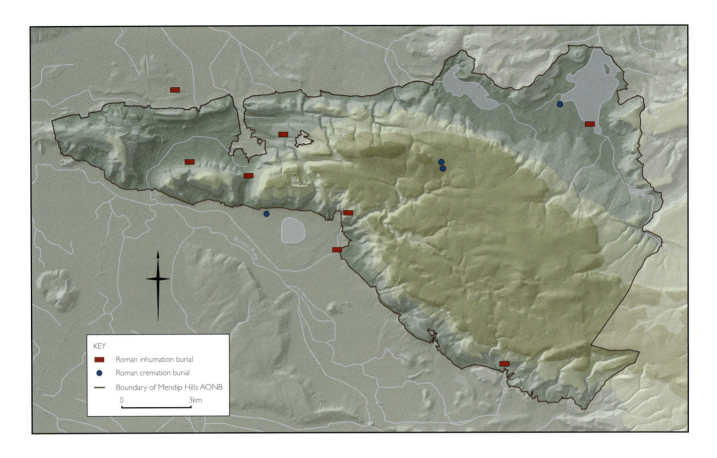

Fig 5.12
The distribution of Romano-British inhumation and cremation burials across the Mendip Hills AONB.

discovered in a wooden coffin in Barton in 1973 and parts of a possible 3rd-century AD stone sarcophagus were found on Old Down when the ground was prepared for a plantation. A group of inhumation burials orientated east–west (with their head to the west) were also uncovered at Stonebridge, near Banwell, and were associated with a number of 4th-century AD coins and an enamelled pelta brooch (Knight 1902, 458).

The early medieval period

The post-Roman landscape (AD 400–1086)

By the early 4th century AD Mendip and its hinterland comprised a diverse range of settlement forms – towns, villas, industrial settlements and farmsteads – the inhabitants of which utilised a wide selection of tools, pottery and ornamental objects. During the second half of the 4th century AD, however, the region began to witness a period of economic deterioration perhaps most clearly visible in the decline of its villa estates. The abandonment of

the villa complexes at Chew Park, Locking and Star brought to an end a period of almost continuous occupation at these sites from the later prehistoric onwards. The desertion of villa sites also removed a key visible element of aristocratic structure, making changes in social organisation more difficult to detect.

By no means all settlements were abandoned, however, and it may only be our lack of expertise in recognising evidence for later occupation which is hampering our understanding of Mendip's post-Roman landscape. Recent dating evidence from Cheddar, for example, suggests occupation may have carried on here into the 5th century AD or later (Webster 2000, 80). At Ilchester and Fosse Lane, excavation has shown that these towns also functioned beyond the supposed end of the Romano-British period. There was, however, a marked decline in urban life, with trade and industry drastically reduced and public services largely withdrawn (Leach 2001b). The intensity of occupation in the towns also waned as Roman military and imperial personnel pulled out. The decline of these market centres had a profound effect on the wider landscape, with the collapse of the market economy removing pressure from the countryside to produce and export surplus crops. It is also generally acknowledged that this period saw a drop in the rural population, which resulted in the abandonment of farmsteads and the removal of more marginal areas from agricultural use. This may have prompted a reversion to a more subsistence-led way of farming, which possibly created a localised pastoral-based economy and radically altered the way the landscape was worked and managed.

On Mendip, these agricultural and demographic changes may have led to a retreat from the higher escarpment slopes, as well as the abandonment of reclaimed areas on the surrounding Levels and Moors. Evidence from the North Somerset Levels has shown that this area was once again claimed by the sea in the later years of the 4th century AD (Rippon 2006). Although a number of factors may have contributed to this, including changes in the natural environment, a failure to maintain the flood defences must have played a significant role and may be interpreted as another sign of the changing socio-economic climate of the region. At the same time as reclaimed areas such as Banwell Moor were being abandoned,

environmental data also indicates a decline in the intensity with which the dry-land areas were being exploited, visible in the archaeological record as an increase in tree pollen (Rippon 2006, 81).

How extensive or long-lived this period of woodland regeneration was is unclear. There are, however, relatively few 'leah' place names on Mendip (Fig 5.13) – denoting a place located close to woodland, in a glade or clearing – which suggests that the incoming Anglo-Saxons did not encounter a landscape dominated by wildwood. The names Ubley and Coley indicate pockets of ancient woodland along the north-eastern escarpment, but groupings of 'tun' place names (particularly evident towards the western end of the region) are indicative of areas cleared long before the Old English speakers arrived (Gelling and Cole 2000, 237). Saxon charter evidence also points towards a relatively open, agricultural landscape, suggesting the incomers largely utilised and developed a long-established pattern of settlements and landholdings (Neal 1976, 77).

The withdrawal of Roman imperial control in the 5th century AD resulted in a sharp decline in the production of manufactured goods,

Fig 5.13
The distribution of 'tun' and 'leah' place names across the Mendip Hills AONB.

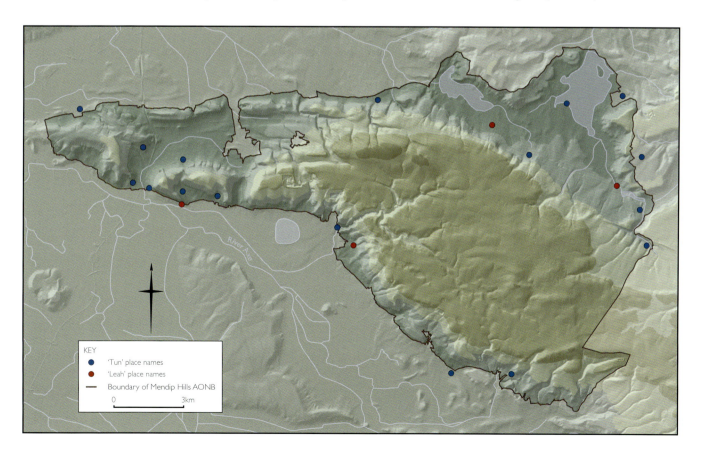

KEY
- 'Tun' place names
- 'Leah' place names
- Boundary of Mendip Hills AONB

0   3km

perhaps most clearly visible in the collapse of the pottery industry. The production of metal artefacts was similarly affected, with the extraction industries of Mendip impacted. The evidence from the industrial settlements of the high plateau suggests these areas were also abandoned by the later years of the 4th century AD, although a lack of modern excavation has restricted our understanding of exactly when and how this process took place. There is some evidence to suggest that Mendip lead continued to be used into the 5th and 6th centuries AD – primarily from burials in lead coffins such as those from Fosse Lane (Leach 2001a, 255). The malleability of lead makes it one of the easiest metals to recycle, however, and in a period of economic decline it seems likely that existing supplies were reused (as was the case with architectural fragments) rather than new sources exploited. This is not to say that extraction and production by individuals and groups did not continue on Mendip, but this would almost certainly have been small-scale compared to the efforts of the Roman administration.

Hillforts, burials and religion

The reuse of some prehistoric hillforts in the post-Roman period highlights the continuing draw of long-standing cultural and ritual centres to the native population. At present there is no excavated material to indicate that any of the Mendip hillforts were reoccupied during the 5th or 6th centuries AD. The evidence for later Roman activity at Dolebury Hillfort, and the (unsubstantiated) reference to finds of Saxon coins (Collinson 1791, 579), raises the possibility that the hillfort continued to form a focus for activity into the post-Roman period and beyond. The reoccupation of hilltop defences suggests they once again became an important nucleus for the surrounding community, possibly forming ritual and administrative centres for the emergent ruling elite. Burrow (1981), for example, has attempted to define a 'territory' around Cadbury Congresbury, and Cadbury Castle has been put forward as a regional centre for commerce and politics. The enigmatic linear earthwork of West Wansdyke, located above the River Avon, incorporates the hillforts of Maes Knoll and Stantonbury, and originally comprised a timber or rubble-faced bank with a sharp-cut ditch along its northern side. The earthwork is thought to be post-Roman in date, possibly having originated as a British defensive work of the 5th or 6th century AD, with its alignment probably defining the course of a tribal boundary (Erskine 2007).

It is perhaps through their burial remains – bones, coffins and occasional grave goods – that the post-Roman population of the region is most clearly visible. The large number of burials recorded by the Revd John Skinner at West Harptree may represent a late and post-Roman cemetery, similar to those found in Henley Wood, near Cadbury Congresbury, and Cannington (Leach and Watts 1996, 75; Rahtz *et al* 2000, 420). At West Harptree the remains of over 100 bodies were discovered in the early 19th century by quarrymen excavating for building stone in a field south of Gournay Court (Fig 5.14). The burials were uncovered within a bank or lynchet and were predominantly aligned east–west (the head to the west), with the bodies 'interred side by side'. A small number of finds were allegedly found associated with some of the burials, including weapons and a 'brass fibula'. All sectors of society were represented in the cemetery, including children and infants, indicating a 4th-century AD or later date for at least some of the burials (BL Add MS 33717, fol 153). The site's close relationship to the former Roman road and to the village of West Harptree could suggest the existence of a settlement at or near this location from the Romano-British period onwards. Indeed, the prehistoric settlement of Pitcher's Enclosure and the medieval stronghold of Richmont Castle are also located close by, which highlights the strategic importance of this area over many millennia.

A second possible late and post-Roman cemetery has been discovered at Winthill, near Banwell, where some of the remains were recorded cutting Roman occupation layers (Hunt 1961b, 26–7). Here a series of inhumation burials was uncovered, including a stone coffin found at the end of the 19th century. The true extent and date of this cemetery is uncertain, but it would appear to have stretched over an area of at least 40m^2, with the number of burials possibly equalling those at West Harptree. The location of the Winthill cemetery may have been influenced by the earlier settlement, or an associated ritual centre possibly focused around a natural spring or nearby hill.

The east–west orientation and row layout of the Winthill cemetery may be considered

Fig 5.14
West Harptree. The remains of over 100 bodies were uncovered in a field above Gournay Court in the 19th century.
(NMR 24818/18)

suggestive of Christian ritual, although caution must be exercised before attributing these burials to Mendip's earliest Christian farmers. Rahtz has pointed out that an east–west orientation can be viewed as a more general trend at this time, one which can also be associated with non-Christian examples, and is not necessarily indicative of specific religious beliefs (Rahtz *et al* 2000, 416). Evidence for early Christianity in the South-West is relatively sparse and largely based on early church dedications and inscribed stones, such as the Culbone stone on Exmoor, which is decorated with a wheel cross (Riley and Wilson-North 2001, 89). The recent examination of a silver amulet from Fosse Lane bearing a chi-rho punched monogram (thought to be an early Christian symbol) has exposed it as a hoax (Minnitt 2008).

The continuing use of pagan ritual sites as cult centres into the post-Roman period is a relatively common phenomenon in Somerset. At Brean Down a small cemetery of east–west aligned burials was discovered to the west of a former Romano-Celtic temple. These burials produced radiocarbon dates ranging from the

5th to the 7th centuries AD, indicating the cemetery was in use long after the temple buildings were abandoned (Bell 1990, 80). It has been suggested that a small east–west aligned building constructed south of the main temple complex in the late 4th or early 5th century AD could represent the Christian use of this former pagan site and may have formed the focus for the later cemetery (Aston and Burrow 1982, 75). A similar east–west aligned structure was identified at Lamyatt Beacon and was again interpreted as a possible early Christian oratory, perhaps associated with a 6th-century AD eremitic monastery (Leech 1986, 274). Excavations at Cadbury Congresbury revealed a series of 5th- and 6th-century AD post-built structures within the hillfort, one of which was interpreted as a timber shrine or temple (Rahtz *et al* 1992). This has led to the suggestion that Cadbury Congresbury was an early monastic site associated with a British bishop, St Congar, with the burials at nearby Henley Wood related to the monastic community.

Aston has suggested that the hillfort at Banwell may have been the location for a post-Roman British monastery, following a similar

THE HISTORIC LANDSCAPE OF THE MENDIP HILLS

model to Cadbury Congresbury (2003, 45). The minsters of Banwell and Congresbury are mentioned in Asser's *Life of King Alfred* in AD 893, and although there is no evidence that Banwell hillfort was occupied in the post-Roman period, the possible early Christian cemetery at Winthill lies close by. British monastic sites in the South-West were put in the hands of the Saxon bishopric by the end of the 7th century AD, and subsequently underwent a period of reformation, which brought them in line with the orthodox Church of Rome (Hall 2003, 53–4). This could have involved their removal from hilltop locations to nearby lower-lying and more accessible sites, a process which may have resulted in the adoption of the fen-edge position at Banwell. Cheddar has also been put forward as a possible Celtic or British monastic centre, primarily on the basis of early church dedications – to St Columbanus, St Nectan and St Petroc (Aston 2003, 46).

The Anglo-Saxon landscape

The Anglo-Saxon Chronicle first records the West Saxons entering Somerset in AD 658, when they defeated the indigenous British population at the battle of Peonnan (usually taken to be Penselwood, near Wincanton) and pushed them back to the River Parrett. The validity of written sources from Anglo-Saxon England has been much debated, with the Chronicle interpreted by some as a retrospective piece of propaganda shaped to fit the political needs of the time (Ecclestone *et al* 2003). With this in mind, many documents do, however, seemingly contain enough genuine information to give us an insight into the changing social and political organisation of the period. Charters granting land to Glastonbury Abbey in the 7th century AD indicate that West Somerset was in the hands of the West Saxon kings by *c* AD 680 (Costen 1992, 82). The archaeological evidence largely supports this, as very few Saxon objects dating to before the 7th century AD have been recovered from the region (the late 5th- or early 6th-century AD spearhead from Worle, at Weston-super-Mare, is a notable exception). The advance of Anglo-Saxon culture across the region is perhaps most clearly visible in the abundance of Old English place names. The distribution of these names over Mendip shows that the majority of Anglo-Saxon settlements were located along the spring line at the foot of the escarpment slope,

although there is also evidence for occasional incursions into the upland areas. Some of the Old English place names are compound personal names and may indicate a desire by the new ruling elite to define authority through the renaming of existing British settlements. In many cases the transition to the new language would have been gradual, however, with some settlements possibly known by both old and new names until the old language passed out of memory (Hooke 2003, 70). Some existing names from the British language were adopted into Old English (mainly those connected to natural features such as rivers and hills), including the name Mendip itself, which probably derives from the Celtic 'mynydd', meaning mountain or hill (Neal 1976, 75).

That some of the prehistoric hillforts and enclosures of Mendip were still prominent features in the landscape when the Old English speakers arrived is demonstrated by names such as Dolebury and Burrington (Neal 1976, 75). Stratford Lane and Stratford Mill get their name from a river crossing on the old Roman road, which suggests that the ancient road remained a main route of communication into the Saxon period. Another possible reference to the Roman road is the name Harptree, a compound of the Old English words 'herepaeth' and 'trew', meaning 'tree by a highway or main road' (Mills 1991, 228). That a network of roads and tracks criss-crossed the region is clear from Saxon charters, which refer to a number of routes or 'ways', including the *Wael Waeg* or 'slaughter-way', the *Smalan Weg* or 'narrow-way' and the *Wryth Wey* or 'twisting-way' (Grundy 1935, 155, 161 and 172).

Place-name evidence can also reflect the ancient topography of the region, such as the presence of heaths, moors or woodland. The significance of 'leah' place names has been touched on before: their distribution indicates the existence of woodland along the north-eastern escarpment of Mendip, on the southern slopes above Cheddar and at the western end of the region (through names such as Ubley, Bradley Cross and Buckley Wood, for example). Areas of ancient woodland also appear as boundary markers in Saxon charters, with 'Loxan Wuda wyrtruman' probably referring to a woodland bank surrounding a once larger extent of the modern Loxton Wood (Grundy 1935, 159; Rackham 1988, 19); *see* Figure 5.15. Some enclosed islands of trees also punctuated the more open landscape of the river valleys,

Fig 5.15
Loxton Wood: aerial photograph showing the remnants of the ancient woodland.
(NMR 24669/04)

which is reflected in minor names such as Woodwick Farm, in Compton Martin.

The woodland of Mendip comprised a range of both dense and more open woodland, suitable for both coppicing and for grazing livestock. Coley may be interpreted as 'charcoal wood or clearing' and is indicative of a settlement on the edge of managed and productive coppiced woodland. These areas of woodland and wood pasture comprised oak, lime, hazel, ash and elm, with the dominance of specific tree species in certain areas evident in names such as Lynhold, above Cheddar Wood, derived from the Old English 'linde' or lime tree (Rackham 1988, 30). The name Hazel Wood, near Compton Martin, is a remnant of the ancient hazel and ash woods that once covered the steeper slopes of the northern escarpment. Hazel Wood was a detached parcel of land belonging to Chew manor, possibly created following the break-up of a much larger multiple estate. The annexing of this area demonstrates the value placed on woodland resources, and highlights their importance within the wider regional economy.

During the early Anglo-Saxon period the agricultural areas of the lower slopes may have comprised an arrangement of regular enclosed fields, probably little changed from the earlier Romano-British field pattern. This system was utilised for both pasture and arable production and was worked and managed from a network of scattered farmsteads and small hamlets. By the beginning of the 10th century a system of common arable fields had developed, drawing people into villages along the foot of the escarpment, and leading to the abandonment of some of the smaller outlying farmsteads. That open arable fields existed around Mendip by the 10th century is clear from the charter evidence, where 'hline' (meaning balk) and 'acre' names appear as boundary markers (Grundy 1935). Habitative-type field names, such as Little Huish, in East Harptree, and Westhewish, in Walcombe, may indicate the location of early settlements abandoned as the common fields were laid out.

Other areas of the lowland landscape continued to be utilised as pasture, meadowland and wetland. The ditched drainage systems of the Romano-British period had long been abandoned and the marshland landscape along the main river valleys would have been exploited for its abundant supply of fish and fowl, as well as being used for seasonal pasture. As the name suggests, Moreton was located within an area of marshy ground in the Chew Valley. Although now lying within the parish of Compton Martin, it formed a separate entry in the Domesday Book, where it was recorded as having a total of 11 villagers and 14 small-holders (Thorn and Thorn 1980, 37, 11). Extensive excavations around this small settlement failed to reveal any evidence for Anglo-Saxon occupation, however (or indeed any occupation earlier than the 12th century), which possibly suggests continuity in land-holding but not necessarily in settlement location (Rahtz and Greenfield 1977, 18).

The higher slopes and upland plateau comprised wood pasture, underwood and open heath, and were utilised as summer grazing for livestock. There is evidence to suggest that specialist stock farms existed on the higher ground in the Saxon period, with Ellick or Ellwick (meaning 'hill farm') an early holding located above Burrington Combe. The significance of field and place names with the element 'wic' – derived from Latin *vicus* – has long been debated, with Costen arguing in Somerset for a correlation between 'wic' settlements and Romano-British occupation (1992, 66). Ellick is located within 1km of the Roman industrial settlement at Charterhouse-on-Mendip, the tumbled remains of which must have been clearly visible in the Anglo-Saxon period. Sutton Wick, in the Chew Valley, is located close to the Roman road and less than 1km from the Roman villa at Chew Park (the upstanding remains of which survived into the 12th century, as noted above); Woodwick Farm is again positioned within ½km of Stratford Lane, with the known Romano-British site at Herriott's Bridge close by.

Two early 'wyrth' names recorded at Ebbor and Green Ore (Ebba's-worth and Green-worth) would again indicate the possible location of early upland farmsteads. Lower Farm (the earlier Cheddarford) was also recorded as a 'separate worth' within a wood in the mid-11th century (Aston 1994, 228). Both Lower Farm and Green Ore had their antecedents in the Romano-British period, and by the early 14th century Green Ore was recorded as an isolated sheep farm held by Hinton Charterhouse. A reference to Aebbewyrth appears as early as 1065 (Neal 1976, 97), and the name has been linked to a deserted settlement identified above Wookey Hole (SHER 25393). These farmsteads form part of a series of deserted medieval settlements

located along Mendip's southern escarpment (Aston 1994; G Brown 2008). One such site was identified close to Carscliffe Farm, Cheddar, where a small quantity of residual Saxon pottery was recovered from the surrounding fields and is suggestive of early land improvement and settlement (SHER 11243, 35963).

The village of Priddy, the only major settlement on the high plateau, is first documented in a lost charter of the late 7th or early 8th century AD (Finberg 1964, 113), and again lies close to an area of Romano-British occupation. The settlement does not appear in the Domesday Book of the 11th century but was mentioned in grants of land dating to the later 12th century (Thompson 2011, 207). The origins of the settlement at Priddy are intriguing, with the name possibly deriving from the British 'pridd' meaning 'earth', perhaps suggesting a pre-Saxon foundation (Neal 1976, 75). The existence of the settlement may be linked to the natural resources of the area – water, minerals and open pasture – and must be viewed within a broader estate economy. The village may have functioned as a specialist workplace, possibly having developed from an area of seasonal shielings (temporary shelters) connected to a system of transhumance and only later becoming an area of permanent settlement. The importance of the region within the surrounding estate structure is reflected in the configuration of land divisions, with the upland boundaries of six medieval parishes converging at Priddy.

Royal, ecclesiastical and secular estates

Immediately following the Saxon conquest Mendip functioned as a royal territory, in a period before the concept of private land ownership. In the following centuries, blocks of land were granted by the king to various ecclesiastical and secular landholders, creating a new aristocratic structure of landholding lords. This process had the dual benefit of cementing allegiances and loyalty to the king, while enabling the emerging ruling elite to sustain a lifestyle suited to their position (Bailey 2002, 11). As an agency of royal policy, ecclesiastical establishments were a particular beneficiary of land endowments and by the end of the Anglo-Saxon period landholding on Mendip was dominated by the king and the Church. Substantial grants of land were made to the bishopric of Wells, the Benedictine house of Glastonbury Abbey and the cathedral priory of St Swithun's at Winchester. Not all endowments were to religious houses, however, with 15 hides at Winscombe and half a hide at Nyland granted by King Edgar to a woman named Aelfswith in the 10th century; the holdings later passed into the ownership of Glastonbury Abbey (Sawyer 1968, 468; Aston and Costen 2008, 139).

In order to retain control over his lords the king retained some important rights over the alienated land, including the right to demand certain military and public services. If these public obligations were not met the land was forfeited to the king. The requirement to provide for the military services demanded was in part responsible for major changes to estate organisation in the late Saxon period, when large estates began to be subdivided to form smaller landholding units. Domesday Book entries for Glastonbury estates record numerous 'thanes' who were supported by small subtenancies, and represent the men retained by the abbey to meet its military obligations to the king (Yorke 1995, 246). Hutton, Winterhead and Elborough were three such estates, and were recorded as 'thaneland before 1066'; a thane is also recorded as holding 1½ hides at Wrington (which included Burrington) from the Abbot. At the time of the Conquest the 30-hide estate of Banwell was regained by the Bishop of Wells. In the late 11th century the estate contained a series of subtenancies – two 5½-hide and three single-hide units – again, possibly representing the holdings of men retained by the cathedral to meet its commitments to the king (Thorn and Thorn 1980, 6, 9).

Other influences in the 10th and 11th centuries further accelerated the break-up of large estates, including a more general growth in population numbers and the ability to sell, purchase and transfer land. Litton, for example, was purchased by Bishop Giso from a thane called Alfred in the reign of King Edward and was held by the canons of St Andrew's as part of their chapter revenues (Kelly 2007, 233–5). The forces of inheritance also played their part, and were connected to a clearer notion of land ownership. Landholdings could be subdivided between family groups, possibly one of the reasons we have estates with 'east' and 'west' prefixes – such as Harptree and Horrington. These estates could in turn be split further, forming a patchwork of smaller land-blocks which came to be known as manors.

The complexity of the seigneurial landholding structure is illustrated by East and West Harptree, which were each recorded at Domesday as being held by two separate landowners. The estate of East Harptree had evidently been even more fragmented in the pre-Conquest period, when the five hides later belonging to the Bishop of Countances were held by Alric and Wulfwy as two separate manors (Thorn and Thorn 1980, 5, 9). This move to a more locally based system of lordship in the 9th and 10th centuries is associated with the creation of manorial centres, parish churches, nucleated villages and common arable fields.

As private land ownership became more clearly defined, estate boundaries were also delineated with increasing precision, as is probably most evident in the carefully recorded bounds of 10th- and 11th-century charters. These boundaries could be defined by topographic features such as rivers, hills and woods or by pre-existing monuments such as barrows, roads and enclosures (the boundary of North Widcombe follows the northern rampart of Burledge Hillfort, for example). Many of the smaller estates created in the late Saxon period and recorded in the Domesday Book are still largely visible in the landscape today through the medieval parish system. The pattern of landholdings on Mendip which developed in the Saxon period allowed each estate access to the range of resources the region had to offer – meadowland, arable, pasture, woodland and open heath. Towards the eastern end of the AONB this has resulted in the formation of a series of long linear estates, which stretched from the valley floor up onto the open expanse of the limestone plateau. This pattern of smaller estates is only broken up by the larger ecclesiastical and royal holdings of Wells, Chewton Mendip and Cheddar (Fig 5.16). To the west the influence of monastic and ecclesiastical landowners was greater, resulting in less fragmentation and the dominance of larger landholding units, such as the estates of Banwell, Winscombe and Bleadon.

The royal estate and palace at Cheddar

The great royal estates of the West Saxon kings provided a base from which royal influence could be promoted and exercised. In Somerset there were important royal centres at Bath, Somerton, Frome, Glastonbury and Cheddar (Fig 5.17), where the royal court could meet

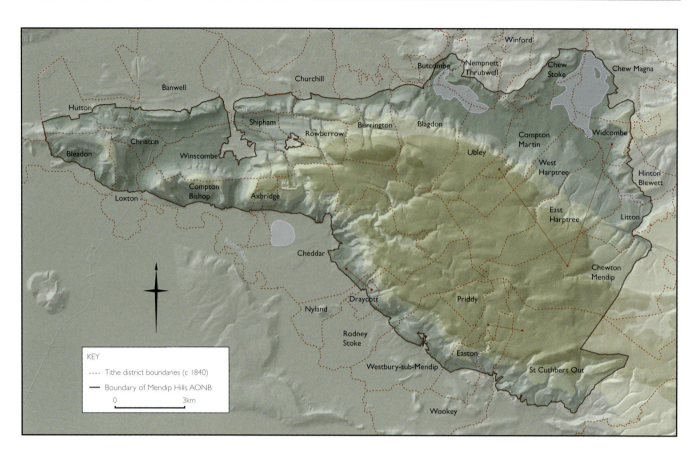

Fig 5.16

Map showing the tithe district boundaries and indicating the general pattern of landholding established by the later medieval period. The solid red lines link detached tithing areas.

and the processes of estate administration could be undertaken. The royal estate at Cheddar had developed into an important centre for the West Saxon kings by the late 9th century AD; its popularity was almost certainly influenced by the extensive upland hunting grounds on Mendip and the richness of the surrounding marshland for hawking. The royal palace is first documented in Alfred's will (probably written between AD 880 and 888) and is mentioned in a number of 10th-century charters. A royal hunting forest at Cheddar is also recorded from the 10th century onwards, perhaps most notably in the *Life of St Dunstan*, written around 1000, which famously describes King Edmund's miraculous escape while riding out from Cheddar Palace on a hunting expedition.

Axbridge formed an important component of the Cheddar estate and was one of the five *burhs* or fortified places set up in Somerset by King Alfred towards the end of the 9th century AD. These were designed to protect the region from attack by the Danes and were located at Bath, Langport, Lyng, Watchet and Axbridge. Some *burhs* were small forts intended as refuges, while others were defended towns

with permanent populations. Axbridge fell into the second category, not only providing a refuge for the occupants of Cheddar in times of unrest, but also creating the potential for urban development and trade. No earthwork defences have been identified at Axbridge, but Batt has suggested that the *burh* was positioned to the south of the market square, covering a low spur of flat land projecting out onto the Levels and Moors (1975, 22–5). Why Axbridge was located 3km from the palace site at Cheddar is unclear, but it could reflect a desire to distance commercial activities from the site of the royal residence. Alternatively, the *burh*'s position – towards the western boundary of the estate – may have been intended to defend the seaward approaches to Cheddar and guard a crossing on the River Axe (Costen 1992, 138). It has been suggested by Blair that the catalyst for the foundation of the *burh* at Axbridge was the restructuring of royal assets at the beginning of the 10th century, involving a shift in focus of the royal residence from Wedmore to Cheddar (1996, 120).

Great royal centres such as Cheddar functioned through a system of dependent landholding units – farmsteads and small

hamlets – which were economically and socially subservient to the central authority. This network of holdings formed an integral part of the estate economy, with each unit possibly performing a specialist function based on the production of grain, cattle, sheep, pigs, dairy products and wood. The farmsteads and hamlets would have been called upon to provide goods and services for the king, including victuals for the royal table when he and the court were in residence. Axbridge played a key role in this system, with the commercial origins of the *burh* defined in the Axbridge Chronicle, which states that if the king did not reside on the estate 'all the supplies gathered were to be sold in the borough market and the money carried to the king's treasury' (Rahtz 1979, 10–11). The *burh's* status as a major trading centre is also illustrated by the establishment of a mint in the town (Fig 5.18), which is known to have operated during the late 10th and early 11th centuries (Bromwich 1971).

The royal palace at Cheddar occupied a fen-edge location, north-west of the parish

church of St Andrew, and was separated from the wider settlement of Cheddar by a curving boundary to the north (now Station Road) and the Cheddar Yeo to the east. There has been much debate about the origins of the palace site, with Blair quite convincingly arguing for

Fig 5.17
Cheddar: aerial photograph showing the town, gorge and former royal palace site (bottom right).
(NMR 24323/27)

Fig 5.18
Anglo-Saxon coins minted at Axbridge.
(01257098001, 01257099001, 01257103001, 01257106001 © The Trustees of the British Museum)

its development from a monastic foundation focused on the existing church (1996). When the West Saxon kings entered Somerset they had already converted to Christianity and were responsible for building minster churches at early royal centres. The existence of a minster at Cheddar in the late 9th and early 10th centuries is largely based upon its topographic position and early documentary references to 'the families (or community) at Cheddar' – possibly alluding to a double minster of men and women (Rahtz 1979, 13). The positioning of the royal palace may therefore have been influenced by the pre-existing minster complex, which could itself have been established on the site of a Roman villa and early British Christian foundation. The subsequent decline of the monastic house at Cheddar may have been inextricably linked to the rise of the adjoining royal centre (Blair 1996, 118–20).

The site of the royal palace was excavated in 1960–2 by Philip Rahtz, who uncovered a sequence of timber halls, stone chapels, ancillary buildings and ditched enclosures dating from the 9th to the 14th centuries (Rahtz 1979). The earliest construction phase included a timber Long Hall, potentially two storeys in height, which was bow-sided and around 24m in length. The building was located within a fenced enclosure and was orientated north–south, with one entrance along its western side and two on the east. Associated with the hall was at least one domestic building – probably of wattle and daub construction – and an 'entrance flagstaff'. No chapel building was found associated with this phase of hall, suggesting that the celebration of religious feasts took place elsewhere, possibly at the minster complex mentioned above. The dating of these structures is largely based on their association with a storm-water ditch located along the northern side of the complex, within which a sequence of coins dating from c AD 845–930 was recovered. The ditch also contained a mass of occupation material, including food bones, stone querns, iron nails, tweezers, knives, a horseshoe and strap ends. Evidence for iron smelting and smithing, and non-ferrous casting and forging (including possibly enamelling), was also found within the ditch fill. All this evidence indicates the existence of a high-status community at Cheddar by the end of the 9th century AD, with its occupants engaged in both domestic and industrial activities.

The timber Long Hall was replaced in the 10th century by a second hall on a different alignment, possibly reflecting renewed royal interest in the site and the development of royal policy. The West Hall was a rectangular building, 17m long and 9.1m wide, with main posts composed of squared timbers set roughly 2.3m apart. Associated with this phase of hall was a small chapel (built over the site of the earlier Long Hall), the building constructed of limestone rubble with ashlar detailing and heavy plaster decoration. The complex also consisted of a number of ancillary buildings, including a fowl house of tripartite arrangement – comprising a store building and dwelling house separated by a circular fenced or walled 'fowl run'. Documentary sources indicate that the king's witan met at Cheddar on at least three occasions between AD 941 and 968, with charter witness-lists suggesting these gatherings involved several hundred people. The royal party spent their days hunting on the uplands of Mendip and hawking on the wetlands; they would have been entertained in the West Hall and feasted on produce from the surrounding estate – beef, mutton, pork, venison, fish and fowl. These gatherings were used to discuss state business, cement political allegiances and observe religious practices.

The West Saxon kings continued to patronise Cheddar into the late 10th and early 11th centuries. This is illustrated by the rebuilding of the West Hall, with the new building constructed in the same location as its predecessor although slightly narrower in plan and with an internal porch or dais at the west end. The hall was roofed in thatch or shingles with the walls possibly made of wattle and daub panels; the building had gable-end entrances and was probably heated by a central fireplace with the smoke vented through a louvre in the roof. A new stone chapel was also built around this period, this time on a larger scale, surrounding the footprint of the earlier chapel building, which had been destroyed by fire. The overall arrangement of the site changed relatively little, however, with the royal complex accessed from the east through two gateways in the surrounding ditched enclosure.

6

The later medieval period

In Westminster Abbey on Christmas Day of 1066 Duke William of Normandy was proclaimed king of England. Continuing unrest, however, meant it was to take at least another five years before the new Norman king could feel confident the Conquest had been completed. The England encountered by the incoming Normans was predominantly rural, well settled and extensively cultivated. In the years following the Conquest there was comparatively little change in the economy of the country. The major industries remained the same – textiles, mining, metalworking, salt production and fishing – and there is little to suggest a reform of agricultural practices occurred under the new Norman estate managers. However, by the late 13th century the population of England had increased significantly, leading to the redevelopment and enlargement of many settlements and the expansion of cultivated areas. This was a period of rising prices, low wages and growing poverty among the rural peasantry. A combination of calamities which occurred during the 14th century served to reverse the upward demographic trend, with the epidemic of bubonic plague in 1348–9 reducing England's population by about one-third. All this had a profound effect on the agricultural landscape, as long-established routines of husbandry were modified and adapted to suit the social and economic circumstances of the age.

The post-Conquest landscape (1086–1539)

The dominance of large royal and ecclesiastical estates on Mendip resulted in more continuity and stability in land ownership in the post-Conquest period than perhaps witnessed elsewhere in England. Cooperation with the new ruling elite saw some institutions prosper. The Bishop of Wells, for example, increased his landholding in the region by gaining new endowments, purchasing land from secular landholders and regaining estates that had previously belonged to the cathedral. The monastic landlords generally held on to their larger estates, although some of their lands in less secure tenure were regained by the Crown and passed to the new Norman lords. In comparison, the Domesday Book records the almost complete dispossession of Mendip's secular lords, as estates were redistributed among the Conqueror's favourites (Thorn and Thorn 1980).

The influence the new ruling elite had on the Mendip landscape is perhaps most clearly visible through the churches and administrative centres they created. Compton Martin, for example, has one of the finest Romanesque churches in Somerset (*see* p 155) and the building can be interpreted as a statement of the piety, wealth and aspirations of the new Norman lord. Without doubt one of the key Norman introductions to the English landscape was the castle, a new type of fortified residence. In the years following the Conquest, Richmont Castle was built at East Harptree, the Norman French name – meaning 'strong' or 'rich' mountain – perhaps illustrating the lord's perception of his recently acquired estate (G Brown 2008, 13). The royal and ecclesiastical landholders also made their mark, with the enlargement of the royal palace at Cheddar and the rebuilding of the cathedral church at Wells. The architecture of these complexes also reflects continental influence, and conveyed messages of wealth, power and grandeur, as demanded by the status of their builders.

Another way the new Norman landholders could project their lordly status was through the endowment of land to monastic establishments. On Mendip the FitzMartin family were one of the principal secular benefactors to monastic houses. They endowed the alien

Benedictine monastery of Goldcliff Priory (Newport) with land in Compton Martin, and the Cistercian houses of Flaxley Abbey (Gloucestershire), Stanley Abbey (Wiltshire) and St Mary Graces by the Tower of London with landholdings in Blagdon. As the nature of churches also changed in the post-Conquest period (and the potential for income from customary dues increased), their new Norman owners were persuaded to grant them to monastic houses. By the mid-12th century Robert FitzMartin had passed Blagdon church and its glebeland to Stanley Abbey, and in 1336 Sir Walter de Rodney granted the advowson of the church of West Harptree to Keynsham Abbey. Bruton held the churches of Westbury-sub-Mendip and Banwell from the bishop, along with their dependent chapels, which included Priddy, Rodney Stoke (Fig 6.1), Churchill and Christon.

In the late 12th and early 13th centuries the influence of the Crown on Mendip began to diminish, as royal land was granted to ecclesiastical houses. The king endowed the Carthusians of Witham Charterhouse with a substantial tract of land along the northern boundary of his Cheddar estate in 1178–9

(Gough 1928, 87–98). In 1204 the royal centre at Cheddar was granted to the Archdeacon of Wells, and after passing briefly back into royal hands it was transferred to Bishop Jocelin in around 1230 (Rahtz 1979, 18–19). The king retained a degree of control in the region, however, through the creation and enlargement of the royal forest of Mendip and the implementation of forest law.

The royal forest of Mendip

Designated hunting forests were an essential component of medieval lordship, and their creation represents one of the most influential changes in estate management in the post-Conquest period. Although certain areas were used as hunting grounds by the Anglo-Saxon kings, the concept of a royal forest – where deer and other wild animals were reserved for the king and protected under forest law – was a Norman innovation (Grant 1991, 3). The South-West was a favoured hunting ground for the Conqueror and his sons, who created and extended a number of royal forests in the region, including Selwood, Kingswood, North Petherton, Neroche and Mendip. The existence of a royal estate was clearly a significant factor in the creation of some of these royal forests, and the presence of a principal royal residence could only enhance a forest's importance to the Crown.

The royal forest was effectively a game reserve with its own administration and jurisdiction. Forest law was primarily created to protect the king's hunting, but it also permitted the monarch to retain rights over land beyond the bounds of his royal estate. Early documents highlight the harsh punishments for offences against forest law under the Norman kings (Grant 1991, 3), but by the late 12th century punishments were more generally in the form of fines imposed by the forest eyres (the highest forest court). Fines could be levied for such offences as killing royal deer, clearing woodland or keeping hounds within the bounds of the royal forest. At its inception the royal forest covered an area roughly comparable to the parishes of Cheddar and Axbridge, but was greatly extended after the coronation of Henry II in 1155. The afforested area then encompassed almost the entire Mendip region, stretching from Worle and Uphill in the west to perhaps as far as Frome in the east (Cox and Greswell 1911, 559; Neal 1976, 91).

Fig 6.1
Rodney Stoke. The church was held by the canons of Bruton as a dependent chapel of Westbury-sub-Mendip.
(DP043806)

The inhabitants of areas under forest law were restricted in the exploitation of their own lands and had to apply for permission to fell areas of woodland within the forest. For example, in 1234–5 the keeper of the Forest of Mendip (the principal local official in charge of the forest) was ordered by the king to issue a licence to the Bishop of Bath and Wells to assart 40 acres of his woods at Cheddar (Cox and Greswell 1911, 559). This licence included an unusual clause authorising the bishop to use the timber from the cleared area as fuel to smelt ore from a mine he had been permitted to open within the royal forest (*Cal Close Rolls Hen III* vol 3, 86, 92–3; Gough 1967, 50–1). Wood was also a primary material used in construction, and the king could award suitable timber from the forest as a favour, often to religious houses. In 1226 the Prioress of Amesbury obtained a grant from the king for 20 tie-beams, for example, from the forest of Cheddar for the erection of her chapel and infirmary (Cox and Greswell 1911, 559). The nature of the woodland within the royal forest is alluded to by a royal order for 3,000 hurdles in 1233, suggesting that managed coppiced woodland formed a sizeable part of the king's estate (Rackham 1988, 23).

The forest was stocked with the indigenous red deer, roe deer and the more exotic fallow deer (Rackham 1988, 23). The bones of all these species were present in deposits from Cheddar Palace but represented a relatively small percentage of the overall assemblage, indicating that venison did not form a main part of the household's diet (Rahtz 1979, 355–6). Venison was valued as a prestigious item in the medieval period, probably being reserved for feast days, and was frequently bestowed as a gift from the king to both his secular and ecclesiastical lords (Bond 1994, 126). In 1221, for example, a licence was granted to Bishop Jocelin to take 4 bucks in the forest of Cheddar, one of several similar grants to the bishop. Live animals were transported as far afield as the island of Lundy, with Henry III granting William le Marshal 10 does and 2 bucks from Cheddar in 1225 (Cox and Greswell 1911, 559–60).

As well as grants of deer, documentary sources also record numerous cases of poaching within the royal forest, an activity which could involve all ranks of secular and ecclesiastical society. At the forest pleas of 1270, the rector of the church of Shipham, together with his clerk, was accused of taking a hart from the forest without warrant. At the same forest court, Brother William from the Carthusian house of Witham Priory, and other members of the household, were accused of poaching a hart from the forest in 1260, and hunting another through Cheddar Wood (Cox and Greswell 1911, 559–60). The cases presented at the forest eyres must represent only a fraction of the true instances of poaching; the benefits undoubtedly outweighed the risks at a time when many struggled to make a living.

Manorial centres

Castles, moats and manor houses

Surprisingly few early manorial centres can be identified with any certainty on Mendip, and in some villages this may reflect the lack of residential lords. In parishes such as East Harptree, Compton Martin and Blagdon, the range of manors, sub-manors and ecclesiastical endowments led to the creation of a diverse assortment of lordly residences. With that said, medieval manorial complexes generally comprised an enclosure or curia, often accessed through a gatehouse, within which all the buildings required for a lordly residence sat. These seigneurial assets would have included an open hall, solar and oratory or chapel, as well as service buildings such as kitchens and stables. Manorial complexes also functioned as the economic and administrative centre for the estate, and as such, comprised offices and farm buildings, as well as structures for processing estate produce – such as mills, bakehouses and brewhouses.

Other lordly appurtenances, including fish ponds, dovecotes, gardens and orchards, were also commonly associated with manorial centres. At Winscombe a dovecote was recorded from at least 1277; the building was located within its own walled yard (Aston *et al* 2011, 74). The foundations of a circular stone building, around 17m in diameter, were identified east of Ludwell Farm, Hutton, and probably represent the remains of a dovecote associated with a secondary estate centre (Isles and Kidd 1987, 49–50). In some cases features such as fish ponds may be the only outward indicator as to the former location of an elite residence. The impressive series of seven stepped ponds at Eastwood Manor Farm, for example, suggests the site was probably the

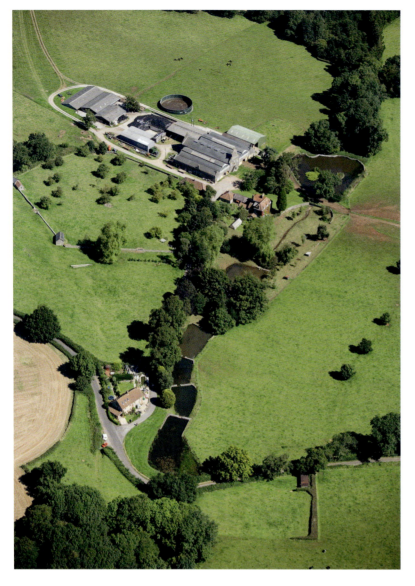

main residence of the Newton family from the 16th century (Fig 6.2).

Some sites which originated as estate centres could later function as farmsteads, which often obscured much of the evidence for their high-status beginnings. When Rutter visited Cheddar in the early 19th century the manorial centre of John de Cheddar had been reduced to the status of a farm, with the 'ancient hall' in use as a stable and granary (Rutter 1829, 183). Crook View Cottage, Christon, functioned as a working farmhouse into the 19th century but had higher-status origins (Fig 6.3). Although altered considerably in the post-medieval period, it has at its core the remains of a medieval house, with a stone arch that suggests a doorway of 13th- or 14th-century date. Although the evidence is incomplete, enough survives to demonstrate that this was once a far larger house, with a long-demolished bay surviving in part as a garden retaining wall incorporating evidence for a possible cruck blade. The likelihood is that this was a former open hall, possibly of cruck construction, distinguished by an internal masonry cross wall. Crook View Cottage would therefore appear to represent the remains of a medieval hall house and was probably the centre of a sub-manor held by the de Cheddar family by the 15th century (Collinson 1791, 578).

Manorial centres could be abandoned at an early date. Excavations carried out at Moreton, for example, uncovered the remains of a structure at the western end of the settlement which was interpreted as a manor house due to its size and superior construction. The stone-footed building was dated to the late 12th or early 13th century and had been deserted by the early 14th century; the abandonment was possibly connected to changes in land tenure or the decline of the de Mourton family. A similar story was revealed during excavations at the moated site of St Cross Nunnery, thought to represent a manorial residence belonging to the Sancta Cruce family, which had probably gone out of use by the later 14th century. The evidence from this site also highlights the numerous and often complex episodes of building and rebuilding which could occur at estate centres. The earliest structure at St Cross Nunnery was represented by a 12th-century timber phase, later replaced by stone-founded buildings constructed over several campaigns during the 13th century and associated with the surrounding moat (Rahtz and Greenfield 1977, 130–45, 107–8).

Richmont Castle

Richmont Castle, at East Harptree, represents the only major castle earthwork within the survey area and occupies a commanding position on the western boundary of the parish, located at the northern end of a steep-sided spur. It is not entirely clear when the castle was built, but it may have originated as a timber structure in the late 11th century when the manor was held by Aselin de Perceval. Aselin held estates in both East and West Harptree and the castle may have functioned as an administrative centre for both landholdings. The castle was certainly in existence by 1138, when it was in the hands of Sir William de

Harptree (created Baron of Harptree), a supporter of Empress Matilda during the time known as the 'Anarchy' (1135–54). Sir William garrisoned Richmont in her defence, but following the siege of Bristol, King Stephen advanced on East Harptree and captured the stronghold (Collinson 1791, 589). Although the subsequent history of the castle is somewhat uncertain, it probably remained the principal residence of the de Harptree family (later known as de Gourney) for much of the later medieval period.

The earthwork remains of the castle (Fig 6.4) have been much degraded, primarily because of stone robbing and mineral extraction, which has served to mask the form of the medieval stronghold. The definable castle earthworks indicate that the complex consisted

Fig 6.2 (opposite top) Eastwood Manor Farm. The impressive series of ponds suggest the former location of an elite residence. (NMR 24666/021)

Fig 6.3 (opposite bottom) Crook View Cottage, Christon. The surviving medieval bay stands to the right of the porch, with various additions to both sides. A modern extension (right) occupies the site of a putative cruck-framed bay, thought to have been the medieval hall. (DP043783)

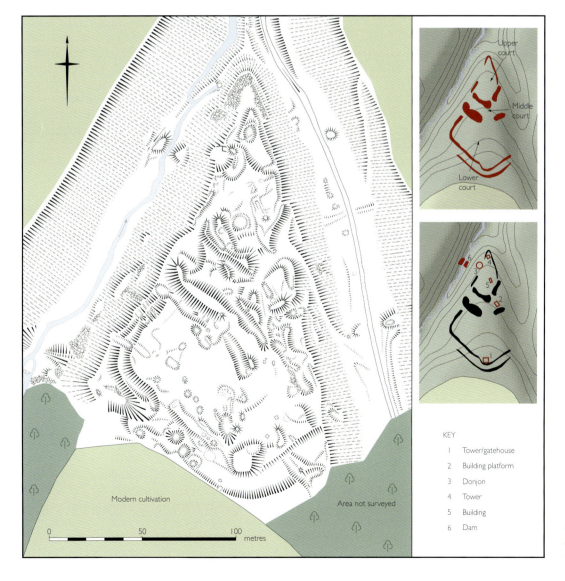

KEY

1 Tower/gatehouse
2 Building platform
3 Donjon
4 Tower
5 Building
6 Dam

Fig 6.4 Richmont Castle: earthwork and interpretation plan.

Fig 6.5
Poppy Cottage, East Harptree: detail of carved leaf ornament on the medieval spolia. The style of the carving is typical of the late medieval period.
(DP086415)

Fig 6.6 (opposite top)
Bickfield: earthwork plan.

Fig 6.7 (opposite bottom)
Late 16th-century map showing the manor house of Bickfield (centre bottom) and the church of Compton Martin (centre top).
(SHS DD/SPY/110, reproduced with permission of Somerset Archive and Local Studies)

of two concentric banks and ditches with a third, possibly earlier, outer bank and ditch to the south (G Brown 2008, 11). These earthworks defined a sequence of enclosed courts – the lower, middle and upper court – within which all the buildings necessary for a lordly seat were housed. The earthwork remains of a possible tower or gatehouse can be seen at the south-east corner of the lower court, and a rectangular building platform is visible at the eastern end of the much more confined middle court. These areas would have contained stables, lodgings, estate offices and other service buildings. Within the upper court a circular keep or donjon, approximately 12m in diameter, was located along the western side of the enclosure, with a second building, possibly a tower, occupying the most northerly point of the spur. A further building was positioned towards the eastern side of the court, with the whole complex probably accessed through a gatehouse and enclosed by a curtain wall. The donjon originally served as a suite of accommodation for the lord, but may have been supplanted by a hall and chamber-block by the end of the 12th century (Impey 1999, 71; G Brown 2008, 13).

The landscape surrounding the castle was also carefully constructed. The castle complex was bounded to the west by a substantial body of water retained by an impressive earthen dam; the dam was overlooked by the donjon from where the walls of the upper court would have been reflected in the sheet of water below. Earthwork evidence also suggests a sequence of smaller ponds were constructed along the valley floor to the east of the castle. The ponds would have been stocked with fish and fowl, but may also have carried more symbolic meaning connected to expressions of lordly display. The lordly imagery also extended to a small pleasure park which occupied the ground along the eastern side of the castle, separating the elite residence from the church and village beyond. This type of medieval designed landscape could be contrived for visual impact, and often displays evidence of a carefully manipulated approach (Richardson 2007, 42–5). Visitors advancing on the castle at East Harptree, for example, would have passed alongside the park pale before turning northwest to approach the lower court. The castle would therefore have been framed by the park, which would have emphasised exclusivity and served to reinforce the power of feudal lordship.

By the 16th century Richmont Castle was in the possession of Sir John Newton and no longer formed the principal residence on the estate. The rather restricted site of the castle may have been abandoned in response to shifting fashions or to the changing social requirements of a lordly residence. During his travels through Somerset in the first half of the 16th century, John Leland commented that 'all the buyldynge of this castle is clene downe'. He went on to say that 'Sir John Newton, now lord of it, hath made his House harde by it of the Ruines thereof upon the very place wher the Graunge of Richmonte Castle was in Gurney's tyme' (Toulmin Smith 1964, 84–5, 104–5). The fabric of the castle was therefore dismantled and carried away to be used in other buildings on the estate.

In the village of East Harptree it is possible to find reused building fabric possibly taken from the castle, in particular high-status 15th-century architectural features identified in at least three houses. These include reused moulded and billeted timber beams and ornate stonework which are inconsistent with the forms and dates of the houses in which they stand. The masonry of an ornately decorated medieval arch was reused in the fireplace of a 16th- or early 17th-century farmhouse at Poppy Cottage, on Middle Street; the stonework originated as a grand doorway or fireplace and was clearly salvaged from a much larger, high-status residence (Fig 6.5). In the neighbouring cottage, once part of the same farmhouse, a substantial roll-moulded timber beam was incorporated into the building. Originally part of a high-status framed ceiling, the beam came from a room approximately 5.2m in width and was truncated to fit within the farmhouse.

Bickfield or Moat Farm

Moated sites occur in a wide variety of situations, but for obvious reasons tend to be found on the heavier land of the river valleys. A water-filled moat could not only serve as a defensive feature, but could provide necessary drainage in lower-lying areas, as well as functioning as a symbol of social status. Where they represented manorial centres their function paralleled their un-moated counterparts. Moats can therefore be surrounded by the normal appurtenances of the manorial curia, such as closes, paddocks, dovecots and fish ponds.

Bickfield, also known as Moat Farm, lies on the heavy clayey soils of the Chew Valley, where natural springs rise, filling the ditch of the moat, and flow north-eastwards to feed the River Chew. Bickfield appears in the documentary record in 1327, when Rogero de Wykefold was listed on the lay subsidy roll for Compton and Moreton (Dickinson 1889, 112). Collinson also states that 'Bykefold' was held as half a knight's fee by Roger de Bykefold from William Martin (1791, 133), all of which suggests that a secondary manor existed at Bickfield by the early 14th century. The manorial complex is situated on the low ground of the Chew Valley, and defines the eastern end of what would have been a small linear settlement. The hamlet may originally have comprised a double row of tofts and crofts but had been reduced to just three households by the early 19th century.

The manor house at Bickfield stands eccentrically within a C-shaped moat (Fig 6.6). The relationship between the house and moat may suggest they represent different phases of construction; however, at present there is no archaeological evidence for earlier occupation on the site, or any indication that the moat once formed a complete enclosure. What is clear is that the orientation of the manor house and the form of the moat were manipulated to create maximum visual impact. The main approach to the complex from Compton Martin was along Bickfield Lane: the visitor then turned north-westwards to be rewarded with a view of the mansion's main facade across the water-filled moat; this is exactly the scene depicted on a map of the late 16th century (Fig 6.7) (SHS DD/SPY/110). To the east of the moated complex was a large enclosure defined by a network of ponds and water-filled ditches. Within this enclosure are the slight earthwork remains of former gardens and orchards, the regularity and orientation of which hint at a degree of formality in their design and suggest a relationship to the late medieval manor house.

While relatively modest in scale, the house at Bickfield displays a number of sophisticated late medieval characteristics which reflect a builder of status and considerable aspiration. It was attributed to the Roynon family, who acquired the manor through marriage in the late 14th century, and the estate was in the hands of John Roynon by the mid-15th century. It subsequently passed to his son William (d 1511), who is described in the documentary record as 'A verie great sheepemaster'

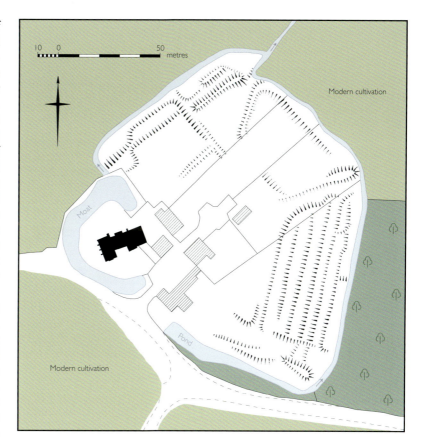

Fig 6.8 (right)
Moat Farmhouse, Compton
Martin, showing prominent
medieval porch and hall
range (centre) and solar
wing (left). The course of the
moat, infilled at this point,
extends left to right at the
front of the image.
(DP069678)

Fig 6.9 (below)
Moat Farmhouse, Compton
Martin: inner doorway of
the porch. It is clearly the
work of an accomplished
stonemason, with finely cut
mouldings and roundels.
(DP069655)

(SHS DD/SPY/60/1), and it seems that the wool trade, based on the manor's grazing rights on the Mendip wastes, is the most probable origin of the wealth that funded building in the 15th century.

The medieval fabric can be read as work of a principal dominant phase, stylistically consistent with the mid- to late 15th century and still reasonably coherent today, despite successive centuries of alteration (Fig 6.8). However, greater complexity underlies this story, and Pevsner describes the house as 'confusing in its evidence' (1958, 175). Irregularities evident in the plan, and the widely varying quality of stone carving found on the doorways and fireplaces, imply a degree of chronological depth: the stone carving defines phases in the limited period between the mid-15th and early 16th centuries, while the plan evidence suggests a potentially longer chronology.

The house claims the medieval domestic prerequisites of a former open hall with solar cross-wing to the west, the wing opposed by a cross-passage with a two-storeyed porch and a vestigial service range beyond. The inner door of the porch is of particularly high quality, with fine detailing carved by a master mason and possibly secondary work of the early 16th century (Fig 6.9). The house shows further refinement in the detail of its plan and form

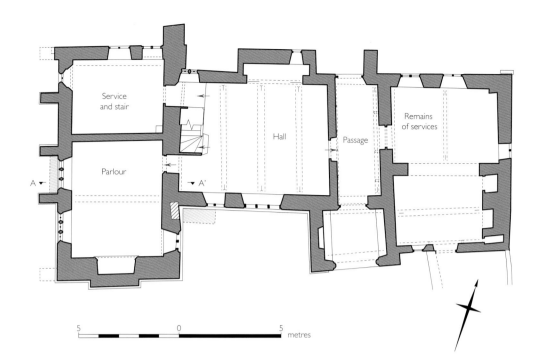

Fig 6.10
Moat Farmhouse, Compton
Martin: plan indicating the
function of spaces within the
house. The well-preserved
solar range is to the left,
with the plan showing
the medieval doorway
associated with the putative
oriel window lighting the
dais and connecting the
hall and parlour. A and A'
represent the position and
direction of the cross section
(see Fig 6.12).

(Fig 6.10). The arrangement within the solar wing is well provided with a neat and comprehensive set of rooms: a parlour on the ground floor, reached from the dais end of the hall; a solar on the upper floor, attained by an internal stair lit by a mezzanine light; and adjoining anterooms, one on the ground floor possibly a service room/offices. Both solar and parlour were heated by ornate carved stone fireplaces; that of the solar has been embellished by a panel of blind-relief tracery, carved somewhat idiosyncratically by an unaccomplished mason (Fig 6.11). The parlour, however, retains elements of a stylish framed ceiling, finely moulded, while the wing is set beneath a four-bay arch-braced roof with curved wind-bracing (Fig 6.12).

Sadly the hall roof has gone, having been replaced probably in 1793, and the service range was reputedly burnt, one perhaps the consequence of the other. But among the confusing evidence there are indications of a once refined open hall, including the scar of an arch-braced roof, an ornate screen bressummer and a putative oriel window lighting the dais. Evidence for the dais oriel is tied in with the arrangement of the medieval doorway between hall and solar wing, this doorway is now cut by the hall's front wall. This apparent contradiction implies a break forward in the front wall, which is explained as a hall oriel standing

at the dais end. A measure of aggrandisement is also evident in the 15th-century windows that survive, lighting the parlour and hall. A further oriel, lighting the solar, is inferred from masonry on the west wall, where a four-centred stone arch, set firmly between two buttresses, projects forward externally at storey height to form the base for a substantial medieval feature now missing. This west elevation, formed by the solar wing, was articulated by up to five buttresses, and stands, on axis, to face the village street, over which the oriel window might well have presided: the whole elevation is a further demonstration of status and sophistication (Fig 6.13).

Ecclesiastical estate centres

Monastic and episcopal estates were probably administered in much the same way as their secular counterparts. In some cases ecclesiastical centres operated as little more than upland sheep farms, with others used as the principal residence of the bishop in office. Holdings of the Bishop of Bath and Wells were extensive on Mendip, particularly along the southern escarpment, incorporating a range of estate centres. They varied from formal moated palaces, such as the lavish episcopal seat at Wells, to more modest residences, such as Westbury-sub-Mendip. These estate centres

Fig 6.11
Moat Farmhouse, Compton Martin: the 15th-century solar fireplace. It was a high-status feature within the house; nevertheless, the nature of the carving is primitive, with imprecise, irregular roundels, and areas where the bas-relief carving was never completed.
(DP069665)

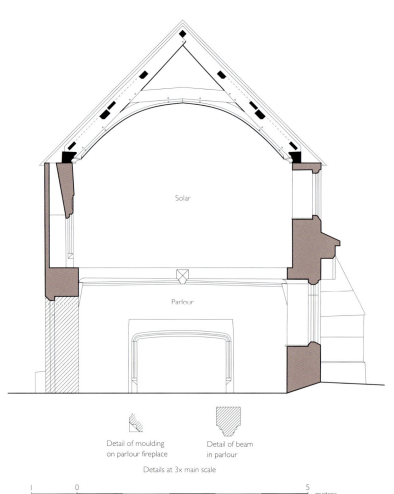

Solar

Parlour

Detail of moulding
on parlour fireplace

Detail of beam
in parlour

Details at 3x main scale

0   5
                                                                      metres

Fig 6.12
Moat Farmhouse, Compton Martin: cross section of the solar wing showing the medieval parlour fireplace and arch-braced solar roof structure.

Fig 6.13
Moat Farmhouse, Compton
Martin. The west elevation
of the solar was elaborated
by large mullioned windows,
as surviving on the ground
floor, and articulated by five
stone buttresses. The stone
arch of a putative oriel
window can be seen between
two of the buttresses.
(DP069647)

were not simply in place to manage the land and collect the dues: they were created to provide a chain of residences which the bishop and his retinue could utilise on their tours of the diocese.

Banwell would appear to have been one of the most favoured centres for many of the bishops of Bath and Wells. Documentary evidence indicates a centre here from at least the 13th century, with a household roll suggesting the existence of a substantial complex by 1337 (Payne 2003, 81–2). The episcopal centre at Banwell was located to the east of the church, with its extent apparently preserved as a tithe-free area on the 19th-century tithe map. The complex sat within an enclosure defined to the north by fish ponds and contained a series of substantial buildings, including a hall and chapel, the remains of which are incorporated in the present house, Banwell Court. The chapel and domestic ranges, attributed in part to Bishop Bekynton (1443–65) (Foyle and Pevsner 2011, 89), were extensively reworked in the 18th and 19th centuries. Along the southern side of the enclosure was a further building range depicted on a map of 1770 and described by Rutter (1829, 134–5) as containing 'a handsome

gateway, a porter's lodge, granaries and other detached offices'; this range had been demolished by 1829.

In the early 13th century the former royal estate at Cheddar passed into the hands of Bishop Jocelin. The manor, known as Cheddar Episcopi, already contained a substantial residence constructed during the reign of King John. This was subsequently replaced by a large stone or cob structure, which was probably constructed in the later 13th century. The building comprised a hall, approximately 20.7m by 12.9m, which incorporated domestic and service accommodation under one roof. The structure remained in use into the 14th century, but had been demolished by 1400, and was possibly replaced by a new range of buildings to the north. The 13th century also saw the complete rebuilding of the chapel at Cheddar, and by 1321 it had received its dedication to St Columbanus. The chapel underwent some modifications in the early 14th century, but is largely represented by the building which survives today (Rahtz 1979, 184–6, 210–16, 378).

Just over 3km from the bishop's seat at Wells was the grand episcopal palace of Wookey. The estate at Wookey was in the hands of the

Fig 6.14
Court Farm, Wookey, viewed from the south, across the site of the medieval curia. The building contains substantial remains of the medieval palace of the bishops of Wells at Wookey. (BB97/09509)

Fig 6.15
Court Farm, Wookey: a 13th-century doorway from the period of Bishop Jocelin. The exceptional quality is testimony to the status and opulence of the palace at that time, with details comparable to contemporary work at Wells Cathedral and bishop's palace. (BB97/09537)

bishopric by 1065, and in 1224–5 Henry III granted a licence to Bishop Jocelin to bring 10 oaks from the royal forest at Cheddar to carry out work on the manor house (Rackham 1988, 23). Documentary evidence also shows that Jocelin made good use of the palace, with four visits recorded between 1231 and 1241 (Hasler and Luker 1997, 22), and successive bishops made regular visits until the estate passed out of episcopal hands in 1548 (Payne 2003, 139). The manorial complex was defined by a large water-filled moat, enclosing an area of over 2ha, positioned adjacent to St Matthew's church on the south side of the village.

Significant remains of the bishop's palace are incorporated into Court Farm, Wookey, including 13th-century features connected stylistically with Jocelin and his work on the west front of Wells Cathedral (Fig 6.14). The most impressive survival is an exceptional two-centred arched stone doorway (Fig 6.15), in the Early English style, which probably dates from the 1230s (Pevsner 1958, 344; Fradgley 1997). The detailing and materials are of the highest quality and give some indication of the status of the palace in Jocelin's time. It was documented in the 1330s that Jocelin 'built magnificently the chapels and chambers of Wells and Wookey' (Hasler and Luker 1993, 115). The doorway, which is set within a wall over a metre thick, may have led into a chapel, hall or other range positioned on the east flank of the palace. Later medieval survivals in the farmhouse include an ambulatory or cloister range (now the main range of the house), which is probably of 14th- or early 15th-century date and appears to have been added to link two 13th-century buildings. The house also retains significant 16th-century remains.

A survey of the manor undertaken in the middle of the century revealed the layout of the estate centre at that time. The main access to the manorial enclosure was from the south-east, through a gatehouse with a porter's lodge. The complex also included an ox and hay house, a stable, pigsty and a cow-house with hayloft, all of which sat within a walled close named 'base cowrte or barton'. A series of other closes, including a garden and orchard, also lay within the moated enclosure, along with a number of fish ponds, a 'fayer large' dovecote and a barn (Hasler 1995, 2–41).

At Westbury-sub-Mendip, Court House Farm represents the remains of an administrative centre or bailiff's residence of the Bishop of Bath and Wells. Comparatively little is known of the overall form of this episcopal centre, which is located north of the church. However, there is one remarkable survival of this complex: a stone dovecote, or barn, probably dating from the 15th or early 16th century. This construction date is based on the roof carpentry, especially the form of the roof trusses. The roof is four bays long, originally with three open trusses, each with distinctive ogee-curved scissor braces (Fig 6.16). Although this form of bracing is extremely rare, an example from Warwickshire has been dated through dendrochronology to 1413–14 (Alcock and Miles 2012, 45).

Court House Farm is the only standing medieval agricultural building identified in the survey area and is an exceptional survival for Mendip. Externally it measures 13.1m by 7.3m, with tall gable walls built with integral nesting boxes, cut through by chimney flues when the building was converted into a farmhouse. The rectangular plan accords with the tenure and status of the site, this plan type being associated with dovecotes belonging to religious houses and manorial sites in the 16th century (Hansell and Hansell 1988, 103–4). Whether the nesting boxes denote a single original function is uncertain, as most of the internal wall surfaces are now plastered. The building has the distinction of being an early agricultural conversion, having been ceiled, floored and subdivided in the early 19th century and given a symmetrical Georgian facade (Fig 6.17). One of the medieval trusses is marked with names, including Samuel Green, alongside which is the date 1811 (or 1817) daubed in red. This might indicate the date at which the domestic conversion took place.

The estate centres of monastic houses are less distinguishable from secular manors than those of the episcopal lords. In many cases monastic granges carried on as secular farms, with numerous phases of later rebuilding removing any trace of their early form. In the 13th century the Carthusian house of Hinton Charterhouse acquired an estate at Green Ore and Whitnells, the holding located

Fig 6.16
Court House Farm, Westbury-sub-Mendip: the extraordinary roof structure. The former barn's substantial scissor-braced trusses were designed to be seen and admired, as well as allowing greater headroom for storage. (DP082354)

Fig 6.17
Court House Farm,
Westbury-sub-Mendip.
The barn was altered to
function as a farmhouse in
the early 19th century and is
now hidden behind the
facade and internal fittings
of this Georgian house.
(DP082363)

on the upland wastes above Chewton Mendip (Green 1892, 130; Thompson 1930, 140). The holding was administered from a grange farm, the main buildings of which were located at the modern-day Rookery Farm, where 14th- and early 16th-century stonework is still evident within the fabric of the farmhouse (Osborne 2008, 181–2). The grange farm lay towards the southern boundary of the holding, which comprised approximately 70ha held in two parcels (Fig 6.18).

The estate also incorporated three extensive sheep runs – Furshill Sleight, Stockhill Sleight and Whitnells – on which the Carthusians pastured around 2,200 sheep (Bettey 1988, 64). By the 14th and 15th centuries monastic sheep flocks were increasingly being managed by tenant farmers, and estate centres or grange farms leased out. Part of the Carthusian holding at Green Ore had been leased to Richard Roynon by 1516, although the estate remained in the hands of Hinton Charterhouse until the dissolution in 1539 (SHS DD/HI 256).

The largest monastic estate on Mendip belonged to the Carthusian house of Witham Charterhouse. Hydon Grange, at Charterhouse-

Fig 6.18
Medieval holding of
Green Ore depicted on the
18th-century enclosure map.
(SHS MAP/DD/WG 50/1,
reproduced with permission
of Somerset Archive and
Local Studies)

on-Mendip, was its most valuable holding and was worth £40 at the time of the *Valor Ecclesiasticus*, an assessment of ecclesiastical wealth compiled in 1535 (Caley and Hunter 1814, vol 1, 158). This may in part be a reflection of the estate's entitlement to mine lead within the royal forest, a right confirmed by the king in 1283 (*Cal Pat Rolls Ed I* vol 2, 73). Skinner believed Lower Farm (the former Cheddarford) to be the site of the principal grange buildings (Gough 1928, 98), where he noted the remains of a mill, fish pond and garden walls, all of which were 'going fast to decay' (BL Add MS 33653, fol 178). There is a documentary reference to a watermill in 1539, and two grist mills 'called or knowne by the name of Chedderford Mills' were mentioned in leases dating to 1660 and 1699 (SHS T/PH/VCH.6, DD/GB 46, DD/BR py 170).

Lower Farm had a significant role in the estate but the existing buildings at the farm present no visible evidence earlier than the 17th century, and it is more generally thought that Manor Farm was the likely location for the main grange farm. The house at Manor Farm is probably of late 16th-century date, although the sequence of phases there raises the possibility that some medieval fabric may have been incorporated into the present house (*see* Chapter 7). Other medieval fabric probably associated with the Carthusian grange is located in the farmhouse at Warren Farm, on the hillside 750m to the south of Manor Farm, where two arch-braced roof trusses and other roof timbers have undergone dendrochronological sampling and produced possible felling dates in the first few years of the 16th century (Arnold and Howard 2011, 2–3). This evidence is discussed further in Chapter 7, in connection with the building's use as a warrener's lodge.

In 1189–91 Cistercian monks at Bruern Abbey, in Oxfordshire, were granted land in West Harptree and Priddy by a local magnate, William FitzWilliam. The bounds of this grant were recorded and it is clear that they formed a compact block of enclosed land around what is today Chancellor's Farm, near Priddy. It is unclear what buildings the grange included, but it is likely that there would have been at least a dwelling house and some agricultural outbuildings. There was also a sheepcote, which was specifically mentioned in 1225. The abbey was granted the right of free warren in 1366, which meant that 'lesser' game could be hunted, and it is likely that the abbey was also

exploiting the lead resources of the area. In 1291 ecclesiastical property was taxed by Pope Nicholas IV and the estate was valued at £2, which was less than other Cistercian granges in the region; however, at the abbey's suppression in the 1530s its value had increased to £4, which may suggest that some time elapsed before the grange reached its full potential.

The farmhouse at Chancellor's Farm is of different phases, with a main range dating from the late 17th century (*see* Fig 7.45). These phases make use of medieval timbers and stonework, most noteworthy being the remains of a high-status roof structure of probable 15th-century date (Fig 6.19). These timbers were carved with decorative blind tracery, and the ornate treatment provides evidence of a high-status 15th-century domestic building. Reuse from the immediate vicinity of Chancellor's Farm is one possibility, as is the idea of timbers being imported from an important medieval site elsewhere – one suggestion being Richmont Castle in East Harptree (Fig 6.20). However, it is possible that the 15th-century roof indicates a grange of Bruern on the site, with administrative estate functions dictating the status of the buildings (Fig 6.21). Such an interpretation may be supported by the fact that the reuse of building materials took place in various phases of building the present farmhouse (Fig 6.22), ranging from the late 17th to the late 19th centuries. This indicates that medieval materials were available for salvage over a lengthy period, presumably from a site close at hand.

The name Chancellor's Farm is intriguing, and it has been suggested that it may derive from a grant to an ecclesiastical institution such as Wells Cathedral; however, this seems unlikely. A more plausible explanation is that it stems from a personal name, possibly that of 'John Chauncler' of West Harptree, who was listed for tax in 1581 when he was paying £5 8s 4d. John Chauncler was clearly an individual of some prominence since this was one of the highest assessments in the parish: it is possible that he owned the farm and that it took his name.

Episcopal and secular parks

To complement their estate centres, private game reserves were created in the medieval period by lesser landholding lords and by the Church. Hunting was an activity which was a

Fig 6.19
Chancellor's Farm, Priddy: medieval timbers reused to form the roof of an extension to the farmhouse built in the 18th century. Most of the timbers are reused, but only the curved, decorated brace, used as a collar, reveals the ornate, high-quality treatment of the medieval building from which the timbers were taken. (DP044114)

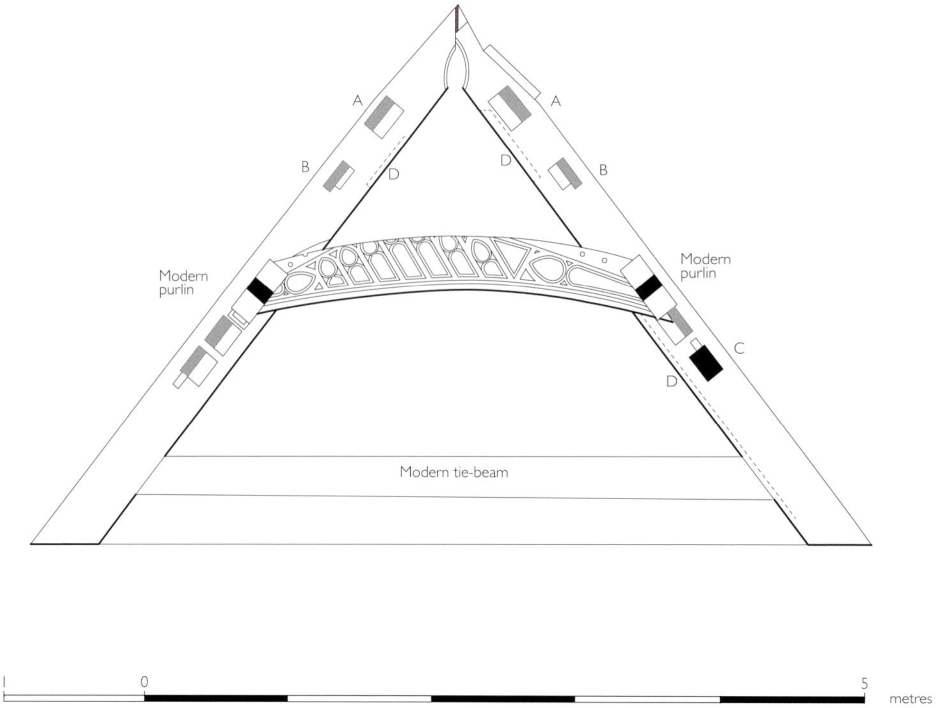

Fig 6.20
Chancellor's Farm, Priddy: cross section of medieval timbers as reused. The principal rafters have a series of redundant mortices showing the arrangement of the original roof purlins and braces (A and D) and their subsequent positions after the timbers were reused (B and C).

Modern purlin

Modern purlin

Modern tie-beam

0   5
metres

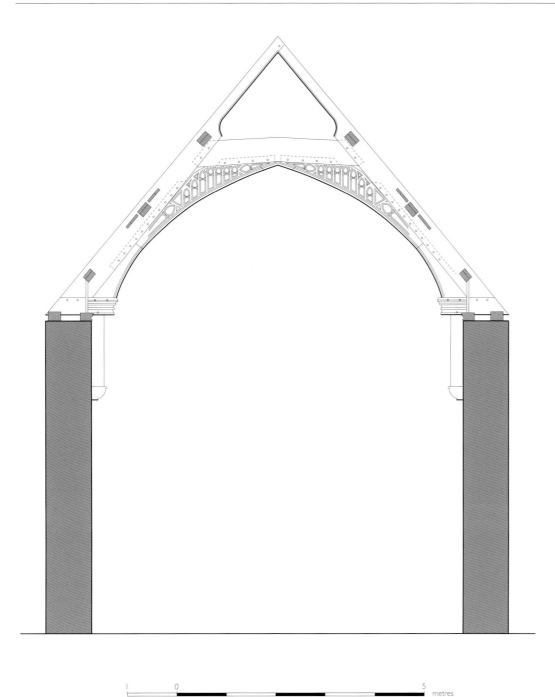

Fig 6.21
Chancellor's Farm, Priddy:
reconstructed cross section
of the medieval roof from
which the reused timbers
were taken, based on
detailed measurements
of the surviving timbers
in various areas of the
farmhouse.

0   5
                                                         metres

preserve of the king and the aristocracy, and therefore the creation of a park defined social status and illustrated a landholder's control over the resources within his estate. A park also provided its patron with a ready supply of venison, and allowed the pleasures of hunting to be enjoyed by the lord and a select group of companions. Deer parks sometimes deliber-

ately incorporated current and past symbols of power, a technique that may have been employed to reinforce the status and authority of the owner. The bishop's park at Banwell (Fig 6.23), for example, had a hillfort at its centre, and Richmont Castle's pleasure park was defined to the north-east by the parish church of East Harptree.

Fig 6.22
Chancellor's Farm, Priddy:
medieval stonework,
probably originally part
of an arched doorway or
fireplace, reused to form a
bedroom fireplace in the
main farmhouse.
(DP044123)

woods and to hold them as a park 'at their will' (*Cal Chart Rolls* vol 4). The disafforestation of Cheddar manor, and the granting of a licence to create a park, were so unpopular with the local peasantry that it led them to riot (Cox and Greswell 1911, 567).

The number of private game reserves multiplied in the 12th century, as the threshold for parks crept down the social scale. Around Mendip, secular lords created deer parks at Ubley, Compton Martin, East Harptree, Chewton Mendip and Rodney Stoke. There were almost certainly more within the region, with cartographic and documentary evidence suggesting the possibility of a deer park at Hinton Blewett, for example. The park at Ubley was in existence by 1280, when five live bucks from Mendip Forest were granted to Rodger de Amery and transported to his park at Ubley, replacing five bucks that had escaped (*Cal Close Rolls Ed I* vol 2, 32).

Parks contained a mixture of woodland and grassland which provided both cover for the deer and a ready supply of food. They could either take the form of relatively open areas supporting pollarded trees, or comprise a series of compartmented enclosures, devised to create a degree of separation between woodland and pasture areas (Rackham 1986, 125). These open areas are sometimes reflected in field names, such as Park Lawn and Great Lawn, recorded within the park at Chewton Mendip. A watercourse or pond was another essential component of a park, and can again be reflected in minor names such as Park Spring, in Compton Martin, and Park Pool, in East Harptree.

Along the northern escarpment of Mendip the parks are located on the lower-lying ground, sometimes incorporating steeper slopes and combes. The parks at East Harptree and Compton Martin were positioned close to the manorial residence, whereas the parks at Ubley and Chewton Mendip are placed on the far boundaries of the estate, possibly sited to avoid agriculturally valuable land. The definable secular parks of Mendip were relatively small, ranging in size from around 37ha (East Harptree) to 53ha (Chewton Mendip); in contrast, the park of the Bishop of Wells at Westbury-sub-Mendip extended to more than 200ha (Fig 6.24). The idea that small medieval parks were areas used to hunt deer on horseback has recently been called into question. Sykes has suggested that the size of these enclosed parks, and the physical

The Bishop of Bath and Wells had at least 10 hunting parks in Somerset (Bond 1994, 134), of which four were located around Mendip. As well as Banwell, the bishop had a string of parks along the southern escarpment at Cheddar, Westbury-sub-Mendip and Wells. The park at Westbury-sub-Mendip is first mentioned in a papal bull of 1178, and documentary evidence indicates that the park at Wells was in existence by 1207 (Greswell 1905, 249; Nott 1996, 1). The park at Cheddar was created after the manor was disafforested in 1337–8, when Bishop Ralph and his successors were given licence to enclose Cheddar's behaviour of the animals within them, indicates that hunting methods must have been limited to the drive, or 'bow and stable', which involved driving deer into nets or towards archers positioned on a platform or stand (2007, 51).

Parks were an expensive luxury to both create and maintain. In particular the perimeter pale or fence had to be constantly repaired, not only to keep deer in, but to keep poachers out. A medieval park pale was traditionally made of cleft oak stakes individually set in a broad, high earthen bank and nailed to a rail (Bond 1994, 140). The boundary bank usually had an internal ditch and the two features were sometimes separated by an open strip of ground known as a freeboard, created to allow access to the pale in order for repairs to be made. The construction of a stone boundary wall was a more expensive option and was often favoured by the Crown and the Church. The park of the Bishop of Bath and Wells at Westbury-sub-Mendip was, at least in part, defined by a stone wall, with the remainder delineated by a fence and section of quickset hedge. In the mid-15th century the Communar of Wells is recorded as paying for three wagonloads of stone and the hire of a labourer to construct two ropes (12m) of wall at Westbury-sub-Mendip (*Cal Wells MSS* vol 2, 76). The responsibility for maintaining the boundary of the bishop's park was made a

customary work spread among his tenants, with those responsible for maintaining sections of wall expected to renovate the stonework every nine years (Nott 1996, 26–7).

A parker or keeper could be employed by the lord to oversee the management of his park.

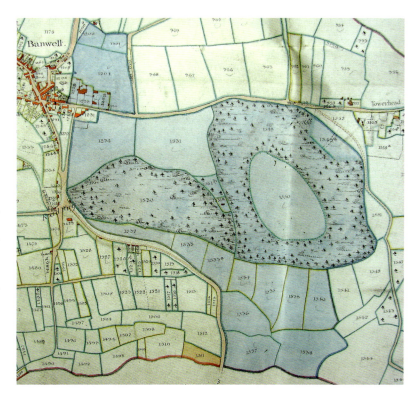

Fig 6.23
Banwell: area of deer park depicted on the tithe map of 1840 with the hillfort at its centre.
(SHS D/P/ban/3/2/3, reproduced with permission of Somerset Archive and Local Studies)

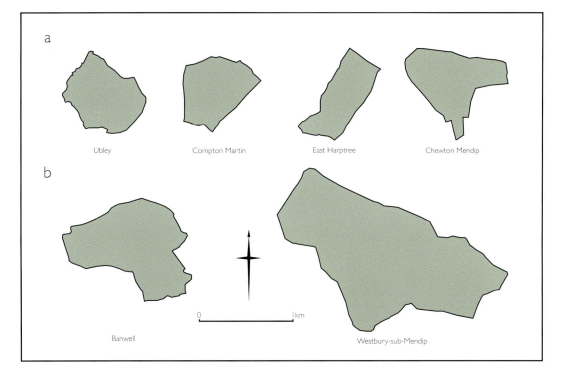

Ubley Compton Martin East Harptree Chewton Mendip

Banwell Westbury-sub-Mendip

0 ——— 1km

Fig 6.24
Extent of deer parks:
(a) secular and
(b) episcopal.

A house or lodge within the park was sometimes provided for the keeper's use, with the structure often positioned on the highest ground – its visible presence possibly aimed at deterring poachers. On the highest point within Banwell Camp, for example, an earthen mound was described in the early 19th century as the site of a park-keeper's lodge. The location is named Lodge Hill on the 18th-century tithe map, and 'within memory of some now living many cartloads of freestone were carried away from this spot' (Rutter 1829, 144). A trial trench was put through the mound in 1958 and revealed a layer of demolition rubble under which was found blue-green roofing slates and stained-glass fragments dating to the later medieval period (Hunt 1961a, 15–16).

Parks were designed to be attractive landscapes, incorporating woodland, open grassland, ponds and streams, and deliberately excluding mundane elements, such as fields, farms and roads. Park pales were intended not only to keep deer in, but also to keep local inhabitants out, creating a sense of exclusion and separation between the lord and his tenants. The creation of these designed landscapes therefore not only caused inconvenience to the local inhabitants, but also served to emphasise social structure (Herring 2003). In 1516 the tenants of Rodney Stoke brought a case in Star Chamber against Sir John Rodney, who, they claimed, had enlarged his park by enclosing part of their common pasture. They stated that he had pulled down tenements and blocked up the common road before installing red deer in the park. In bringing this case the peasants of Rodney Stoke also demonstrated that social hierarchy could sometimes be challenged. Indeed, the enlargement of the park proved so unpopular that some of Sir John's tenants allegedly broke down his park pale and attacked him with a pitchfork (Bradford 1911, 34, 73–5, 79–80).

Rabbit warrens

Rabbits and other small game, such as hares, woodcock, partridge, swans and pheasants, were often raised within deer parks. Rabbits were a valuable commodity for both their meat and their skins, and so warrens were another form of conspicuous display. The breeding of rabbits in warrens using specially constructed artificial burrows – long, low earthworks sometimes called pillow mounds – rapidly gained popularity during the early 13th century. The number of rabbits increased as the medieval period progressed, and more warrens were developed outwith the bounds of parks (Bond 1994, 145–6).

Some warrens on Mendip are only known through place-name evidence, with others identified through the physical remains of pillow mounds. Several warrens lie within, or close to, deer parks and may themselves be medieval in origin. Other rabbit warrens are positioned on the higher ground beyond the edge of cultivated land and represent a later phase of estate improvement (*see* Chapter 7). Place-name evidence suggests the former location of a warren within the episcopal park at Wells, with pillow mounds and building remains at Warren Hill, near Cheddar, which may represent the vestiges of a warren belonging to the Bishop of Bath and Wells. In 1516 a warren at Rodney Stoke was mentioned in the Star Chamber proceedings and was almost certainly associated with Sir John Rodney's deer park, the enlargement of which caused such local anger (Bradford 1911, 79).

On one of the highest points of the bishop's park at Banwell, the earthwork remains of a pillow mound can be seen lying within

Fig 6.25
Banwell: earthwork plan of cruciform pillow mound.

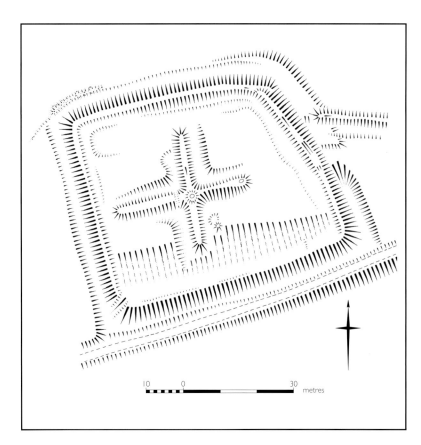

10   0   30
metres

a subrectangular enclosure. The earthwork feature takes the form of two banks placed in a cruciform formation and surrounded by shallow ditches; the banks are 5.5m wide and stand up to 0.8m high (Fig 6.25). The east–west arm of the monument is slightly longer than the north–south, at 39m, and the pillow mound is positioned towards the western boundary of the enclosure. A small trench was put through the western arm of the pillow mound in 1961 but no dating evidence was recovered (Evans 1980, 48). Although unusual, this cross-shaped pillow mound is not unique: other examples have been recorded at Port Talbot (South Glamorgan), Chirbury (Shropshire), Swinton (Yorkshire) and elsewhere (Williamson 2007, 59–60). The form and location of the warren at Banwell would indicate a medieval or early post-medieval date for its construction, and its cruciform shape may suggest a function beyond that of simple practicality. Stocker and Stocker (1996) have argued that rabbits and their pillow mounds carried symbolic meaning. The form and alignment of the pillow mound at Banwell, and the area's association with an early monastic centre, could imply a symbolic parallel with the fabric of the church.

The churches of Mendip

In most Mendip parishes the church is the oldest surviving structure, and represents a physical record of the changing fortunes of the area it served. Their special status has often resulted in the greater preservation of early fabric than witnessed in domestic buildings. The developing form of church buildings can therefore provide us with valuable information on social, cultural and liturgical changes over time, as well as indicating the wealth and piety of both individual patrons and the community as a whole. In addition, by looking at the setting of churches in the landscape we can attempt to understand the nature of church foundations; through analysing the plan form of villages we can begin to create a picture of the development of rural settlements and consider whether their churches were primary or secondary components (Fig 6.26).

Churches in the landscape

The vast majority of Mendip churches were integral to the medieval village plan. Only a very few churches stand apart from the main

Fig 6.26
The distribution of churches considered in the study.

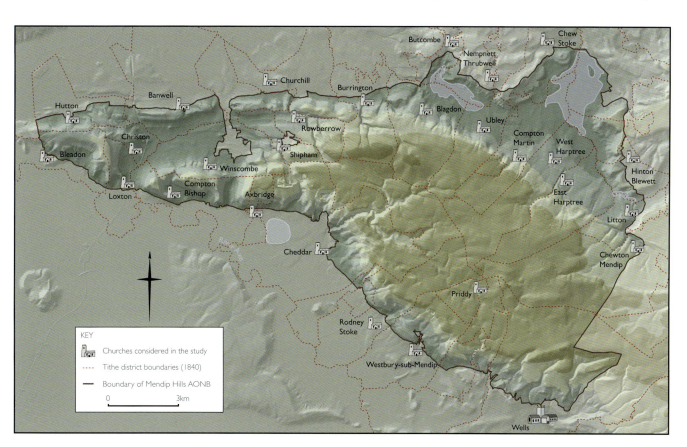

focus of settlement (notably Churchill and Rowberrow), which indicates a degree of settlement stability in the region. Closer examination of their landscape setting, however, reveals that the churches within our study area can be divided into two main categories: those associated with topographic features (such as springs, trees, river crossings and knolls) and those associated with a manorial enclosure (either lying at its centre or towards one of its entrances).

Springs were clearly an important element in the foundation of a number of Mendip churches. Perhaps the most obvious examples are Banwell and the cathedral church at Wells, both of which represent important early church foundations and, along with Cheddar, formed part of a regional structure of Anglo-Saxon minster churches. It may be no coincidence that all three of these sites have produced excavated evidence for Romano-British activity, suggesting the churches may have occupied locations with pre-existing landscape significance. The likelihood that at least some cult sites were absorbed into Christian ambition has been observed by previous scholars (eg Blair 2005). Rattue has

noted, however, that although the springs at Wells were the focal point of the minster settlement, there is no indication of their 'Christianisation' in the 8th century AD, which suggests the creation of St Andrew's Well (Fig 6.27) may be linked to a later Christian era (1995, 58).

A close association with wells and springs was not just confined to the higher-ranking churches. On Mendip examples have been identified at Axbridge, Blagdon, Ubley, Compton Martin, West Harptree, Nempnett Thrubwell, Winscombe and Chewton Mendip. In some of these cases the church may have preceded the development of the village, having originated as an earlier isolated religious centre which subsequently attracted settlement to it. At West Harptree, for example, evidence for a post-Roman cemetery to the south of the church (see Chapter 5) may suggest this location was adopted at an early date in order to 'Christianise' a site of pagan significance. A similar situation may have occurred at Chewton Mendip, where evidence for Romano-British activity was recovered close to the church. Here, the church is located on a small promontory overlooking Chew Head, the

Fig 6.27
St Andrew's Well and the cathedral church of Wells.
(OP05566)

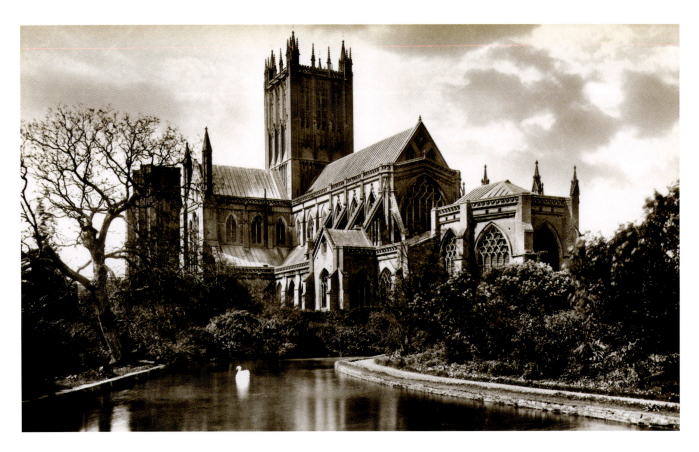

source of the River Chew, a location which may have held particular cult significance. At Wookey Hole the source of the River Axe was evidently a place of sacred importance for millennia and was named 'Holy Well' in the 15th century (Rattue 1995, 39). The unnamed spring at Compton Martin may be a further example; it issues beside the churchyard and represents the source of the River Yeo.

We cannot presume that all churches associated with springs and wells were early foundations. There is always the possibility that churches established within existing settlements were located close to springs for practical or liturgical reasons. The work of Rattue, for example, has identified evidence for the use of springs and pools for baptism in a period prior to the practice being undertaken indoors (1995, 66). Stocker and Everson have gone on to suggest that the need to perform the baptismal function may have resulted in some 10th- or 11th-century churches also adopting spring-side locations (2006, 65).

The second category of church foundations includes those which were associated with a manorial curia, either constructed within the enclosure or close to one of its entrances. The

often close geographical relationship between churches and manorial centres has long been recognised in Somerset (eg Aston 1988). Examples of Mendip churches which clearly lie within the manorial enclosure (close to its centre) include Shipham, Loxton, Hutton, Westbury-sub-Mendip and Litton. This relationship may indicate that these churches developed from a proprietorial church attached to the hall of the manorial lord, as the 10th and 11th centuries saw a proliferation of new churches built by local landholders. There are also a larger percentage of churches which would appear to have been located adjacent to the curia gate, either inside or outside. These include the churches of Christon (Fig 6.28), Rodney Stoke, Churchill, Rowberrow and West Harptree. These church sites may have been selected for their accessibility, as their position would have allowed the church to be used by both the manorial family and the wider community (Blair 2005, 389).

There are a number of less certain examples – such as Ubley, Compton Martin, East Harptree and Compton Bishop – where estate centres have moved or been completely lost. At Compton Bishop, for example, the manorial

Fig 6.28
Christon: aerial photograph showing church located adjacent to curia gate (centre).
(NMR 24669/19)

Fig 6.29
Compton Bishop: earthwork
plan showing the location
of a possible former
estate centre adjacent
to the church.

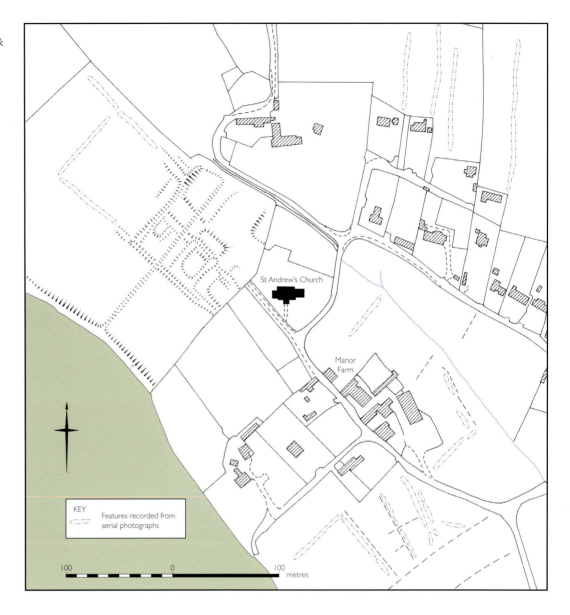

centre, now Manor Farm, lies on a former open space or 'green', which would indicate that it represents a later foundation. Earthwork evidence suggests the possible location of a second estate centre to the north, close to the church, which may imply that the church was positioned towards the entrance of a manorial curia associated with an earlier hall (Fig 6.29). It may be wrong to assume that the church is always the secondary element, however. In one-third of our examples there is evidence to suggest an earlier stimulus for the found-ation of the church – such as a spring or natural feature. A similar percentage represent dependent chapels, including Churchill and Christon, which were both dependencies of Banwell and could have had their origins in the pre-parochial estate structure. Early religious centres may therefore have been appropriated by manorial lords eager to establish control over a source of traditional power.

Church buildings

Local churches which developed in the late Anglo-Saxon period were probably constructed in timber or stone rubble, with lower-ranking churches unlikely to retain any early upstanding fabric. The only visible evidence we have on Mendip for these early religious buildings takes the form of fragmentary remains. These include part of a 10th-century grave marker at the church of St Andrew, Banwell, and an 11th-century piscina at Blagdon (Fig 6.30);

although these are both reset, they may well relate to earlier buildings on the site. The herringbone work on the exterior of the chancel at St Mary, Christon, may also be considered a stylistic legacy from the 11th century. Higher up the social scale, the excavated remains of two phases of an Anglo-Saxon chapel at Cheddar (*see* Chapter 5) demonstrate the significance of materials, with the chapel representing the only stone-built structure on the site.

During the late Anglo-Saxon period much of England moved away from the pastoral system based primarily on minsters to one focused on local churches. The formal creation of the parochial system – represented by a network of local parish churches serving a discrete community – did not occur until the 12th and early 13th centuries, however. The 12th century was also a period of unparalleled church rebuilding, with wealthy patrons constructing parish churches on a scale previously unseen. This is borne out by the visible evidence from Mendip, where a close examination of the developing physical form of the region's churches has revealed clear chronological trends in relation to building activity. These include a period of very substantial alterations during the 12th century. In the main, existing churches were rebuilt; few parish churches would have been entirely new, and it is perhaps notable that so much substantial or vestigial Norman fabric survives in the region (well over half the churches investigated display evidence of 12th-century fabric).

Perhaps the most striking example of Romanesque architecture in the study area can be seen at Compton Martin, where the form of the church, endowed with the full array of nave, clerestory, aisles and chancel in the 12th century, is testament to the high status of the benefactor. This is reflected also in the quality of the extraordinary spiral-fluted column placed, perhaps symbolically, at the east end of the south arcade (Fig 6.31). The carving is exceptional, and finds few parallels even among the finest cathedrals and abbeys of the period; a comparable example survives in the Norman fabric of York Minster. At Chewton Mendip, too, part of the Norman nave and chancel remain *in situ*, as do remnants of the Norman chancel arch. Evidence from here and elsewhere (including East Harptree, West Harptree and Cheddar) indicates that some of the region's Norman churches were of consider-

Fig 6.30
Church of St Andrew, Blagdon: the 11th-century piscina reset in the south wall of the chancel. (Olivia Horsfall Turner)

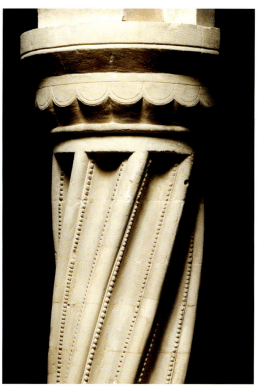

Fig 6.31
Church of St Michael, Compton Martin: detail showing the spiral-fluted column at the east end of the 12th-century south arcade. The quality of the stone carving is exceptional for the period. (DP081988)

able size. Norman fabric at St Lawrence, East Harptree, for example, suggests that the 12th-century nave was as wide as it is today. In contrast, the narrow, small-scale chancels at Westbury-sub-Mendip and Rodney Stoke would suggest that they represent original Norman fabric. Likewise, at Holy Trinity, Burrington, there is a small chancel that has been widened out at its western end in order to join with the wider setting of the aisles, which suggests that the chancel may well be 12th century in date. At Christon and Loxton the Norman nave and chancel still survive, if on a somewhat smaller scale than seen elsewhere, with both churches simply refenestrated rather than expanded in the later medieval period (Fig 6.32).

Fig 6.32
Comparative church
plans: (a) Christon,
(b) Priddy and
(c) East Harptree.

a

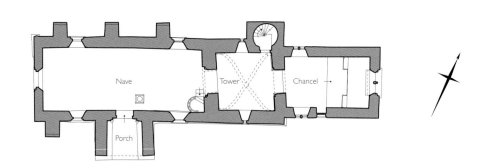

b

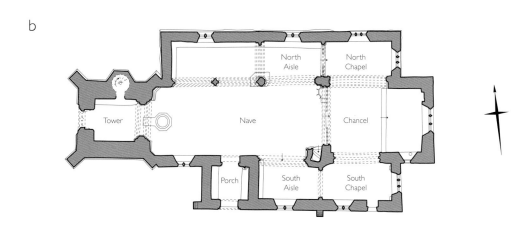

c

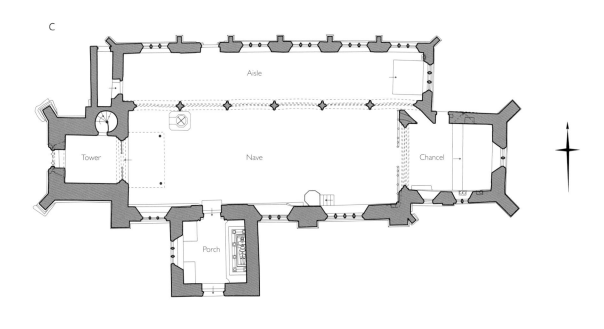

THE LATER MEDIEVAL PERIOD

The 13th century on Mendip may be categorised as a period which witnessed substantial alterations to church fabric. Although this work is identifiable at over two-thirds of the churches in the study area, it is more often manifested in the proportions of a nave or chancel rather than in Early English mouldings or carving. Remodelling in this period was predominantly, though not exclusively, associated with the re-edification of east ends. Examples of remodelling can be seen at churches at Cheddar, Compton Bishop and East Harptree, all of which have large chancels and Early English piscinae. This is congruent with patterns distinguished elsewhere in the country, and reflects developing liturgical requirements. It also corresponds to the clerical responsibility for chancels that was laid out in diocesan statutes from the 13th century onwards. The rebuilding of chancels is not something that is prevalent in later centuries (although there is some evidence of remodelling at Blagdon and Bleadon in the early 14th century), which perhaps reflects the fact that by that point they largely satisfied liturgical needs.

The modest alterations carried out during the 14th century are largely confined to aisle building; examples of this can be seen at Cheddar (the north and south aisles), Churchill (south aisle) and Priddy (eastward two bays of the north aisle). The addition of aisles can be attributed to a variety of factors, including the desire for more lay space within the church. This was not connected to population growth,

however, for this was a period of decline, with the epidemic of bubonic plague in 1348–9 affecting an already waning population. The addition of aisles was connected to new devotional practices and the demand for chapels, additional altars and lights. The expenditure involved in constructing an aisle may have been made more viable through rising wage levels and higher disposable incomes.

The 15th century was a period of very substantial alterations to church fabric, almost on a par with the rebuilding of the post-Conquest period. The alterations included the addition of substantial aisles, rebuilt naves, porches and towers, as well as refenestration. This work gave many Mendip churches their distinctive character through the deployment of decorative parapets, pinnacles and sculptural decoration. There are a number of sites where the design of the tower incorporated niches for sculpture. At Chewton Mendip, for example, the figure of Christ as the saviour of the world, surrounded by censing angels and angels holding instruments of the Passion, still survives. The churches at Winscombe, Banwell and Cheddar all had Annunciation scenes, though the figures survive only at the latter two.

The majority of Mendip towers probably date from the 15th century or the very end of the 14th century, such as Banwell. These perpendicular towers have in many ways overshadowed a number of earlier medieval towers, such as Christon (Fig 6.33), Loxton and West Harptree. A 12th-century tower arch

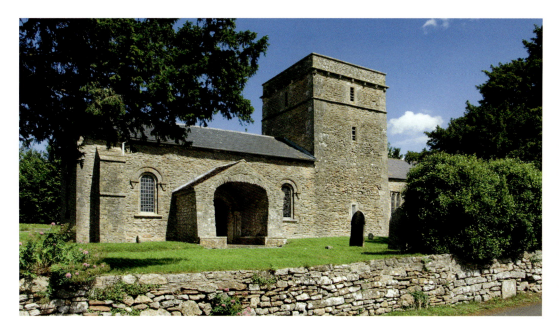

Fig 6.33
Church of St Mary, Christon. The Norman tower, standing between the nave and chancel, is a reminder of an earlier type of medieval church tower in the county. These were largely superseded by the imposing perpendicular towers for which Somerset is renowned. (DP043742)

Fig 6.34
Church of St Mary Magdalene, Chewton Mendip. The tower is among the tallest in the county and was probably still under construction in the 1540s.
(DP044508)

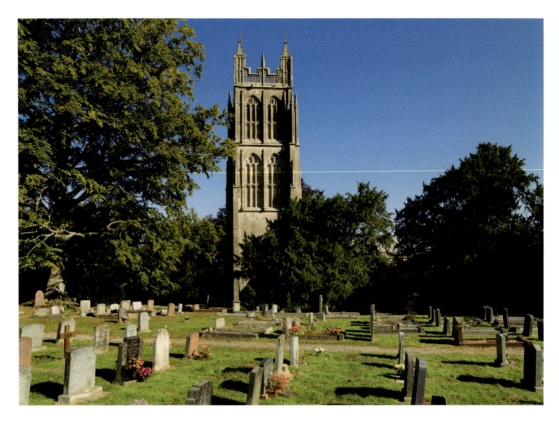

Fig 6.35
Church of St John, Axbridge: one of only a few churches in the Mendip area with a central tower. The church's status within the market town was a major factor in the choice of this complex plan form.
(DP044512)

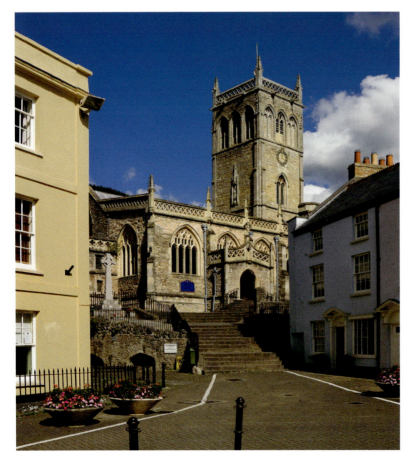

also points to a lost west tower at Westbury-sub-Mendip, with irregular bay-spacing at Bleadon indicating a former central tower. Although there is no surviving evidence of a Norman tower at Compton Martin, given the church's size and evident significance it is very probable that there was one. Similarly, Chewton Mendip's tower (Fig 6.34) is one of the latest examples (probably still under construction in the 1540s), but given the importance of the site, it is likely that there was also an earlier tower. In many cases, therefore, the 15th-century work may have obscured or swept away earlier phases of building, giving the impression of more monolithic, and later, structures than were actually the case.

The positions of the Mendip church towers are also worthy of note, as they are predominantly located at the west end of the nave. In fact, the only central crossing tower (apart from the Norman central tower at Christon and probably Bleadon) is at Axbridge (Fig 6.35). At Loxton (and possibly Shipham) the Norman tower was located on the south side of the nave and also functioned as the entrance porch. The clear preference for west towers may be ascribed to the evolutionary pattern of the majority of churches: beginning as smaller foundations and gradually developing, only adding towers in the later medieval period. Constructing a tower at the west end was by far the most practical option. The alternative was to create a crossing tower, which would have been more complicated and expensive to build, and would have required the renewal of the existing fabric.

At a number of Mendip churches it is evident that the 15th-century naves that are now standing are also rebuildings of earlier structures. At Banwell and Cheddar, for example, parts of what was once external tower fabric are now contained within the interior of the nave, demonstrating that the earlier nave was lower. At these locations – both large foundations with early origins – the raising of the nave roof went hand in hand with the addition of a clerestory. The decorated form of the windows at Cheddar suggests that this augmentation was carried out in the 14th century, while the clerestory at Banwell appears to have been added in the 15th century.

The rebuilding of a nave could also occur without the imperative for increased lighting and aggrandised space. At Rodney Stoke, for example, although the nave is narrow and may therefore have been constructed on the footprint of the original Norman nave, a section of the tower's north-east diagonal buttress descends below the current roofline, showing that the tower was built in respect to an earlier, lower nave. Given that the tower can be dated to the late 15th century, it seems likely that the rebuilding of the nave must have taken place after that date. In contrast, at Hutton the tower's eastern face bears the scar of a higher roofline, which implies a taller, narrower, earlier nave. At Ubley, evidence of a rebuilt nave is given not by a change in the height of the roof, but by the lack of alignment between the chancel, chancel arch and the nave, which suggests that the nave may have been rebuilt with the position of the earlier chancel ignored. There is also evidence of partial rebuilding of nave walls, for example at Priddy, where the nave walls appear to have been extended at the west end in order to join the new tower to the existing fabric.

The accretive nature of Mendip churches is perhaps most evident in the development of aisles. It is worthy of note, however, that there are some churches within the group that never had any aisles, including Christon, Nempnett Thrubwell, Loxton, Shipham and Rodney Stoke (Loxton's south aisle dates to 1926). The absence of aisles might indicate simply the small size of the parish, such as Christon, or might be ascribed to the foundation's chapel status: for example, Nempnett Thrubwell as a chapel of Compton Martin. A unique example of a church without aisles is Bleadon, where a project was initiated in the 15th century to erect a two-bay north aisle but then abandoned, with the remnants of the half-finished arcade left immured in the north nave wall. The rationale for such a decision remains unknown, but such striking change of intention seems to indicate the impact of an external event: perhaps the death of a patron, the sudden redirection of resources elsewhere or the realisation that the nave fabric was not sufficiently stable to have an arcade inserted.

The vast majority of the churches with aisles received them in the 15th century, though some of these may have replaced earlier aisles. A small number of existing aisles were also extended at this time, such as the two bays added to the 13th-century south aisle at Chewton Mendip and the two-bay extension of the 14th-century northern aisle at Priddy. These cases suggest that the construction of an aisle was specific in its purpose and related to the needs of the community at a given point in time. Of those churches which do have medieval aisles, there are some that have only one and some that have two. The latter can be divided into two groups: those churches where the north and south aisle were built at different dates, and those churches where they were built contemporaneously.

Churches with only one medieval aisle include Compton Bishop, East Harptree (Fig 6.36), Hutton, West Harptree and Westbury-sub-Mendip, all of which were constructed in the 15th century. We can also include in this group Blagdon, which was rebuilt in 1822 and again in 1909, with a plan sketch of the church prior to the 1822 work showing a north aisle. One of the last churches to have a single medieval aisle added was Hinton Blewett, where the north aisle was constructed in the early 16th century. The style of the arcade piers – comprising the typical combination of four shafts and four chamfers – indicates the longevity of this particular motif. When considered as a group, the equal incidence of north and south aisles would suggest that there was no particular iconographical or associative significance attached

Fig 6.36
Church of St Laurence, East Harptree, showing the nave (centre) remaining aisleless on the south side. The church was extended in numerous phases, with a substantial north aisle added in the 15th century. (DP044504)

to the position of the aisle. Instead, a number of factors probably influenced the decision, including the position of the church within the churchyard, the location of the church in relation to the settlement and the landscape of the churchyard itself.

Churches with two medieval aisles of different date include Axbridge, Burrington and Litton, all of which have 15th-century aisles but with the south aisle added slightly earlier than the north. At Ubley both aisles are again 15th century in date, but the north aisle was added earlier than the south. The incidence of aisles indicates that in the 15th century there was continued growth in the need for space, presumably reflecting a continuing desire for additional altars and ancillary liturgical space. Often it is not possible to establish from the fabric evidence the exact length of time that elapsed between the construction of one aisle and the construction of the other, but in most cases it may not necessarily have been very long. At Churchill, however, the fabric evidence indicates that the north and south aisles were the product of two entirely separate circumstances (the south, 14th century, and the north, 15th century), though the earlier aisle was also re-edified in the 15th century. In the other cases where there is little stylistic difference between the aisles it is difficult to establish whether the provision of a second aisle was anticipated at the time of the construction of the first or whether it was a

response to continually changing factors: both are a possibility.

Churches with two medieval aisles built at the same date include Compton Martin, Cheddar, Banwell and Winscombe, and of these, the latter two have 15th-century aisles. The 12th-century aisles at Compton Martin indicate that a high-status aisled church was planned from the start, though the south aisle was rebuilt on an enlarged scale in the 14th century. At Cheddar the story is slightly more complex and obscure, as, although both aisles were built in the 14th century, there is a change in the pier forms of the south aisle. These subtle differences suggest that a decision was taken during the construction of the aisle to alter the form of the arcade piers – which perhaps indicates a change of mason.

At Banwell, the building of the aisles appears to have coincided with the reconstruction of the nave and the raising of its roof, but given the church's high status it is probable it had aisles in an earlier phase. The existence of an aisled Norman church at Winscombe is corroborated by evidence for the bases of Norman pillars that were discovered beneath the existing pillars of the nave (Eeles 1929, xli). Although the two aisles at Winscombe have identical features, indicating that they were both built in the 15th century, there is fabric evidence to suggest the north aisle was a rebuilding of an earlier aisle (the north buttress on the tower does not descend to the ground, and a section of the north aisle wall devoid of a plinth may be the remnant of that earlier aisle). Whether this was the re-edification of a 12th-century aisle is unclear, as the consecration of the church in 1235 implies the building also underwent a phase of rebuilding in the 13th century.

In general, the presence of aisles may be considered as an indicator of the status of the church: the more significant the church was, the more likely it was to have aisles, and to have two aisles built in one phase. Consequently, Compton Martin had two aisles even in the Norman period, as did Winscombe; Cheddar had two aisles built in essentially one phase (despite the nuances noted above) and Banwell had two 15th-century aisles, possibly replacing earlier examples. These churches were among the largest in the Mendip area, positioned within settlements associated with major springs. Both Banwell and Cheddar were manors belonging to the see of Bath and Wells. Their status is underlined by the evidence of the 1291 *Taxatio*, in which there were two churches with significantly higher valuations than the others – Cheddar (valued at £26 13s 4d) and Banwell (valued at £31 6s 8d). The provision of two aisles may express the financial resources available at a large church or the demands of a larger congregation, and may also reflect a notion of decorum as to what an important ecclesiastical centre should look like.

Another notable feature of Mendip's churches is that in the majority of cases where there are both medieval aisles and a later medieval west tower, the tower pre-dates the aisles. More than half the churches studied have a later medieval (that is, not Norman) west tower and one or two medieval aisles. Of these, two-thirds had their tower built before the aisles were added. Of course, the caveat should be added that it is possible that there were earlier towers which were later rebuilt. Overall, though, a general trend in the sequence of tower–aisle phasing is discernible and potentially significant. Towers were built to house bells and as status symbols, while aisles were built in order to afford space for ancillary altars, lights and sometimes tombs, as well as being acts of devotional construction themselves. The significance of tower-then-aisle phasing is therefore that it suggests that the desire to build impressive towers, involving considerable investment, preceded the desire to expand the liturgical space of the churches.

Church houses

The 15th century saw the emergence of church houses as a specific building type, largely established in response to ecclesiastical intolerance of secular activities within the nave of the parish church. These buildings could be erected by parishioners to function as a large adaptable space for communal use, typically the celebration of festivals and feasts, and for parish ales from which funds could be raised and charity administered to the poor. Church houses were usually located adjoining or close to the churchyard, and were sometimes constructed on open areas or common greens. As a highly distinctive building type they can be recognised by their long plan form and large upper room, reached by an external stair and open to the roof, often accompanied by a ground-floor room with a smoke bay or large fireplace. E H D Williams identified 21 examples of church houses within the historic county of Somerset (1992, 16). Further examples have since been recognised, including three candidates identified during the course of this project, at Hinton Blewett, Wookey and East Harptree.

One of the best-preserved examples, illustrated by Rutter in 1829, stands just beyond the AONB boundary to the north, at Chew Magna, where the elaborate gable end of the church house forms the facade, looking onto the street alongside the entrance to the churchyard. This exceptional survival is 99ft (30m) long and retains arch-braced collar trusses, probably the result of two phases built in the late 15th and early 16th centuries. Of the newly identified candidates, that at Wookey also lies just outside the AONB, this time to the south, where one wing of the mansion known as 'Mellifont Abbey' retains an arch-braced collar-trussed roof of a similar period, although on a comparatively modest scale and alternatively interpreted as part of the medieval rectory. However, Holmes reported that, in the 18th century, 'when the place was rebuilt, the house in the churchyard, mentioned in the Terrier of 1634, was brought in as offices for the enlarged house' (1885, 86). A 1557 survey of the manor gives details of the church house, described as 'a hall a kychen and a loft over that under one ruffe [roof] containing 4 feldes [bays]' (Hasler 1995, 15). At East Harptree another example is the Waldegrave Arms public house, which contains collar trusses of a late medieval roof, the number, open form and decorative treatment of which suggest the building originated in the late 15th or early 16th century as a church house. The building is located close to the parish church on an area of former open common, which further strengthens the case for a communal use.

A similar story can be seen at Church Cottage, Hinton Blewett, where the vestiges of a probable church house have been identified along the south side of the churchyard, with the building located at the eastern end of a former linear green (Fig 6.37). Detailed investigation of the building identified a smoke-blackened roof truss of probable 15th-century date as the earliest component of the structure. The medieval truss comprises principal rafters and a cranked collar, with the rafters formerly clasping a diamond-shaped ridge piece. The extent of the original building is no longer certain, but the truss suggests it originally comprised a tall single storey open to the roof. Differential smoke staining between the east and west sides of the truss also suggests an open hearth or perhaps a smoke bay originally located at the western end. In the late 15th or early 16th century a substantial ceiling was inserted which covered the full extent of the range and defined a long ground-floor room, reflecting the typical elongated single-room plan identified with church houses. The beams indicate that, by this phase at least, the building had stone-rubble walls and that a large fireplace existed at the west end, possibly replacing the earlier smoke hood. Evidence for a blocked first-floor doorway also points towards the likely existence of a characteristic external stair.

Fig 6.37
Church Cottage, Hinton Blewett: the elongated single-room plan form typical of church houses (not to scale).

The medieval settlement pattern

On and around the limestone plateau is a combination of small market towns, villages, hamlets and individual farmsteads. A typical Mendip parish contains a principal occupation area accompanied by at least one other focus of settlement, such as a hamlet or farmstead. In the medieval period the largest parishes had a greater number of population centres, including townships with their own common fields. The former royal estate of Cheddar, for example, had a diverse range of settlement forms which included the medieval market town of Axbridge, the port of Hythe, the hamlets of Carscliffe and Bradley Cross, and upland farmsteads such as Milkway and Piney Sleight.

A number of factors could have led to this diverse settlement pattern. A complicated tenurial arrangement (in many cases stretching back to the Saxon period), combined with an increasing population, may have formed the background for the growth of these separate settlement foci. The proliferation of sub-manors led to the wide dispersal of settlement, perhaps as the properties of thegns or freeholders disintegrated under the impact of partible inheritance. The endowment of land to ecclesiastical houses also influenced settlement patterns – leading to the creation of separate administrative centres established to run these often distant holdings. These foundations could attract secondary settlement in the form of cottages and tenements of the peasantry who worked the estate. Wooded areas, such as Cheddar and East Harptree, developed a more dispersed pattern of settlement, as farmland was cut from tracts of forested land.

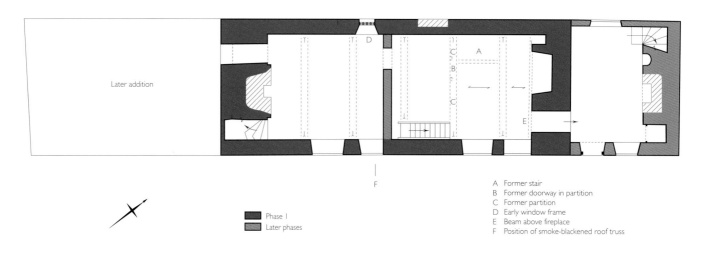

Later addition

F

Phase I
Later phases

A Former stair
B Former doorway in partition
C Former partition
D Early window frame
E Beam above fireplace
F Position of smoke-blackened roof truss

Settlement form

A small number of Mendip settlements can be characterised as medieval market towns – typically defined by an ordered arrangement of plots focused on an open space – usually connected to royal or ecclesiastical centres. However, by far the most dominant settlement form during the medieval period was the nucleated village. These were chiefly located along the spring line at the foot of the limestone escarpment and were surrounded by a patchwork of common fields. These settlements were generally characterised by a group of peasant tofts and crofts focused on the parish church and, in some cases, one or more manorial centres (Fig 6.38). Many of the villages are represented by linear forms, often

Fig 6.38
Aerial photograph showing settlements strung out along the spring line at the foot of the limestone escarpment. (NMR 24322/48)

articulated by a single street, some of which can appear straggling and poorly nucleated. Alternatively, they could be focused on a central space or 'green', such as Shipham and Winscombe, defined by no more than a loose cluster of farmsteads and closes. There are also examples of settlements which developed along watercourses, for example Chewton Mendip and Litton, the latter being represented by a rather haphazard arrangement of tenements focused on a crossing on the River Chew. A few of the larger settlements may be termed polyfocal, including Westbury-sub-Mendip and Blagdon. In most cases these villages developed from the fusion of a number of small hamlets or separate settlement zones, sometimes reflecting multiple estate centres.

In contrast, the smaller hamlets of the region are all generally defined by relatively simple morphologies. Approximately 75 per cent of minor settlements within the project area are linear in nature, either stretched along a road or trackway or laid out at the end of arable plots. The hamlets range in size from no more than two or three holdings to large linear settlements stretching for over 500m, but all exhibit some sign of social, economic or religious dependency on another place. The clustered settlements tend to be grouped around road junctions and river crossings, sometimes focused on a mill and often located towards the boundary of the parish. Some settlements evidently developed next to secondary manors or within areas of different tenurial holding, possibly representing freehold farms or monastic endowments. A number of hamlets developed within areas of cleared woodland or on common-edge locations, with a few bearing 'green' or 'end' suffixes (Fig 6.39). Many of these settlements comprise little more than a loose straggle of farmsteads or cottages set along a sinuous road or around the edge of

a small area of common grazing; examples of green-edge settlements can be seen at Lower Milton, Sutton Wick and West Horrington.

The smallest component in the medieval settlement pattern was the isolated farmstead – usually represented by a small cluster of buildings focused on a central yard. Most parishes included a number of individual farms, often located in more marginal areas, many of which represent holdings that have their origins not in expansion over arable land, but in enclosure from waste, woodland or heath. Archaeological and place-name evidence suggests some of these farms may have been founded in the pre-Conquest period, possibly having originated as areas of seasonal settlement, with others the result of population and settlement growth in the early Middle Ages. A number represent specialist upland stock farms, with some the product of endowments to monastic houses (such as Green Ore and Temple Hydon), and others clearly established to support a mixed farming regime. Other apparently isolated farms can be the product of amalgamations, having begun life as small hamlets.

Settlement origins and development

When examining the character of Mendip's medieval villages what is perhaps most noticeable is that almost without exception they were successful, and have continued in use to the present day. These villages have therefore evolved and changed through time, which has often resulted in their early form being masked by later development. That said, by examining their plan form in detail it is sometimes possible to gain an insight into their origins, as well as to define subsequent episodes of expansion and contraction.

A number of settlements within the study area are arranged in such a way as to suggest they were the result of conscious and deliberate planning. These can take the form of regular linear rows, comprising rectangular plots arranged in an orderly line along one or both sides of a main street. For example, Rodwell has suggested the main town streets of Wells were laid out in a planned episode, possibly as early as the 10th century, aligned on the marketplace and the Anglo-Saxon minster church (2001, 120). Draycott perhaps represents one of the clearest examples of planning, where a double row of tofts and crofts line

Fig 6.39
Chewton Mendip: the small linear settlement of East End as depicted on an estate map of 1740.
(SHS DD/WG/MAP/1, reproduced with permission of Somerset Archive and Local Studies)

a north–south aligned street. The axis of the street mirrors the configuration of the surrounding fields and clearly indicates that the settlement was laid out over pre-existing furlongs. Draycott developed from a solitary farmstead recorded at the time of Domesday, and would appear to have been established in a single episode by the Augustinian canons of Bristol, possibly by the late 1200s.

The 12th and 13th centuries also saw a proliferation of new town creations, many of which were established on the estates of ecclesiastical landholders. The port of Rackley, for example, was first mentioned in 1179 and developed as a trading centre after Richard I granted a charter to the Bishop of Wells in 1189. The settlement was located along the old course of the River Axe and comprised a single east–west aligned street. Rackley is now reduced to a loose group of four or five houses, some including possible medieval fabric, but field evidence indicates it originated as a double row (Fig 6.40). The earthwork remains of building platforms, tofts and boundary features are evident in pasture fields on the north side of the main street, with the settlement evidently inserted into a pre-existing pattern of strip fields (Fig 6.41). Rackley's failure to succeed as an urban centre was almost certainly a result of its close proximity to the towns of Axbridge and Lower Weare, the latter also a failed port and new town foundation. Rackley continued to function as a small port throughout the Middle Ages, with a dispute regarding the use of the river in 1390 mentioning cargoes of salt, iron and fish (Bettey 1986, 59; Aston and Leech 1977, 117).

Perhaps more common on Mendip are towns and villages where evidence of planning can be associated with the reordering or expansion of an already established settlement. The town of Axbridge, for example, originated as a Saxon *burh* and had attained urban status by the time of the Domesday survey when it was recorded as a borough and supported 32 burgesses (Thorn and Thorn 1980, 1, 2). The settlement later experienced a phase of reordering, taking the form of a double row of plots centred on the market square and church. Excavations to the rear of properties on both the north and south sides of the High Street produced ceramic evidence suggesting a 12th- to 13th-century date for this phase of reordering (Everton 1978, 7; Everton and Kirk 1982, 4). The earliest surviving fabric of St John's church dates from

the 13th century, strengthening the suggestion that the town experienced a period of significant investment at this time. The settlement also underwent a wave of expansion to the west, possibly in the 13th or 14th century; this separate suburb, owned by the manor of Compton Bishop, did not form part of the town

Fig 6.40
Rackley: aerial photograph showing the surviving buildings alongside the old course of the River Axe. (NMR 26590/01)

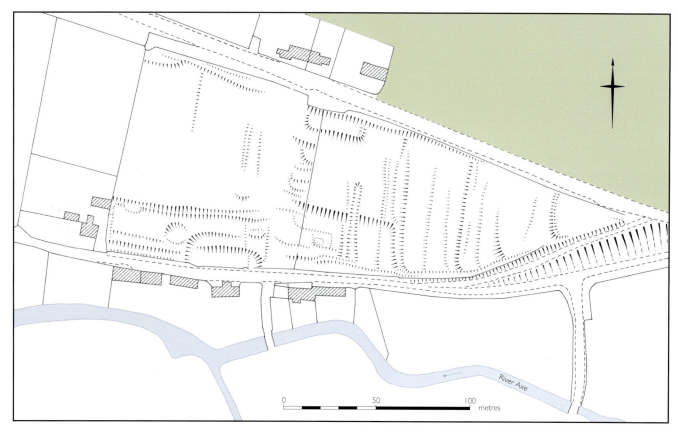

River Axe

0   50   100
                        metres

Fig 6.41 (above)
Rackley: earthwork plan
of settlement.

Fig 6.42 (below)
East Harptree: an ornate
fireplace of the late medieval
period. The timber bressummer
is embellished with blind
tracery whose style suggests
a date in the 15th century.
(DP069754)

proper until the early 17th century (Everton 1975; Richardson 1998, 10).

Multiple phases of planned expansion can be identified elsewhere on Mendip, including the villages of Compton Martin, East Harptree and Compton Bishop. Architectural investigation has helped reveal the medieval core of East Harptree, suggesting it was focused along High Street and on the area of St Laurence's church.

Evidence in the buildings includes an intact late medieval fireplace (Fig 6.42), with carved timber bressummer, and roof trusses encapsulated within refashioned terraced houses along the High Street. A high proportion of 16th-century buildings were also identified in this area, which suggests a degree of settlement stability (Fig 6.43). This rather poorly nucleated village would appear to have developed adjacent to a large, linear open space or green, in a similar way to Hinton Blewett and North Widcombe, part of which had been infilled by the later Middle Ages. Regular plots along the eastern side of the green would suggest the settlement experienced an episode of planned expansion into what had formerly been arable strips, with test-pit evidence indicating colonisation by the 12th century (L Ross, pers comm). The development of a separate settlement zone around Proud Cross may have been stimulated by the creation of Richmont Castle in the late 11th or early 12th century, with the substantial Norman church also reflecting this period of significant investment (Fig 6.44).

The smaller hamlets of the region have also revealed evidence for episodes of possible planned expansion. For example, Walcombe, to the north of Wells, was first documented in the 11th century and probably originated as a small cluster of tenements at the head of 'The Combe' (Fig 6.45). Only a few holdings were evident along Walcombe Lane by the mid-18th century, but field evidence has highlighted the former location of a regular row of at least eight adjacent tofts and crofts along the east side of the road. The plots were approximately 20m in width, with tofts located bordering the street frontage and crofts behind extending for up to 200m. Two houses along this frontage retain possible medieval fabric, most notably Walcombe Cottage, whose deceptive cottage exterior conceals a late medieval framed ceiling with moulded beams, fireplace and framed medieval doorway. These tofts and crofts were inserted into pre-existing furlongs, which accounts for their regularity in size, and indicates an episode of conscious and deliberate development.

The nearby settlement of Upper Milton also displays clear evidence of expansion over arable fields. Here, the hamlet formerly comprised a double row of tenements set along the Old Bristol Road, positioned on a sheltered west-facing terrace (Fig 6.46). The initial focus of

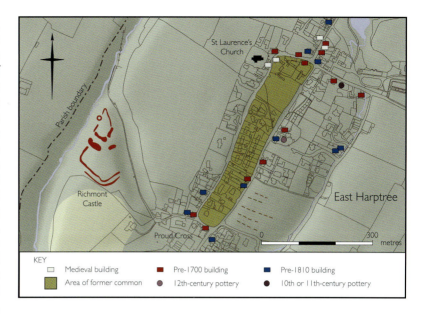

Fig 6.43
East Harptree: the distribution of medieval and post-medieval buildings.

Fig 6.44
East Harptree: reconstruction showing the village as it may have looked at the beginning of the post-medieval period.

KEY

⟨⟩ Features recorded from aerial photographs   ■ Walcombe Cottage

0   50   100 metres

Fig 6.45
Walcombe: earthwork plan of settlement showing the remains of tofts and crofts inserted into pre-existing furlongs.

occupation was probably around Upper Milton Manor, although the existing manor house contains no visible medieval fabric. Earthwork evidence indicates that at some point there was an expansion of settlement northwards from the manorial complex into pre-existing fields, with the form of the plots or crofts defined by the underlying contour strips.

As well as expansion over arable land, new settlements were also created on areas of

former woodland or waste. For example, within the manor of the Bishop of Wells at Easton, a group of small farmsteads collectively known as Hope were established on the common edge sometime during the 12th or 13th century. Hope comprised three holdings located on a sheltered south-facing slope above Ebbor Wood, sited between 110m and 200m apart, each defined by a cluster of buildings and yards set within a subrectangular enclosure (Fig

168

6.47). The regular form and layout of the farmsteads and attached land would suggest they were constructed in a single operation, possibly with a degree of planning in mind.

The creation of new farmsteads may not have been confined to more marginal land. At Chewton Mendip, for instance, the earthwork remains of a number of abandoned farms would suggest these sites may, at some point, have comprised two farmsteads set side by side (Fig 6.48). This pattern of paired farmsteads could suggest individual holdings were subdivided, perhaps during a period of social or economic pressure, with the holdings later brought back together, or in some cases completely abandoned.

Much of this evidence suggests that planning, in one form or another, was one way in which some settlements of Mendip came to take on their present form. Although settlement reordering can be evident, it is often difficult to assign a reason or secure date to the process. From the very limited dating evidence from Mendip, a 12th- or early 13th-century date for the majority of reorganisation may be tentatively put forward. The reasons behind the process may be harder to quantify, however. The theory that manorial lords were the principal agents in village planning has recently been called into question, with some scholars highlighting the power of peasant communities to shape the landscape in which they lived and worked (eg Lewis *et al* 2001, 172–9). On Mendip, the evidence from Draycott, Rackley and Hope suggests acquisition by an ecclesiastical lord could influence settlement planning. At Compton Martin, significant investment by the FitzMartin family in the post-Conquest period (perhaps most clearly visible today through the exceptional Romanesque parish church) may be linked to the reorganisation of the village plan. Another settlement which experienced a clear phase of lordly investment was East Harptree, with the construction of Richmont Castle in the late 11th or early 12th century. The planned addition to the settlement appears to date from around the same time and may be connected to a broader phase of investment by the de Harptree family.

The reasons for what would appear to be planned additions to settlements such as Walcombe and Upper Milton are perhaps less easily defined. It may be the expansion of these settlements was related to an increase in

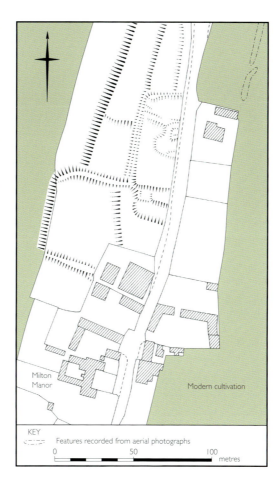

Fig 6.46
Upper Milton: earthwork plan of settlement showing evidence of expansion over arable fields.

the rural population, and the adoption of new agricultural methods in the 12th and 13th centuries. A similar argument can be made for the creation of the new holdings on the upland wastes and the subdivision of established farmsteads. The development of other settlements may have been influenced by practical or economic factors, such as the existence of a medieval market grant. The substantial expansion of the settlement at Cheddar may in part be linked to its status as a market centre. One of the key elements of the town is a grid-based street plan located to the north of the royal palace complex. This regular grid of streets suggests a more intensive episode of growth than witnessed in other villages on Mendip, with excavation indicating a 12th- or 13th-century date for colonisation (Hollinrake and Hollinrake 1997). In some cases the acquisition of a weekly market grant or annual fair may have led to the disruption of settlement morphology through the deliberate creation of an open green or marketplace within or attached to the settlement. At Priddy, for example, the core of the present village

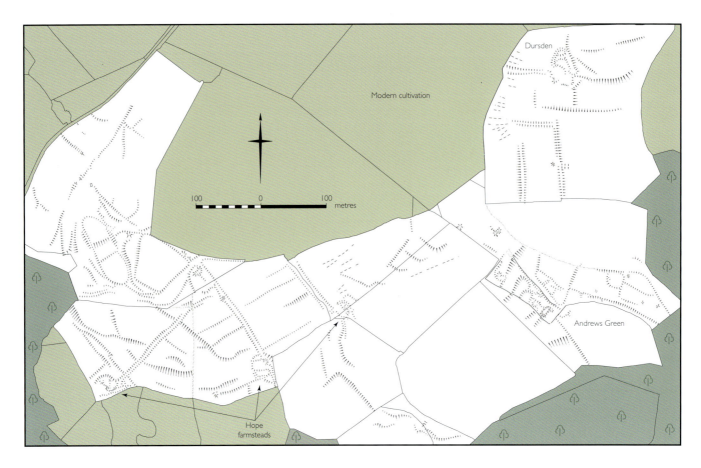

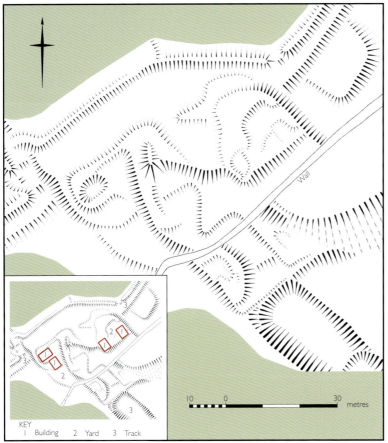

KEY
1 Building 2 Yard 3 Track

is centred on a triangular open space which is used to this day to hold the annual sheep fair.

Some of the larger settlements display evidence that they developed from a number of separate settlement foci. The village of Blagdon, for example, comprises three settlement zones, represented by East End, West End and Street End; the latter probably developed in the post-medieval period as a centre of industrial activity (Neal 1976, 85). The village of Westbury-sub-Mendip also adopted a poly-focal plan, comprising two or possibly three nuclei linked together by lanes (Fig 6.49). The northern element is formed by Old Ditch, which probably originated as a separate hamlet, and which was laid out at the head of the combe and has a regular single-row extension at its western end. A second nucleus existed to the south, focused on a central green, now much encroached upon, and surrounded by a complex pattern of closes and lanes; 10th- to 12th-century pottery has been recovered from this area of the village (B Lane, pers comm). The administrative centre for the Bishop of Wells was located on the west side of the green, adjacent to the church, forming a third and possibly the earliest focus for settlement.

Fig 6.47 (opposite top)
Earthwork plan showing
the landscape around the
farmsteads of Hope,
Andrews Green and
Dursden.

Fig 6.48 (opposite bottom)
Chewton Mendip: earthwork
plan showing paired
farmsteads.

Fig 6.49
Westbury-sub-Mendip:
aerial photograph looking
north over this large
polyfocal settlement.
(NMR 24322/21)

The desertion and shrinkage of settlement

Settlement shrinkage, or complete abandonment in some cases, was a widespread phenomenon during the later medieval and early modern periods. The evidence from Mendip illustrates, however, that contraction was in many cases not the product of a single event or a particular period in time; it was a continuing process, often experienced over many generations. It is perhaps worthy of note than none of the main settlements of the region were completely abandoned, as happened elsewhere in the country. Many did, however, experience a period of decline, often reflected in gaps in the settlement pattern or visible through the earthwork remains of abandoned buildings, yards and closes. Reasons for this may be diverse and complex. The changing pattern of residential and non-residential lords, and their varying policies of estate management, may have combined with social, economic and climatic factors to influence the changing settlement pattern.

The region's smaller hamlets and farmsteads appear, perhaps unsurprisingly, to have been more vulnerable to the effects of change than the larger towns and villages. Winthill, for example, a hamlet in the parish of Banwell, shows clear evidence for a number of phases of settlement decline (Fig 6.50). Intermixed with the existing holdings are earthwork platforms, trackways and closes, indicating the location of former farmsteads and suggesting that the hamlet was originally more densely settled. Some of these holdings were abandoned at an early date, with others amalgamated in the second half of the 19th century; these different episodes of abandonment reduced the size of the settlement to that which we see today. A similar story can be seen at Walcombe, where fieldwork and cartographic evidence has highlighted the different phases of abandonment, with some holdings lost during the later 18th and 19th centuries and others deserted long before. At Moreton, excavations have shown that some holdings within this linear township were deserted by the 13th century, with others abandoned during the later 14th or early 15th century (Rahtz and Greenfield 1977, 90–122).

Although the evidence from Moreton suggests an episode of settlement shrinkage in the 13th century, the most clearly identi-

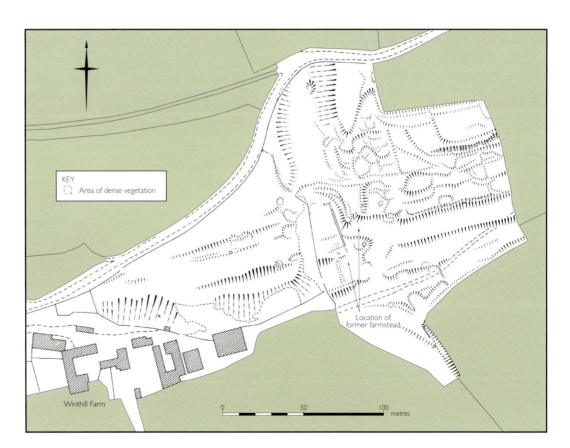

KEY
☐ Area of dense vegetation

Location of former farmstead

Winthill Farm

0   50   100
                        metres

Fig 6.50
Winthill: earthwork plan showing former areas of settlement.

fiable period of decline was in the 14th and 15th centuries. The effects of the epidemic of bubonic plague in 1348–9 on an already shrinking population, followed by other 14th-century calamities, paved the way for later settlement decline. On Mendip this is perhaps most clearly seen with regard to the more marginal holdings on the common edge. The farmsteads of Hope, for example, seem to have been abandoned by the early 15th century. Hope appears in the documentary record in 1402–3, when three tofts were granted to the Carthusian monks of Hinton Charterhouse. Two of the holdings comprised 30 acres of land and 4 acres of woodland, and were held by John Goundenham and his wife, Agness, and William Nyle and his wife, Joan, for a rent of 8½d. The third toft was less than half the size and was held by a certain Robert, his wife, Matilda, and Isabelle ate Hye (Brett 2007, 22–3). The use of the term 'toft' would indicate the farm buildings had decayed by this time, a suggestion perhaps strengthened by the use of a locative surname for one of the tenants.

It is possible that the farmsteads at Hope were abandoned, as the area was converted to pasture for sheep and cattle. Indeed, a large sheep enclosure was constructed immediately east of the farmsteads (*see* Fig 6.66). Another farmstead which may have experienced a similar fate is Dursden, which lies to the north-east of Hope and has now been largely levelled through the processes of modern agriculture. Comparatively little is known of this holding, but Nicholas de Duddesdene is recorded in the 13th century, and pottery dating from the 12th or 13th century was recovered from the site (Everton 1967, 23–4; TNA PRO E 326/2970). The two deserted farmsteads of Ramspits, Westbury-sub-Mendip, may also have been casualties of agricultural reform. These holdings are recorded in 1463, when Bishop Bekynton leased two tofts and two fardels called 'Rammespytte' to Raynold Baker and Isobel, his wife; the use of 'toft' again suggests the buildings of the farmsteads had been abandoned by that time (Pattison 1991, 95–111). Flights of fossilised arable strips are evident along the escarpment slopes below Ramspits, and are again indicative of the change from an arable-based economy to a largely pastoral regime (Fig 6.51).

Fig 6.51
Ramspits: aerial photograph showing the earthwork remains of the medieval farmsteads (centre right) and fossilised arable strips (top left). (NMR 26656/49)

Panel 6.1 Christon: a 'shrunken' medieval settlement

The small village of Christon is located on the sheltered south-facing slopes of Flagstaff Hill, towards the western end of the Mendip range (Fig P6.1.1). The settlement lies hard against the south-western boundary of the parish and overlooks the broad valley of the Lox-Yeo river. Today the village is poorly nucleated, predominantly strung out along Banwell Road, and displays clear evidence of contraction. The 'shrunken' settlement at Christon was first identified by R L Clarke, who interpreted the earthwork remains as a series of 'squalid cottages straggling up the hillside' (1969, 8–17; 1970, 8–14; 1973, 18). Recent archaeological and architectural research has revealed a more complex story, however, involving several phases of settlement expansion and contraction. The core of the medieval settlement was located towards the eastern end of the modern village, adjacent to the church and principal manorial

centre. The small Norman church of St Mary the Virgin, positioned outside the gate of the manorial curia, was a dependent chapel of Banwell and possibly formed the earliest focus for occupation.

The upstanding remains of Christon Court date to the 17th century, but the earthwork evidence for further buildings, low terracing and boundary features suggests a much longer history. At the time of Domesday, Christon was recorded as part of Uphill and was held by four men-at-arms under the lordship of Serlo de Burci (Thorn and Thorn 1980, 37, 2). The manor of Christon is first mentioned in 1186 in the Great Rolls of Henry II, when it was in the hands of Sir Wyein (Ywerne) de Chricheston. It subsequently passed to William de Oiselier and Mabel, his wife, who were ordered in 1204 to pay to the Prior of Bruton an annual alimony of 8 shillings from their chapel (Knight

Fig P6.1.1
Christon: aerial photograph showing the village surrounded by the earthwork remains of former settlement and fields.
(NMR 24821/4)

1915, 285). In 1548 the principal manor at Christon was sold by the Pokeswell family to John Payne. At that time the estate was worth £140 and included the chief mansion, a dovehouse and an orchard, as well as tenements, the common upon Christon Hill and the advowson of the parish church (Bristol Record Office [BRO] AC/D/10/1). Christon continued to function under multiple owner-ships throughout the medieval period. Thomas de Cheddar held land in the parish during the 15th century, and the estate passed through marriage to the Capel family and remained in separate ownership until 1652 (Collinson 1791, 578). As we have seen, the centre for this sub-manor was probably located north of the church at what is now Crook View Cottage.

The earthwork remains of abandoned village tenements predominantly lie along Flagstaff Road, a well-defined hollow-way which extends north-westwards from the churchyard (Fig P6.1.2). At the lower end of this route are a series of subrectangular plots – typical peasant tofts and crofts – which lie perpendicular to the road. The buildings of Manor Farm (formerly Christon Farm) can still be seen to occupy one of these plots. The tofts and crofts are terraced into the hill-slope and their width, and possibly their length, may have been influenced by the pre-existing ancient field system which underlies the later landscape. The form of the earthwork remains would suggest that the tenements were possibly abandoned at different periods. There is clear evidence within one of the plots for buildings and a yard, accessed from Flagstaff Road via a sunken ramp (a). Although it had been abandoned by the early 18th century, these well-defined earthworks imply that the tenement continued in use longer than its neighbouring holdings, where no such occupation remains survive. The earth-works also indicate that this tenement may be the product of engrossment, the enclosure formerly subdivided lengthways and possibly having originated as two holdings of roughly equal size.

At the higher end of Flagstaff Road are further tenements, some of which may represent a less ordered phase of expansion. The size of these terraced plots is again evidently influenced by the existing field system, and an assemblage of 12th- to 13th-century pottery has been recovered from this area (Clarke 1969, 15). Map evidence indicates that at least one of these tenements was occupied during the early 18th century (BRO AC/PL 52); the former location of this building is represented by a terraced platform on the west side of the road (b). At the northern end of Flagstaff Road, the axis of the main village street turns westwards, leading towards the common strips of West Field. On the north side of this route are a series of small closes, building remains and trackways which overlie a complex pattern of ancient fields. The earth-works roughly follow the same alignment as the medieval settlement pattern and field system, and may represent a further expansion into more marginal land. A single holding named 'Cadice' is depicted here in the early 18th century (BRO AC/PL 52); the tenement was abandoned sometime in the second quarter of the 19th century (c). A trackway (lined on one side with orthostats) now cuts through these remains, forming part of a formal approach from Christon Court to Barleycombe Cottage, a late 19th-century shooting lodge.

The evidence from Christon clearly illustrates that settlement contraction was not the product of a single event or a particular period in time. Some tenements in the village were probably lost in the 14th or 15th century, the casualties of social, economic and envir-onmental change. Other holdings held on, and may even have prospered, accumulating land as their neighbours left in search of a better life elsewhere. Changes in the old routines of husbandry, the loss of people and facilities, and antisocial behaviour may all have combined to undermine settlement stability and fuel migration (Dyer and Jones 2010, 37–45). Enclosure and consolidation during the 16th and 17th centuries were perhaps a further catalyst for settlement decline, as the old system of open-field agriculture was swept away and the separate manorial estates at Christon were united under the same lordship. The last phase of abandonment occurred in the first half of the 19th century and was almost certainly linked to the wholesale agricultural reforms of the period – reflecting the final move from feudalism to capitalism.

Fig P6.1.2
Christon: earthwork plan.

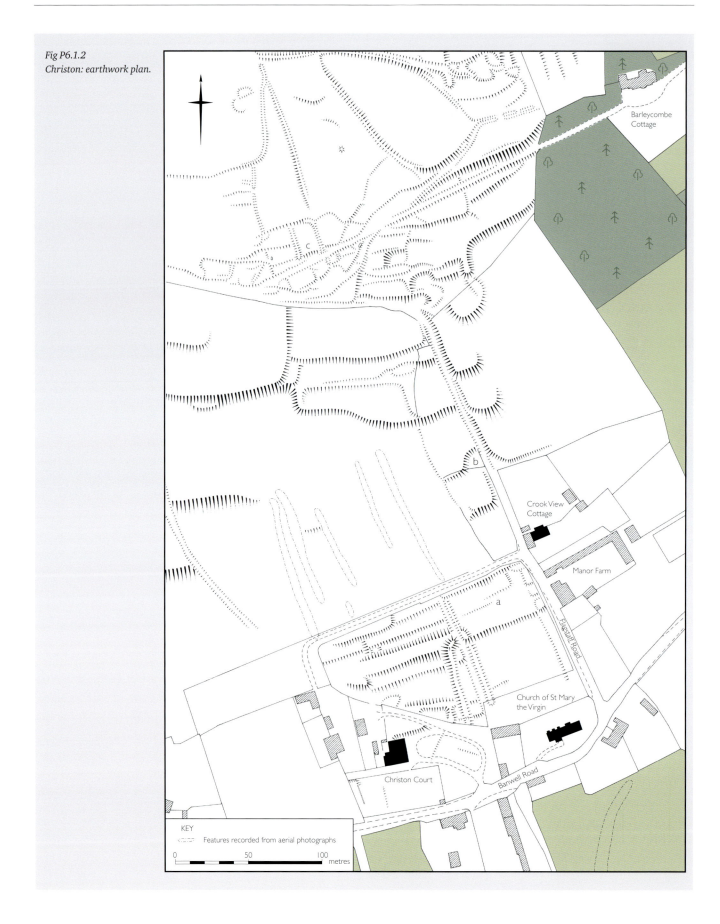

KEY

Features recorded from aerial photographs

0   50   100
                metres

The medieval buildings of Mendip

The buildings of the farmstead: the earthwork evidence

Many of the holdings established in the medieval period continue in use to the present day. As a result, the early form of their buildings has been destroyed by numerous phases of repair and rebuilding. The best evidence we have for the form of these medieval structures is therefore often from those holdings which failed. A number of farmsteads were lost during the medieval period, while others succumbed to the changing agricultural and economic climate of the 18th and 19th centuries. The earthwork remains of early desertions provide us with our clearest picture of the structures that made up the medieval farm. By nature these examples are largely from the upland areas, on the margins of cultivation, where holdings were more vulnerable to the environmental and social changes of the Middle Ages. They therefore also represent some of the smaller, less productive holdings, which may be reflected in their size and form.

What is perhaps striking is the scale and simplicity of the medieval buildings identified on Mendip. They are generally represented by one- or two-cell rectangular structures, with only a few displaying evidence for internal partitioning. These internal divisions are visible as discrete level changes across the interior, indicating that partitions, where they did exist, were of timber construction (Fig 6.52). Many of the buildings occur in pairs, with single doorways sometimes apparent as gaps in the wall footings. Where walls are visible through the turf they are formed by roughly coursed stones, which probably supported a timber superstructure infilled with wattle and daub. Some buildings may have been constructed entirely of timber and furnished internally with clay or beaten-earth floors. Excavated evidence from the Chew Valley suggests a move away from buildings constructed using earthfast posts during the 13th century (Rahtz and Greenfield 1977). Surrounding the farm buildings were a series of yards and closes defined by ditches, fences or stone walls; some yards were possibly covered by a metalled surface of gravel or cobbles.

The field remains of spread stone walls and slumped platforms make the accurate measurement of buildings difficult. However, approximate external dimensions indicate that the medieval buildings ranged in length from around 4m to 18m, and in width from 4m to 8m. The buildings would appear to fall into two main categories: those structures which are around 4m in width and generally between 4m and 10m in length, and buildings

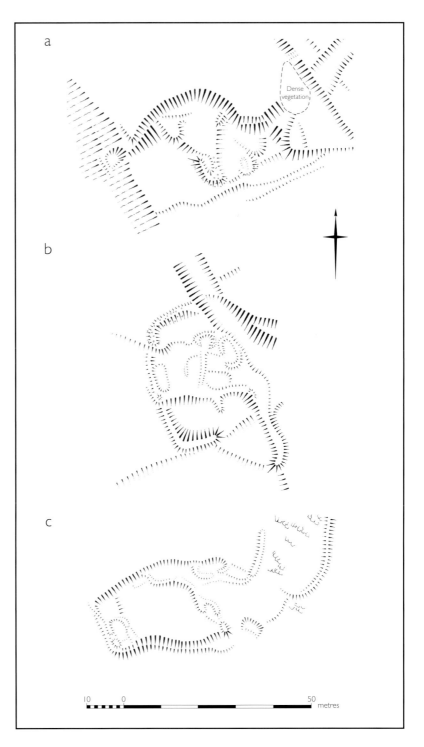

Fig 6.52
Earthwork plans of farmsteads: (a) Hope, (b) Lower Hope and (c) Rodney Stoke.

between 6m and 8m in width and up to 14.5m in length. In general, buildings displaying the narrower plan tend to be grouped together. At Hope each farmstead had a paired arrangement of buildings, both of which were around 4.5m wide and either 5m or 8.5m long. At Ramspits a narrow-plan building 18m in length was recorded; its unusual size possibly suggests that it performed a specialist function. There are a few sites where both categories of building plan appear side by side. The settlement above New Road, Rodney Stoke, for example, has a building on the western edge of the farmstead around 9m long and 6m wide, with a possible annex at its northern end; the remaining three structures around the yard were approximately 4m in width and between 5.5m and 10m in length. The earthwork remains also indicate differences in building form, with some structures surviving as stone footings and others as simple platforms possibly indicative of wholly timber construction.

Differences in the scale, number and construction techniques applied to buildings on any one plot may be a reflection of the wealth and status of the occupant (Dyer 1986, 26). Farmsteads comprising the narrower-plan buildings alone could therefore represent the holdings of the lower-ranking peasant farmers. It is also possible that variations in building size within a single holding could reflect different phases of construction or rebuilding, with dwelling houses perhaps more likely than agricultural buildings to be remodelled and enlarged. Structural variations can also be an indication of the different functions each building performed. In holdings such as Hope, for example, the larger building would probably have been the dwelling house, with the small, single-cell structure used as a workshop, as an animal shelter or for storage. The use of a building could also change in response to the specific needs of the peasant farmer, with agricultural and ancillary buildings sometimes converted for domestic use.

Medieval village houses: the architectural evidence

It is from the latter part of the 13th century that upstanding examples of the area's earliest houses survive, picking up the sequence of evidence provided by excavation and earthwork remains. Contrary to common perceptions, these buildings were not necessarily of imper-manent construction, as is testified by their ability to endure right up to the present day. Construction was predominantly of cruck form, with roofs and often walls carried on cruck blades, paired to form trusses, and fashioned from the curved trunks and limbs of the oak tree or sometimes elm. Vestigial evidence for cruck construction was found at Christon, for example, but a far more significant example stands in the same valley, on the opposite side of the Lox-Yeo river. In the hillside hamlet of Barton, West End Farmhouse is an extraordinary Mendip survival, the earliest known cruck house in Somerset (Fig 6.53). Dated by dendrochronology to 1278–9 (Miles and Worthington 1999, 111), it represents the remains of an open hall, with smoke-blackened timbers from an open fire and tapering cruck blades rising from about a metre above the ground to just below the saddle-type apex (Fig 6.54). The house was probably built as a grange farm for the Barton estate owners, the Dean and Chapter of Wells (Penoyre 2005, 47).

The 13th-century survival at West End Farmhouse can be considered exceptional in a regional context and even more so in Mendip. However, it has become evident that numerous houses whose appearance is relatively modern do in fact have earlier medieval structures at their core, or occupy similar footprints to their medieval predecessors. The often deceptive external appearance of houses is highlighted by West End Farmhouse, which the statutory list entry describes as having a 'modern appearance', although evidently this masks a 13th-century structure. Evidence from the two principal village house surveys, and from other houses visited by invitation, presents a more detailed picture, offering clues about continuity in the occupation of farmhouse sites and the likely characteristics of medieval houses. Surprisingly few medieval roofs were encountered, and likely survivals are often fragmentary and display plain carpentry that hinders dating on stylistic grounds. Clues to medieval origins may also come from solitary features whose style is characteristic of the period, or from thick walls of 0.7 to 0.8m (28 to 32in) that can also indicate a possible medieval date. Similar insights are offered by stratigraphy evident in the layers of building fabric, with wall joints and features characteristic of the 16th century, for example, implying earlier hidden phases. At High Hall, Compton Martin, complex evidence implies a pre-16th-century

phase in what presents as a row of 19th-century cottages, with traces of medieval construction.

Assigning status and function to these houses is not straightforward. Many of the houses investigated were used as farmhouses right into the 20th century, with village farms based on relatively modest landholdings. Similar findings resulted from a previous study of vernacular buildings on the North Somerset Levels (Rippon 2006, 154–89). The majority can be described as peasant farmhouses, including those of assured tenants on the estate of the bishops of Wells at Westbury-sub-Mendip. These old auster farms were ancient enclosed tenements, with inherited customs, rights and responsibilities that descended through generations of the same family. Some houses, however, may have stood at a slightly higher social level, and distinctions can be difficult to draw between the medieval farmhouses of the wealthier peasant farmers and smaller hall houses at the centres of minor estates.

Evidence from the project has added to a growing understanding of the characteristics of the medieval peasant farmhouse in North Somerset, revealing comparatively modest houses with low roofs and eaves, wide plans

and simple two-room layouts with opposed entries or a cross-passage. At Westbury-sub-Mendip, Hollow House retains this basic plan and form, despite the addition of a porch, upper floor and possible former stable in line to one end (Figs 6.55 and 6.56). The original part of the house has a width of 6m and a length of 13m, excluding later additions; the dimensions are comparable with abandoned house remains examined through earthwork survey. The roof structure is modern, but the irregular thick walls and plan proportions point to a medieval date, which is corroborated by a wooden-framed doorway with four-centred arched head, which is characteristic of the 15th century (Fig 6.57). This doorway connects the two rooms: a hall/kitchen to the south and chamber or parlour to the north. Both rooms were probably open internally to the roof apex, although the absence of the historic roof timbers makes this impossible to clarify, and both have inserted fireplaces and ceilings of likely 16th- or early 17th-century date.

Other houses in the village share some of these characteristic features, as well as massive fireplace bressummers spanning the entire width of the house, suggesting possible smoke hoods later reduced to form fireplaces.

Fig 6.53
West End Farmhouse, Barton, Winscombe. The exterior hides a late 13th-century cruck-built house, the oldest of its type yet identified in Somerset. (DP163847)

Fig 6.54
The cruck truss at West End Farmhouse, Barton, Winscombe, dated by dendrochronology to the years 1278–9. (DP163844)

Fig 6.55
Hollow House, Westbury-
sub-Mendip: plan of the
ground floor, showing the
original footprint of the
medieval two-unit house.
The opposed entries
probably opened directly
into the main room or hall,
which would have been open
to the roof. The slightly
smaller bay to the right
was probably a parlour or
service room, originally
unheated, with a
15th-century doorframe
(A). Both bays were sealed
and fireplaces were inserted
in two phases during the
16th and 17th centuries.

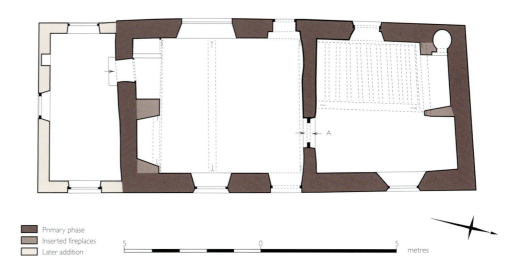

■ Primary phase
■ Inserted fireplaces
□ Later addition

5   0   5
                          metres

However, these houses lack specific medieval details, which makes a date attribution highly tentative, while others may reflect 16th-century building or rebuilding on a medieval footprint. Examples include the Old Red Lion on Free Hill (Fig 6.58), Box Bush Villa on Duck Lane (Fig 6.59) and Crow Lane Farm, where a medieval origin is unproven, but fabric of the 16th century may be inserted within the walls of an earlier house. Box Bush Villa retains a framed ceiling and fireplace that may have been inserted into an earlier house in the

Fig 6.56
Hollow House, Westbury-
sub-Mendip. It originated
as a medieval two-unit
farmhouse with opposed
entries, and is now fronted
by a porch. The left-hand
bay is an addition, possibly
originally a stable or byre.
(DP068893)

16th century. At Crow Lane, for example, the former farmhouse dimensions give the recognisable footprint of 6m by 14m: this is just one of numerous potential medieval houses with vestigial surviving fabric.

By the early 1520s, Westbury-sub-Mendip had around 38 tenements, including cottages and some freehold farmsteads (SHS DD/CC/31559), and their remnants and footprints survive in several of the village houses. One example is a house called West End, on the Stoke Road, which retains irregular stone-rubble walls, around 0.8m thick, a two-room plan with opposed entries and a massive full-width bressummer in the hall. The plan dimensions of approximately 5.4m by 12.1m are also consistent with medieval examples, but in this case the visible fabric of the house may be largely of the 16th century. The adjoining property, West End Cottage, represents an in-line addition, which may have originated as a stable, barn or byre.

Documentary evidence for this category of two-unit house has been identified in a 16th-century survey of the customary tenants

*Fig 6.57 (left)
Hollow House, Westbury-sub-Mendip: medieval doorframe, probably of the 15th century, with chamfered, four-centred arched head, now truncated where the jambs meet the heads. (DP069282)*

*Fig 6.58 (below)
The Old Red Lion, Free Hill, Westbury-sub-Mendip, viewed from the rear. The two-unit farmhouse is of modest scale and proportions, with very low eaves and a short but wide footprint. In this case the two bays are of contrasting phases: that to the left of the central chimney is the earlier, probably dating from the late 15th or early 16th century. The roof was originally covered with reed thatch. (DP068880)*

Fig 6.59
Box Bush Villa, Duck Lane,
Westbury-sub-Mendip.
The substantial fireplace
and framed ceiling were
probably added to an earlier
house, possibly in the late
16th century.
(DP068914)

of the Manor of Wookey (DHC 96M, 96 add M, box 4/5). This document, dating from 1557, has been interpreted as describing over 20 examples, many comprising a hall, chamber and stable arranged in line, with the hall used for cooking (Hasler and Luker 1997, 233–45). Although the survey dates from the post-medieval period, the form of houses described almost certainly reflects a direct continuity of form with the customary farmhouses of the medieval period in Mendip. The most basic form of house mentioned in the survey comprised a single room, open to the roof. Later additions and alterations make these examples difficult to identify among the surviving building stock, although the earliest surviving phase of the Old Red Lion at Westbury-sub-Mendip may be an example (*see* Fig 7.27).

Until very recently, the two-unit house had been considered uncommon in Somerset (Somerset Vernacular Building Research Group 2008; Penoyre 2005). However, it is clear from the Mendip evidence that medieval houses of this plan type, with low eaves and roof, were once commonplace. The medieval three-room house is arguably more easily identified among surviving houses that were altered and extended during ensuing centuries. However, likely examples of the three-unit plan among the houses investigated in Mendip are notably fewer in number than potential two-unit candidates. The three-unit house is represented in the 1557 survey of Wookey, but accounts for less than a third of the buildings listed in the survey.

The identification from vestigial evidence of the two-unit class of peasant farmhouse marks a significant shift in understanding, one that is also becoming apparent elsewhere in the country (eg De Boise 2010). Similarly, the identification of known and putative medieval houses possessing wide plans and squat roofs concurs with emerging thinking on the form of early houses at or before the threshold of the surviving building stock, where precursors are thought to have been built around very low but wide cruck trusses (Alcock and Miles 2012, 155). The Mendip evidence also presents examples where, despite the absence of medieval roof structures, the roofs that replaced them are also squat and wide, allowing for only a low half-storey upstairs, as at Hollow House.

In Mendip the search for longhouses – in which livestock and humans occupied accommodation accessed through a shared entry and set beneath a single roof – has been less fruitful. Of the few candidates put forward during the last fifty years, one has been discounted at Orchard Cottage, Winscombe (Somerset Vernacular Building Research Group 2012), while at Sherborne Farm, near Litton, the evidence is fascinating but ambiguous. Here, a two-room range stands on sloping ground, with the characteristic long end positioned downhill of suggested opposed entries and a parlour (Fig 6.60). Such long bays, or units, are thought to be a key feature of the longhouse, being used to house livestock, but at Sherborne Farm the explanation may be that they were more a conventional room, perhaps a hall or kitchen with fireplace. The contours of the site may account for the changing floor levels, which are seen widely in Mendip, simply as a reflection of topography.

The original walls and roof coverings of these very early village houses are long gone or heavily concealed within the fabric of houses still in use. In Westbury-sub-Mendip all the houses investigated are built of local stone rubble, but the irregular nature of these early rubble walls, which incorporate straight joints and numerous patches, indicates that they were repaired and even rebuilt over the centuries. West End Farm, Barton, has clay-bonded rubble walls, a type identified in other houses in the Somerset Levels (Penoyre and Penoyre 1999; Rippon 2006). Later houses in Mendip were limewashed, and it is likely that this method of protecting walls from attrition by rain and wind was also used for medieval house walls. No certain evidence of timber-framed walls was found in the rural buildings investigated, although this method of construction is immediately evident in surviving urban medieval buildings in Axbridge. In the rural examples a marked absence of dressed-stone detailing for window and door openings suggests that timber was the principal means available for the builders of most peasant farmhouses.

Wooden-framed windows were seen at a number of houses, although ascribing dates to these features is difficult, as the form continues into the late 16th century and beyond. However,

Fig 6.60
Sherborne Farm, Sherborne, Litton, viewed from the front, with the medieval range to the right.
(Barry Jones)

at Sherborne Farm, Litton, a small two-light wooden window frame with no rebate for glazing is probably medieval. Similarly, framed and pegged timber doorways, with four-centred arched heads, typically medieval in detail and form, were also identified in a number of houses, including Sherborne Farm and Walcombe Cottage, Walcombe.

Few of the houses sampled in Westbury-sub-Mendip appear to retain medieval roof timbers, which otherwise would clarify carpentry techniques and structural forms. However, at Sherborne Farm the surviving roof timbers are plain, nearly squared, with straight principal rafters, a diamond-set ridge piece and butt purlins, chamfered and stopped. In other villages, medieval roof trusses are visible only at the apex, with the rest concealed by later fabric or removed completely. In two of these examples a distinctive apex joint was seen, including at Church Cottage, Hinton Blewett, and in a 'fossilised' truss encapsulated in a partition at 2 High Street, East Harptree. These apex joints have been categorised as the 'Mendip Type' (Type M), with five examples identified by the mid-1990s by the Somerset Vernacular Buildings Research Group (Penoyre 1998). Roofs were probably covered by water reed or wheat straw thatch (Williams 1991, 133), although evidence from Moreton indicates that some more prestigious 13th- to early 14th-century buildings were roofed with stone tiles and supported a glazed ridge crest (Rahtz and Greenwood 1977, 101).

The majority of the medieval village houses were probably open internally to the roof apex, with only part of the house lofted or, in rare cases, floored over a single room to give an upper chamber. The specific evidence associated with these early ceilings is scarce and difficult to identify, and even in houses where associated fabric may have survived it is likely to be hidden by plaster surfaces and later alterations. Sometimes thick, steep-sided transverse beams, perhaps with hollow chamfers, and closely spaced, square-section timber joists can be seen as evidence of such ceilings, as is present in the southern bay of the Old Red Lion in Westbury-sub-Mendip (Fig 6.61).

The most impressive evidence of medieval ceilings in the Mendip area, as elsewhere,

Fig 6.61
The Old Red Lion, Free Hill, Westbury-sub-Mendip: interior, with bressummer extending the full width of the house, possibly to front a smoke bay, but reduced by a smaller inserted hearth. The squared plain joists, closely spaced, are also characteristic of the early floors built from new or inserted into farmhouses in the late 15th and 16th centuries. (DP068871)

comes from the framed ceilings that begin to appear in farmhouses in the late 15th and early 16th centuries, perhaps influenced by their adoption in manor houses, as found at Moat Farm, Compton Martin. These comprise a series of crossing beams forming a framed structure of great strength and considerable decorative quality. They consumed large amounts of timber, involved sophisticated carpentry and were expensive to construct, and therefore reflect the appreciable attainment of wealth by the builder. At Sherborne Farm, Litton, in the parlour of the north range, a fine medieval framed ceiling was inserted into an earlier bay, probably in the very late 15th or early 16th century (Fig 6.62). Another example at Walcombe Cottage, Walcombe, has smaller beams, but these are highly decorated with rich mouldings. Such framed ceilings, with varying details, are a defining feature of medieval and 16th-century houses in the area, whether inserted into formerly open medieval houses as at Sherborne Farm or built as part of a two-storey arrangement from the start. Local examples dated by dendrochronology include two ceilings in houses on Thomas Street in Wells, one at no. 28, dated to 1485, and the

other at no. 26, with a date range of 1494–1526, in a house with a roof dated to 1511 (McDermott 2006, 92). However, the framed ceiling is long-lived and is found in numerous houses where the details and form are evidently of the late 16th or early 17th century.

This sum of evidence seen during the investigation of rural houses in Mendip indicates that many of the two-cell buildings identified within the nucleated settlements represent the vestiges of medieval structures. It also indicates that at the end of the medieval period the building stock of Mendip, at least in part, comprised two-cell, single-storey houses and not the three-unit houses traditionally associated with this period and region. Evidence from across Mendip demonstrates that during the latter part of the 15th and early 16th centuries open houses were being ceiled in, while at Walcombe there is evidence suggesting that around the same time two-storey dwelling houses were being constructed. Documentary evidence from Wookey shows that these two-unit houses remained the dominant type in the second half of the 16th century, and that many were still open to the roof in the medieval manner.

Fig 6.62
Sherborne Farm, Sherborne, Litton: a framed ceiling of four-compartments inserted into an earlier house, possibly in the late 15th or early 16th century. (Barry Jones)

Medieval agriculture and land use

The common fields

In the medieval period Mendip was characterised by a complex mixture of pasture and arable fields, deer parks, meadow, woodland and waste. This varied landscape, combined with its diverse settlement pattern, meant that in most parishes there could never have been a fully developed common field system comparable with the much-studied Midland System. However, by the 12th century the main nucleated village in each parish would have been associated with open-field arable, comprising at least two common fields, which usually coexisted with extensive areas of upland and lowland grazing, common meadowland, wood pasture and parcels of enclosed land. Each peasant householder within the settlement had their own strips distributed over the open fields, and retained certain defined rights and responsibilities over the use of the common ground.

The open fields of the medieval period were generally located close to the settlement, and comprised bundles of strips, called furlongs, within which the same crop would normally be grown in any one year. Furlongs were grouped into blocks to create fields, the basic unit for fallowing, with a single field remaining unsown each year in a rotational system. In an area such as Mendip the abundance of upland and lowland pasture reduced the pressure for year-long fallow, although the nutritional benefits to the soil from grazing animals on the common fields were significant (Aston 1988, 97). Soil fertility would have been improved by spreading manure from yards and animal houses (along with domestic rubbish) over the strips and furlongs, as well as by folding sheep flocks on the open fields after cropping.

In Northamptonshire, D Hall has shown that under the Midland System most villages had at least 80 per cent and some as much as 90 per cent under the plough (1995, 3). The figures for Mendip are more difficult to calculate, as the extent of pasture, particularly common grazing on the upland and lowland wastes, often went unrecorded. At Hutton an estate survey of the early 14th century recorded the demesne as comprising 355 acres (144ha) of arable dispersed across the open fields, suggesting around 70 per cent of the lord's land, exclusive of the common waste, was under the plough. In 1428 the canons of St Augustine's Abbey, Bristol, still held 70 per cent of their demesne land in East Harptree under arable cultivation (Beachcroft and Sabin 1938, 38). The main crops cultivated were wheat for baking and barley for brewing, with oats and black peas grown as fodder (the latter was also valued for its beneficial effect on the following crop). Secondary crops could include apples for cider making, reeds for thatching and flax for the production of linen (Coward 1978, 36–41 and 46–7).

Estate surveys from the manors of Sandford and Cheddar Hanhams reveal that by the early years of the 16th century arable represented only around 30 per cent of a tenant's recorded holding, with the remainder largely held as meadow and pasture (IHR Seymour papers vol 12, fols 57–64 and 67–71). This would indicate a shift away from intensive arable farming towards a more livestock-based economy by the end of the medieval period. These surveys also indicate that arable land in some parishes could be spread over a large number of fields. For example, at Sandford a whole range of fields, furlongs and closes are recorded as under cultivation, including common arable within Buttons Field and North Field. Tenants in the manor of Cheddar Hanhams predominantly held their arable in East Field and West Field, although smaller areas of subdivided arable and individual crofts and closes were also periodically under the plough.

The complex, irregular pattern of fields may in part be a result of the process of piecemeal enclosure and subdivision, but could also be attributed to earlier arable expansion, when areas were added and brought into cultivation from former woodland and waste. The system of taking in parts of the common waste for arable crops is well known in the South-West (eg Riley and Wilson-North 2001, 116, 126; Riley 2006, 110–11). Such enclosures can sometimes be reflected in close or furlong names: for example, 'le Doneacre' (Downacre) recorded at Hutton, 'Heath field' at Draycott and 'the old downe field' at Rowberrow (Coward 1978, 41; SHS T/PH/bmd/1 and D/D/Rg/85). Fieldwork has identified an area of strip lynchets above Bleadon's former West Field which had reverted to common grazing by the mid-17th century, and possibly represents an episode of earlier arable expansion. This flexibility to expand the area in arable cultivation may have prevented a fully developed common field system from developing in many Mendip parishes.

Individual farmsteads were generally associated with a series of crofts, closes and paddocks located adjacent to the holding. In Rodney Stoke the settlement above New Road is surrounded by traces of its former field system, lying at an altitude of around 245m (Fig 6.63). These remains comprise a series of closes defined by earthen banks and containing the vestiges of cultivation ridges, displaying an interlocking pattern of furlongs (G Brown 2008, 20–5). The form of these closes and paddocks not only demonstrates that they were created in a piecemeal fashion from waste, but also indicates the holding worked a classic

medieval infield and outfield system. The south-facing slopes closest to the settlement were ploughed to provide the main cereal crops for the holding. Fields were later added to the north, which also display evidence for cultivation, possibly indicating an episode of arable expansion. The outfield was defined by a ditch and bank and may have been periodically cropped after it was manured by livestock.

Strip lynchets

Evidence for open-field agriculture is perhaps most clearly visible in areas where individual strips survive as lynchets – long narrow terraces spread across the hillside. Lynchets were generally created through the action of the plough and are indicative of episodes of arable cultivation. They tend to be best

Fig 6.63
Rodney Stoke: earthwork plan of settlement and surrounding fields.

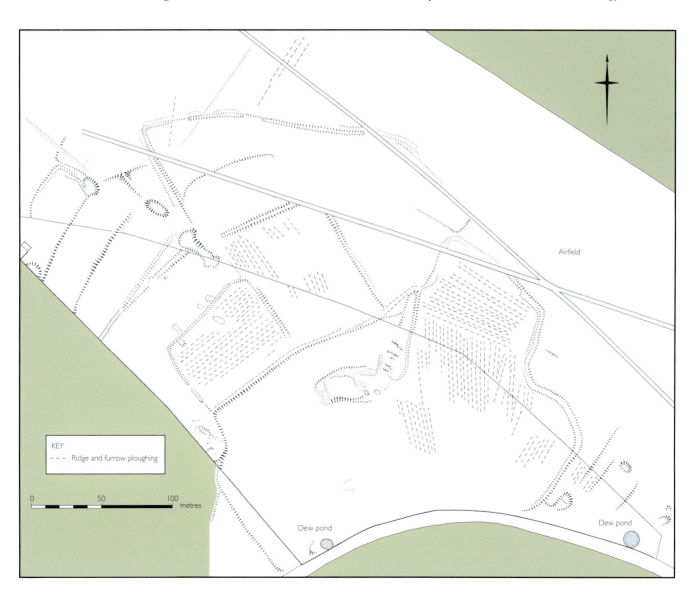

KEY
- - - Ridge and furrow ploughing

0   50   100
metres

Airfield

Dew pond

Dew pond

Fig 6.64
Christon: strip fields.
(Elaine Jamieson)

preserved on the higher slopes, particularly along the southern escarpment, in areas which experienced less intensive episodes of farming. Some strips follow the contour of the hillside, creating impressive terraces standing over 2m high, with others running up and down the slope and surviving as slight scarps or low banks (Fig 6.64). A small excavation at Carscliffe Farm suggested that the lynchets in this upland area were probably created sometime in the 11th century and continued in use for around 300 years, before reverting to pasture (SHER 35963).

The diversity and complexity witnessed in some of Mendip's medieval field systems is probably the result of strips being fitted into varied topography. Existing strips could be modified and extended, such as those recorded at Ramspits, where separate blocks were combined to form strips up to 290m long (Pattison 1991, 102). Where detailed examination of fields has been undertaken, a degree of regularity has been identified which would suggest strips could be carefully laid out. At Walcombe, for example, the strips immediately surrounding the settlement have straight and relatively parallel sides and comprise two main groups: those 15m in width (three perches) and those 20m in width (four perches). The former were clustered together, which may suggest they formed a discrete block created in a single episode. The consistency in strip width would indicate that equality in size was important to the individuals or community who laid them out. This may be particularly true of fields closest to the settlement, where soil was generally more fertile and strips were more convenient to work.

A sinuous network of trackways connected the settlements to the open fields and the areas of common grazing land beyond. Some were evidently established before, or in conjunction with, the laying out of the open fields, with parcels of strips often conforming to their course. Boundaries could also take the form of broad headlands or balks between the furlongs (some around 10m wide) which allowed access to the cultivated land and enabled the use of large plough teams. It is also clear that these boundaries could be laid out prior to the formation of the strips and used in their setting out. This is particularly evident in the western half of Stoberry Park where the open fields are divided by two roughly east–west aligned balks, forming three separate blocks (Fig 6.65). The strips within each block were set out in relation to the southern boundary of their land parcel, which resulted in the splaying of strips as these boundaries curved, and left the strips within each block on a slightly different alignment. This would indicate that each block was laid out separately, possibly representing individual furlongs, and may be indicative of sequential development.

The upland commons

Beyond the open-field arable lay areas of common pasture where livestock could be grazed when not folded on the fallow. The upland and lowland wastes of Mendip provided abundant common grazing which was intensively exploited during the medieval period. All the settlements within the bounds of the forest had common rights over the upland pasture, and special grazing rights could also be granted in conjunction with endowments of land to monastic houses. An endowment of half a hide of waste upon Mendip, for example, was granted to the Benedictine priory of Goldcliff, Monmouthshire, which was later to form the source of a dispute between George Bredyman and Sir George Speake, the then lord of the manor of Compton Martin, which illustrates how rights of common pasture could be

Fig 6.65
Stoberry Park: earthwork plan of strip fields.

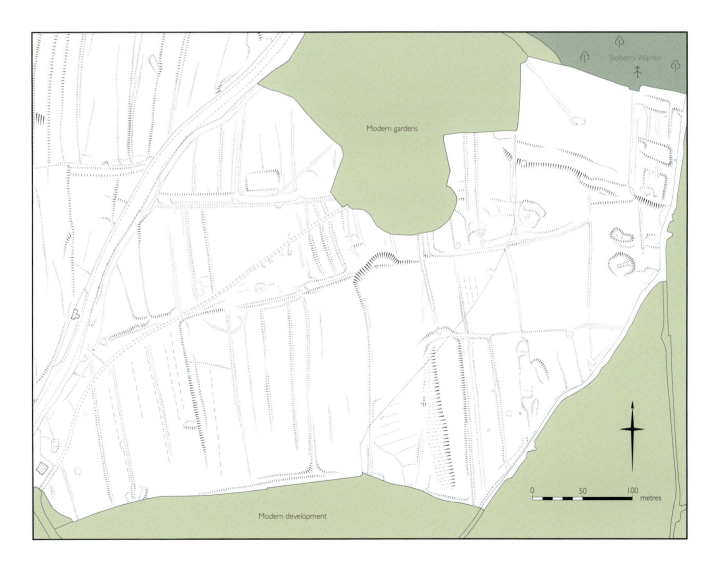

jealously guarded (Collinson 1791, 131; SHS DD/SPY/60/1).

The upland landscape of Mendip was largely one of expansive open heath, criss-crossed by a network of tracks and drove-ways, and pitted with the scars of mineral extraction. Although there is little direct archaeological evidence for medieval mining on the upland commons, documentary sources indicate that mineral extraction was probably being carried out by the Bishop of Bath from at least the 12th century. As well as mining on his own manors, the bishop was also granted a licence by the king in 1235 to begin exploration for metal-bearing ore at Hydon, and to use timber from 40 acres (16ha) of woodland at Cheddar in the production of iron. The grant would suggest the right of the king to control all mining operations within the royal forest. Lead mines were most highly valued for their potential to produce silver, and extreme measures were sometimes undertaken to safeguard the precious argentiferous ore. For example, in the early part of the 14th century

the bailiffs at the bishop's mine near Priddy insisted on the ore being transported to Wookey for processing, in an attempt to prevent the silver content being stolen by unscrupulous employees. A furnace was built at the bishop's palace to allow smelting to be carried out under supervision until trustworthy workmen could be found (Gough 1967, 49–56).

During the summer months large flocks of sheep, kept primarily for their fleece, roamed freely over the open commons. There are numerous documentary references to sheep-cotes, primarily connected with monastic houses, though field evidence for these structures is yet to be forthcoming. On Bruern Abbey's estate at Priddy a sheepcote was documented in 1225, and on the estate of Hinton Charterhouse at Green Ore a sheepcote is depicted on a map of around 1700 (Chadwyck Healey 1897, 39; SHS DD/WG C924). The lasting features, however, tend to be the permanent enclosures which were used to separate different types of sheep, to contain sheep or for facilitating activities such as milking and lambing. Rectilinear enclosures have been recorded from aerial photographs at Rowberrow Warren, Charterhouse-on-Mendip, Piney Sleight and Green Ore. A rectangular earthwork enclosure at Charterhouse clearly overlies the Roman occupation remains, and may also represent a medieval stock enclosure (Fradley 2009, 61).

Enclosures have also been identified on the higher ground towards the common edge. For example, at Andrews Green, above Ebbor Gorge, a trapezoidal sheep enclosure lies close to the medieval settlements of Hope and Dursden. The enclosure is almost 120m in length and is defined by a combination of grass-covered banks and drystone walls (Fig 6.66). The enclosure has entrances at its north-west and south-east corners, and the remains of a sheep-creep are still visible in the wall along its southern side. The enclosure was clearly reused in the post-medieval period, when a small structure was incorporated into its north-western corner and a cottage built in its interior. Also within the enclosure are the earthwork remains of a much smaller building, possibly an earlier shepherd's hut, and a dew pond, a necessity when caring for large numbers of livestock on the limestone escarpment (G Brown 2008, 12–13, 29).

On the open waste the landholdings of individual estates were defined by a series

Fig 6.66
Andrews Green: earthwork plan of trapezoidal sheep enclosure.

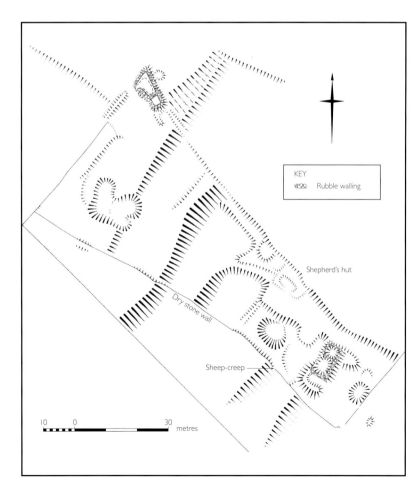

KEY
Rubble walling

Shepherd's hut
Dry stone wall
Sheep-creep

10 0 30 metres

of boundary markers, which could include artificial features such as barrows, boundary stones or mining rakes. The upland commons were also punctuated by wayside crosses, used to define estate boundaries, to mark routeways and possibly to signify religious places. These crosses would have served to reinforce the Christian faith to those who passed them by. The former location of some of these crosses is marked on 16th- and 17th-century maps, though there is little to indicate their presence today. Paine's Cross, in Ubley, was depicted as an upstanding feature on a map of 1809, but was evidently dismantled soon after (SHS MAP/DD/WG/MAP7). At East Harptree the head of a sculptured cross was uncovered in the 19th century during the demolition of a cottage near Proud Cross. The carved stonework, depicting the crucifixion, dates from the late 12th or early 13th century and may represent the vestiges of one such wayside cross (Fig 6.67).

Fig 6.67
East Harptree: head of a late 12th- or early 13th-century sculptured cross depicting the crucifixion, found near Proud Cross.
(© Somerset County Council Museums Service)

7

The post-medieval period

The post-medieval period can be characterised as an age of unprecedented social, cultural and economic change. In the early years of the 16th century the Mendip Hills would have appeared familiar to its former medieval inhabitants, but by 1900 the landscape was changing beyond all recognition. The redistribution of landholdings in the beginning of the period, combined with wider social and cultural influences, provided some with the wealth and incentive to create new and often extravagant forms of elite residence. This percolated down the social scale, with lesser lords and the farming gentry adapting and improving their homes in the desire for increased comfort and sophistication. In contrast, unparalleled demographic change resulted in the erosion of living standards for those reliant on wages, which resulted in increasing social stratification.

To sustain the growing urban and rural population of England, new agricultural practices were adopted and large areas of open farmland and waste were enclosed and brought into arable cultivation. These fundamental developments, largely carried out over the course of the 17th and 18th centuries, resulted in a profound transformation of the rural landscape.

The post-medieval landscape (1540–1900)

The beginning of the post-medieval period is marked by the Reformation and the dissolution of the monasteries, which saw the estates of monastic institutions broken up and redistributed among the ruling elite (Fig 7.1). The buildings of these monastic centres were either

Fig 7.1
Manor Farm, Charterhouse. The dissolution of the monasteries saw Charterhouse Hydon, as the farm was previously known, pass into secular hands, with an episode of rebuilding following soon after.
(DP044400)

torn down or adapted to suit the needs of their new secular owners. This mirrors a wider episode of rebuilding that saw many medieval structures either completely swept away or modified and adapted to suit the changing requirements of post-medieval life. The stronghold of Richmont Castle, for example, was finally abandoned, the buildings and outer walls were dismantled and the stone was reused elsewhere. The Reformation, and the liturgical changes it brought, also had an influence on the fabric of the church, with images of saints defaced or destroyed, wall paintings white-washed and internal fittings repositioned.

During the 17th century the Civil Wars (1642–51) brought a period of social and political unrest. There was a degree of support in the area for the Parliamentarians who, when gathering on a hill near Chewton Mendip in August 1642, were joined by many villagers 'bringing pitchforks, dungpeeks, and such-like weapons' (BL E.112[33]). From there a force of 6,000 men with two cannons marched towards Wells. The next day they fired their cannons against the bishop's palace, where the main body of the Royalist force was ensconced, and, after a brief encounter, the Royalists withdrew. The Parliamentarians entered Wells and broke the cathedral's stained-glass windows and attacked the palace, destroying symbols of Catholicism. Over the following two years there was further damage to the ecclesiastical buildings to such an extent that it was still noticeable twenty years later (Wroughton 1999, 16 and 252–4). The advent of puritan austerity, and the introduction of church rates and poor relief, undermined the need for community fundraising feasts and provision for the poor. This saw many church houses fall into decline or adapted for other uses. At Hinton Blewett the church house was adapted to serve as a dwelling by the 17th century, and the church house at East Harptree was converted to a public house.

The century after the Civil Wars saw the Mendip landscape gradually transformed into an area largely composed of enclosed fields, open wastes and large enclosed rabbit warrens. These fundamental changes represent a period of wider agricultural improvement undertaken in response to an increasing demand for foodstuffs, largely driven by demographic change and a desire for increased profits. The enclosure of the common fields led to the amalgamation or engrossment of more marginal holdings, with some smaller hamlets reduced to no more than a single farm. The settlements and houses of Mendip also experienced considerable change, as the more successful members of the farming classes, influenced by new fashions and ideas of comfort and convenience, invested in improvements to their homes.

The later 18th century saw a step change in the scale and nature of landscape change, with piecemeal private enclosures giving way to extensive systematic enclosure of the common wastes by parliamentary Act. By this means large areas of former sheep walks were divided and enclosed, which created distinctive new field systems, dominated by large rectilinear enclosures. Inflationary rises during the French Revolutionary and Napoleonic Wars (1793–1815) led to these new parcels of land being continuously exploited for grain production. The Wars also saw volunteer militia and independent companies being raised throughout the country 'in case any of those wretched and detestable slaves called Frenchmen … should ever attempt to invade the venerated and beloved shores of this land of real liberty' (Knight 1902, 421).

The adoption of improvement farming techniques in the period after the Napoleonic Wars saw a further episode of landscape reorganisation, as more areas of the upland were enclosed, plantations were established and holdings were consolidated to form larger tenanted farms. Many new farm complexes were created in response to agricultural developments which encouraged improved efficiency in farmstead layout. These new improvement farms were planned around a central yard and were often the catalyst for the destruction of many of the older agricultural buildings. New cottages were built and existing buildings subdivided to form smaller domestic units, which housed the rural workforce of industries such as cloth manufacturing and mineral extraction.

Mendip manor houses in the 16th and 17th centuries

The profound change, religious upheaval and persecutions of the middle of the 16th century established the basis from which ensued the relative stability and opportunity of the Elizabethan period. The redistribution of monastic estates after the Reformation provided wealth and incentive, while changing social and cultural influences brought experimentation and creativity in the design of new and often extravagant forms in the great house. The same influences affected the thinking of many lesser manorial lords, who sought the prestige and social standing conferred by building in new and substantial ways. In Somerset the wave of Elizabethan great-house building was particularly strong: numerous courtier and gentry houses were built from the 1560s onwards, as epitomised by great houses such as Montacute House, built for a successful lawyer, Sir Edward Phelips, in the 1590s (Summerson 1977, 76).

On Mendip the assimilation of medieval mansions and their adaptation into something new was far closer to the norm than was the construction of a new house entirely from scratch. In the earlier part of the 16th century medieval, traditional forms continued to dominate, particularly in plan terms, with the hierarchical focus on the hall entered through the cross-passage, and the separation of best chambers and services at opposing ends of the house. However, other changes were

apparent. The superior manor houses adopted the enclosed fireplace and ceiled hall, and provided complex suites of rooms for the lord, including parlours and subsidiary chambers. Some of these elements were present in the design of Moat Farm in the 15th century (*see* Chapter 6), but others were not. The open form of the hall in particular had been superseded by the end of the 16th century by a fully floored arrangement with an inserted hall ceiling and chamber above. At Hutton Court, in the northwest of the region, the grand medieval manor house was restyled and augmented by the addition of new ranges and stylish fenestration, which created a larger and more fashionable house, but one which remained fundamentally medieval in plan form.

In the Mendip Hills and the adjoining parishes there are no surviving great Elizabethan houses of a class that would rival the likes of Montacute House, Fairfield House or North Cadbury Court. However, the influences that brought these houses to their accomplished Elizabethan forms were present in Mendip and did bring about new building in many of the manors (Fig 7.2). At Banwell, for example, Bishop Thomas Godwin (1584–90)

Fig 7.2
Location map showing the manor houses mentioned in the text.

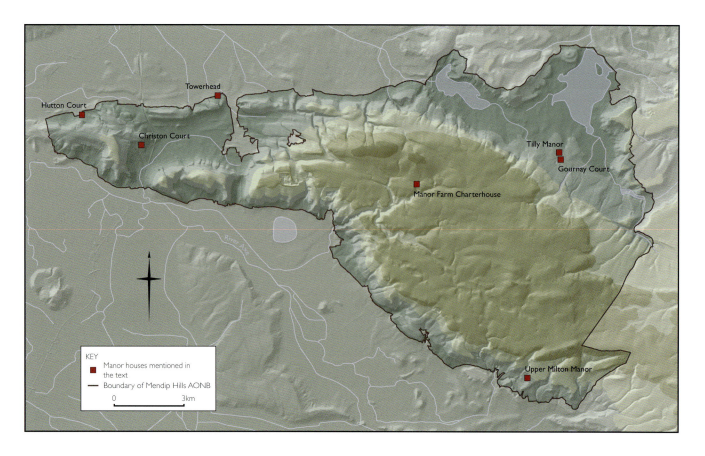

built a new mansion, not to replace the medieval palace of the bishops of Bath and Wells, but on a new site beyond the eastern fringes of the town. This mansion, known at various times as Towerhead or Ockingham House, was destroyed in 1840 (Knight 1902, 405), but was described by Rutter as being in the contemporary [Elizabethan] style, with a porch bearing the motto 'Godwyn – wyn God wyn all' (Rutter 1829, 135).

One of the region's most important Elizabethan houses remains standing, though much reduced, at Manor Farm, Charterhouse-on-Mendip. After the dissolution, the Carthusian estate of Witham Charterhouse was acquired by the Maye family. Letters patent issued by Henry VIII on 12 September 1554 granted 'the manor or grange of Hydon lying within the parishes of Witham Frarye Blagden and Predye' to Robert Maye (BRO 5139/339; *see also* Gough 1928, 94, fn 1). By 1577 it was the seat of John Maye Esquire, Robert's descendant and Sheriff of Somerset (BRO 5535/13). Considering John Maye's position in the county, and documents that identify Charterhouse Hydon as his chief residence, the mansion must have been suitably grand; over a century later it was still referred to as 'the great house at Charterhouse' (SHS DD/GB 114).

The surviving fabric of the Mayes' 'great house' is primarily of post-dissolution date, although it incorporates reused medieval timbers and may include walls from this earlier period. Stylistic evidence dates the principal phase and its distinctive ashlar south facade to the later part of the 16th century (*see* Fig 7.1), while a number of high-status characteristics set it apart from other houses on Mendip. The facade, orientated towards the combe leading from Cheddar, is exceptional in its use of large ashlar blocks, as is the extensive use of mason's marks, which testifies to an elite and well-organised workshop (Fig 7.3). Additional stylistic evidence supports a late 16th-century date, especially the very thick mullioned and transomed windows with ovolo mouldings, a parallel for which can be found in North Cadbury Court, Somerset, in a range built between 1589 and 1593 (Penoyre 2005, plate 10). Similarly, a highly distinctive twisted finial on a gable at Manor Farm (Fig 7.4) is comparable to finials at the impressive Elizabethan range of Barrington Court (Penoyre 2005, 116).

The manorial complex was described in *c* 1671 as a 'ffayer stone house, two gardens, a

Fig 7.3
Manor Farmhouse, Charterhouse: detail of mason's marks, indicative of the use of a well-ordered mason's workshop. (DP044396)

Fig 7.4
Manor Farm, Charterhouse: late 16th-century twisted finial on gable of the south facade. (DP044415)

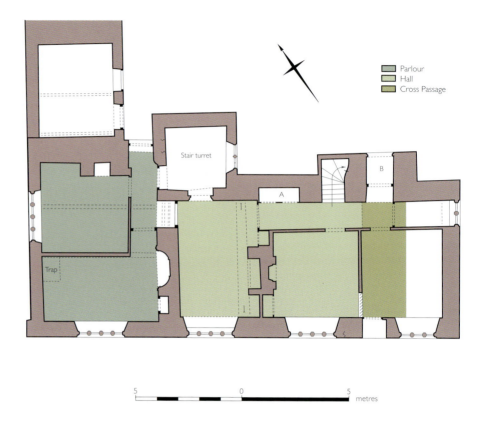

Fig 7.5
Manor Farm, Charterhouse:
plan showing areas of
former parlour, hall and
cross-passage. A: lateral
chimney stack; B: later
porch and stair.

Parlour
Hall
Cross Passage

Stair turret

B

A

Trap

5   0   5
         metres

Fig 7.6
Manor Farm, Charterhouse:
late 16th-century fireplace
with an entablature resting
on fluted pilasters with a
diamond motif at the base.
It once carried two shields,
presumably each bearing the
Maye family coat of arms.
(DP044434)

courtyard with all convenient offices, a large barne, two stabells and all hings [things] fitting for a manner house' (SHS DD/GB 151). However, during the 18th century its status diminished to that of a leased farmhouse, and by the early 19th century the house was described by the Revd John Skinner as 'gone to decay' (BL Add MS 33653, fol 178). The house we see today forms only a part of the Maye mansion, which was truncated at least once in the middle of the 19th century, when a wing and porch were removed from its east end (Fig 7.5). What remain are the former hall with lateral chimney stack, the position of the cross-passage, to its east a rear stair turret and a substantial parlour wing with an impressive stone chimney piece (Fig 7.6).

Map evidence (Fig 7.7) shows something of the larger house, with this forward-projecting east wing, an arrangement that would have relieved the flat uniformity of the facade we see today (SHS DD/STL/3). The front wing could have contained a chapel, but alternative functions might include a parlour or kitchen. However, despite possessing high-status characteristics, in its surviving curtailed form the house at Manor Farm Charterhouse does not reflect the sophisticated or extensive forms and plan arrangements typical of the great houses of the Elizabethan period. Its plan is limited simply to the standard hall with passage and parlour found in many farmhouses, and it lacked the fully developed articulation of the

H-, E- or U-shaped plan, or the depth of the double-pile plan that was to emerge in the ensuing century.

At Upper Milton Manor, in the parish of St Cuthbert Out, the U-plan with front wings was chosen for the modification and enlargement of an existing house, probably in the mid-17th century (Fig 7.8). This work is attributed to Arthur Mattock, Receiver General for the Bishop of Bath and Wells (Reid 1979, 22), who, as an aspiring official, provides a likely candidate for the aggrandisement of a comparatively modest house. This restyling created a U-plan frontage with courtyard and central entrance facing onto the Old Bristol

Fig 7.7
Manor Farm, Charterhouse: detail of 1842 map showing east wing and porch, now missing.
(SHS DD/STL/3, reproduced with permission of Somerset Archive and Local Studies)

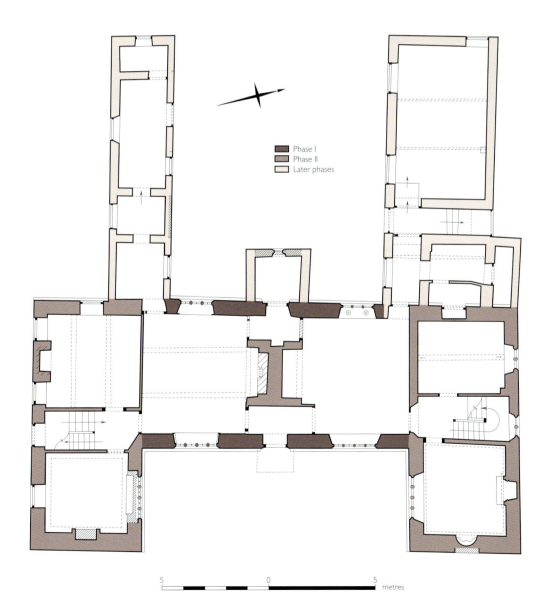

Phase I
Phase II
Later phases

Fig 7.8
Upper Milton Manor: plan. In the mid-17th century two symmetrical wings were built across the curtailed ends of the earlier central range.

Fig 7.9
Upper Milton Manor:
main front facing the
Old Bristol Road.
(DP164510)

Road, designed to impress travellers on the main route from Wells to Bristol (Fig 7.9).

The precise origins of Upper Milton Manor house are somewhat unclear. What we do know is that it initially consisted of a stone-rubble house of at least two units, with a major building phase in the early 17th century, as demonstrated by stone-mullioned windows that contrast very slightly with the windows of the wings. The earlier house probably had a cross-passage, with the entrance position as today, but, perhaps during Mattock's remodelling of the house, the cross-passage was blocked by the insertion of a massive internal chimney stack. This provided back-to-back fireplaces on the ground and first floors and created a 'lobby-entry' plan, a plan form not typical in Somerset and which generally occurs as a result of adaptation. However, the remodelling of the house conferred a degree of sophistication significantly above that achieved in the previous house. The gables facing the road were given stylish oval windows in sunken panels, typical of the second half of the century, and internally the plan was also more refined and reflective of the period, providing a series of separate rooms, with those on the upper floors reached by new staircases added in the centre of each wing (Fig 7.10).

The culmination of the work at Upper Milton Manor was the achievement of a harmonious and up-to-date U-plan house, despite compromises inflicted by the retention of earlier fabric. However, the same could not be said of all the mansions where remodelling took place. A number of manor houses in Mendip were

Fig 7.10
Upper Milton Manor: the
high-status stair in the south
wing with deeply moulded
closed string and pierced
flat vase balusters.
(DP044845)

Fig 7.11
Christon Court, Christon.
The Georgian facade masks
a range of the Vaughans'
17th-century mansion.
(DP043758)

altered significantly in the 17th century but would appear not to have achieved a coherent form. For example, at Christon Court, much of the manor house originates from the 17th century, despite the Georgian appearance of the facade (Fig 7.11). The manor was purchased by Francis Vaughan in the middle of the 17th century, and Francis went on to unite the manorial lands under his single ownership. Much of the present house is attributable to the Vaughans, although the irregular plan form and sequence of roof structures indicate that it is the product of various phases of addition during the 17th and early 18th centuries.

The scale of Christon Court during the 17th century surpassed considerably the size and extent of the present building, as is demonstrated by an inventory drawn up after the death of Lady Ann Smythe, who gained title from the Vaughan family (BRO AC/D/10/78). The inventory, dated 1699, mentions 12 well-fitted chambers, including a hall, porch, 2 parlours and a nursery, as well as 4 garret rooms. Francis Vaughan's house was said to be a fine, old mansion with a richly decorated porch, which bore a Vaughan coat of arms, now reset in the garden wall (Collinson 1791, 578; Rutter 1829, 163). Despite internal alterations in ensuing centuries, the house retains features of the Vaughans' mansion, including panelling

and an ornate fireplace with a carved oak mantelpiece, surmounted by the Vaughan arms and bearing the date 1672 (Fig 7.12).

In contrast, Gournay Court at West Harptree is a complete mansion of the 17th century, despite major renovations in the 1900s and the possibility that earlier fabric may be

Fig 7.12
Christon Court, Christon:
fireplace with carved oak
mantelpiece surmounted by
the Vaughan coat of arms.
(DP043763)

incorporated on the east side (Pevsner 1958, 334). Gournay Court is a substantial manor house built of red sandstone and of two and a half storeys with a basement beneath the main range. The facade is symmetrical with seven bays and a central two-storey entrance porch supporting an open gallery or loggia. All three floors have vertical cruciform windows, the exception being over the porch, where there is a three-light mullioned and transomed window. The facade is dominated by four large gables with ball finials, but somewhat incongruously in the centre a smaller ogee-shaped gable sits rather awkwardly, giving the impression of an afterthought.

The building of Gournay Court seems to have been begun by Francis Buckland, who married Elizabeth Warner of Fifield, Hants, whose combined initials F.B. and E.B. appear in the spandrels of a fireplace in the 'bay room' (Cox 1936, 43–4). Francis might well have been building in the early 17th century and was still alive in 1623. His son John married Elizabeth Phelips, daughter of Sir Robert Phelips of Montacute, and the arms of Buckland and Phelips are carved in the outer porch doorway (ibid, 43–4). The style of the building is arguably more indicative of a date in the mid-17th century, perhaps prior to the Civil Wars, and so with both inscribed initials and arms, John and Francis Buckland are each credited with roles in the building of the house (Reid 1979, 1).

Tilly Manor (Fig 7.13), also in West Harptree, is again attributed to the 17th century, with an overmantel bearing the date 1659 (Reid 1979, 2). The house is named after the Tilly family, but passed into the hands of the Bucklands, who held it until the end of the 17th century. The house shows much evidence of the reuse and resiting of architectural details, and there has been considerable speculation about the original form and appearance before its extensive reconfiguration, perhaps in stages during the 18th and early 19th centuries. One commentator wrote that 'Only the central portion of Tilly Manor remains, but it is said that originally it had "wings" on either side; and the remaining portion was at one time loftier' (Anon 1936, 46). In its current form –

Fig 7.13
Tilly Manor, West Harptree, with reconfigured front facade largely characteristic of the late 17th century. (DP082032)

with a double-pile plan and hipped roof with no gables, and classically inspired detailing – Tilly Manor reflects the development of the manor house by the end of the 17th century. By this time the extensive U-, H- and E-shaped plans were overtaken by the compact double-pile plan, two rooms deep. The gabled roof and horizontal ranks of mullioned windows were superseded by the hipped roof and vertical-format windows, while the central entrance and classical symmetry, the pediment and the wider vocabulary of classical architecture prevailed.

Agriculture and settlement in the 16th to early 18th centuries

Throughout the years of social, religious and political turmoil in the 16th and 17th centuries, the agricultural story is largely one of gradual change. During this period the population of England doubled (Smith 1978, 207), and with this demographic change came inflationary pressures, particularly in relation to foodstuffs, as the 16th and early 17th centuries saw real wages steadily declining because of an over-stocked labour market. Those individuals dependent on wages (such as day labourers) experienced a gradual erosion of their living standards, which led to widespread depriv-ation. In the late 16th and early 17th centuries the population of England's towns also began to swell, largely due to the influx of migrants, creating an ever-increasing demand for both agricultural produce and manufactured goods. For the farmers and artisans who supplied the market, the long-term effects of inflationary rises produced unequalled opportunities for profit (Wrightson 2002, 129–34). This new prosperity was reflected in a general rise in living standards, visible through an unpreced-ented phase of rebuilding and an ever-expanding range of material culture.

Areas such as Mendip, with access to extensive commons, had the ability to more easily absorb demographic change. Holdings could be subdivided if necessary, which could relieve some of the pressures created by a rising population. Rural industries also eased the burden on communities coping with demo-graphic change. Mining and manufacturing could supplement the income of those tenants with limited land. Industry also attracted immigrant cottagers who travelled to areas they thought could sustain them; these cottagers eked out a living in good times but could face chronic distress in years of industrial or agricultural depression. Cottages began to spring up on the edges of townships, along roadsides and on the boundaries of commons, often comprising no more than a modest building and garden plot. At Charterhouse-on-Mendip the excavation of a small stone-built structure (approximately 10m long and 5m wide) revealed evidence for occupation spanning little more than a generation. The cottage was evidently constructed around 1680 and had been demolished by around 1720 (Tofts 2008, 19–43).

Exploitation of the wastes: duck decoys and rabbit warrens

The desire by landholders to find more profitable ways of exploiting the resources of their estates extended to the upland and low-land wastes. In these areas of poor soils, rough moor and marshland, enterprising landlords adopted more specialised forms of exploitation. These included the establishment of extensive rabbit warrens on the uplands, and the con-struction of duck decoys on the wetlands at the foot of the limestone escarpment.

A duck decoy is an artificial pool of water, usually square or rectangular, with a number of curving 'pipes' – tapering channels covered by netting supported on a framework of hoops – leading from it. Wildfowl were encouraged onto the pond and then lured up the curving pipes by small dogs before being trapped in nets at the end (Williamson 1997, 101). During the 17th and 18th centuries at least four duck decoys were constructed on the Levels and Moors along the southern margins of Mendip. At Rodney Stoke a decoy was in operation by 1635, and had been rebuilt by the mid-18th century when an estate survey records 'the new decoy' located towards the eastern boundary of the parish (Aston and Bettey 1998, 133; SHS MAP/D/P/rod.s 20/1/3). Aerial photography has shown that this small decoy had six long pipes radiating from a central rectangular pond; a small stone structure to the east may also have formed part of the decoy complex. Little more than 400m to the east is evidence of a second decoy site, the earthwork remains of which suggest that it also comprised a central pond with six radiating pipes (McDonnell 1984, 29).

Fig 7.14
*Aerial photograph showing
the remains of the duck
decoy at Nyland.
(NMR 24657/02)*

A further two duck decoys – Hythe Lane and Nyland (Fig 7.14) – were located near Cheddar. The ditched enclosure of the former was depicted on the Ordnance Survey 1st edition map, at which time the area was still partially wooded. The decoy had six curving ditches

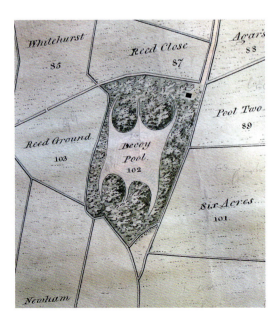

Fig 7.15
*Estate map of 1813 showing
the duck decoy at Nyland.
(SHS DD/PO/79,
reproduced with permission
of Somerset Archive and
Local Studies)*

leading away from a rectangular pond, but its remains were completely destroyed in 1981 (McDonnell 1984, 27). The decoy at Nyland was first documented in 1668, and was depicted along with an associated structure on a series of estate maps (Fig 7.15). In 1678 the decoy was let out for an annual rent of £55, the lease also requiring the tenant to deliver '100 cupple [pair]' of wildfowl yearly for the lord's table (Dennison and Russett 1989, 148–53). Towards the end of the 18th century Collinson commented on the pool's ability to attract 'a great number of wild ducks, teal, widgeon, sea-pheasants, and other fowl' (1791, 606).

Rabbit farming was another way landlords could diversify their interests. Although rabbits needed careful tending they could be raised on poor soils, and the heather and gorse of upland areas provided an excellent habitat (Williamson 2007, 18–20). In the 16th and 17th centuries rabbits were highly valued for their meat and fur, which made commercial rabbit farming a profitable venture. Enterprising landlords were therefore quick to establish warrens on the upland commons of Mendip. The creation of these large commercial enterprises led commoners in the 1660s to petition against the warrens, as they were competing with their rights to graze cattle on the upland 'to the utter ruin of them and their poore families' (Aston and Bettey 1998, 135).

Warrens were widespread across Mendip, at places such as Ubley, Charterhouse-on-Mendip, Rodney Stoke, East Harptree, Chewton Mendip, Dolebury, Pen Hill, Shute Shelve and Rowberrow. The archaeological evidence for the warrens largely comes in the form of pillow mounds – long, low rectangular mounds used for housing rabbits, often surrounded by a shallow drainage ditch. Pillow mounds come in a wide variety of sizes and can be found singly or in groups, sometimes joined together into complex forms. At Rowberrow a sequence of four pillow mounds (the most southerly measuring 88m in length and standing up to 1.2m high) is visible running down the slope of a north-facing spur; the earthwork remains of one are shown in Figure 7.16. The warren on Shute Shelve Hill is similar in form, comprising three pillow mounds, one of which has clearly been enlarged. The excavation of a pillow mound at Shute Shelve revealed that it was defined by a retaining wall and capped with large stones, with the ditch also lined with flat stones (Sylverton 1956, 5–7). At Ubley the pillow mounds lie intermixed with the rakes and spoil heaps of former mining activities, and on Pen Hill the largest human-made burrow in the region (measuring over 210m in length) survives within an area of improved grassland. Other warrens, such as East Harptree and Rodney Stoke, display little evidence for such artificial burrows and may simply have comprised a walled enclosure containing suitable plant cover to shelter and sustain the rabbits.

Perhaps one of the best-known and longest-surviving rabbit warrens was Dolebury Warren (Fig 7.17). Here a series of pillow mounds were placed within the bounds of the ancient hillfort, probably as it formed a ready-made enclosure (*see* Fig 4.27). A series of slightly curving linear pillow mounds are clearly visible within the camp, along with the only example of a circular pillow mound yet discovered in the region. The rabbit warren was in operation when John Strachey visited the site in the early 18th century, at which time it was run by a Mr Jones of Langford (Williams 1987, 61).

Earthwork evidence indicates more than one phase of activity within the warren, with the relatively modest first phase comprising a series

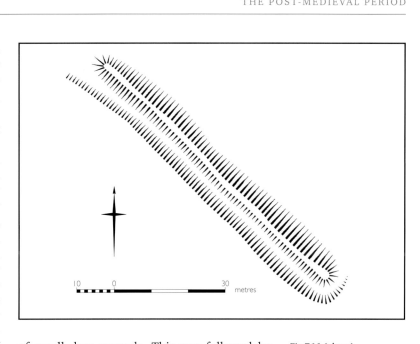

of small, low mounds. This was followed by massive expansion, not in the number of mounds but in their individual scale, with a series of large, well-formed linear mounds constructed across the interior (Bowden 2009, 15). Rabbit farming clearly continued at Dolebury after some of the slighter pillow mounds had gone out of use, as is perhaps most clearly demonstrated by a vermin trap inserted into the top of one of the mounds. These traps are generally thought to have been used to

Fig 7.16 (above)
Earthwork remains of a pillow mound, Rowberrow.

Fig 7.17 (below)
Aerial photograph showing the warren within Dolebury Hillfort, which includes pillow mounds, vermin traps and a warrener's lodge. (NMR 1462/105)

Fig 7.18
The warrener's lodge at
Dolebury, located on the
highest point of the hill.
(Abby Hunt)

catch the various vermin that preyed upon the rabbits (such as polecats, wild cats, weasels, foxes, rats and stoats), although Allcroft was told by the warrener that those at Dolebury Warren were for catching rabbits (Allcroft 1908, 691–3; Williamson 2007, 78). The traps were still in use in 1885 and are mainly of a cruciform arrangement, constructed of stone,

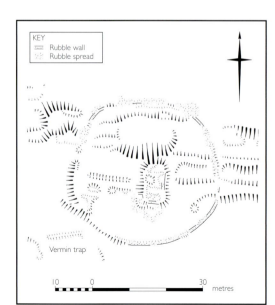

Fig 7.19
Earthwork plan (detail)
showing the remains of the
warrener's lodge, Dolebury.

with the arms designed to funnel predators into a central trap (Dymond 1885, 17).

Also within the warren at Dolebury is a subcircular walled enclosure defining the highest point of the hill (Fig 7.18). At its centre lies a well-built masonry structure, 8.1m in length and 5.6m in width (Fig 7.19). This feature has traditionally been interpreted as a warrener's lodge and was in ruins by 1830 (Dymond 1883, 106). At Charterhouse-on-Mendip the extensive warren originally had two lodges, one represented by the farmhouse at Charterhouse Warren Farm. To the west the 'ruins of Rowborough Lodge' are marked on a map of 1761; the building is now visible as grass-covered footings above the southern side of Velvet Bottom. The sometimes contentious nature of rabbit farming, partiularly on areas of upland common, may suggest these buildings functioned on a symbolic as well as a practical level. They often occupied commanding positions, mirroring deer-park lodges, and could have been perceived as symbols of lordly authority (Williamson 2007, 84).

At Charterhouse Warren Farm the lodge was a substantial structure with a rectangular footprint approximately 12.5m in length and 8.5m wide (Fig 7.20). The size and proportions of the building are noteworthy: it has a wide plan with walls over 0.8m thick, and a high ratio of roof slope to walls in cross section (Fig 7.21). The form of the building's two roof trusses are indicative of the late medieval period. This all points to the possibility of an earlier and perhaps alternative function. The roof timbers were sampled for tree-ring dating and produced possible felling dates in the early 16th century, but the results were inconclusive and at least one of the timbers is known to be reused (Arnold and Howard 2011, 2–3).

Fig 7.20
Warren Farmhouse, Charterhouse. The modern-looking exterior masks a house of much earlier origins. (Elaine Jamieson)

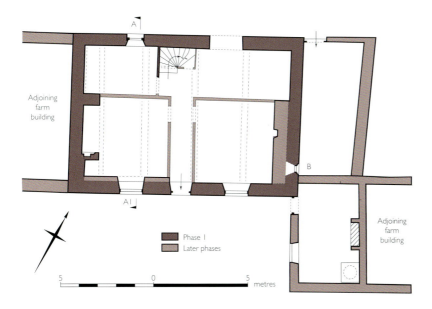

Fig 7.21
Warren Farmhouse, Charterhouse: plan showing rectangular footprint of lodge building, highlighting the wide plan form, and indicating the location of the stone single-light window surround (B). A and AI represent the position and direction of the cross section (see Fig 7.22)

Adjoining farm building

A

AI

B

Adjoining farm building

■ Phase I
■ Later phases

5   0   5
metres

Fig 7.22
Warren Farmhouse,
Charterhouse: section
showing wide plan form
and roof trusses, which, if
reused, were taken complete
and re-erected without
adaptation or reduction.

If reused, then the roof trusses were taken complete, rather than as individual salvaged timbers. Furthermore, the building was erected to this wide plan and substantial scale to allow the trusses to be reused without adaptation or reduction (Fig 7.22). One further indication is the existence of a stone single-light window surround characteristic of the 16th century. Despite the body of evidence the interpretation of this enigmatic building is, as yet, inconclusive, and the available facts imply either a pre-Reformation building of the early 16th century, or the reuse of the roof structure and other materials from such a building. What is certain, however, is that by the late 17th century the building was in use as a warrener's lodge. In a document ascribed to the 1670s the Charter-house warren is described as 'well stored with game and a new lodge yt cost £300 bilding and let for £65/00/0' (SHS DD/GB 151).

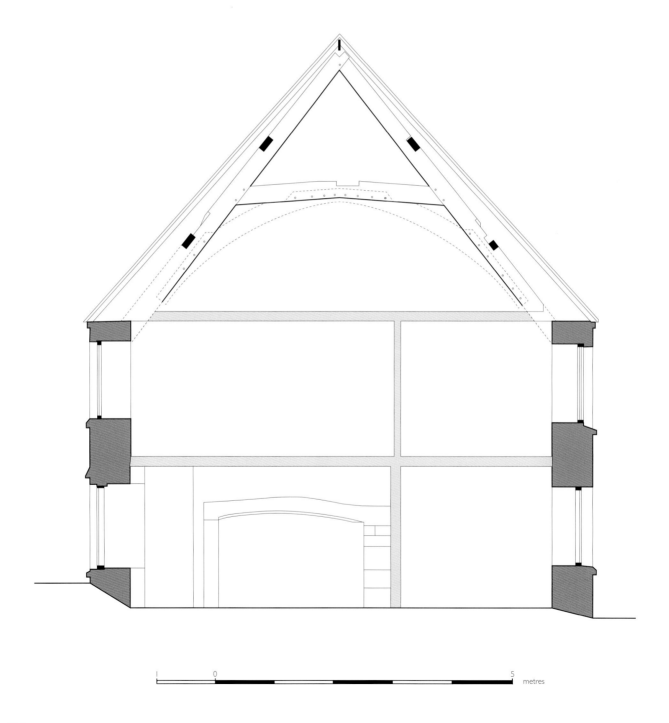

0   5
metres

Improvement farming and the enclosure of the common fields

As the demand for agricultural produce continued to grow during the 17th century, improved farming techniques were increasingly adopted by landlords keen to raise productivity and estate profits. These included the widespread use of manure to enhance soil fertility and the planting of new root crops and artificial grasses to sustain larger flocks. Records show that artificial grasses were being sown in Compton Bishop by the late 1680s, suggesting these new farming techniques were being embraced by at least some Mendip landholders.

Improvement agriculture was considered best employed on land held 'in severalty', that is, in small enclosed fields reserved for the sole use of the owner rather than within commonly worked open-field systems. Some piecemeal enclosure of the common fields occurred on Mendip during the 16th and 17th centuries, but it was not until the early 18th century that a wholesale reordering of the open fields was finally achieved. In Christon, for example, the scattered arable strips of the glebeland recorded at the beginning of the 17th century had been consolidated and predominantly laid to pasture by 1703, which left several flights of former open arable strips fossilised within the glebeland's newly enclosed North Field (Fig 7.23). In Litton, land in the community's South Field was recorded as 'lately enclosed' in 1733, and in Chewton Mendip an estate survey of 1740 defined 'The Common Field Inclosure', within which a small number of strips were still held in common (SHS DD/WG/MAP/1 and DD/WG box 9, no. 8).

Enclosure, carried out by common consent, resulted in the abolition of the small, scattered land parcels that typified open-field agriculture. The long-held rights of individuals over the land (which could include a tenant's right to graze livestock on the stubble after harvest and to fold sheep on the fallow in the winter) were also extinguished. The open-field strips were bundled together to create new land parcels bordered by fences, hedges or stone walls. Often, but not always, the newly enclosed fields were laid out following the pattern of earlier holdings and furlongs. In Stoberry Park, for example, the pre-parkland field boundaries define subrectangular enclosures that respect the course of the earlier open arable strips. At Bleadon the blocks of fields visible today

largely reflect the pattern of the common-field furlongs depicted on a map of the mid-17th century (SHS T/P11/SFY/1). In other areas enclosure and consolidation did not always go hand in hand. The common strips surrounding Draycott, for example, were fossilised on a map of 1775, suggesting the holdings of

Fig 7.23
Former open arable strips fossilised within North Field, Christon.
(NMR 24821/11)

individual farmers were still intermixed when enclosure occurred (SHS MAP/D/P/rod.s 20/1/3). Examples such as this possibly reflect areas where later agreements to comprehensively reorder fields through consolidation and exchange proved harder to achieve.

Rural settlement and housing in the 16th and 17th centuries

The 16th and 17th centuries were a period of extensive rebuilding on Mendip, a phenomenon witnessed across much of England. This period of transformation was first brought to wider attention by W G Hoskins, who termed the process 'the great rebuilding', which he assigned to the period between 1570 and 1640 (Hoskins 1953). Since he first set out these ideas, academic research has challenged this concept, pointing to greater regional variation and extending the time frame over which the characteristics of the medieval house were transformed. The associated waves of building may not have been unprecedented, but their impact on the houses and settlements that went before was substantial, obscuring the evidence of earlier medieval structures and presenting the impression of a comprehensive renewal. In Somerset, however, this notion of wholesale renewal was challenged by E H D Williams, who stated, 'It is now clear that the "Great Rebuilding" of the 16th and 17th centuries in Somerset usually involved modernizing an existing medieval house, rather than building a completely new one' (1976, 78). On Mendip a comparable picture emerged from the buildings evidence, and on investigation the majority of houses attributable to this period of transformation demonstrated some degree of retention of earlier fabric.

Although the long-term effect of rebuilding was to be dramatic and widespread, the process was far more gradual, taking shape over two centuries. At the start of the 16th century the medieval houses described in Chapter 6 remained dominant throughout Mendip, and were gradually improved during the course of the 16th century by the insertion of ceilings, stairs and enclosed fireplaces with chimney stacks. However, in a few houses where aspirations and funds coincided, the framed ceiling and enclosed fireplace had been imposed by the late 15th or early 16th century, which widens the chronology for the move away from medieval forms. Over the course of the 16th century the early influence of these domestic fashions spread, and the fully floored house form became the standard. The methods by which the householder attained these comforts varied considerably according to means, leaving evidence of the owners' and tenants' circumstances imprinted in the range of domestic adaptations and compromises, as well as the new buildings put up for their use.

In Westbury-sub-Mendip, for example, the houses investigated revealed numerous instances where only a single component within a house, perhaps a single-room addition or inserted framed ceiling, originates from a particular period. Twenty farmhouses that displayed some 16th- or 17th-century fabric were examined in the parish. Of these, only four were judged to be complete houses of that period, with two-room or three-room plans, and, out of these, at least two showed evidence that they incorporate the remains of earlier buildings. Although later alteration undoubtedly accounts for some loss of coherent houses of the period, the extent and position of surviving 16th- and 17th-century fabric within the houses examined suggests that later alterations were not of a comprehensive nature, and in many cases would not reasonably account for the absence of earlier fabric. One example, at Upper Old Ditch Farm, Lynch Lane, includes fragments of earlier phases in conjunction with an expensive framed ceiling dating from the 16th or early 17th century, within a house that was extended and improved again in a much later campaign (Figs 7.24 and Fig 7.25). The development of the house reflects a characteristic in the Mendip hill-slope settlements which saw great emphasis on piecemeal improvement, and rather less on building new farmhouses of the substantial three-room plan typical in other areas of Somerset.

In the Mendip villages the relative wealth and status of the customary tenant or yeoman farmers, as reflected in their houses, show that the two-room plan remained acceptable as the basis for a respectable farmhouse. As the 1557 survey of the customary tenants of the Manor of Wookey demonstrates, the two-unit house remained the standard plan well into the middle of the 16th century, typically comprising hall/kitchen and chamber (DHC 96M, 96 add M, box 4/5; Hasler and Luker 1997, 233–45). The documentary record and the surviving houses tell us that, in such farmhouses, the hall

Fig 7.24
Upper Old Ditch Farm,
Westbury-sub-Mendip.
The late 18th- or
19th-century development
of the farmhouse focused
on extending to the side of
the earlier building, and
turned the main axis of
the farmhouse to face the
road frontage.
(DP068933)

Fig 7.25
Upper Old Ditch Farm,
Westbury-sub-Mendip:
16th- or early 17th-century
parlour or hall ceiling,
reflecting investment in
a reasonably high-status
domestic phase focused
on one individual room.
(DP068931)

was still a multifunctional space, used by the household for cooking, eating, socialising and possibly still for sleeping. In some cases the fabric evidence suggests that the two rooms may originate from contrasting phases, but this does not necessarily indicate that the original phase formed a single-room plan. Instead, the likelihood is that the phases within these customary tenant farmhouses reflect a sequence of changes involving only partial rebuilding. The work of successive phases may or may not have broken out beyond the medieval footprint, and often retained a relatively low form with a squat upper floor under a steep roof. Over the course of the period a sequence of modifications might result in the attainment of an additional room or two, usually a kitchen and/or parlour, and the provision of an additional bedchamber above, usually unheated. The result, unlike at Upper Old Ditch Farm, was a coherent dwelling with recognisable plan for the period.

The Old Red Lion, Westbury-sub-Mendip, is a case in point (Fig 7.26). The house, which sits on a sloping outcrop of bedrock on Free Hill, represents continuity of occupation from the medieval period, with the earliest identifiable

phase probably of the late 15th or early 16th century and comprising just one room: a hall with cross-passage, or opposed entries, at the uphill end (Fig 7.27). The hall retains a massive bressummer spanning the full width of the house, which is indicative of a substantial fireplace later reduced in size. The roof over this single room is not smoke-blackened, but has good-quality mortice and tenon joints, and butt purlins that are typically associated with the 15th and 16th centuries in Somerset (McDermott 2006, 94–5). The lack of smoke-blackening suggests that the hall always had a first floor, but the absence of a suitable stair projection or alcove probably implies a missing stair in the position of the later bay to the north; alternatively, a ladder stair may still have sufficed.

The house was modified and extended in subsequent phases – firstly, in the late 16th or early 17th century, at the uphill end, with a single-bay parlour created above the passage, either as a new addition or more likely an upgrading of an earlier second bay. This room matches the width of the earlier hall and reuses some late medieval fabric. The result is

Fig 7.26
The Old Red Lion,
Westbury-sub-Mendip,
looking south-east and
showing the cross-passage.
(DP068882)

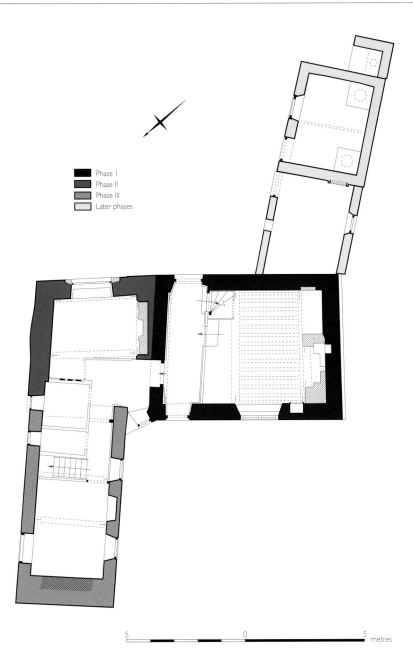

Fig 7.27
Plan of the Old Red Lion,
Westbury-sub-Mendip,
showing phases of piecemeal
development.

Phase I
Phase II
Phase III
Later phases

5   0   5 metres

a reasonable two-unit house. In the mid- to late 17th century, a much narrower wing, with thinner walls, was built to the front of the parlour, extending towards Free Hill Lane. This addition is more typical of the later 17th-century farmhouse plan in that the footprint is narrow in relation to the width. It probably contained a separate kitchen and a service room, allowing food preparation and cooking to be removed from the hall. The sequence of three roofs shows a diminishing quality of timber and carpentry techniques from hall, to parlour, to

kitchen. The two-room plan often suited the village farmhouse, where there might be limitations affecting the width of the plot. Here at the Old Red Lion the third room, the kitchen, was provided in a projecting wing, which thereby avoided extending the frontage.

The alternative means of providing a two-cell farmhouse was to begin from scratch. Such building could create the same fundamental plan but allowed for other improvements, including a full first floor with decent bed-chambers and possibly an attic garret of a

Fig 7.28
Plan of Knyftons
Farmhouse, Westbury-
sub-Mendip, showing new
two-unit farmhouse of the
16th century.

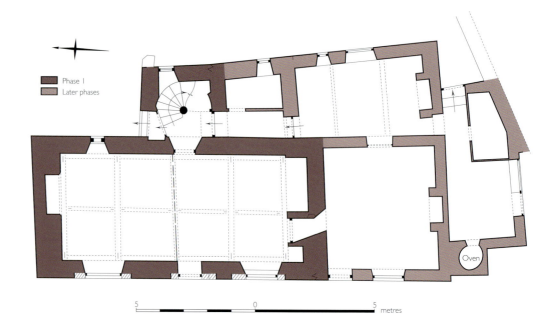

Fig 7.29
Knyftons Farmhouse,
Westbury-sub-Mendip:
interior showing framed
ceiling and fireplace with
four-centred arched head.
(DP068940)

half-storey above. The resulting form was much taller and more stylish, with high eaves and a more substantial appearance. If the expense could be spared, freestone, such as Doulting, would be the preferred choice for window and door surrounds. However, this degree of expense was not a prerequisite, even on the grandest of farmhouses, with less costly hardwoods such as oak or elm frequently used, sometimes on the same elevation. The availability of freestone in terms of cost and scarcity in the Mendip area is one factor that may be

responsible for the limited survival of original windows and doorways in the region's 16th- and 17th-century houses. The walls were built from local stone rubble, limewashed or rendered, and the roof was usually of reed or straw thatch, and less commonly covered in imported stone slate.

An example of a new two-unit farmhouse was built in Westbury-sub-Mendip in the 16th century. Known as Knyftons, the house was probably built on an established village farm plot and may well reflect some aspect of this in its form and position (Fig 7.28). The house was entirely new, with the principal ground-floor rooms comprising hall/kitchen and parlour, originally separated by a timber plank and muntin screen, now only retained on the first floor. Fireplaces were built in the end walls and the parlour was given an expensive freestone fire surround (Fig 7.29). Instead of by a cramped stair in an alcove or wall thickness, at Knyftons the upper floors are reached by a winder stair contained in a substantial projecting stair turret, which gives the house a T-shaped plan (Fig 7.30).

The means by which this type of 16th-century two-room farmhouse was augmented to form a three-unit house was relatively straightforward: by the provision of an extra bay, either in line or in a wing to the front or rear. The chief advantage was the extra room provided, frequently a kitchen, which left the hall to function as a more salubrious and higher-status space. There was plenty of scope for providing the three-room in-line plan by adapting earlier medieval houses, and although identification of such cases is not always clear, there are many Mendip examples. These include two houses in East Harptree: the Old Rectory (Fig 7.31), on Church Lane, and what is now a row of three cottages on Middle Street (Poppy Cottage, Sumac and The Cottage). Both might potentially include earlier fabric in areas of the walls.

Examples of new-built three-room plans also survive on Mendip. Wellington House, Westbury-sub-Mendip, for example, was probably built in the early 17th century to replace an existing farmhouse (Fig 7.32). The house retains a number of 17th-century features, including ceiling beams, substantial kitchen and hall fireplaces, and a high-status freestone chamber fireplace (Fig 7.33). At Coley Court the three-room plan was reached by the aggregation of two phases in close succession during the late 16th or early 17th century, beginning with a two-unit house and extended by the provision of a substantial in-line kitchen to one end. The kitchen retains an exceptional fitted dresser of the period, although the

Fig 7.30
Knyftons Farmhouse, Westbury-sub-Mendip: stair with solid wooden newel and winders. (DP068942)

Fig 7.31
The Old Rectory, East Harptree: a three-unit in-line plan that may be adapted from an earlier medieval house. (DP086348)

*Fig 7.32
Wellington House,
Westbury-sub-Mendip:
plan showing new three-unit
farmhouse of the early
17th century.*

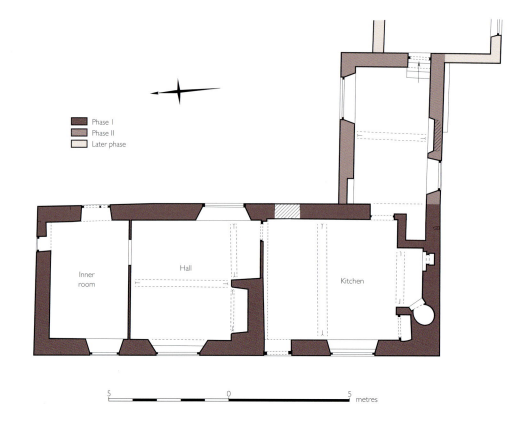

*Fig 7.33
Wellington House,
Westbury-sub-Mendip:
17th-century freestone
chamber fireplace with
the initials LW carved in
the spandrels.
(DP069253)*

cupboards were given new panelled doors in the 18th century.

A variation on the three-unit farmhouse plan also came to the fore in this period. This is exemplified by Combe Farmhouse, Compton Martin, which appears to be a new house on a newly colonised plot. The tall sectional form and T-shaped plan are familiar from Knyftons. The third, central, bay provides a small inner room, a service room between the passage and the kitchen, in a distinctive arrangement found elsewhere in Somerset. Combe Farmhouse retains many original features, including a stair with flattened vase balusters that show a marked development in style and sophistication compared to the newel stair at Knyftons.

Up until the middle of the 17th century the principal means of embellishing the interior of Mendip's village farmhouses was carved timber and stone mouldings on beams, fireplaces and doorframes. Although decorative plaster ceilings and friezes were used at high-status farmhouses in the period, few examples were seen during the project. An exception was at Combe Farmhouse, where the principal bed-chamber is embellished with a fascinating classical plasterwork chimney piece (Fig 7.34). This includes a simple roll moulding on the edge of the fire opening and an elaborate frieze of mythical serpents or seahorses. The frieze is flanked by low-relief scrolled consoles of a flattened, almost two-dimensional, quality, giving the impression that this is the work of an artificer who was unfamiliar with classical architectural detail, and perhaps one used to working from drawings rather than objects. The chimney piece is finished with a finely moulded plasterwork mantelshelf in the form of a box cornice, while a similar mantelshelf survives in the bedchamber at the north end of the house. In this instance the fireplace retains the moulded timber bressummer exposed. The plasterwork, with its delicate classical details, appears at odds with the heavier quality of the timber mouldings typical of the remainder of the interior. This contrast, taken in conjunction with the position of the inscription in a first-floor chamber, may allude to the initials and date commemorating a marriage, rather than the construction of the house (Fig 7.35). The house was owned by the Tilly family during the 17th century, and parish records note that one Nathaniel Tilly married Gertrude Hurle in 1660/61 at Compton Martin church (D Hart, pers comm).

Fig 7.34
Combe Farmhouse, Compton Martin: 17th-century chimney piece with classical plasterwork frieze. (DP099725)

Fig 7.35
Combe Farmhouse, Compton Martin: plasterwork chimney piece showing initials and date, possibly commemorating a marriage. (DP099718)

The village farmhouses of Mendip, by the close of the 17th century, had developed a long way from their medieval predecessors, and yet the fundamental spaces within the house remained the hall, parlour and kitchen, with cross-passage or opposed entries associated with the hall. The classical frontage – with symmetrically placed entry and associated stair hall – was yet to take precedence, although it was presaged by the coming together of cross-passage and rear stair. The symmetrical facade was also foreshadowed in the two-unit farmhouses, where the passage or entry was naturally placed close to the centre of the house, as at Lower Farm, Charterhouse-on-Mendip, where the high status of the Maye family also influenced the classical style of the door case.

The enclosed fireplace and chimney was established as a prerequisite for all but the humblest of cottages, and in the houses of the customary tenant and yeomen farmers provided heating in two or more rooms on each of the main floors. The problem of positioning fireplace and chimney stack within the house plan was resolved in a number of ways during the period, but the lateral fireplace, as seen in the medieval hall at Moat Farm for example, did not become commonplace in Mendip. The preferred placement was in the gable-end wall, or internally, in the form of a transverse division between hall and passage. In both cases the predominant arrangement of stacks in relation to plan was to provide an inglenook fireplace positioned towards one side of the room, with a slender monolithic stone jamb often used instead of a substantial masonry jamb, and space allowed for a stair, doorway or curing chamber alongside. The use of the monolithic jamb, however, seems to have been more closely associated with the more modest farmhouses and those of the earlier part of the period; the carved stone surrounds seen in the higher-status farmhouses became the desired standard during the mid- to late 17th century.

In the house of the humble husbandman or cottager, the inglenook with monolithic jamb and timber bressummer remained the standard right through the 18th century. These lesser dwellings first appear as surviving cottages from around the mid- to late 17th century, although their presence in the village make-up in earlier periods is virtually certain. For example, the 1586 rent roll for the manor of Westbury-sub-Mendip lists six cottages in the manor at that time, and there are six noted in a later survey dated to 1634 (TNA LR 2/257; SHS DD/CC/13324). These smaller houses were the dwellings of the village husbandman, artisan and labourer, who might be engaged in subsistence farming, working in the typical range of rural industries – leather and textiles, baking and brewing, mineral extraction and processing.

Such dwellings might be built on the margins or wastes, possibly with the acquiescence of the landlord, as seems to have been the case at what is now Nut Tree Cottage in Westbury-sub-Mendip. Here the Bishop of Bath and Wells took rent from the occupiers of what was in form and location nothing more than a pair of squatter cottages (Fig 7.36). The earliest phase is a very small single-room cottage of one and a half storeys, and is perched above a low cliff with a sheer drop, now directly adjoining the house, where a small outshot was added (*see* Fig 7.36c). The original cottage had a direct entry from the front, and a corner inglenook fireplace at the opposite end, which served all the household purposes. A low attic or loft was reached probably by a tiny winder stair, and the thatch-roof was typically very tall and steep, with low eaves. It is difficult to assign a date to such a humble cottage, but its characteristics imply a date in the late 17th century or perhaps a little earlier. In the mid-18th century a second, slightly larger, cottage was added against the original gable-end chimney stack (Fig 7.37).

Opposite Nut Tree Cottage stands a row of three houses illustrating a further contrasting house type (*see* Fig 7.36b). This row developed piecemeal from a single dwelling, now known as no. 2 Free Hill, which probably originated in the late 16th or early 17th century. It reflects a higher social standing compared to that of Nut Tree Cottage, and comprised a two-storey form with a one and a half room plan. The principal room includes the typical off-centre inglenook fireplace (Fig 7.38), while the half bay to the north was originally unheated, and probably a service room. The scale and detail of the house, including ground-floor ceiling beams with large stops and hollow chamfers, reflect a position in the middle of village society. Probably in the late 17th century a second house, now called Dunelm, was added to the south end; again the pre-existing chimney stack in the gable wall was utilised, but in this instance a smaller single-room plan was provided with end passage and inglenook fireplace.

a

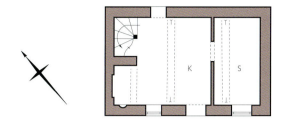

Fig 7.36
Comparative cottage plans:
(a) Havenmead Cottage,
Easton, a mid-18th-century
cottage with a one and a
half unit plan representing
kitchen (K) and service
room (S); (b) no. 2 Free
Hill/Dunelm Cottage,
Westbury-sub-Mendip;
(c) Nut Tree Cottage,
Westbury-sub-Mendip.

b

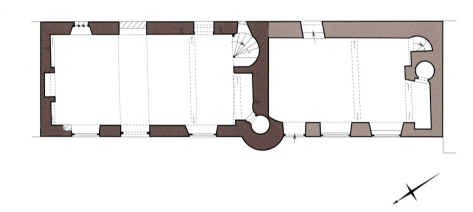

c

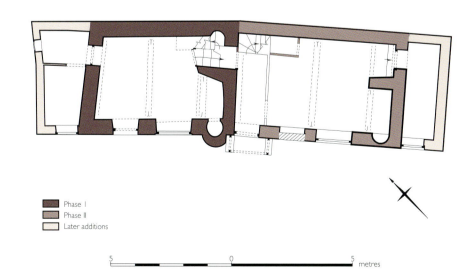

■ Phase I
■ Phase II
□ Later additions

5   0   5 metres

Fig 7.37
Nut Tree Cottage, Westbury-sub-Mendip. The mid-18th-century cottage was built against the chimney stack of an earlier single-room one and a half storey dwelling.
(DP068890)

Fig 7.38
No. 2 Free Hill, Westbury-sub-Mendip: typical off-centre inglenook fireplace with stair alongside.
(DP068902)

Farmsteads of the 16th to 18th centuries

As we have seen, numerous farmhouses of the 16th and 17th centuries remain in the Mendip area; however, in contrast, only very few upstanding farm buildings of the period survive. Of those, most have been altered significantly as a consequence of agricultural developments which resulted in the replacement of many pre-improvement farm buildings with new purpose-built structures, especially during the 19th century. The clearest evidence for the form and layout of the 16th-century and 17th-century farmstead, therefore, comes from holdings which were completely abandoned prior to agricultural improvement.

The buildings of these deserted farmsteads are usually represented by low stone footings or level platforms, often terraced into the slope and surrounded by enclosure walls. The remains generally define rectangular structures, and where walls are visible, were constructed of roughly coursed stone. Pre-improvement farmsteads could comprise a range of buildings beyond the ubiquitous farmhouse – including a barn, stables or stalls and outhouses. More specialised structures such as a kitchen, bakehouse or brewhouse could also be incorporated in the farm complex, although the function of these heated service buildings could overlap. Farmsteads were often laid out with the barn and dwelling house set parallel to one another, although not always directly opposite. An alternative plan was to have the buildings set side by side in a linear arrangement, with both formats including an adjoining 'backside' or farmyard. Additional buildings, where they existed, were often irregularly placed around these two main structures, forming a compact grouping (Fig 7.39). Most Mendip farmsteads were relatively modest. The barn was the most substantial agricultural building and was a dual-purpose structure, used for cereal

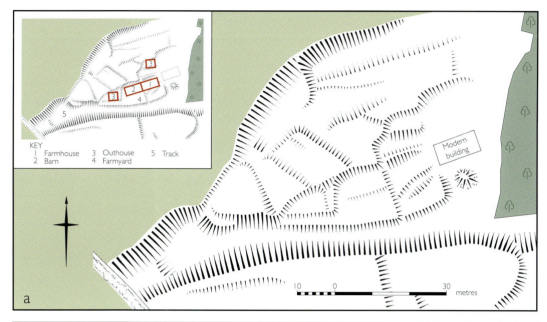

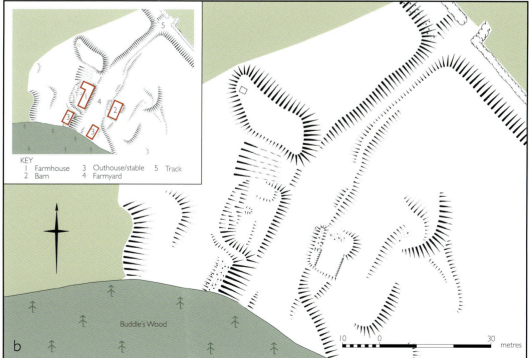

Fig 7.39
Earthwork plans showing (a) the linear arrangement of farmhouse and barn at Payne's Pond, Chewton Mendip, and (b) the parallel arrangement of farmhouse and barn at Neat Place, Chewton Mendip.

processing and sheltering livestock, with storage for hay and fodder.

Farmhouses and barns tended to be similar in size – around 12m in length and 7m in width – which sometimes makes it difficult to differentiate them through earthwork remains alone. So it is by way of later estate maps that the functions of such buildings can often be determined, although complexity within the earthworks can sometimes suggest a domestic use. At Neat Place, Chewton Mendip, for example, the farmhouse lay on the west side of the yard and was an L-shaped building, 17m in length, possibly representing a three-room plan. This holding was the largest in the district, and the size of the farmhouse, along with the range of buildings in the farmstead (including a barn, stable and outhouses), was undoubtedly a reflection of the economic status of the farm. At Chancellor's Farm, near Priddy, the main range of the farmhouse, which dates from the 17th century, measures 13.5m long by 5.2m wide, but provided, originally, a two-room plan only. The barn, which is situated at a distance from the house in a separate yard, measures 18.2m long by 5.6m wide, but is one of the larger examples on the Mendip uplands.

Barns were more often than not relatively small, with the few upstanding examples indicating they were of rendered stone and would originally have been thatched (Fig 7.40). The arrangement of openings in these structures is unclear, but they may have been furnished with either a single large door or two opposing entrances. The barn at Chancellor's Farm, which was planned with two distinct spaces divided by a stone cross wall, had a larger compartment originally with relatively narrow opposed doorways, 1.45m wide, on the long walls. Both elements of the barn also had high pitching doorways and ground-level doorways in the gable walls. At Sacrafield, in Chewton Mendip, the barn was offset from the dwelling and had its long axis terraced into a steep slope (Fig 7.41). This arrangement would suggest the building had a single large entrance at ground-floor level, with the loft possibly accessed via an opening on the upslope side. At the beginning of the 18th century the holding was entirely pastoral, and the barn would have been used to store winter fodder and shelter livestock. The farmstead also included a 'mowbarton' or stackyard, where hay or cereal crops could be stacked in ricks, probably raised

Fig 7.40
Sherbourne barn,
Sherbourne: a traditional
Mendip barn.
(BRBR/Litton/1810, Bristol
Region Building Record,
University of Bath)

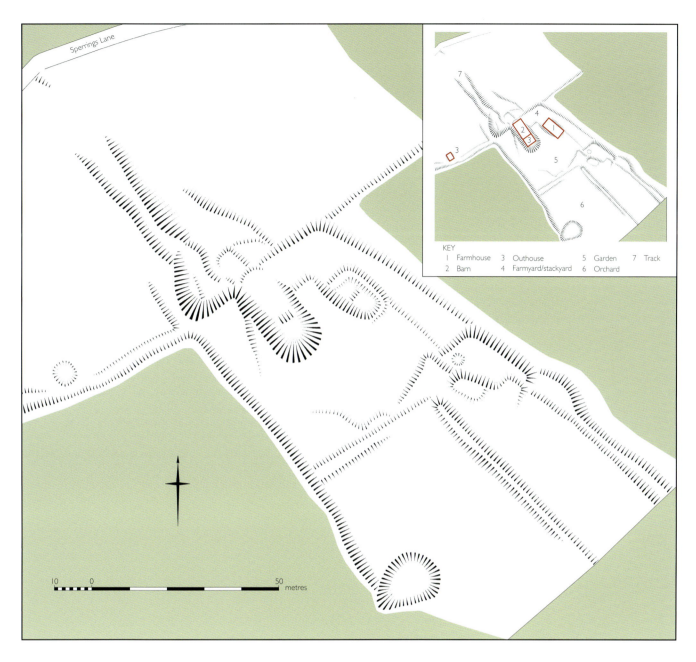

Sperrings Lane

KEY
1 Farmhouse 3 Outhouse 5 Garden 7 Track
2 Barn   4 Farmyard/stackyard 6 Orchard

10   0   50
                                    metres

on staddle stones, and broken up as and when they were needed. Stackyards were located adjacent to the farmstead and functioned as an extra storage area, effectively reducing the need for a large barn.

Other specialist yards, including an 'oxbarton', also appear in the documentary record, as do gardens, paddocks and orchards. Apple growing was an important aspect of the rural economy, and small orchards were often found beside farmsteads. A site with a northerly aspect, sheltered from the westerly winds, was deemed most suitable for apple growing, with fruit raised along the northern Mendip

escarpment producing cider 'strong, palatable and highly esteemed' (Billingsley 1797, 124). Few traces of this industry have been identified within the farm buildings of the region, however. Cider making required equipment such as a crusher and a press, sometimes housed in a purpose-built cider house or 'pound house', although this sort of activity could equally have taken place in a barn or outhouse.

As well as being used to store hay and fodder or to shelter livestock, outhouses may have performed specialised functions. For example, a 17th-century estate survey records the buildings of Daniel Burge's holding in Priddy as

Fig 7.41
Earthwork plan of Sacrafield, Chewton Mendip, where the barn was offset from the farmhouse and terraced into a steep slope.

Fig 7.42
Earthwork plan of Ellick,
near Blagdon, where the
farmstead comprised at
least four buildings with
attached yards.

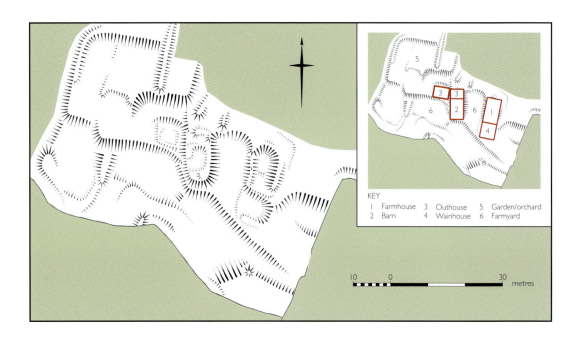

KEY
1 Farmhouse 3 Outhouse 5 Garden/orchard
2 Barn   4 Wainhouse 6 Farmyard

10   0   30 metres

Fig 7.43
Ellick, near Blagdon:
reconstruction drawing
showing how the farmstead
may have appeared
around 1600.

comprising two outhouses called 'shop' and 'wainhouse' (SHS DD/WG/4/1/2). Outhouses could take the form of one- or two-bay free-standing buildings, or could be attached to a barn or dwelling. At Ellick, near Blagdon, the farmstead comprised at least four buildings with attached yards and closes, with the barn and dwelling house positioned on opposing sides of a central yard (Fig 7.42). A small structure was attached to the north side of the barn, with an outhouse to the west forming an L-shaped range which faced onto a second yard. To the south of the dwelling was a further outhouse, possibly a wainhouse, as the single-bay building appears to have been open on one side (Fig 7.43).

Holdings could also contain a stable for horses or pack ponies, or a stall for cattle or oxen. A barn and stable or stall would be the minimum agricultural buildings required for holdings engaged in a mixed farming regime – allowing the harvest to be stored and providing shelter for draught animals. In contrast, the only essential building for pastoral farming was

a barn for storing winter fodder. In both the documentary and archaeological record there is little evidence of specialist buildings for livestock, such as a cow-house or shippon, although this function could have been served by an outhouse or barn. There is, however, some evidence for sheep-houses or sheepcotes on the larger upland farmsteads, with a building called 'the shepe pen' depicted on a map of Green Ore dated to around 1700 (SHS DD/WG C924). The form of these buildings is unclear, but documentary evidence indicates they were roofed in thatch, and examples elsewhere suggest they were probably long, narrow single-storey structures (eg Dyer 1995). A general lack of shelters for overwintering animals on Mendip is commented on at the end of the 18th century by John Billingsley: with regard to outhouses and cattle sheds, he states that on dairy farms 'a shameful inattention prevails' and that during the winter months cattle are 'almost universally served with their provender in the field' (Billingsley 1797, 32).

Chancellor's Farm

The range of earlier farm buildings on Mendip was therefore generally relatively sparse, and even where provided, farm buildings were meagre in scale and construction. Exceptions did apply, however, one notable example being Chancellor's Farm, which despite its location on the high Mendip plateau, approximately 270m above sea level, was provided with a range of substantial buildings in the 17th and 18th centuries (Fig 7.44). The estate of Chancellor's Farm was licensed by Queen Elizabeth on 20 April 1567 to Sir John Newton and to his heir Henry (BL Lansdown Charter 675). By the late 17th century Chancellor's Farm was owned by Charles Buckland of West Harptree, who leased it to George Savidge in December 1697 for the term of three lives. By the middle of the 18th century the farm had developed to include 'a dwelling house, out-houses, barnes, bartons stables, penns and courts', as described in a lease dated September 1768 (SHS DD/TD Box 23).

Chancellor's Farm stands out today as a little-altered, traditional farmstead, the house and farm buildings settling into the lee of the rugged landscape, with walls of local Carboniferous Limestone rubble and typical Somerset-tiled roofs that replaced the earlier thatch. The buildings, arranged over sloping ground in separate upper and lower yards, are interspersed among closes, bounded by irregular stone walls, whose varied character reflects contrasting periods in the development of the farmstead (Fig 7.45). The farmhouse is the focus of the upper yard and is the earliest building to survive, probably dating from the mid- to late 17th century, although it includes

Fig 7.44
Chancellor's Farm, Priddy: view looking east across upper yard towards mid-to late 17th-century farmhouse. (DP044088)

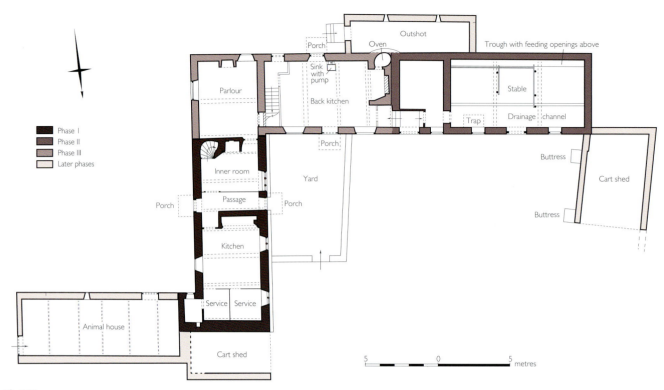

Fig 7.45
Chancellor's Farm, Priddy:
plan of house and upper
yard showing multiple
phases of development over
the 17th and 18th centuries.

Fig 7.46 (right)
Chancellor's Farm, Priddy:
surviving window shutter
in the 17th-century
farmhouse.
(DP044132)

Fig 7.47 (far right)
Chancellor's Farm, Priddy:
surviving plank screen to the
south of the cross-passage in
the 17th-century farmhouse.
(DP044130)

reused medieval and 16th-century fabric. It retains a wealth of vernacular details, including window shutters (Fig 7.46), doors, fireplaces and plank screens (Fig 7.47). During the late 17th or early 18th century a substantial free-standing stable was built in the upper yard at 90 degrees to the house. Shortly afterwards an extension to the house comprising parlour and back kitchen, or bakehouse, was built to link the two. Alongside are gardens and former orchards, with later additions including a pigsty, cart shed, animal shelter and byre.

In the lower yard the farm buildings centre on the substantial stone barn described above, which was probably built in the late 17th or early 18th century. The original opposed doorways are blocked, but are indicative of threshing and so the production of corn crops and straw, functions evidently maintained or revived in a later period, as proved by the secondary timber threshing floor and inserted winnowing doors. A rickyard once stood behind the barn, the only evidence of which is now abandoned staddle stones nearby. Adjoining the barn a later byre and shelter-shed face into a stock-yard, reflecting the later shift to pastoral farming. These were added between 1809 and 1829, as was an adjacent rectangular pond, serving yard and field (SHS DD/WG/MAP 7 and DD/TD/38).

Agricultural improvement in the 18th and 19th centuries

The 18th and 19th centuries witnessed philosophical, scientific and technological advances that defined an era of wide social and economic change. The national population once again started to grow significantly, a process that accelerated towards the end of the 18th century. As we have already seen, this demographic trend was not in itself new, but the rate of population change was unprecedented, with the population of England increasing from 6 million in 1751 to just under 14 million in 1831 (Lawton 1978, 314–16). There was also further expansion in England's urban centres, a process fuelled by rapid industrial growth, which created an ever-expanding market for agricultural produce. In a period of rising grain prices and falling rural employment, there was increasing pressure on landowners to boost cereal production through the adoption of improved farming techniques. The rise in the

number of estate surveys undertaken in this period is testament to the increasing desire of landlords to find more profitable ways to exploit the resources of their estates.

Parliamentary and private enclosure

Perhaps the most visible aspect of this period of agricultural improvement was the reclamation of the upland and lowland wastes. The drainage and reclamation of the lowland areas around the foot of the Mendip Hills had begun in the medieval period, and, after a phase of stagnation in the late 17th and early 18th centuries, was finally completed in the 19th century, when the remaining commons were enclosed under Act of Parliament (Williams 1970, 82–168).

The transformation of Mendip's open sheep walks began in 1771 with the enclosure of the common grazing land in Ubley. Although some larger estates enclosed areas of the plateau through private agreement, as occurred at Chancellor's Farm in the 18th century, the bulk of enclosure was achieved through parliamentary Act. Following Ubley's lead, the majority of Mendip parishes enclosed and improved their upland commons over the next three decades, although a few, such as Hutton and Loxton, were not enclosed until the mid-19th century, with Burrington the last to be awarded an Enclosure Act in 1913 (Fig 7.48).

The Mendip enclosures were seen as a way of improving rates of production and, at least in part, as a solution to the problems of over-stocking on the commons. John Billingsley observed that 'commons of every description, when inclosed and cultivated, are capable of supporting at least three times more stock than they did in a state of nature' (Billingsley 1797, 54). Like many parishes on Mendip, when the commons of Blagdon were reclaimed in 1787 the process involved improving old mining areas, as well as extensive tracts of upland grazing. Land was divided, allotted and enclosed by the appointed commissioners. On Mendip these new enclosed fields were usually upward of 1.5ha, but where field sizes were smaller, around Priddy for example, this was often the result of complex ancient grazing rights or ingresses by the mining community (Williams 1972, 113). The process of enclosure required the commissioners to take into account the rights of different individuals and groups over the designated area. In Blagdon, for example, land was allotted by the

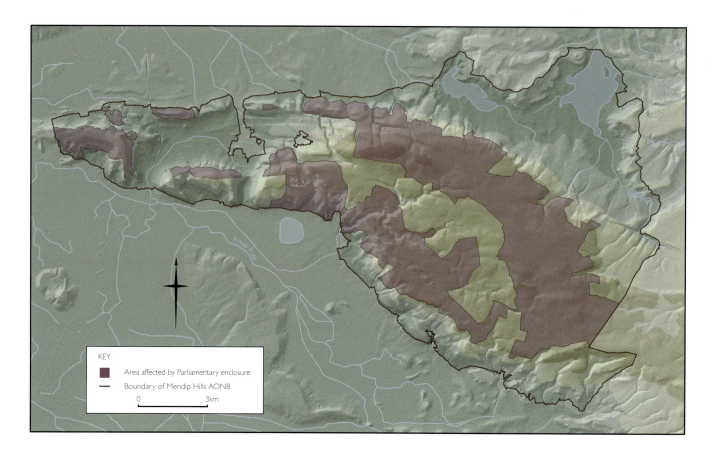

Fig 7.48

Map showing areas affected by parliamentary enclosure across the Mendip Hills AONB.

commissioners to the poor of Compton Martin, although the field remains suggest these strips were never fully enclosed (Fradley 2009, 36). Some allotted areas were too small for practical use and proved too expensive for individual tenants to improve. These undersized and often distant land parcels were later bundled together to form larger fields, sometimes worked from new improvement farmsteads.

The uplands of Chewton Mendip were enclosed in 1797, with approximately 2,000 acres (809ha) of open common replaced by an ordered network of regular geometric fields. These regimented enclosures were defined by straight boundaries, formed by either drystone walls or quickset hedges, especially hawthorn (Fig 7.49). Walls were preferred across the high plateau, despite the limited protection offered to sheltering stock, and were encouraged by the abundance of local Carboniferous Limestone, which today gives the landscape its distinctive character (Fig 7.50). The same limestone geology and the resulting effects of percolation led to a lack of surface water, meaning that fields were often provided with stock ponds, sometimes constructed towards the corner of the enclosure or across a boundary to allow

their use from multiple fields. A network of new, straight roads was also created, which improved access to the upland enclosures from the valley farmsteads. These broad corridors comprised a metalled road surface flanked by green verges; the latter were originally intended for the passage of livestock on the hoof.

Between 1770 and 1819, 18 parliamentary Enclosure Acts were passed for the Mendip Hills, with the period of greatest intensity taking place between 1780 and 1799, when 11 Acts were approved for the enclosure of approximately 6,410ha (Williams 1972, 103). But rather than concluding the process, the Acts marked only the beginning of change that was to continue through the first half of the 19th century and beyond.

Improvement-period farmsteads

The impact of enclosures upon the development of Mendip farmsteads was not straightforward. The combination of private and parliamentary enclosures brought change over a considerable period in the 18th and 19th centuries and saw the gradual adaptation of existing farmsteads, both in the ring of settlements surrounding

Fig 7.49
Aerial photograph showing
the ordered grid of regular
geometric fields indicative
of parliamentary enclosure.
(NMR 24736/5)

the hills and on the private and ecclesiastical estates on the high plateau. Where new fields were set out on the former commons and wastes, this did not lead immediately or universally to the creation of new farmsteads and new buildings standing within precise rectilinear fields. Instead, a combination of circumstances, including the land allocations distributed by the enclosure commissioners and the wider demand for grain crops, created complex patterns of ownership and farming practice that delayed this process in many cases until the late 1830s and 1840s.

Behind all this, however, was the desire on the part of the landowners and improvers to increase productivity, efficiency and profit, in the face of often poor and tradition-bound farming practices. The development of Chancellor's Farm during the 18th century illustrates the gradual nature of private enclosure and farm improvement. In 1712 the farmstead stood at 49 acres (20ha) and included a close of 7 acres (3ha) called 'Newland' and a 'sleigh called Saunders Hill' (SHS DD/SAS/c/82). The name Newlands may refer to a recent private enclosure, while the sheep sleigh was a long-established area of grazing common over which the farm held rights. In 1754 a description of the farm records 'all that sleigh or sheep sleigh adjoining and

belonging to the said farm, called Saunders Hill, … containing by estimation five hundred acres, part of which sleigh, is now inclosed with a stone wall' (SHS DD/SF 3961). An interesting set of 18th-century accounts also survives for Chancellor's Farm. During the period 1775–7 the accounts reveal a great deal of work on walls and hedging on the farm, possibly new work or otherwise extensive repairs. Labour and cart hire were recorded for 20 'ropes' or lengths of wall, and a total of £22 13s 3d was

Fig 7.50
The stone walls of the
upland plateau that
help give the area its
distinctive character.
(DP081863)

Fig 7.51
Lower Farm, Charterhouse-
on-Mendip: yard wall
with integral bee-boles.
(DP115035)

comprising 236 acres (95.5ha), and was let from the Charterhouse Estate of Wellbore Ellis Esquire to a tenant farmer named William Stevens (SHS DD/STL 1). Between the late 17th and late 18th centuries the range of functions accommodated within the farmhouse at Lower Farm became more distinct, with the addition of a back kitchen and ancillary service rooms freeing the domestic spaces from activities more closely associated with the farmyard. An associated yard wall, built to retain the hill-slope where the back kitchen was erected, provided integral bee-boles, giving an important source of honey and encouraging the pollination of crops (Fig 7.51). In the middle of the 19th century the irregular cluster of small farm buildings was augmented and partially replaced by a substantial new farm building that was considerably larger than any of those previously in use on the farm. This 'barn', which extended the farm group into a close to the north, was built of stone rubble with a slate roof, and was of two storeys, providing extensive storage on the upper floor, with areas of direct feeding into mangers for horses and livestock below (Fig 7.52).

At other established farms in the period the evolution of the farm plan might result in a more regular, formal layout, with a rectangular single-courtyard arrangement enclosed with buildings on all four sides. The transformation of the in-line arrangement of farmhouse and

spent between February and July 1768 on producing lime that was ploughed into the land (SHS DD/TD box 17). By 1829 the farm-stead comprised 272 acres (110ha), a massive increase that almost certainly came about because of enclosure (Penoyre 2005, 155).

At Lower Farm, Charterhouse-on-Mendip, the pre-1800 farmstead plan was irregular, based on an earlier farmhouse, probably of the 17th century. In 1761 the farm recorded a considerable acreage for Mendip at that time,

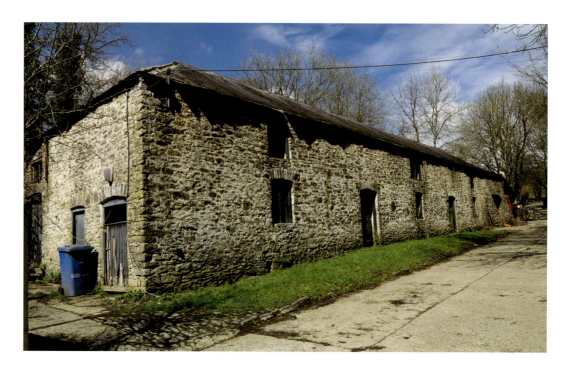

Fig 7.52
Lower Farm, Charterhouse-
on-Mendip: mid-19th
-century two-storey 'barn'.
(DP115048)

barn/stable might well follow this pattern, as took place at Pen Hill Farm, St Cuthbert Out. Here the farmhouse, perhaps dating from the 16th or 17th century, still stands in line with the earlier barn, but in sequences of phases built alongside, a rectangular courtyard developed, with buildings for managing livestock, including animal pens and open-fronted sheds.

Alternatively, such modest linear-plan farmsteads, as found at The Cottage on Middle Street, East Harptree, and West End and Dags Hole Farms, Westbury-sub-Mendip, eventually might be stripped of their land and fall out of agricultural use, with the barns converted into cottages to accommodate growing numbers of landless labourers and industrial workers. This process, a widespread consequence of agricultural improvement, was referred to in connection with the origins of poor rural housing in Somerset in the early 20th century. Writing in 1915, William G Savage, medical officer of health for Somerset, commented that in the 1760s to the 1790s: 'The large farmer, who threw, perhaps, half-a-dozen farms together, pulled down many of the cottages, or allowed them to fall into ruin, maintaining only sufficient house room for his own labourers, whom he frequently crowded

into the old farm houses' (Savage 1915, 46). The process was seen in East Harptree, where some of the village's characteristic rows of estate cottages actually developed piecemeal from the conversion of a village farmstead into estate workers' dwellings.

Billingsley noted that many of Mendip's farms were modest in scale and farmed only a 'small proportion of arable' (1797, 34), with the remainder concentrating on livestock and root crops. Throughout the 18th and 19th centuries at Westbury-sub-Mendip, many of the village farms would have matched this description closely, perhaps typically farming between 30 and 60 acres, and with the old farmhouse and a few very small farm buildings sited together within the village. The land comprising the farmstead might be distributed in parcels throughout the parish, initially including grazing rights on the commons then superseded by an allocation of the enclosed common. Farms derived from these origins continued through the 20th century and remain legible in the village landscape today, with small traditional farm buildings of rubble construction, augmented by large prefabricated agricultural sheds of the mid- to late 20th century (Fig 7.53).

Fig 7.53
Westbury-sub-Mendip: Old Ditch area, showing Stream Farm and small traditional farm buildings of rubble construction. (DP069259)

Fig 7.54
Priddy Green with
St Cuthbert's Farm behind.
(Elaine Jamieson)

St Cuthbert's Farm, a holding of the Bishop of Bath and Wells, stands hard against Priddy Green, with the yard reputedly used as part of the trading ground on fair days (Fig 7.54). From the exterior the farmhouse appears to date from the late 18th and early 19th centuries, but it has a more complex history, derived from a number of earlier phases of indeterminate date, the oldest of which have left scant remains. The farm is shown on an estate map of the bishops of Bath and Wells in 1827, with two buildings fronting the green: a long, slender farm building bounding the edge of the green and a square-plan building corresponding to part of the farmhouse (SHS DD/CC/T/7183). In the will of one Joseph Church, yeoman, dated January 1823, the property is described as a 'dwelling house, garden and premises, with thirty acres of pasture' held for lives from the Bishop of Bath and Wells (document held in private collection). Within a few years, the premises had undergone radical transformation, with the house extended and the long farm building shown in 1827 demolished. A new, substantial, L-plan range is shown on a map of 1837–8, positioned further back from the Green (SHS D/D/Rt/M/3701). However, building fabric evidence shows that this L-plan building was put up in two phases, presumably only a few years apart, with a large raised barn built first, then a stable added later. This accretive arrangement provided a substantial hay barn, with modest opposed doorways on the long walls, and a byre beneath reached from a small yard on the slightly lower ground to the south-west. This forms a bank-barn arrangement, although the rear entry is reached via a set of steps not by an incline or bank. In two later phases an additional byre, sheep shelter, pigsty and further stable were added.

As the parliamentary enclosures took hold on Mendip during the late 18th century, the first new farmsteads were established on the former upland commons. For such farms Billingsley recommended a mixed farming regime, with the proposed system including the use of fallow crops – such as turnips, cabbages and potatoes – and the planting of artificial grasses on which to maintain a 'great flock' of sheep (1797, 78). However, the lure of high grain prices during the Napoleonic Wars resulted in many farmers cropping their new upland land parcels continuously. Commenting in 1807, Billingsley recorded that it was the general practice on Mendip to have six or seven successive crops of corn without an intervening fallow or fallow crop (1807, 47). The process had an enduring impact on farming on the Mendip upland, continuing through much of the first half of the 19th century, when Thomas Dyke Acland, another agricultural commentator, reported that farmers 'grew oats without manure as long as the land would bear it', with the enclosures eventually laid to pasture when the land became unproductive (Acland and Sturge 1851, 73). These same allotments were then reploughed and leased for growing potatoes, a system in operation in Upper Rains Batch field when Skinner visited Charterhouse-on-Mendip in 1820 (BL Add MS 33656, fol 25).

Billingsley estimated that the cost of building a farmstead of 100 acres (40.5ha) 'with a farm-house, barn, stable, stalling, barton, pool, and pig-stye, should not exceed three hundred pounds', and that this would increase rental per acre from 20 to 25 shillings per annum

(1797, 62–3). Hazel Warren and Fernhill farms stood, historically, in the parishes of Ubley and Compton Martin respectively. Both were probably built by the time Billingsley (Fig 7.55) first published his *General View of the Agriculture of Somerset* (1794) and were located close to land owned by him. It is conceivable that Fernhill Farm, then known as Funnel Farm, was the subject of Billingsley's recommendation of a 'semicircular farmyard at Compton Martin', though most of his description is limited to the explanation of the farm's hay rick (Billingsley 1797, 68).

Of the two farms, Hazel Warren, originally known as Dory's Farm and later as Ubley Hill, was built between 1772 and 1791, and stood at the centre of a modest landholding built up in that period by one Thomas Dory (SHS DD/SAL/C1696/3/3). The buildings of the farmstead were particularly well constructed, with stone dressings and quoins, including the window surrounds, throughout the farmhouse, even used on the original rear outshot (Fig 7.56). The farmhouse originally had a symmetrical frontage of three bays, with central entrance, and internal chimney stacks and stone copings at the gable ends. It was soon extended to one end and the original quoins were reused on the new corners. The first farm buildings were equally lavish in their use of dressed-stone detailing, and comprised a cart shed, barn, stable and byre contained in an

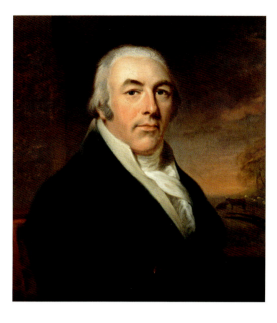

Fig 7.55
John Billingsley, painted by Joseph Hutchinson (1747–1830).
(© Victoria Art Gallery, Bath)

L-plan building to one side of the house. This was later augmented by the addition of animal sheds, including a large shelter-shed and a pigsty. The architectural treatment of the house was notably conservative in its use of stone mullions, hood moulds and iron-framed casement windows. In contrast, the farmhouse at Fernhill Farm was built using a Gothic style, with an ogee-arched doorway to the front and 'Gothick' windows, but neither the farmhouse nor the farm buildings benefited from the expensive ashlar quoins used at Hazel Warren

Fig 7.56
Hazel Warren Farm, Ubley: late 18th-century farmhouse constructed in a conservative style.
(DP086425)

Farm. The semicircular farm buildings and a large barn were built in phases probably in the 1790s and early 1800s, but have been altered extensively.

When the land surrounding the warren at Charterhouse was enclosed the former lodge was adapted to become the farmhouse for a new farmstead that became known as Warren Farm. By the early 19th century the building stood in a landscape transformed by enclosure, with large rectilinear fields bounded by drystone walls, and the pre-existing lodge at the junction of four large fields. This followed the improvement model, but was achieved conversely by constructing the system of fields to respect the earlier structure. The building was refenestrated with sash windows and given a central entrance and double-pile plan, with kitchen to the front and stair and ancillary service rooms to the rear. The farm buildings were added incrementally, with the first phase occurring in line with the farmhouse, and comprising a stable and large barn, the latter with large opposed entries, later reduced in size. Beyond this, to the west, a rectangular pond was provided, and slightly later a long animal shed was built extending south from the farm buildings, an arrangement achieved by the early 1840s (SHS MAP/DD/STL 3). In the mid- to late 19th century a new phase of substantial addition to the east saw the farmstead augmented by an L-plan range containing a brewhouse, three cart sheds, stable, byre, calving or foaling pen and separate storerooms.

However, this story of new farmsteads established on newly enclosed land is not typical of how the landscape was managed and changed in the decades after the Enclosure Acts were passed. Because of the process of allocating land within the area of new enclosures to those with existing rights, the new fields on the Mendip plateau were often farmed remotely from the villages on the lower slopes, and were not consistently provided with new buildings. Some small field barns were put up to alleviate the problems associated with this remote method of farming. Only after the demand for cereal crops dwindled and the land was depleted did the impetus to set up new upland farmsteads really come to the fore (Williams 1972, 114).

The process continued during the middle of the 19th century, and on the higher ground above Cheddar and Rodney Stoke, Bristol Plain Farm was built among enclosures that had been laid out about thirty years previously. In 1821, in the enclosure award for Cheddar, Priddy and Rodney Stoke, the associated land is shown as newly enclosed and allocated to the Duke of Buckingham (SHS D/P/rod.s/20/1/2). The area, later defined as 'Bristol Plain', is further subdivided into a number of rectangular strips let to a variety of tenants. In about 1859 sales particulars appear to show the sale of land by the Duke of Buckingham and Chandos, including 'Lot 43 – An enclosure known as Bristol Plain … supplied with water', totalling 86 acres (35ha) and which was in the hands of 'sundry tenants' (SHS DD/X/HIL/1). There is no mention of any farmhouse or buildings and none are shown on the accompanying plan, nor any field boundaries – indicating that very little had happened to the land since enclosure. Shortly afterwards Bristol Plain Farm was established as a new farmstead near the junction of four large fields, with a circular pond positioned judiciously across the intersection, accessible to stock in all four enclosures. The buildings of the farmstead reflect the expectations of income to be derived from the investment, and in typical Mendip fashion were very modest, built in rubble, with a rendered double-fronted farmhouse and an L-shaped range of farm buildings intended principally for livestock.

Numerous other farms, displaying varying degrees of economy in their construction, characterised this last period of farm building, including King Down Farm, a short distance to the north of Bristol Plain, which was built in phases during the mid-19th century. Williams determined that at least 60 new farmhouses, plus a further 10 that were possibly new, were established on Mendip during the main period of parliamentary enclosures (Williams 1972, 114). This last wave of new farm building on Mendip in the middle of the 19th century coincided with a general improvement in farming prospects, after a period of suppressed conditions during the 1830s. The expenditure on individual upland farms in this period was modest, but the cumulative investment across the upland must have been considerable. For some of the larger farmers in the area, and certainly on the landed estates, investment in farmhouses and farm buildings continued through the middle of the century into the 1880s, but much of this was piecemeal improvement and expansion on existing farms.

Model farms: Eastwood Manor Farm

We have seen that investment in Mendip farms in the 19th century was typically piecemeal. The exception to this was the extraordinary early Victorian model farm constructed at Eastwood Manor in the late 1850s. It was reputedly designed by Robert Smith, who had been employed as agent to Frederick Knight, the famous reclaimer and improver of Exmoor (Jones 1972, 919). The farmstead, or homestead as it was called in the 1860s (HEA SA 02543/SC01628), was designed at a time when the nation's estate owners and landed farmers were being inspired to build and improve on their home farms, influenced in part by the exertions of Albert, Prince Consort.

The farm at Eastwood Manor was designed upon the most advanced principles of industrial farming, utilising integration and organisation of function and process. These were based on the central idea of fattening cattle under cover, which both improved the yield on the animals themselves and improved the condition of the valuable manure used for conditioning the land, which at Eastwood Manor Farm was collected in a 3,000-gallon (13,640l) slurry tank beneath the steading (Jones 1972, 920). The farm combined an astonishing array of functions and activities within a single structure covering over an acre (0.4ha) of ground, and was built using the most up-to-date industrial construction methods and materials, although wrapped in a highly architectural veneer of ashlar stonework (Fig 7.57). This external elaboration, however, did not conceal what was an entirely functional internal plan, with five large parallel ranges, articulated by gables on the main facade to the south-east, accommodating mechanised and intensive farming activities, including chaff cutting, threshing, cake crushing and turnip slicing.

Originally the farm stood at the centre of a 900-acre (364ha) estate (Jones 1972, 919) with prime arable and pasture land, which the owners, a Mr and Mrs Taylor, the latter being heiress of Gournay Court in West Harptree, transformed along the most informed lines. The farmstead provided accommodation for rearing sheep, pigs and cattle, with water-powered mechanised facilities for processing cereal crops, including grist and flour mills, and flax processing, in conjunction with other estate functions such as a sawmill, carpenter's workshop and blacksmith's forge (ibid, 920); *see* Figure 7.58. With its architectural and principled design, the farmstead encapsulated contemporary notions of beauty and profit, though the expense was considerable, as noted in a sale catalogue which described the farm as 'A model covered homestead … recently constructed on the most approved principles, and at a very large cost' (HEA SA 02543/SC01628).

Fig 7.57
Eastwood Manor Farm, East Harptree: view of south-east elevation of principal cattle sheds. (DP069528)

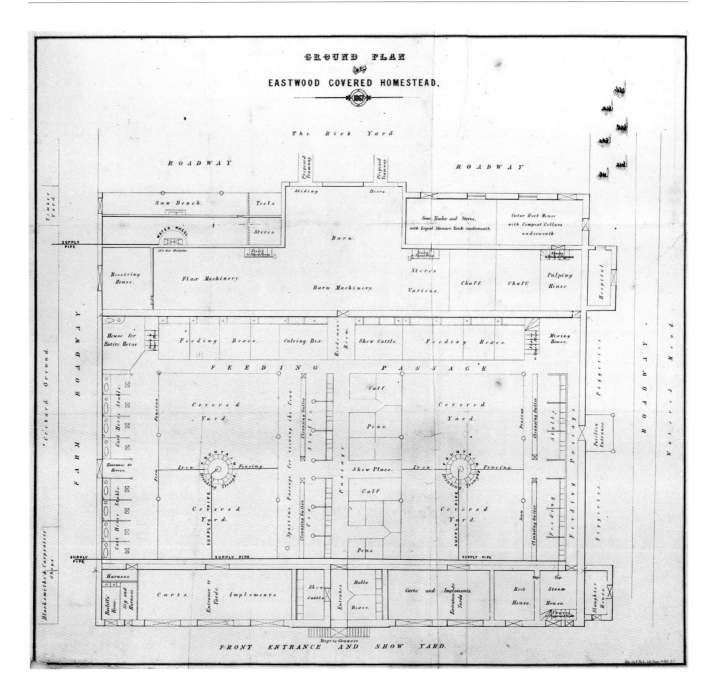

Fig 7.58
Plan of Eastwood
Manor Farm.
(BB90/12827)

The farmstead was arranged on two main levels, with a further half-basement level on the downhill side, to the north-east. The lower levels were primarily for animal husbandry and processing feed and crops, while the upper floors were for storage, largely straw and grain. The farmstead was arranged round a central range, emphasised externally by an eccentric pronounced gable standing high above the associated roofline of the two covered yards. The central range comprised a storage barn and granary on the upper level, reached by two external flights of stone steps. To the rear a large threshing barn stretched across the back of the building, adjacent to the power source: a 27½ft (8.4m) diameter waterwheel. The covered yards, designed for fattening bullocks, were treated with a mix of embellishment and utilitarianism, each furnished with an ornate central water fountain (Fig 7.59). They were provided with generous viewing galleries with industrial latticework balustrades, which looked on to the stock and the central fountain in each yard.

The same contrasting treatment sets apart the industrial interior construction from that of the architectural exterior. The latter makes widespread and expensive use of cut stone, with rusticated quoins and numerous other carved details, and only a slight concession given to brickwork used on arches into the covered yards and cart and implement sheds. The two end ranges, flanking the covered yards, were each treated with a stone finial in the shape of a corn sheaf, while further elaboration included quatrefoil piercings and, on the north-east side, two small projecting bays embellished with elaborate bargeboards and stone panels with carved stone sheep and cattle heads. To allow open access between the covered yards and associated stalls beneath the central range, the latter was built on two arcades with cast-iron columns and brick aches, with the viewing gallery and barn floor supported on fabricated wrought-iron beams (Fig 7.60). This type of arcade was in widespread use in industrial and railway architecture of the time, and reflects honestly the industrial nature of the farm processes for which the building was designed. The use of iron for both structure and covering was ideal for the large uninterrupted space required for the covered fattening yards.

This example of high Victorian farming was an extraordinary manifestation of contemporary thinking, and yet probably never profited on the great expense invested in its construction. It stands, however, as a testament to improvement farming in the Mendip area and what was achieved on a comparatively small Mendip estate during this era of agricultural improvement in the middle of the 19th century.

Fig 7.59
Eastwood Manor Farm, East Harptree: ornately designed fountain in centre of cattle yard. (DP069512)

Fig 7.60
Eastwood Manor Farm, East Harptree: interior of cattle sheds showing viewing galleries, cast-iron columns and wrought-iron beams. (DP069492)

The homestead, as it was known, was only part of the improvements made at the Eastwood Estate during the period, with the other main areas to benefit being the house, park and gardens.

The industrial landscape

Travelling through the Mendip Hills today it has the appearance of a tranquil agricultural region, but in previous centuries the hills and combes would have echoed to the sound of industry. One of the chief industrial activities was mining, with lead, calamine, manganese, silver and iron ore all extracted. Coal was also mined, with a small colliery established in Litton towards the end of the 18th century (Bodman 1990, 14). Stone quarrying was another extractive industry that was widespread in the region and one that continues to this day. Up to the mid-19th century the majority of buildings on Mendip were constructed from local stone, usually won from a small quarry established close by, which gave the villages their own distinctive character. The demand for local stone increased during the 18th and 19th centuries, for use in both

major engineering works – such as roads and railways – and for wider agricultural improvements. Limestone was utilised in the construction of the new enclosure walls that sprang up across the uplands, along with the improvement farmsteads that followed.

Improvement farming involved a lengthy process of soil enhancement which, along with clearing, levelling, ploughing and harrowing, included the application of lime. The use of lime to improve the soil can be traced back to the medieval period, but it was only during the late 18th and 19th centuries that more permanent structures were built for its production. Just under two-thirds of the limekilns recorded on the Ordnance Survey 1st edition map lie within areas of parliamentary enclosure, and many improvement farms had their own limekilns (Fig 7.61). The limekilns were predominantly rectangular in plan, and were usually located adjacent to the quarry from where the limestone was sourced, often positioned close to a roadway. Limekilns comprised a bowl or pot – a circular hole lined with stone and surrounded by thick walls – with a draw hole at its base. The structures were generally terraced into the slope for ease

Fig 7.61
The distribution of limekilns across the Mendip Hills AONB.

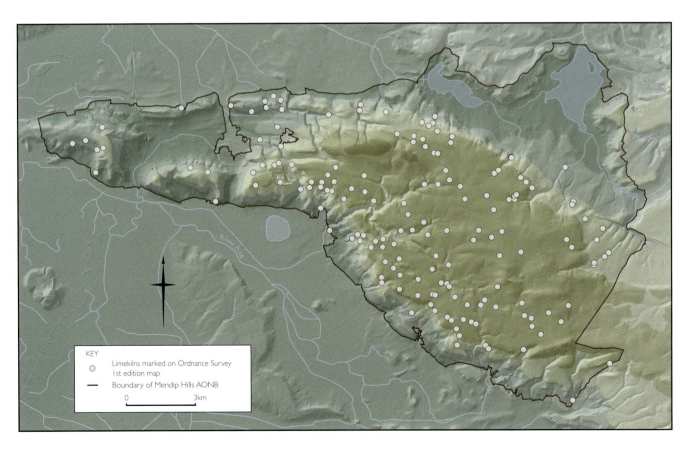

of both construction and loading (Fig 7.62). Billingsley described the form of Mendip limekilns as 'that of a French bottle', and estimated the build cost of a single kiln in 1797 to be around £13, with the structure producing enough lime to manure 3 acres (1.2ha) per week (1797, 90–1).

Manufacturing industries included the production of textiles, edge tools, paper, gunpowder, cider, beer and cheese, as well as the hand-knitting of stockings. When Daniel Defoe travelled through Cheddar in the early 18th century he commented on the system for cheese production in the region:

The Milk of all the Town Cows, is brought together every Day into a common Room, where the Persons appointed, or trusted for the Management, measure every Man's Quantity, and set it down in a Book; when the Quantities are adjusted, the Milk is all put together, and every Meal's Milk makes One Cheese, and no more; so that the Cheese is bigger, or less, as the Cows yield more, or less, Milk. By this Method, the Goodness of the Cheese is preserved, and, without all dispute, it is the best Cheese that England affords, if not, the whole World affords. (Defoe 1968, 278)

Textile manufacturing was largely concerned with the production of woollen broadcloths and lighter cloths called Spanish medleys. The primary centres for cloth production were Wells and Frome, with Axbridge, Chewton Mendip and the Harptrees all involved in the industry. It was usually organised in the 'putting-out' system, and largely undertaken in the homes or workshops of the local craftsmen. The move towards mechanisation in the late 18th century, along with the development of a more centralised factory system, saw cloth manufacturing decline in rural areas, and it disappeared almost completely by the early 19th century.

Cloth production led to the creation of fulling mills along many of the region's fast-flowing watercourses. At Coley a fulling mill was documented in 1675 and was still in operation when Collinson passed through the area in the late 18th century (1791, 587). Upstream the fulling mill at Sherborne was powered by a small tributary of the River Chew and was in operation until at least 1770 (Bodman 1990, 17). After fulling, broadcloths and medleys were transferred to timber racks where the cloth was stretched on tenterhooks to dry; several fields surrounding the lower mill at Sherborne are named 'Rack Close' on an estate map of 1761 (SHS MAP/DD/CC/338). Fulling had ceased at Sherborne by 1839, although the mill continued to grind grain until 1883. By the early 19th century the majority of fulling mills had ceased to operate, as the manufacture of cloth was increasingly centralised on the towns of Frome and Bradford-on-Avon.

The clear, fast-flowing waters of the Mendip region were also a key factor in the

Fig 7.62
A limekiln. These were generally terraced into the slope for ease of loading.
(Elaine Jamieson)

Fig 7.63
A 17th-century map of
Mendip showing mining
districts, now in Wells
and Mendip Museum.
(DP158767, reproduced by
permission of Wells and
Mendip Museum)

Harptree, was being used to produce paper in 1816 when Charles Gumm was the papermaker, but had reverted to grinding corn by 1830 (Ross 2004, 34). Local tradition says that the mill at Sherborne was later used as a button factory, as Elihu Tucker was recorded as a button dealer in the Litton census returns of 1851 (Atthill 1984, 63). In contrast, the mill at Wookey Hole was rebuilt and enlarged after its acquisition by William Sampson Hodgkinson in 1852, and continued in operation until 1972.

Post-medieval mineral extraction

There is a wealth of documentary and field evidence relating to mining and prospecting for metal-bearing rocks on Mendip (Fig 7.63). A comprehensive history of mining on the Mendip Hills has been told by J W Gough in his book entitled *The Mines of Mendip* (1930, reprinted 1967), first published within a generation of the last mines closing. Mineral extraction in the region is an activity that stretches back to at least the Romano-British period (*see* Chapter 5), and by the 16th century mining was formalised in four main divisions or 'Liberties'. These were administered by the four 'Lords Royal of Mendip' – the Bishop of Bath and Wells, and the lords of Chewton, Charterhouse and Richmond (Harptree) – who issued licences to mine and claimed 'lot-lead' (which was 10 per cent of any produced on their land). They also administered their own courts, and enforced and enhanced the complex set of mining rules and customs which applied over the whole area. Each of the four lordships had its own 'minery' where ore was brought to be washed and smelted before being weighed. The weight of lead determined the 'lot' or tithe due to the lord, which was collected by his officer, the lead-reeve. The mineries were known as Priddy Minery, Chewton Minery, Harptree Minery and West Minery (Gough 1967, 69–111).

establishment of paper works around the foot of the escarpment slope. The earliest reference to papermaking in the region dates to 1610 at the Wookey Hole Mill, and by the early 19th century there were paper works at Rickford, Sherborne, Banwell, Compton Martin, West Harptree, Wookey and Cheddar (Atthill 1976a, 168). Many of these mills were small family concerns producing paper by hand and employing a small number of local people. The paper works at Sherborne Upper Mill, for example, had been established by 1823 and the first papermaker, John King, appears to have been a partner in the paper mill at Compton Martin. By 1825 the mill at Sherborne was in the hands of Thomas Gilling, who came from a family of papermakers connected with the paper works at Cheddar (Bodman 1990).

In an age of increasing commercialisation the smaller paper works struggled to turn a profit, with many going out of business by the mid-19th century. Herriott's Mill, in West

The archaeological evidence is explicit. Aerial photographic transcription shows a sea of mounds and hollows, either circular or linear, marking the areas of former mining operations that stretch from Bleadon in the west to Green Ore in the east (Fig 7.64). A particular concentration is apparent over the central plateau – around Charterhouse-on-Mendip, Priddy, Chewton Mendip and East Harptree (Fig 7.65) – reflecting the four main lead-mining districts. Other concentrations can

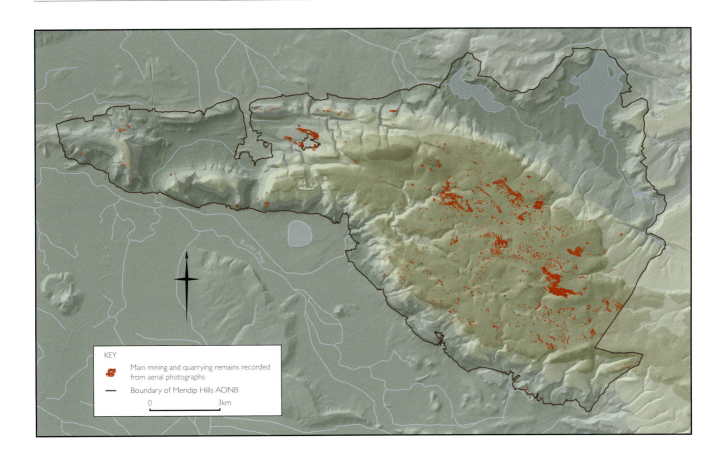

Fig 7.64
Map showing the extent of main mining and quarrying remains recorded from aerial photographs.

Fig 7.65
Smitham Hill, East Harptree: Cornish-style stone and brick chimney. This is the only remaining example of its kind in the region.
(DP163838)

be seen around Shipham and Rowberrow and represent the main focus of the calamine industry. This pitted and scarred landscape was known locally as 'gruffy ground'. Ore was commonly dug out from a discrete pit or shaft, the sides of which were sometimes supported by a drystone lining. The spoil removed from these pits was usually dumped close to the area of excavation, often around the lip of the hollow. When a pit became too deep to work easily it was abandoned and a new one opened up a short distance away. Ore was normally found in thin veins or lodes, and the pits commonly form lines following the mineral deposits. Rakes are narrow linear trenches that follow a vein of ore (Fig 7.66).

Fig 7.66
Earthwork plans showing examples of mining remains: (a) pits and (b) rakes.

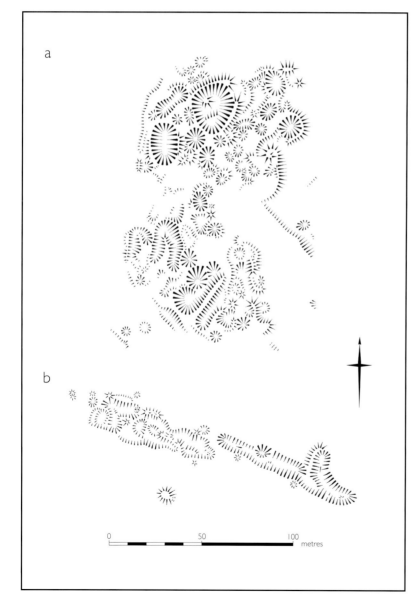

Calamine and iron ore mines

Calamine, or *lapis calaminaris*, was a key ingredient in the manufacture of brass and was being extracted on the Mendip Hills from the 16th century. By the end of the 17th century, mines had been established in the western part of the hills at Rowberrow, Shipham, Winscombe and Burrington. The first decade of the 18th century saw the founding of the Bristol Brass Wire Company, which grew to become one of the largest brass manufacturers in Europe. Mendip calamine was considered the best in the country, and the mines were kept busy supplying mills around Bristol, Birmingham and beyond. A process for extracting zinc (also known as spelter) from calamine was discovered by William Champion, who went on to establish a works near Warmley in 1746 primarily concerned with the manufacture of zinc from calamine ore. The demand for calamine therefore grew during the 18th century and was probably at its peak around 1800. Soon after the industry went into rapid decline, and in 1839 Sir Henry de la Beche (the first director of the British Geological Survey) noted that calamine working on Mendip had all but ceased (Farrant 2008, 37).

Shipham and Rowberrow were the main centres for the calamine industry in the region. The modern villages now sit amid a landscape of long-abandoned pits, shafts and rakes (Fig 7.67). When Collinson visited the area at the end of the 18th century, Rowberrow consisted of around fifty houses with the vast majority of its inhabitants employed in mining. After the decline of the calamine industry, however, many of these cottages were abandoned. The vestiges of this once-thriving community can be seen strung along Rowberrow Bottom, surviving as the rubble footings and earthwork remains of buildings, enclosures and yards. To the south of the settlement was the dressing floor, where the ore was washed, baked, picked and sifted, before finally being put in bags to be hauled to Bristol. Perhaps the most distinctive feature of this processing area is a flight of terraced stone-revetted platforms, approximately 65m in length, which can still be seen along the wooded valley bottom. At the height of the industry, the baking or burning process created such toxic conditions in the combe that Collinson commented 'very little wood thrives

KEY

Earthwork features

Cut features

Extent of settlement on Ordnance
Survey 1st edition map

0   1km

near the village, the fumes arising from the burning of the calamine being very destructive to their foliage' (1791, 599).

By the late 18th century, calamine was also being extracted in the east of the region. Returns for the East Harptree mines clearly illustrate that by the 1790s calamine was the principal mineral raised in the district, with quantities of calamine far outweighing those of lead. The industry at East Harptree would appear to have been relatively short-lived in comparison to Shipham and Rowberrow. Although several leases were granted for the extraction of calamine during the 19th century, it would appear relatively little ore was raised after the middle of the century. When the Revd John Skinner visited East Harptree in 1830 he noted that calamine was still being dug in the area of Richmont Castle. He also noted that to the north of the castle, where the valleys converge in Harptree Combe, a building had been constructed to wash the ore before it was transported by cart to Bristol (BL Add MS 33717, fol 166).

The extraction of iron, mostly in the form of yellow ochre, was also undertaken on Mendip.

This industry was in operation in the west of the region during the 18th century, with mining recorded above Hutton and Banwell by around 1750. Pits and spoil heaps again provide the evidence for this period of activity, with nowhere immune to the prospector's pick. A string of pits across the interior of Banwell Camp, for example, are testament to the efforts of individuals and adventurers keen to locate and extract any profitable seams of iron-bearing ochre. By the end of the century ochre was being raised above East Harptree and Chewton Mendip, though quantities were relatively small. It was not until the second half of the 19th century that greater efforts were made to extract iron-producing ore, presumably as more traditional minerals were proving harder to obtain. Mr W Thomas was granted a licence to work iron ore on the Waldegrave Estate in 1867 (which included the area around Wigmoor Farm), an enterprise which continued until 1871 (Gough 1967, 247). Iron mining was also carried out for a short time in the 1870s in Lodmore Wood on Chancellor's Farm. In 1890–1 iron and a little copper were raised near Ebbor Rocks, with evidence for this short

Fig 7.67
The distribution of pits, shafts and rakes around Shipham and Rowberrow, mapped from aerial photographs.

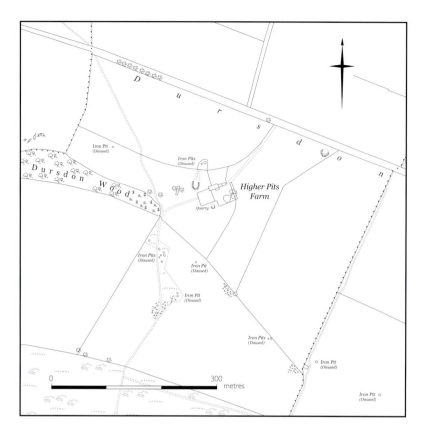

period of industrial activity evident on the Ordnance Survey 1st edition map, where a series of disused 'iron pits' is recorded around Higher Pits Farm (Fig 7.68).

The 19th-century lead industry

The enclosure of the upland wastes largely brought to an end the age-old system of adventurers working individual lead pits on Mendip. Exploration in the early 19th century was largely carried out by enterprising landowners, such as Dr Benjamin Somers of Langford, who was prospecting for ore and reworking the old slag deposits on his Ubley Warren estate by the 1820s (Clarke and Stanton 1984, 35). When the Revd John Skinner visited Charterhouse-on-Mendip in August 1824, he commented that Dr Somers had engaged miners from the village of Rowberrow to work the old slag grounds and had constructed a smelting house in the Blackmoor Valley to process the material (BL Add MS 33677, fol 105); *see* Figure 7.69. The less efficient processing techniques employed by earlier operations left large quantities of refuse material which contained a sufficient lead content to make resmelting commercially viable. This process was easier and cheaper than sinking new shafts to win fresh ore, although some optimistic landlords continued the search for profitable seams during the first half of the 19th century.

Dr Somers held the lease for the Chewton and Priddy mineries in the 1830s and 1840s, and was involved in prospecting operations right across the hills until his death in 1848 (Gough 1967, 183). By the 1850s Mr Edward Barwell of Harptree Court, in partnership with Mr T S Wright, negotiated the lease for the Chewton Minery and new exploration works started. Shafts were sunk in the hope of locating profitable seams of ore, but these efforts proved unsuccessful and attention soon focused on reprocessing old mining debris. In the first half of the 19th century reprocessing operations were largely undertaken using traditional methods, and a lack of technical expertise hampered the ability of enterprising landlords to turn a profit. However, by the mid-19th century Mendip had attracted the attention of Cornish mining engineers who brought with them knowledge of more sophisticated processing techniques (ibid, 184). These included round buddles (tanks for

Fig 7.68
Ordnance Survey 1st edition map showing the distribution of iron pits around Higher Pits Farm, near Ebbor Rocks.

Fig 7.69
A 'Mendip Miner' as depicted by the Revd John Skinner in the early 19th century. (Add MS 33673, folio 113v © The British Library Board)

washing and separating the ore) and reverberatory furnaces, where ore was smelted using rotary fans driven by a steam engine.

The 19th-century lead working at Charterhouse-on-Mendip

In 1844 the Mendip Hills Mining Company (MHMC) embarked on a new phase of mining at Charterhouse-on-Mendip, initially concerned with reopening old mines and sinking new shafts in the Blackmoor Valley (primarily on the Ubley and Charterhouse rakes). These mining trials proved an expensive failure, however, and were abandoned by 1846. In the same year Lord Clifden leased his lands and slag grounds around Velvet Bottom to the MHMC, which then turned its attention to exploiting the old mining waste. A large open trench was dug into the slag heaps and driven up the centre of the valley; by 1847 the trench was 200m long and up to 7m deep, and contained continuous beds of slags up to 4m thick (Clarke and Stanton 1984, 35). These extensive open works are a distinctive feature of the Velvet Bottom and Blackmoor valleys, and have served to destroy most of the evidence for earlier mineral extraction and processing in the area.

Enough viable slag was extracted via this method to necessitate the preparation of dressing floors and a smelt mill. By 1847 work on the furnace and engine house had begun in the Velvet Bottom valley, with a boiler and steam engine brought to the site from Bristol to power the fans. Brickwork flues were constructed to carry the draught from the fans to the three blast furnaces which, along with deposit chambers and condensing flues, were largely in place by the end of 1847. The condensers were looped into the main flue, which ascended the hillside directly above the furnace building, ending in a vertical chimney. The complex also included a small furnace to smelt the lead into pigs, and a store for coal and coke; by 1849 a reverberatory furnace was also in operation (Clarke and Stanton 1984, 37).

In 1848 the MHMC also leased the slag grounds in Ubley and Blagdon parishes from Dr Somers, with the lease including existing buildings and machinery. Work on the Ubley slag grounds began in the spring of 1849, and new dressing floors were constructed soon after. The first dressing floors on the Ubley and Blackmoor grounds were located at a high level, on top of the slag deposits, with the material drawn up to the floors using a tramway and winding machinery powered by a steam engine. Later, new floors were built on the valley bottom to allow material beneath the original floors to be quarried. By the autumn of 1849 a reservoir had been created towards the upper end of the Blackmoor Valley, and a reverberatory furnace had been built to smelt the material produced by the dressing floors (Clarke and Stanton 1984, 39).

By 1855 a Pattinson plant had also been set up in the Blackmoor Valley. This plant improved the recovery of silver deposits using a process patented by Mr Hugh Lee Pattinson some two decades earlier (Gough 1967, 194–5). Pattinson found that as molten lead cooled it crystallised, and the crystals contained a lower silver content than did the molten metal. By moving the lead crystals down a sequence of pans and repeating the process, the remaining metal became greatly enriched in silver (Raistrick and Roberts 1990, 7). In 1967–8 the main building of the Pattinson plant was partly excavated, which revealed a linear range comprising four rooms; this range was connected to a circular chimney by a stone-lined flue which climbed the hillside above the plant. A second structure to the north-west was also excavated and found to represent a small stable, with the open-fronted building divided internally by a timber partition forming two stalls (Hawtin 1970, 173).

In 1861 the MHMC passed into the hands of Treffry & Co., a Cornish firm, and it was under its ownership that the smelt mill and flues at Blackmoor were either rebuilt or improved. Today this processing works is largely represented by the remains of its masonry flues (Fig 7.70), partly refurbished in 1982, in front of which lie heaps of glassy black slag. The older Velvet Bottom smelt mill survives slightly better, with a range of structures including the engine house, furnace building and flues still visible, shrouded in trees on the north side of the valley. The buildings survive as stone footings, tumbled walls and grass-covered earthworks (Fig 7.71). The engine house is represented by a two-cell structure, 22m long and 12m wide, north-east of which lies the furnace building. This more substantial structure is terraced into a steep slope and divided internally, both rooms measuring approximately 20m by 14m, with evidence for a cobbled floor in the western room. Also

*Fig 7.70
Masonry flues in the
Blackmoor Valley.
(NMR 4804/40)*

forming a series of ponds in which the run-off water from the buddles could settle and clear.

Processing sites were dependent on the supply of water, and by 1847 the MHMC had dammed the springs at Lower Farm and directed water along 1800m of launders. These launders were rectangular wooden troughs – 0.3m wide and 0.2m deep – which traced the contour of the slope along the east side of the Longwood Valley and round into Velvet Bottom (Clarke and Stanton 1984, 36–7). Sections of the launder were carried along the ground in cuttings, with others raised on posts. A short section of surviving cutting was recorded from aerial photographs on the northern side of Velvet Bottom, with rock-cut stretches also visible in the woods below Lower Farm (Fig 7.73). The water was carried by the launders down to the dressing floor, where it supplied the buddles and the steam engine.

Horses were also used in conjunction with steam power at the Charterhouse mines. Horse whims have been identified adjacent to the Charterhouse and Ubley rakes, to the west of Ubley Warren Farm, and were used to raise ore from the vertical shafts. The horse whim at the Ubley rakes is represented by a raised circular platform around 14m in diameter, with a central stone socket in which a metal pin rotated, working the winding gear (Burgess 1971, 5). Horses were also employed at the processing sites to transport concentrates from the dressing floors to the smelt mill, and to power machinery. At the south-western end of the Velvet Bottom smelt mill site is the earthwork remains of a circular platform, probably representing a horse engine used to drive crushing machinery. The circular platform is 17m in diameter and is terraced into a steep slope, with the feature slighted on the eastern side by later quarrying. A series of platforms identified to the south-west of the horse engine possibly represent areas where the slag was picked by hand before being carried to the crushing roller.

evident at the site is a series of other smaller structures, two of which appear on the 1st edition Ordnance Survey map of 1885; the map was produced within a decade of smelting operations being abandoned.

Dispersed along the Blackmoor and Velvet Bottom valleys are the remains of flights of circular buddles, some of which retain evidence of their stone-revetted sides. When in operation the buddles would have comprised a very low cone-shaped floor and central boss, onto which slimes were fed. With the help of mechanical stirrers, the material flowed outwards to the edge of the tank, with the heavier ore deposited closest to the centre and the lighter waste towards the edge. The buddle was then dug out and the lead ore lying in a narrow zone near the central boss was retrieved; the process was repeated until material with a sufficient lead content for smelting was produced. The straight-sided circular buddles which adorn the valley floors ranged in size from 6.6m to 9.9m in diameter, and are grouped in batteries of five or more (Fig 7.72). Dams were also constructed across the valley in Velvet Bottom,

After 1878 the smelting of lead was given up altogether at Charterhouse, although the buddles continued to be worked, with dressed material prepared and sent to be smelted at Bristol. The final closure of the lead-works at Charterhouse in 1885 was probably a result of falling lead prices and the exhaustion of cheaply accessible ore, which made the enterprise economically unsustainable (Gough 1930, 195).

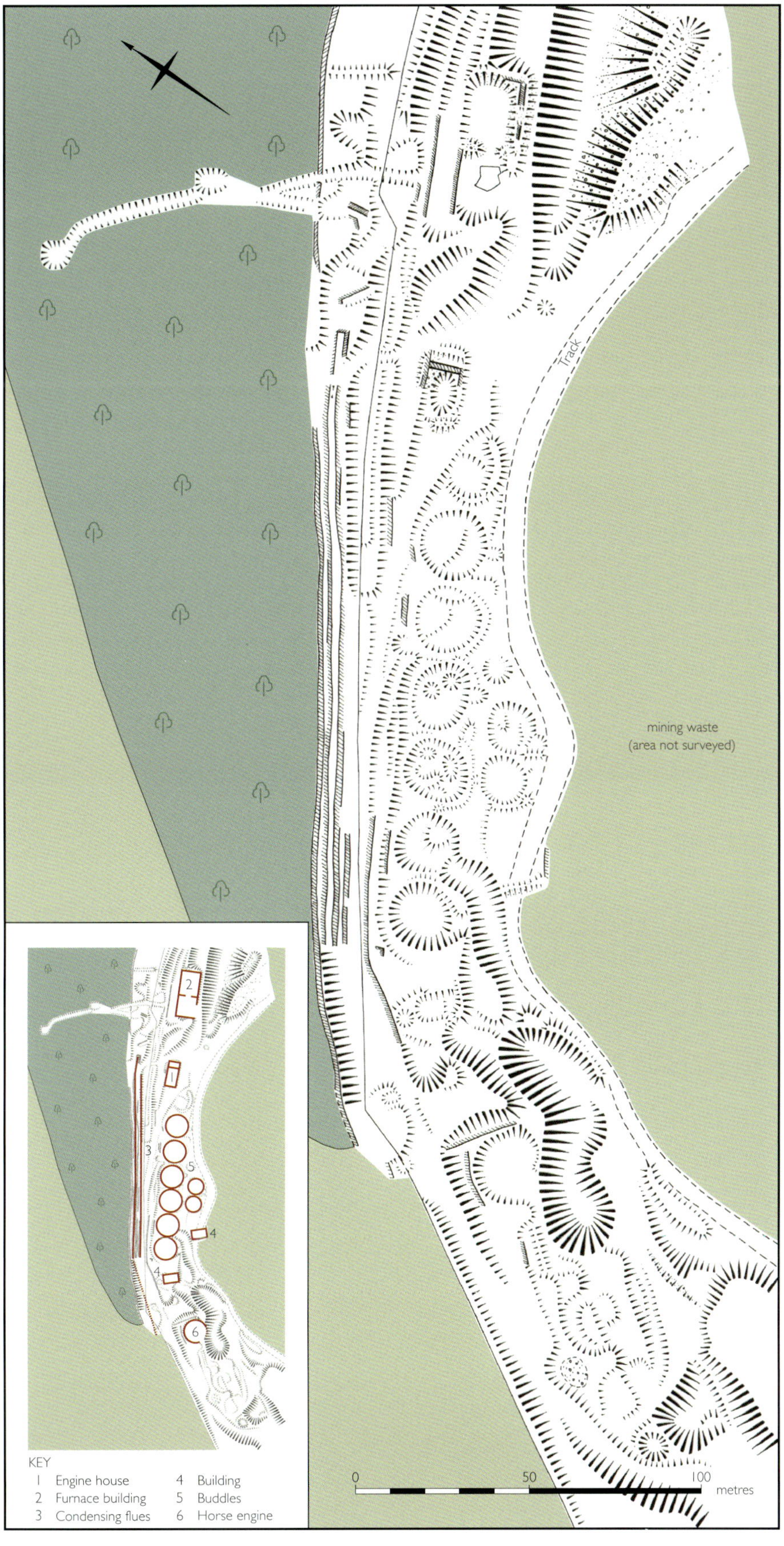
Track
mining waste
(area not surveyed)
0
50
100
metres
KEY
1 Engine house
2 Furnace building
3 Condensing flues
4 Building
5 Buddles
6 Horse engine

Fig 7.71
Earthwork plan of the Velvet Bottom dressing floor.

Fig 7.72
Aerial photograph showing
open works, spoil heaps and
buddles at Velvet Bottom.
(NMR 24331/4)

Fig 7.73
Remains of the cutting below
Lower Farm that carried the
launder to Velvet Bottom.
(DP115016)

Panel 7.1 The changing landscape of West End Division, Chewton Mendip

Today West End Division, Chewton Mendip, consists of a small number of dispersed farms surrounded by rolling pasture fields and mixed woodland. If you look closely, however, you will see the earthwork remains of a surprising number of abandoned farmsteads and cottages, surrounded by small closes and fields, and intermixed with the pits and spoil heaps indicative of mineral extraction. There are few places on Mendip that illustrate better the changing nature of the post-medieval landscape. A rich cartographic record, combined with a wealth of archaeological and architectural information, can be used to demonstrate how the settlement pattern developed through time, and how changes in agriculture and industry influenced this transformation.

West End Division (Fig P7.1.1) encompasses a lobe of land towards the south-western corner of Chewton Mendip parish and forms part of an estate that has been in the hands of the Waldegrave family since the mid-16th century. It is bounded to the north by the parish of Litton and to the west by Eaker Hill and Niver Hill, which define the edge of the uplands. The form of the fields and the nature of the holdings within West End Division – predominantly ring-fenced farms – suggest the area had its origins in a period of assarting from woodland or waste. The medieval development of the region has been touched on before (*see* Chapters 5 and 6), and the general pattern of settlement changed relatively little until the early 19th century. Fieldwork has, however, revealed a layer of information not visible in the cartographic or documentary record, identifying farmsteads abandoned before the first estate surveys were undertaken and highlighting the value of a holistic approach to the study of settlement development.

By the 18th century, West End Division comprised around 27 holdings linked by a complex network of roads and tracks. The farms in the area were relatively small by today's standards: the majority of tenants worked between 20 and 40 acres (8 and 16ha), with a third of the holdings covering no more than 10 to 20 acres (4 to 8ha), and three comprising less than 10 acres (4ha). Estate records indicate that a number of farms were subdivided in the 17th century. A holding towards the north of the district named Sacrafield (later known as Payne's Pond) was divided between Susan and Robert Haskins, with each tenant allotted around 20 acres of land. The farmhouse was also split, with Susan occupying the 'hall, entry and chambers over' and Robert 'the kitchen parlour, buttery and chambers over'. This would indicate the dwelling almost certainly had a two-room plan, possibly with an entrance lobby, and had a fully floored upper storey. The earthwork evidence supports this, indicating the holding had an in-line range of farm buildings and faced onto a small yard. The division of Sacrafield would appear to have been relatively short-lived, as by April 1720 the holding had been brought back together under a new tenant (SHS DD/WG/4/1/2).

Each farmstead in West End Division was surrounded by its own network of small enclosed fields defined by banks, hedges and hollow-ways. Later land improvement has left little archaeological evidence for farming practices, but the documentary sources give us an insight into how the land was utilised during the 18th century. At this time mixed farming predominated in the region, although three of West End's smaller holdings were entirely pastoral by the end of the century. On most tenements at least 20 per cent of the land was in arable cultivation by 1794, with a quarter having as much as two-thirds under the plough. The 1801 crop returns show that oats predominated, accounting for almost half of arable production, with wheat representing a third. Barley, peas and potatoes were also grown in far smaller quantities, but only a few acres of beans and turnips were cultivated. Two medium-sized tenements at Priddy (which lay within the West End Division of Chewton Mendip) were under permanent grass, representing specialist stock and dairy farms with extensive grazing rights on the upland wastes.

Customary rights permitted tenant farmers to graze stock on the commons and allowed individuals or groups of tenants to prospect and extract minerals from the wastes under licence. This was permitted on condition they followed

Fig P7.1.1
Extract from an estate
map of 1794 showing the
West End Division of
Chewton Mendip.
(DP069312. Estate
map property of Earl
Waldegrave, reproduced
by permission of the
Waldegrave Estate)

the mining code and a 'lot' or tithe was paid to the lord of the manor. Within the lower-lying enclosed areas mining customs did not apply, and the extraction industry was more directly controlled by the lord of the manor. The earthwork remains of mineral extraction – represented by a series of shafts, pits and spoil heaps – survive within West End Division (Fig P7.1.2). The densest concentration of pits and shafts was recorded to the west of Eaker Hill Farm in an area of former common, with further mining remains evident within the enclosed ground on the lower slopes of the hill and in Buddle's Wood (formerly Grove Ground).

Here the remains of shafts, spoil heaps, dressing waste and a leat survive under a canopy of coniferous plantation.

Lead extraction in the area was at its peak during the 16th and 17th centuries. However, the following century saw the industry's decline, with mining activity increasingly focused on the extraction of calamine. By the end of the 18th century calamine ore was being raised on Eaker Hill and in the area around Green Ore. In contrast to the lead industry, calamine extraction would appear to have been relatively short-lived and was probably in decline by the early 19th century. A concen-

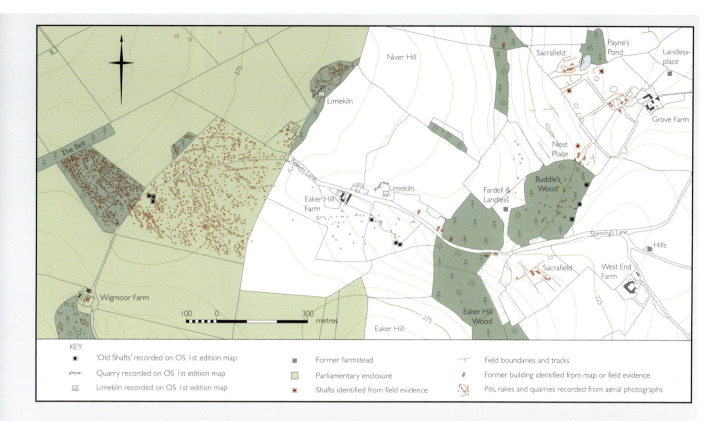

Fig P7.1.2
*West End Division:
settlement remains and
areas of former mining
and quarrying.*

KEY

⊡	'Old Shafts' recorded on OS 1st edition map	■	Former farmstead	⊤	Field boundaries and tracks
〰	Quarry recorded on OS 1st edition map	▨	Parliamentary enclosure	▮	Former building identified from map or field evidence
⌂	Limekiln recorded on OS 1st edition map	⊡	Shafts identified from field evidence	⁖	Pits, rakes and quarries recorded from aerial photographs

tration of cottages along Reeves Lane and
Sperrings Lane may represent the homes of
labourers employed in these various episodes
of mineral extraction. Some of these cottages
were abandoned by the early 18th century;
others were the product of new building work
undertaken around 1800. A number of these
cottages survive to this day and reflect the ebb
and flow of industrial activity in the region.

The enclosure of Chewton Mendip's common
grazing land at the end of the 18th century
had a significant impact on the rights of tenants,
and shaped the way the landscape was
managed and farmed. Although the Act saw
each tenant allocated land within the area of
new enclosures, documents indicate that many
had relinquished their small allotments by the
early 19th century. This land, combined with
allotted areas in hand, was amalgamated to
create Wigmoor Farm, a large new holding
above Eaker Hill. The buildings of this improvement farmstead were constructed around a
subcircular yard, and included a stable, barn
(with ground-floor stalling and a threshing
floor above), open-fronted animal shelter, and
a farmhouse and offices. Billingsley stated that
this 440-acre (178ha) farm cost just under

£3,600 to establish in 1802. He estimated a
further £400 would be required to construct
additional buildings (such as a dairy house,
wagon house and pigsty) and for the cost of
rearing the boundary fencing of the distinctive
rectilinear fields (Billingsley 1807, 45–6).

The creation of Wigmoor Farm was the first
step in a programme of far-reaching estate-led
improvements undertaken during in the 19th
century. In West End Division most of the
tenements were brought in hand by the 1830s,
which facilitated a comprehensive reordering
of the agricultural landscape. This process
included the construction of 'The Grove' (later
Grove Farm), a completely new improvement
farmstead built about 1830 (Fig P7.1.3). The
relatively modest farm buildings of 'The Grove'
were constructed around a courtyard, and
included an open-fronted animal shelter, barn,
stables and large farmhouse. The construction
of this new improvement farm coincided with
the consolidation of many of the surrounding
tenements, with land brought together to
create larger, more efficient units. During this
process many of the buildings, yards and closes
of earlier farmsteads were swept away and
are now only visible through their earthwork

Fig P7.1.3
Grove Farm surrounded
by the earthwork remains
of former farmsteads.
(NMR 24736/41)

remains. Only a few pre-improvement farm buildings were retained and utilised as out-barns or shelter-sheds for livestock, with others converted to provide accommodation for the growing number of landless labourers.

The census returns show that the number of houses in the parish as a whole dropped by almost a quarter between 1831 and 1841, more than in any other decade of the 19th century. The few farmsteads that remained in West End Division were enlarged and renamed. These included West End Farm and Cole's Farm, the buildings of which were improved, either through the enlargement of existing structures, or by constructing anew. It is within these farmsteads that the fragmentary remains of earlier structures can be found, such as the 17th-century timbers in the farmhouse at Cole's Farm. This process of estate-led improvement was not simply confined to the farming landscape. Plantations and shelter belts were also created, such as Eaker Hill Wood and 'The Belt' (located to the north of Wigmoor Farm), some of which were established on former mining areas unsuitable for agricultural production. The first few decades of the 19th century also saw the creation of a small pleasure park to the north of Chewton Priory, and the construction of a new turnpike road linking Wells and Bath.

Mendip: a healthy situation?

The natural resources of the Mendip Hills were not only exploited by adventurers and industrialists, but were also harnessed by those wishing to promote improved health and well-being. The rapid growth of industrial centres during the 19th century created increasingly desperate living conditions severely affecting the health of their inhabitants. As the urban masses underpinned the commercial wealth of the places in which they lived and worked, improved living standards were seen as essential to commercial growth. The Mendip Hills, like other landscapes such as the seaside, acquired a status and significance which diametrically opposed that of the unhealthy industrial urban environment. Ironically, this was despite the fact that some of these land-scapes simultaneously supported dangerous and environmentally unhealthy industries, such as lead mining in the case of Mendip. This led to two parallel strands of development on Mendip: the creation of infrastructure to convey a clean water supply to the city, and the construction of institutions devoted to health.

The Bristol Waterworks Company

By the mid-19th century the 'excessive mortality' recorded in the city of Bristol was ascribed to poor drainage and a lack of clean and easily accessible water. The Bristol Waterworks Company was established in 1846 by Act of Parliament with the aim of remedying the problem by supplying clean water to Bristol. The company concluded that springs at Barrow Gurney and at Harptree Combe and those forming the River Chew at Litton and Chewton Mendip were most suitable for the task. This was due to the quality and quantity of the waters in these areas, and their naturally elevated position above the city. It was calc-ulated that the Mendip Hills sources could supply Bristol with 4,000,000 gallons of water per day, and the works to convey the water to the city were designed to cope with even greater volumes (Clarke 1850, 112–15).

The construction of the engineering works to carry water from the Mendip Hills to Bristol – known as the Line of Works – began in earnest once royal assent had been given to the parliamentary Act. Included in the Act was also a requirement for the company to supply water in the Chew Valley to compensate for the water

taken from the river; this was achieved through the construction of reservoirs at Sherborne and Chew Magna. The springs at Chewton Mendip and Litton were collected below ground level by culverts, and the water was conveyed in several branches to East Harptree, where it entered a stone-lined tunnel above the village. At Harptree Combe a tributary aqueduct fed more water into the main line, which was then carried across the combe by way of a 105m long, ovoid wrought-iron tube supported by tapered masonry piers. The Harptree Combe aqueduct was designed by the company's engineer James Simpson, and was completed in 1851 (Fig 7.74). Beyond the aqueduct the water passed back into a stone tunnel and then, near West Harptree, it passed again into a line of undulating cast-iron pipes towards Compton Martin. At each extremity of undulation, the

Fig 7.74
The Harptree Combe aqueduct.
(DP068727)

water pipe was connected to a vertical tube so that air could be expelled to the surface, which reduced the amount of resistance to the flow of water. Dotting the landscape, these valves remain an above-ground indicator of the route of the Line of Works (Fig 7.75).

The Mendip Hills landscape was even more dramatically changed when parliamentary approval was given for the construction of the first of the great Mendip Hills reservoirs – Blagdon. Work began in 1891 on the dam crossing the valley of the River Yeo; to aid the scheme a railway line was laid and a station built on the south side of the dam, and the work was finally completed in 1901. In order to deliver the water from the reservoir to Bristol, a pumping station was built on the eastern side of the dam. The water was pumped a distance of around 6½km to North Hill, near Chew Stoke, where it joined the Line of Works en route to the company's storage facilities at Barrow Gurney. Designed by the civil engineering firm T & C Hawksley of Westminster, the Gothic revival-style pumping station was designed to house four steam-powered beam engines located in two engine halls that projected eastwards from a large boiler room (Fig 7.76).

Fig 7.75
A valve on the Line of Works.
(DP068724)

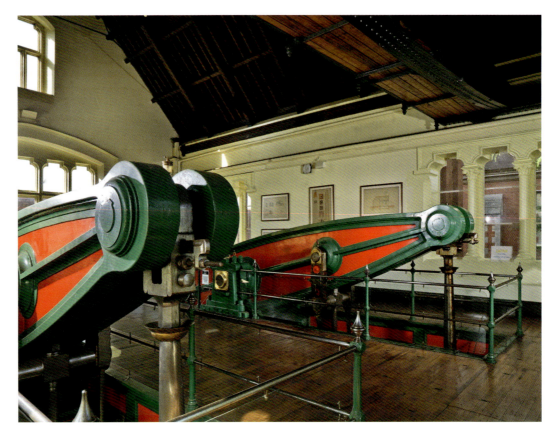

Fig 7.76
Yeo Pumping Station: two steam-powered beam engines in the building's south wing.
(DP068771)

Built in red brick with ashlar detailing, including ball finials, the building had a chimney stack that bore a resemblance to St Mark's campanile in Venice (Fig 7.77); it stood nearly 40m high before the top 15m of the tower was removed in 1954.

Institutional health on the Mendip Hills

It was from the middle of the 19th century that the Mendip Hills acquired its most notable institutions devoted to health, created as a result of philanthropic benevolence, private enterprise and state responsibility. They were established primarily because of the belief that the landscape and natural environment of the area sustained good health, and even improved mental and physical well-being. Contemporary attitudes towards mental health care, for example, are reflected in the parliamentary select committee report of 1808, which recommended that 'new asylums were to be in an airy and healthy situation with a good supply of water and which may afford a probability of constant medical assistance' (Marshall 2006, 126).

The Lunatics Act of 1845 compelled all counties to build asylums for the insane poor, although the Somerset justices had already established a committee to build a county asylum in the previous year. In 1844 the partnership of George Gilbert Scott and William Bonython Moffatt won the competition to design the Somerset County Pauper Lunatic Asylum, which was to be located approximately 2km north-east of the centre of Wells. Built to house 350 patients, the asylum was ready to admit its first patients in March 1848. It was designed in Scott and Moffat's favoured 'Elizabethan' style, and comprised a central administration block flanked by corridor-plan ward wings (Fig 7.78). Echoing contemporary prison and hospital designs, the asylum plan separated male and female patients and also the different classes of patient, with each class having its own airing ground. The airing courts were an important feature of the design of the asylum, as fresh air, exercise and suitable work were considered essential elements in the treatment of the patients. Octagonal stone shelters were erected in the airing yards and these were roofed to provide patients with a level of protection from rain and sun (Fig 7.79).

Tuberculosis sanatoria

The importance of a healthy situation was particularly relevant with regard to the treatment of tuberculosis, which at the end of the 19th century was believed to cause around one in eight deaths in England and Wales.

Fig 7.77
Yeo Pumping Station: drawing showing the east elevation of the Gothic revival-style building, including the elaborate chimney stack. (DP068765, reproduced by permission of Bristol Water plc)

Fig 7.78
Somerset County Pauper
Lunatic Asylum.
(DP068746)

Fig 7.79
Somerset County Pauper
Lunatic Asylum: octagonal
stone shelters in one of the
airing yards.
(DP068735)

Fig 7.80
St Michael's Free Home
for Consumptives.
(DP068712)

In 1818 John Mansford, member of the Royal College of Surgeons, published his findings into the 'Influence of Situation on Pulmonary Consumption' and concluded that the area around Axbridge was highly favourable for consumptive patients. St Michael's Free Home for Consumptives was therefore built approximately 1km north-east of the town. The sanatorium and its chapel, run by the Community of St Peter, an Anglican sisterhood devoted to nursing, were designed in the Gothic revival style by the architect William Butterfield (1814–1900), and opened on 28 September 1878 (Fig 7.80).

Initially the sanatorium accommodated 12 male and 12 female patients, but capacity was soon increased to 50 with the opening of a new wing in 1882. The original building was built on three levels, each with access to the gardens: the ground floor/basement comprised a hall for male patients and the kitchen; above this was the male ward, which opened onto a quadrangle and lawn; and the top level comprised the female ward. Wards for the severely ill flanked the chapel and had shutters that opened onto the nave, so that the patients could hear services from their beds. The sanatorium had its own mortuary and cemetery (Fig 7.81). The mortuary was demolished and the stone used to construct an extension to the sanatorium (Hassell and Wilson 2005, 29). In support of the tenet that pulmonary tuberculosis patients should be fed well in order to aid recovery, the sanatorium also had its own farm with hens, geese, ducks, goats and pigs, and a fruit and vegetable garden.

Fig 7.81
Headstones moved from
the former sanatorium
cemetery.
(DP068695)

Nordrach-upon-Mendip Sanatorium for the treatment of pulmonary tuberculosis could be described as one of the most historically significant health institutions in England. It opened in 1899 and its establishment was the direct result of the 'open-air' treatment received by Dr Rowland Thurnam at the influential Nordrach sanatorium of Dr Otto Walther (1853–1919) in the Black Forest. Following his recovery, Thurnam assisted Walther for nearly a year before setting out to find a suitable site for an 'exactly similar sanatorium in England' (Thurnam 1899, 50). After two years inspecting and rejecting sites, Thurnam eventually selected a site high on the Mendip plateau and began admitting his first patients on 1 January 1899.

Situated approximately 1.7km east of the Blackmoor Valley, the Nordrach-upon-Mendip Sanatorium was established in the grounds and adjacent fields of Willoughby's House. The 1885 Ordnance Survey map shows the site originally comprised two buildings set parallel to one other; one building was probably the farmhouse to Willoughby's Farm and the main sanatorium building was built extending from

it. The original entrance to the sanatorium was at the east of the site and swept along the southern edge of the grounds (a lodge was later added next to the entrance) before arriving at a turning circle to the front of the former farm buildings.

The new sanatorium building (Fig 7.82) comprised a two-storey, five-bay, stone house, orientated to face south-east, and overlooking a newly formed lawn. When completed, the sanatorium stood in 65 acres (26ha) of grounds, and could accommodate around 40 to 45 patients. The patients were housed in the main sanatorium block and in a variety of timber bungalows that were located in rows at right angles to each other in an adjacent plot to the north-east. The sanatorium building was designed with the 'open-air' treatment in mind, with surviving fabric including horizontally hinged two-centred arched windows, the lower portions of which appear to have included inward-opening casements with window seats below.

The 'open-air' treatment also extended to the communal dining hall, which was timber-framed and covered with a corrugated-iron

Fig 7.82
Nordrach-upon-Mendip: the sanatorium building. (DP068749)

Fig 7.83
Nordrach-upon-Mendip:
the timber-framed
dining hall.
(DP068751)

roof (Fig 7.83). It initially contained a large number of windows, with the north-west gable end being almost entirely glazed. The dining hall was built on the north-west of the sanatorium block, adjacent to the kitchen, and may have initially been detached. To the north-east of the dining hall was a rose garden, and at the edge of the lawns was a verdant area of undulating ground among trees which was known as 'The Dell', a popular area for outdoor relaxation along with 'The Glass Shelter' on the lawn. The sanatorium had its own laboratory, and as well as providing for the 'open-air cure', the sanatorium also used more technically advanced treatments, including vaccines and artificial pneumothorax and ultraviolet ray treatment.

Following the success of Nordrach, Mendip Hills Sanatorium was established in the now derelict Hill Grove country house, near Green Ore. Previously known as Pen Hill House and Hillgrove Farm, the house was adapted as a sanatorium around 1900. It was considered suitable as a sanatorium for sufferers of pulmonary tuberculosis because of its altitude of around 240m, its remoteness and its extensive grounds. An assessment of 1902 exhorted: 'It would be difficult to imagine a more secluded and attractive spot for the open-air treatment.' As well as the adapted two-storey house, the sanatorium had several huts in the grounds for patients to sleep in, and revolving shelters for daytime outdoor rest. Many of the chalets were set out on a long, narrow building platform to the north-east of the house and faced south. Evidence from historic postcards suggests that there were two sizes and styles: both forms had pitched roofs, and were timber-framed and covered with horizontal, feathered boards, with each having verandas to their fronts, either at the gable end or along the long elevation. The larch and pine woodland within the 160 acres (65ha) of grounds was laid out with walks, which were so well covered as to afford protection to the patients from the excesses of the Mendip weather.

8

The 20th century and beyond

In many ways the early 20th century represented a continuation of the social and economic changes instigated in the previous century. These included the modernisation and regeneration of some of Mendip's domestic and institutional buildings, including improved water supply and the installation of electric lighting. To meet the demands of an increasing urban population, the Bristol Waterworks Company was empowered to obtain water from the foot of Cheddar Gorge and began work on a new reservoir at Cheddar in 1927. In contrast, the period also witnessed a general decline in traditional rural industries on Mendip: mining in the region came to an end with the closure of St Cuthbert's lead mine in 1908 and agricultural production dropped, largely as a result of cheap foreign imports (Gough 1967, 203; M Williams 1976, 119). The impact of the two world wars also left its mark on the region, though the agricultural improvement and enclosure of previous centuries ensured this was perhaps less intrusive than in some other areas of the South-West.

The 20th-century landscape

The agricultural depression that began in the last decades of the 19th century saw much of the improved land on the plateau revert to rough grazing. The more fertile lower slopes continued to support a mixed farming economy, although more emphasis was put on stock farming, which led to larger areas of permanent pasture. However, with the advent of war in 1914, and the blockades that followed, the Mendip landscape saw an intensification of agricultural production. This was short-lived, however, and production fell back once again during the depression of the interwar period. The outbreak of the Second World War put greater emphasis on the home production of foodstuffs, with the government offering

financial incentives to farmers to plough up areas of pasture for cereal production. The legacy of this on the plateau was an improvement in the quality of the grazing land, which led to a substantial increase in dairying in the post-war period (M Williams 1976, 123). Agricultural changes also led to a drop in the overall number of farms in the region, as the scale of individual holdings steadily increased.

During the Second World War the relatively isolated and rural nature of the Mendip landscape made it an ideal location to site a network of military installations. By the beginning of 1943 the whole of the Mendip Hills became part of the strategic defence of the country, with the area declared a military exclusion zone when it was turned into a vast arsenal of equipment and munitions. The war was also responsible for delaying the plan to create the largest of the Bristol Waterworks Company's reservoirs in the Chew Valley; the scheme was not completed until 1956 (Fig 8.1).

The post-war period saw the afforestation of substantial areas of the uplands, as plantations were established at Rowberrow Warren, Stockhill and East Harptree Woods. The Forestry Commission, established in 1919 to help restock the timber felled during the First World War, was responsible for planting a total of 484ha of coniferous and mixed woodland on Mendip. These plantations were not established on improved farmland, but on more marginal areas, including former mining sites which were unsuitable for agricultural production. On other parts of the plateau 19th-century plantations and shelter belts were removed, such as the plantations surrounding Fernhill Farm and Rookery Farm, which effectively opened up the landscape once more. The consequence of 20th-century improvement on the lowlands was one of subtle change, as some hedges were grubbed out and walls demolished to create larger, more efficient fields. This was

particularly evident around settlements such as Westbury-sub-Mendip and Draycott, where a patchwork of small fields had continued into the early 20th century.

Market gardening flourished on the fertile southern slopes of Mendip, particularly around Cheddar, where strawberries and flowers were cultivated by an army of smallholders. Produce was transported to market along the Cheddar Valley railway, which also served the quarries at Sandford, Cheddar and Wookey. The Cheddar Valley line, however, was one of the many victims of the Beeching axe, with the passenger service being withdrawn in 1963 and freight traffic eastwards from the Cheddar quarries ceasing in 1968 (Atthill 1976b, 140). Some railway buildings still survive and have been converted to new uses, such as the stations at Cheddar and Axbridge, and the old track-bed is still clearly visible on aerial photographs snaking its way through the landscape. Freight traffic was transferred to the roads and the removal of the old rail-track enabled the construction of the Axbridge bypass, which opened in 1967. Perhaps the biggest change

to the road network, however, came with the construction of the M5 motorway, which slices through the western end of the hills; the Lox-Yeo Valley section opened in 1973.

The second half of the 20th century also witnessed the spread of new housing developments in the towns and villages, particularly around major centres such as Wells and Weston-super-Mare, as well as the regeneration of the existing housing stock. Traditional agricultural buildings were superseded, on many farmsteads, by large open sheds more suitable for modern farming practices, reflecting the continuing process of agricultural change.

The First World War

Following the outbreak of war in August 1914, the inhabitants in the villages and towns surrounding the Mendip Hills were quick to answer the call to arms. At Wells, on 14 August, a meeting was held in the marketplace which was addressed by the mayor, the bishop and several other dignitaries appealing for volunteers 'to take up arms on behalf of their country' (*Somerset & West of England Advertiser* 21 August 1914, 8). Some 28 men were recruited, and the following week they marched to the railway station accompanied by a detachment from the Regular Army, the Wells band and well-wishers. A local volunteer defence force was also established on the Hills. In September 1914 a unit was formed at Wookey Hole for 'the defence of the realm' (*Somerset & West of England Advertiser* 11 September 1914, 8) and similar forces were recruited elsewhere. A memorial at Shipham commemorates the village's war dead (Fig 8.2).

As well as recruiting men for the war effort, the military were also keen to acquire horses. Their standards were clearly high, as on one occasion in 1914, 200 horses were inspected at Wells but only 18 accepted (*Somerset & West of England Advertiser* 14 August 1914, 8). Bourton Farm, near Axbridge, was used as an army remount centre and mule stable (NMR ST 45 NW 75). The approach to the farm was lined with elm trees, and as a precaution against the mules damaging the trees their trunks were painted with tar. At one time 600 mules were brought to the farm for assessment.

Fig 8.2
Shipham: village memorial commemorating the war dead.
(DP100275)

No permanent accommodation was provided for the soldiers, however, who were billeted in the hay barns (Jordan 1994, 81).

The effect of the military activity on the landscape of the Mendip Hills was not as dramatic at this time as on other places such as Dartmoor or Salisbury Plain, where large tracts of land had been acquired for training by the turn of the 20th century. Unlike these areas, the Mendip Hills were a more enclosed landscape, with the majority of the uplands divided into fenced and walled fields. These would have been unsuitable for large formations of troops, particularly for the cavalry and artillery, which needed large 'open' and unencumbered areas in which to manoeuvre. What training was undertaken was on a much smaller scale, and soldiers were encamped either in or near villages. In April 1915, for example, three regiments were billeted at Blagdon (Winter 2007, 160). There was also a camp at Cheddar in the winter of the same year, and it was from here that a battalion of the Warwickshire Regiment exercised on the Hills against the Gloucesters, who were stationed at Blagdon. The manoeuvres included trench digging, but

where exactly this occurred is now unknown (*Somerset & West of England Advertiser* 5 March 1915, 8).

In May 1915, 150 members of the University of Bristol Officer Training Corps Reserve camped at the head of Burrington Combe and took part in military training on Black Down (Fig 8.3) – practising skills such as weapons training, field-craft and trench digging (*Bristol and the War* 1 June 1915; *Bristol Times and Mirror* 29 May 1915). The archaeological evidence for these practice trenches remains elusive, however, although other examples have been identified elsewhere. At Hutton, for example, a trench system was identified on aerial photographs located on rising ground along the contours on Elborough Hill (Fig 8.4). It comprises a firing line and a support trench 20m to the rear. Linking these two trenches are three communication trenches. The front line is crenulated in much the same way as those so familiar on the Western Front and other theatres of war. The crenulations on the support line, however, are larger but more fragmentary. As the name implies, this line provided support and a reserve of troops to

Fig 8.3
Members of the Bristol Officer Training Corps Reserve at Blagdon Camp. (BRO 43207/27/4/1, Bristol Record Office)

Fig 8.4
Aerial photograph showing
First World War practice
trenches on Elborough Hill.
(RAF FNO 37 RV 6023
11-JUL-1942, Historic
England [RAF
photography])

those on the firing line. The three communication trenches are zigzag trenches; they extend beyond the support line to an area of scrubland and denser vegetation which would have been ideal cover for the troops as they approached the trenches. The trench system appears to be incomplete, since two of the communication trenches are less developed compared to the central one. Also, the northern part of the support trench does not appear to be linked to the rest of the system and is on a slightly different alignment. In addition, there may have been features such as saps, which provided forward listening positions in front of the firing line, and shelters along the communication trenches which are present on more developed systems, such as those on Salisbury Plain (Brown and Field 2007).

The remains of trenches also survive to the east of Burrington Camp, although these do not form part of a linked system as at Hutton (NMR ST 45 NE 112). At Burrington there are five trenches, each measuring approximately 16m by 3m, with the spoil on either side of the long axis. These also appear to be practice trenches and not designed for any tactical defence, since they do not make best use of the

ground. Although it is unclear when they were dug, it could either have been by the Home Guard during the Second World War or, more likely, during the First World War.

The Second World War

Following the evacuation from Dunkirk in 1940, invasion of the British Isles became a real threat, and a complex network of land defences was rapidly constructed across the country. The Mendip Hills, with the Levels and Moors to the south, was an ideal natural defence line and formed part of the GHQ (General Headquarters) Green Stop Line. The Stop Line skirted the southern side of Wells and formed part of Bristol's outer defences, comprising an anti-tank ditch, pillboxes and anti-tank obstacles. The ditch was still visible on late 1940s aerial photographs to the south of Park Wood but has since been backfilled for much of its length (SHER 15876). Pillboxes were placed strategically along the Line in order to give maximum fields of fire, but at the same time they were carefully concealed. They were also sited elsewhere on Mendip, such as the example in Ubley Wood which was built of concrete and stone rubble (NMR ST 55 NW 67).

In response to the German campaign of long-range bombing, an array of countermeasures was deployed which included early warning systems, anti-aircraft guns and fighter aircraft. There were several military installations to the north-west of the Mendip Hills, including factories and an RAF station at Weston-super-Mare. Defending these sites were anti-aircraft gun emplacements and a network of barrage balloons; there was also local defence in the form of trenches and air-raid shelters (Priest and Dickson 2009, 63). One gun position was on Bleadon Hill, where there was a troop of two 3in (7.6cm) guns which were later replaced by four 3.7in (9.4cm) guns (Dobinson 1996, 486). Within the immediate area were a barrage-balloon site, barracks, two air-raid shelters and ammunition storage (ST 35 NE 112). The gun position was ideally sited since it was just below the crest of the hill, which provided good lines of sight but at the same time a degree of concealment from the probable aircraft approach route from the south-east. Searchlights were sited round the Weston aircraft factories, with their headquarters at Banwell; other searchlight emplacements were situated at Star, Cheddar and Westbury-sub-

Mendip (Brown 1999, 151–5). Sadly, despite all these countermeasures, in September 1940 German aircraft dropped their bombs over the village of Banwell, killing 5 people and injuring 50 more.

Although the Mendip Hills did not become a major training area during the Second World War, a small-arms range was established at Yoxter (Fig 8.5) just prior to the war. Situated on the ridge between Charterhouse-on-Mendip and Priddy, the present range covers an area of 191ha and is the only military training facility on the western hills. It was established in 1933 when a 600yd (550m) rifle range was constructed. By 1938 there was no permanent camp apart from a couple of huts, which were presumably stores, and soldiers were accommodated in tents (Brown 1999, 189–93). An additional butt, a grenade range and some buildings including air-raid shelters were later constructed (Truscoe 2008); to the rear of the butts a large 'danger area' restricted access during firing periods. Initially the range was established to train Territorial units; however, during the Second World War it increased in importance when more army units arrived for training. Driver training for tank crews also took place, with the old mining rakes presumably making ideal obstacles for the tanks to negotiate.

Black Down: a landscape of denial and deception

Aircraft landing obstructions were a common feature on wide, open spaces throughout the country and were intended to prevent enemy aircraft landing invasion troops. The type of obstacle varied depending on the available resources. On Black Down, earthen mounds and stone cairns were used on the summit of the hill and on the gently sloping ground to the south. Each mound is surrounded by a slight ditch and measures up to 1.7m high and 4m in diameter, with the whole complex covering an area of around 146ha. The mounds are set out in a regular grid pattern with 3 longitudinal rows which are crossed at right angles by 11 much shorter rows. All the rows comprise two lines of staggered mounds. The barrow cemetery on Beacon Batch forms part of the obstacle, with one barrow actually on a grid line. Three other prehistoric barrows continue the northern row but on a slightly different alignment, with another, shorter, row set at right angles to them. In contrast, the stone cairns are mainly on the southern and eastern sides of the system and are generally lower than the earthen mounds (Fig 8.6).

During the early years of the war, airfields and later urban areas were subjected to prolonged strategic bombing by the German

Fig 8.5
Aerial photograph showing the small-arms range at Yoxter.
(NMR 26592/4)

Fig 8.6
Black Down: the regular
grid of anti-landing
obstacles set out on the
summit of the hill.
(NMR 22007/30 [Jim
Hancock Collection])

air force. To counter this bombardment a decoy programme was initiated throughout the country in late 1939 under the direction of Col Sir John F Turner (Schofield *et al* 1999, 271–86; Dobinson 2000). The system on the Mendip Hills was the southernmost of a network of bombing decoys that ringed the city of Bristol. The wide, open and unimproved expanse on Black Down was an ideal setting for an elaborate landscape of decoys which were designed to confuse and deceive enemy bombers. The system on Black Down was unusual in that it attempted to replicate the entire city of Bristol with displaced lighting, and made use of marshalling yard lights to depict the various areas (Dobinson 2000, 146). The anti-aircraft mounds were incorporated into this scheme, with double rows of mounds capped by illuminated glowing boxes used to simulate streets. Some precisely located lighting systems replicated Bristol's railway patterns – imitating stations and marshalling yards – all of which was intended to lure the enemy aircraft into dropping their bombs on open country.

On Black Down there were six 'QL' sites (lighting sites), two of which also had a 'QF' (fire sites) function, and a 'Starfish' or Special Fire (SF) was a few hundred metres to the south, near Tyning's Gate. These sites were some of the most sophisticated decoys

developed, and were based on the principle of diversionary fires (Schofield *et al* 1999, 274). The sites would have worked together: the QL sites simulated a target, with the QF and Starfish simulating a successful hit. An example of a combined site was C82c, which consisted of firebreak trenches enclosing a number of structures on which fires were lit (ibid, 283–4; Truscoe 2008, 61).

The order to initiate the system was received by telephone at Lower Farm and was passed to the control buildings (Brown 2011, 361). There were two control buildings on the Black Down escarpment that housed the operating equipment for the lighting and decoy fires. The buildings comprise two rooms with an outer blast-wall protecting the single entrance (Fig 8.7). Another control building was at Tyning's Gate, where there was also a Z-battery anti-aircraft rocket battery position. This battery is possibly one of only two surviving examples in Britain: it comprises at least 18 emplacements for rocket launchers and the remains of 4 storage shelters (Schofield *et al* 1999, 281).

Part of the denial and deception programme also entailed putting obstructions on the reservoirs surrounding the Hills. Hundreds of rafts of unhewn tree trunks were placed on Blagdon and Cheddar reservoirs (Jones 1946, 41). These bodies of water were also clearly good navigational markers, and in 1942 the rim of Cheddar reservoir was painted grey in order to make it less obvious to enemy aircraft (Brown 1999, 151).

Prisoner-of-war camps

In early 1941 thousands of Italian prisoners of war were brought to Britain after the capture of Tobruk and incarcerated in camps around the country. Two of these camps were on the outskirts of Wells (Thomas 2003), and although they were demolished at the end of the war they have been plotted from aerial photographs (Truscoe 2008). Penleigh Camp was located on the north-western edge of Wells, along the Wookey Hole road. Stoberry Camp was constructed in the park of Stoberry House, on the northern edge of the city, part of which has now disappeared under modern development.

The camp at Stoberry covered an area of about 4ha and was accessed via College Road on its western side (Fig 8.8). It appears to have been separated into four distinct zones, with two accommodation zones to the north and

Fig 8.7 (above)
Black Down: one of the control bunkers for the bombing decoy site. (NMR 24330/43)

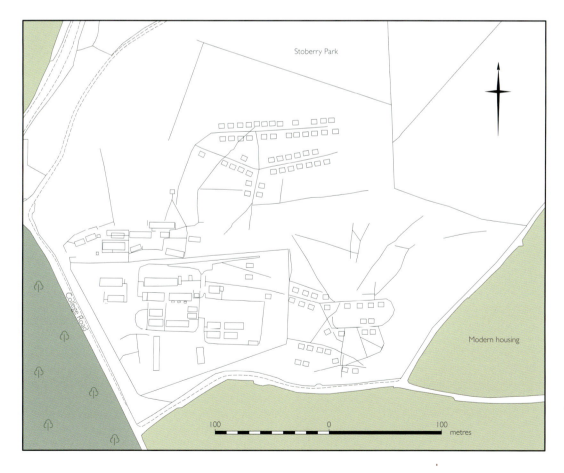

Fig 8.8 (left)
Stoberry Park: prisoner-of-war camp recorded from aerial photographs.

east, both defined by square parchmarks and interpreted as stances for tents. There were 47 probable tents in the northern zone and 27 in the southern zone. On the southern side of the camp entrance there are several much larger parchmarks contained within a perimeter, and although their function is unclear, they may have been administrative and recreational buildings as well as guards' accommodation and cookhouses. On the northern side of the entrance are further parchmarks, with one of those beside the entrance probably the guardroom.

Many of the prisoners worked on local farms, and some settled in the area after the end of the war. A prisoner from Stoberry Camp named Gaetano Celestra designed and made a concrete statue depicting the legend of Romulus and Remus, the traditional founders of Rome.

This statue can be seen on Pen Hill, and stands as an important legacy of the prisoner-of-war camps at Wells (Fig 8.9).

The defence of a nation: the Home Guard and Auxiliary Units

During the Second World War the majority of the towns and villages had their own Home Guard detachments. Formed in May 1940 as the Local Defence Volunteers, these units were mainly responsible for the defence of installations and manning pickets and road-blocks. Some weeks later, in July, they were renamed the Home Guard, and those units on Mendip became affiliated to the Somerset Light Infantry.

Much of the Home Guard training on Mendip took place in quarries and on open ground, and therefore the impact on the landscape was minimal. However, military skills were also practised elsewhere. A number of two-man battle trenches, more commonly referred to as slit-trenches or foxholes, have been identified within Stoberry Park and on Black Down. The trenches measure approximately 2m by 0.8m, and have been partially backfilled. Within West Twin, an Iron Age enclosure on Black Down, a line of three closely spaced trenches have upcast on alternate sides. All were probably dug as part of a training exercise during the Second World War, probably by the Home Guard, since none are tactically sited. The efforts of the Home Guard were not always confined to training, however. When Spitfires shot down an enemy bomber over Mendip, the Charterhouse Home Guard captured the surviving airmen after an armed confrontation at Warren Farm (Brown 2011, 360).

Another volunteer force were the Auxiliary Units. These operated in small detachments and were trained to carry out covert operations from their operational bases, which here were mainly in caves. Their training, like that of the Home Guard, was undertaken at various places on the Hills, including Ebbor Gorge, Cheddar Gorge, Dolebury Warren and Winscombe Quarry (Brown 1999, 99). There were a total of 11 operational bases within the Mendip Hills AONB. The bases were carefully camouflaged: the base at Denny's Hole, for example, was marked by a metal threshold across the entrance to the tunnel which opens up into a deeper cave used as the operational base. The one at Chewton Mendip was an old mineshaft

Fig 8.9
Pen Hill: concrete statue of Romulus and Remus designed by Gaetano Celestra. (DP044496)

in the woods, while at Green Ore it was a corrugated-iron shelter camouflaged with grass and brambles (ibid, 75–88). These bases not only housed the unit but also an array of equipment, explosives and provisions.

The Royal Observer Corps

The Royal Observer Corps (ROC) evolved from the Metropolitan Observation Service in 1941 (Cocroft and Thomas 2003, 174–86). Its principal role was to identify aircraft, both friend and foe, and chart their movements. This was done from a network of posts which were generally located on high ground with good fields of observation. The information was reported up the chain of command where it was correlated with data from other posts and forwarded to fighter squadrons where necessary. Later in the war, despite the introduction of radar, the ROC continued to perform an invaluable task particularly in identifying low-flying aircraft which would presumably be below radar cover. The ROC was finally disbanded in May 1945.

There were four observation posts within the area of the Mendip Hills AONB: Winscombe, West Harptree, Westbury Beacon and Bleadon. They were all established in 1938 and formed part of No. 22 Group whose headquarters were at Yeovil. There appears to be no standardised form for these wartime posts: some were constructed of brick or concrete, while others were sandbags and corrugated iron. During the early 1940s these were replaced by two types of 'Orlit' posts that were distinguished by whether they were sited on the ground or elevated. Each consisted of a box of pre-constructed concrete panels measuring 10ft by 6ft 8in (3.05m by 2.03m). The post was accessed from one side via a low hardwood door (Cocroft and Thomas 2003, 175).

The demise of the ROC in 1945 was relatively short-lived since in January 1947 it was re-formed, but with a slightly different role. Initially it continued to report aircraft sightings, but six years later, in 1953, with the threat of nuclear war, it was responsible for the monitoring of the passage of fallout following a nuclear attack. In order to fulfil this role its posts were resited underground. The first to be resited was at Bleadon in 1959, followed by Winscombe and West Harptree in 1960 and Westbury Beacon in 1961.

These monitoring posts were designed to accommodate up to four people. They were made of reinforced concrete, cast on site, and covered in earth to increase protection from radiation. The only noticeable features above ground were the entrance shaft, which was sealed with a steel hatch; next to this was a mushroom-shaped casting which carried the Ground Zero Indicator; there were also two ventilators with steel or wooden louvres, the bomb power indicator and a probe for the fixed survey meter (Cocroft and Thomas 2003, 180). A vertical ladder led to the underground bunker, which comprised the monitoring equipment as well as all the facilities required for the detachment to live in such a confined space (Fig 8.10). The monitoring posts at

Fig 8.10
Westbury Beacon: Cold War ROC underground monitoring post with entrance shaft (left), fixed survey meter probe (centre) and ventilators (right). (Elaine Jamieson)

Winscombe and Westbury Beacon remained in service until 1968, while Bleadon and West Harptree were operational until 1991, when they were finally decommissioned at the end of the Cold War following the collapse of the Soviet Union.

The historic landscape of the Mendip Hills AONB in the 21st century

Looking over the Somerset Levels and Moors towards the steep-sided southern escarpment of the Mendip Hills range (Fig 8.11), it is hard to imagine how the landscape must have looked over half a million years ago when early humans first visited the region. As we have seen, these groups encountered a climate comparable to southern Europe, and hunted deer within a landscape composed of broad-leaved deciduous woodland. The changing character of the natural environment is one of the dominant themes in the early history of the Mendip Hills. These changes, experienced over long periods of time, dictated migratory patterns and landscape exploitation and helped shape the form of the hills we see today. In this modern age of changing climatic conditions, it may become easier for us to imagine the challenges these early humans must have faced

in adapting to the substance of the landscape around them.

The first communities on Mendip utilised the distinctive natural features of the area – its steep-sided gorges, caves, swallets and springs – all of which may have been imbued with legends of the ancestors and the mythical past. The continuing attraction of these natural features has emerged as a recurring topic in this book. The region's springs and watercourses clearly played an important role in the development of social and ritual landscapes from prehistory onwards. They have been highlighted as an important factor in the foundation of a number of the region's earliest churches, for example, which may suggest a pre-existing understanding of the special qualities of place. Evidence for a lasting fascination with the region's caves and swallets is also apparent in their prolonged use as ritual and ceremonial sites throughout prehistory, and in their continuing draw in later centuries – attracting diarists, artists, scientists and philosophers alike. Today, the caves and rocky gorges are a magnet for climbers, cavers and tourists, anchoring the past with the present and setting cultural patterns that reinforce the perception of Mendip as a special and unique place.

The Mendip landscape we now see before us is not purely a natural construct, however. It

Fig 8.11
Looking over the Somerset Levels and Moors towards the steep-sided southern escarpment of the Mendip Hills.
(DP057759)

has been fashioned over many generations and is a product of its past. Human intervention has helped define the character of the Hills: from the initial small-scale clearance of deciduous woodland for cereal and stock farming in the Neolithic, to a more comprehensive reordering of the landscape in the later prehistoric and Roman-British periods. Subsequent adaptations, including the setting out of the open fields around the foot of the escarpment, utilised land divisions laid down centuries before, encapsulating the past in the present and creating a historic grain which is still visible in the landscape today. The construction of ritual and ceremonial monuments on the uplands during the prehistoric period has left a lasting, if somewhat enigmatic, testament to the traditions and beliefs of the region's earliest farmers. It is perhaps not surprising that clergymen such as the Revd John Skinner were drawn to investigate them four millennia later, as tangible relics of past belief systems.

The story of habitation in the region is one of a surprising degree of continuity, with spring-line locations favoured as settlement loci over many hundreds of years. In some ways this has made past occupation more difficult to detect on Mendip, but it also indicates a degree of stability and time-depth inherent in the modern pattern of farms, hamlets and villages. This continuity is also visible in the archaeological record. To take an example, the prehistoric roundhouse at Chew Park was replaced by a timber rectangular building in the early Romano-British period, which in turn was superseded by a stone-built villa complex a few generations later. The upstanding buildings of the region are also testament to the longevity of the settlement pattern, with the continued adaptation and modernisation of pre-existing structures a key finding from the project's programme of architectural investigation. Court House Farm, Westbury-sub-Mendip, for example, has the accolade of being an early barn conversion and demonstrates how adaptation can be vital to survival. The Mendip Hills in the 21st century are a living place and the people who now occupy the farmhouses, village houses, cottages and former barns create their own history, adding to a long story of continuity and adaptation.

The closure of the last lead-working site in the early 20th century brought to an end an industry which had influenced and shaped Mendip since at least Roman-British times. The

easily extractable lead resources of the region were fundamental to the Roman administration establishing a fort at Charterhouse-on-Mendip in the 1st century AD, and the subsequent growth of the associated settlement over the following years. Continued exploitation at many extraction sites has served to both destroy and reveal evidence for past industry. It has also influenced how large areas of the plateau can be worked and managed today. The aerial survey transcription undertaken as part of this project has mapped the pitted and scarred landscape which forms a lasting legacy of this bygone industry. Exploitation of the region's natural resources still forms an important component of the Mendip economy, with the pits and rakes of lead extraction superseded by the large, dramatic stepped quarries of the post-war aggregate industry.

There is a long and vibrant tradition of archaeological enquiry on Mendip, and the work and ideas put forward in this book will hopefully stimulate further research and help develop new approaches to understanding the historic landscape of the Hills. The study of past landscapes has come a long way from the days of antiquarian investigation by the likes of John Strachey and the Revd John Skinner, but there is still a great deal further to go. There are many unanswered questions regarding the historic landscape of the Mendip Hills. What role did the Priddy Circles play in the lives of the Neolithic groups who hunted and farmed across the Hills? Where did the communities who constructed the hundreds of Bronze Age barrows live, and what were the belief systems that drove them to construct these round mounds? When were the earliest coaxial field systems set out and what part did they play in shaping later land divisions? Targeted research into later periods should prove rewarding. More work looking at the development of the region's medieval settlement pattern would help refine some of the ideas advanced here, and further investigation of the area's vernacular architecture would represent a fruitful area of study.

Ultimately this publication demonstrates that the Mendip landscape we see today is one which has been shaped over many thousands of years, and it is a story that continues to evolve. How we use and manage the landscape over the coming years will influence how it is viewed and appreciated by future generations.

APPENDIX 1

Site gazetteer

The major archaeological sites discussed in this text are listed below with their National Grid references and National Record of the Historic Environment numbers (in brackets) where applicable. Detailed records for the sites are available using these numbers from the Historic England Archive at Swindon and via PastScape (www.pastscape.org.uk). Most of the sites on this list are on privately owned land and permission for access should be sought.

Major cave, rock shelter and swallet sites

Aveline's Hole ST 4761 5867 (ST 45 NE 2)
Badger Hole ST 5324 4795 (ST 54 NW 15)
Brimble Pit Swallet ST 5079 5080 (ST 55 SW 133)
Charterhouse Warren Farm Swallet ST 4936 5457 (ST 45 SE 60)
Chelm's Combe Rock Shelter ST 4632 5445 (ST 45 SE 1)
Gough's Cave ST 4670 5391 (ST 45 SE 10)
Hay Wood Cave ST 3409 5830 (ST 35 NW 14)
Picken's Hole ST 3968 5501 (ST 35 NE 15)
Soldier's Hole ST 4686 5400 (ST 45 SE 13)
Sun Hole ST 4673 5408 (ST 45 SE 11)
Totty Pot ST 4825 5356 (ST 45 SE 3)
Wookey Hole ST 5319 4801 (ST 54 NW 14)

Long barrows

Beacon Batch ST 4844 5717 (ST 45 NE 17)
Pen Hill ST 5633 4868 (ST 54 NE 34)
Priddy Hill ST 5141 5342
Priddy Long Barrow ST 5141 5091 (ST 55 SW 63)

Henge monuments and standing stones

Gorsey Bigbury ST 4842 5582 (ST 45 NE 15)
Hunters Lodge ST 5590 4978 (ST 54 NE 16)
Priddy Circles ST 5409 5304 (ST 55 SW 4, ST 55 SW 124, ST 55 SW 125, ST 55 SW 126, ST 55 SW 127)
Deer Leap Stones ST 5179 4876 (ST 54 NW 37)
Wimblestone ST 45 NW 33 (ST 4334 5848)
Yarborough Stone ST 3903 5783 (ST 35 NE 4)
Standing stone, Green Hill ST 5288 5136
Standing stone, Prior's Hill ST 5646 4792

Major barrows and barrow groups

Ashen Lane ST 5150 5160 (ST 55 SW 34)
Ashen Hill ST 5399 5200 (ST 55 SW 5)
Beacon Batch ST 4847 5721 (ST 45 NE 17)
Black Down barrows and flat cemetery ST 4742 5842 and ST 4738 5823 (ST 45 NE 38, ST 45 NE 42)
Bristol barrows ST 5452 5255 (ST 55 SW 7)

Hunters Lodge disc/bell barrow ST 5591 5009 (ST 55 SE 8)
Longwood ST 4843 5549 (ST 45 NE 19)
North Hill (Priddy Nine Barrows) ST 5384 5157 (ST 55 SW 74)
Pool Farm barrow ST 5374 5415 (ST 55 SW 25)
Stockhill ST 5571 5097 (ST 55 SE 9)
Tyning's Farm ST 4700 5635 (ST 45 NE 58)
Westbury Beacon ST 5005 5075 (ST 55 SW 56)

Prehistoric field systems

Bleadon Hill ST 3382 5752 (ST 35 NW 5)
Dolebury Warren ST 4617 5873 (ST 45 NE 108)
Flagstaff Hill ST 3785 5774 (ST 35 NE 2)

Hillforts and hill-slope enclosures (earthwork sites)

Banwell Camp ST 4094 5900 (ST 45 NW 6)
Burledge Hillfort ST 5826 5850 (ST 55 NE 4)
Burrington Camp ST 4780 5878 (ST 45 NE 43)
Burrington Ham enclosure ST 4871 5831
Dolebury Camp ST 4501 5895 (ST 45 NE 3)
Longbottom Camp ST 4574 6584 (ST 45 NE 12)
Pitcher's Enclosure ST 5492 5549 (ST 55 NW 32)
Rowberrow Camp ST 4644 5682 (ST 45 NE 13)
West Twin ST 4771 5763 (ST 45 NE 7)
Westbury Camp ST 4920 5112 (ST 45 SE 31)

Major Romano-British sites

Banwell villa ST 3981 5927 (ST 35 NE 40)
Chew Park villa ST 5680 5930 (ST 55 NE 3)
Locking villa ST 3649 6061 (ST 36 SE 7)
Star villa ST 4353 5868 (ST 45 NW 3)
Charterhouse-on-Mendip amphitheatre ST 4988 5651 (ST 45 NE 25)
Charterhouse-on-Mendip fort ST 5039 5579 (ST 55 NW 2)
Charterhouse-on-Mendip settlement centred ST 5014 5624 (ST 55 NW 1)

Castles and moated sites

Bickfield/Moat Farmhouse ST 5480 5870 (ST 55 NW 3)
Richmont Castle ST 5613 5580 (ST 55 NE 10)

Deserted or shrunken settlements

Chewton Mendip paired farmsteads ST 5747 5321
Christon ST 3784 5754 (ST 35 NE 2)
Compton Bishop ST 3962 5540
Dursden ST 5265 4933 (ST 54 NW 39)
Ellick ST 4969 5745 (ST 45 NE 75)
Hope and Lower Hope farmsteads ST 5222 4891 (ST 54 NW 38)
Neat Place, Chewton Mendip ST 5737 5304
Rackley ST 3947 5486 (ST 35 SE 6)
Ramspits ST 5149 4930 (ST 54 NW 41)
Rodney Stoke settlement ST 4889 5161 (ST 45 SE 46)
Sacrafield, Chewton Mendip ST 5738 5265
Sacrafield/Payne's Pond, Chewton Mendip ST 5736 5334
Upper Milton ST 5459 4750 (ST 54 NW 40)
Walcombe ST 5515 4703
Winthill ST 3974 5846 (ST 35 NE 12)

Relic medieval field systems

Carscliffe ST 4772 5246 (ST 45 SE 4)
Christon ST 3791 5788 (ST 35 NE 51)
Litton ST 5949 5400 (ST 55 SE 35)
Westbury-sub-Mendip centred ST 5079 4965
(ST 54 NW 78, ST 54 NW 79, ST 54 NW 41)
Rodney Stoke ST 4891 5167 (ST 45 SE 46)
Stoberry Park/Walcombe centred ST 5532 4663

Duck decoys and pillow mounds

Banwell pillow mound ST 4030 5876 (ST 45 NW 5)
Dolebury Warren ST 4499 5895 (ST 45 NE 105, ST 45 NE 126)
Nyland duck decoy ST 4528 5028 (ST 45 SE 64)
Rodney Stoke duck decoy ST 4787 4847 (ST 44 NE 15)
Rowberrow Warren pillow mounds ST 4611 5812 (ST 45 NE 77)
Shute Shelve pillow mounds ST 4256 5535 (ST 45 NW 8)

Mining remains

Chewton Minery ST 5470 5150 (ST 55 SW 92)
East Harptree/Smitham Chimney ST 5537 5463 (ST 55 SE 43)
Higher Pits Farm ST 5349 4894
St Cuthbert's lead-works ST 5449 5057 (ST 55 NW 49)
Shipham ST 4454 5740 (ST 45 NW 76, ST 45 NW 77)
Rowberrow ST 4474 5796 (ST 45 NW 42)
Velvet Bottom and Blackmoor valleys centred ST 5036 5548
(ST 55 NW 34, ST 55 NW 48, ST 55 NW 50)

Military remains of the 20th century

Elborough Hill trench system ST 3679 5835 (ST 35 NE 177)
Black Down anti-landing obstacles and bombing decoy centred
ST 4790 5713 (ST 45 NE 73, ST 45 NE 91, ST 45 NE 94,
ST 45 NE 98, ST 45 NE 100)
Burrington trenches ST 4798 5875 (ST 45 NE 112)
Stoberry Park prisoner-of-war camp ST 5524 4643 (ST 54 NE 152)
Westbury Beacon monitoring post ST 5001 5077 (ST 55 SW 138)
Yoxter Range ST 5111 5428 (ST 55 SW 139)

Radiocarbon dating

Radiocarbon (^{14}C) is a naturally occurring radioactive isotope of carbon that is formed in the upper atmosphere when cosmic radiation interacts with nitrogen atoms. It is unstable, with a half-life of 5730±40 years. Once produced, radiocarbon mixes rapidly through the atmosphere and enters the terrestrial food chain through photosynthesis. This means that the ^{14}C content of land plants and animals is in equilibrium with the contemporary atmosphere. When an organism dies it ceases to take up radiocarbon, and so over time the proportion of ^{14}C in the dead organism decreases. By measuring the proportion that remains, the elapsed time since death can be estimated. The ratio of ^{14}C in the material of unknown age to that in a modern standard is multiplied by the half-life to determine the age.

Most radiocarbon results undertaken for archaeology are reported as radiocarbon ages measured on the conventional radiocarbon timescale in units 'before present' (BP). Calibration is an essential step in using radiocarbon measurements to estimate the calendar date of archaeological samples. It is necessary because the production rate of radiocarbon in the atmosphere is not constant, but varies through time. This means that we need to convert the radiocarbon measurement of a sample to the calendar scale using a calibration curve made up of radiocarbon ages on samples of known calendar date (Fig i.1).

The terrestrial calibration curve for the northern hemisphere (IntCal13: Reimer *et al* 2013) has been used to calibrate all the radiocarbon results used in this publication.

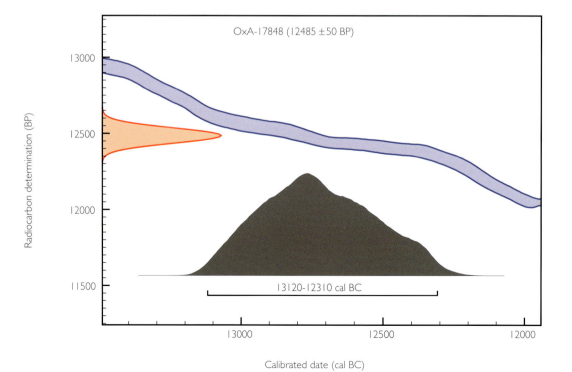

Fig i.1
Calibration of radiocarbon date OxA-17848 from Gough's Cave using the IntCal13 calibration data (Reimer et al *2013). The blue is the calibration curve made up of samples of known calendar dates, the red is the radiocarbon result in units BP and the grey is the calibrated date.*

Marine isotope stages

The different isotopes of oxygen preserved in the tests ('shells') of foraminifera have been instrumental in developing a framework for global climate change. Foraminifera combine oxygen in the calcite in their shells, and this is present in two different forms – the atomically heavier ^{18}O and atomically lighter ^{16}O. The precise isotopic composition of the foram test reflects the isotopic concentrations in the water from which the oxygen is derived, and these concentrations vary according to changes in the global volume of ice. By analysing samples from forams through long cores, a history of ice build-up and decay can be plotted, showing peaks and troughs of isotope ratios that reflect cold and warm periods respectively.

The first extensive application of this methodology was applied to a deep-sea sediment core (V28-238) and the graph of results showed that 23 peaks and troughs occurred in the last 800,000 years (Shackleton and Opdyke 1973). These periods have been numbered by counting back from the present-day interglacial or Holocene period – marine isotope stage 1 (MIS 1) – with usually interglacial peaks (warm episodes) having odd numbers and glacial peaks (cold but not necessarily ice-dominated events) even numbers (Fig i.2).

Fig i.2
Oxygen isotope trace from deep-sea sediment core V28-238 (after Shackleton and Opdyke 1973).

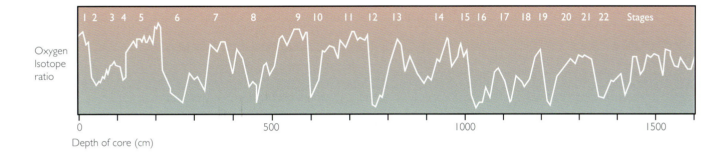

Anglian: a glacial period in the Middle Pleistocene of Britain, equivalent to the Elsterian Stage of northern continental Europe, preceding the Hoxnian Stage.

assart: farmland formed by the clearance of areas of woodland, common or forest. It gives rise to a distinctive landscape characterised by small, irregular-shaped fields, sometimes conjoined into larger units.

Aurignacian: an Upper Palaeolithic stone tool tradition, usually considered associated with both Homo sapiens and Neanderthals throughout Europe and parts of Africa, characterised by the production of flaked blade tools.

aurochs (*Bos primigenius*): ancestors of domesticated cattle, thought to be extinct from Britain by the end of the Bronze Age.

backed blade: a blade with one edge blunted by the removal of tiny flakes.

ballista bolt head: the head of a large bolt or arrow fired from a ballista (a large military catapult). The Roman examples from Hod Hill were made of iron and pyramidal in form with a conical socket.

barbed-and-tanged arrowheads: triangular-shaped flint arrowheads of the later Neolithic and Early Bronze Age in Europe. They are distinctive in having a short rectangular tang on the base opposite the point, with symmetrically set barbs either side.

bargeboard: board fixed to the gable end of a roof to hide the ends of the roof timbers.

bâton percé: an Upper Palaeolithic implement made of antler and perforated with one or more cylindrical holes at the crown end, thought to be used in the manufacture and throwing of spears.

bee boles: niches in a wall to accommodate bee hives.

bell barrow: a bowl-shaped mound separated from its surrounding ditch by a level berm, and in profile, therefore, presenting a slightly flattened bell-like shape.

berm: a level area separating the ditch top and rampart base of an Iron Age hillfort or other earthwork, often associated with the **box rampart** type of construction.

bifacial knife: a stone implement worked in such a way as to produce a cutting edge that is sharp on both sides.

bilaterally barbed point: a projectile point or harpoon with barbs on both edges.

bivallate: (of earthworks) comprising multiple circuits of bank and ditch.

blade-points: unifacial hafted weapon-heads made by retouching blades, and diagnostic of the early Upper Palaeolithic in Britain.

blast furnace: a furnace used for smelting, where metal ore, coke and limestone are loaded into the top of the structure and hot air is blown into the bottom, which produces several chemical reactions and allows molten metal and slag to be extracted from the bottom.

bout coupé hand-axe: a type of hand-axe widely considered to be a cultural and typological marker for the Middle Palaeolithic in Britain.

bowl barrow: a mound in the shape of an inverted pudding bowl with slopes of varying profile, sometimes with a surrounding ditch and occasionally an outer bank.

box rampart: a type of rampart found on Iron Age hillforts, formed with a timber frame, where horizontal struts are linked to vertical posts with an earthen core.

bressummer: a horizontal beam supporting the wall above, especially in a jettied building or over a fireplace.

broadcloth: a dense, plain woven cloth, historically made of wool.

buddle: a shallow inclined container in which ore is washed.

burin: a specialised bone or antler scoring tool with a bevelled point.

butt purlins: horizontal longitudinal roof timbers tenoned into either side of the principals.

cake crushing: preparing compressed 'cakes' of animal feed (typically linseed).

chaff cutting: preparing husks of corn or other seed.

chamfer: the splayed face resulting from the removal of the angle or arris along a piece of timber.

chert: a form of microcrystallite quartz that can be broken to form very sharp edges.

Class I henge: a circular or oval area enclosed by a bank with an internal ditch broken by a single entrance.

collar: a horizontal member in a roof spanning between a pair of inclined members – blades, principal rafters or common rafters – and located about halfway between wall-plate level and apex.

cranked collar: a collar with a sharp natural bend producing a blunt point.

Cromerian: an interglacial period in the Middle Pleistocene of Britain and northern Europe, preceding the Anglian glaciation.

cross-passage: a passageway running from the front to the back of a building, often separating the hall and service rooms in a medieval house.

cruck: one of a pair of inclined timbers (blades), usually curved, set at bay lengths; they support the roof timbers and can also support the walls.

disc barrow: a circular ditch and external bank defining an area of 40m or more. The level interior is sometimes occupied by one or occasionally two small mounds.

double-pile plan: a house plan consisting of a rectangular block two rows deep.

framed ceiling: a ceiling that is carried by a visible timber framework.

furlong: a block of individual units or strips in an open-field system.

'Gothick': of or in an 18th-century form of the Gothic revival style.

greenstone: a general term for igneous or metamorphic rock, made into axes and widely traded in Neolithic Britain.

hide: a former measure of land used in England, typically equal to between 60 and 120 acres (24–48ha), being the amount that would support a family and its dependants.

hipped roof: a ridged double-sloping roof.

hood mould: a moulding over a door or window that deflects rain.

horse whim: a horse-powered windlass, usually for raising ore or water from a mine.

interstadial: a minor period of less cold climate during a glacial period.

karst: a limestone landscape that includes caves, sinking streams, closed depressions and dry valleys.

lateral chimney stack/fireplace: a stack or fireplace located in the side wall of a building.

leaf-points: bifacial hafted weapon-heads often broadly leaf-shaped in outline, and diagnostic of the early Upper Palaeolithic in Britain.

'lobby-entry' plan: a building plan in which the front entrance opens into a lobby opposite an axial chimney stack.

lynchet: a ridge or ledge formed along the downhill side of a plot by the action of ploughing.

microliths: very small flint tools dating from the Mesolithic period.

minster: a large and important church, typically.

MIS: *see* Notes for the reader (marine isotope stages).

mortice and tenon joint: a joint comprising a hole or recess (mortice) which is designed to receive a corresponding projection (tenon) to join or lock the parts together.

Mousterian: a Middle Palaeolithic stone tool culture associated with Neanderthal man and consisting of five or more stone-artefact traditions in Europe whose characteristic tools are side scrapers and points.

mullioned and transomed window: a window with both vertical and horizontal members separating window lights.

newel stair: a spiral stair ascending round a central supporting newel.

ogee-shaped: double curve, concave and convex, creating an S-shape.

oriel: a projecting window resting on brackets or on corbels, or a bay window at the high end of a medieval hall.

orthostat: an upright stone or slab forming part of a structure or set in the ground.

ovolo moulding: wide convex edging to a panel, beam or other building element.

palstave: a type of chisel characteristic of the Middle Bronze Age in Europe, typically made of bronze and shaped to fit into a split handle rather than having a socket for the handle.

pelta brooch: a pelta-shaped brooch, having an ornamental form resembling a Roman shield.

periclinal fold: a type of fold similar to an anticline where the rocks are folded upwards, but plunging at each end.

periglacial: relating to very cold conditions.

plank and muntin screen: an internal partition composed of vertical studs grooved to accept boards.

platform cairn/embanked platform cairn: a low, flat-topped mound of earth and/or stone, sometimes with a bank encircling the top of the mound.

quatrefoil piercing: an aperture of an ornamental design of four lobes or leaves, resembling a flower or clover leaf.

quoin: an external angle or corner of a wall or building, often defined by a quoin stone.

reverberatory furnace: a furnace that is naturally aspirated, usually by the convection of hot gases in a chimney flue.

ring cairn: a circular bank of earth and/or stone defining a level central area.

round barrow: a circular mound of earth and/or stone (stone examples are often called cairns); the main period of construction occurred in the Early Bronze Age.

rusticated quoins: dressed stones at the angles of a building where the masonry has received an exaggerated treatment to give an effect of strength.

shippon: a cattle shelter, often open-fronted.

solar: a private upper chamber in a medieval house, often accessed from the high end of the hall.

Spanish medleys: cloth made of variegated wool.

spindle whorl: a whorl or small pulley used to weight a spindle.

staddle stone: a stone, typically formed of an upright with an overhanging top, supporting a framework or rick.

stadial: a period of lower temperatures during an interglacial (warm period) separating the glacial periods of an ice age.

stone cairn: *see* **round barrow**.

swallet: a natural depression or hole in the surface topography caused by the removal of bedrock, often through the action of water; also known as a sinkhole.

tie-beam: a horizontal beam connecting two rafters in a roof or roof truss.

toft: a house, especially a farmhouse, and outbuildings.

univallate: (of earthworks) comprising a single bank and ditch.

vase balusters: vertical supports, of vase form, for a handrail.

vertical cruciform window: a window with a single vertical and a single horizontal member separating window lights where the top lights are proportionally smaller than the bottom.

vertical-format windows: windows that are proportionally taller than they are wide.

wainhouse: a covered cart-store.

witan: an Anglo-Saxon national council or parliament. Also called a witenagemot.

REFERENCES

Acland, T D and Sturge, W 1851 *The Farming of Somersetshire*. London: John Murray

Alcock, N and Miles, D 2012 *The Medieval Peasant House in Midland England*. Oxford: Oxbow

Aldhouse-Green S, Pettitt, P and Stringer, C B 1996 'Holocene humans at Pontnewydd and Cae Gronw caves'. *Antiquity* **70**, 444–7

Allcroft, A H 1908 *Earthwork of England*. London: Macmillan

Allen, J R L 2001 'Sea level, salt marsh and fen: Shaping the Severn Estuary levels in the later Quaternary (Ipswichian-Holocene)', *in* Rippon, S (ed) *Estuarine Archaeology: The Severn and Beyond*. Archaeology in the Severn Estuary **11**. Bristol: Severn Estuary Levels Research Committee, 13–34

Andrews, P and Fernández-Jalvo, Y 2003 'Cannibalism in Britain: Taphonomy of the Creswellian (Pleistocene) faunal and human remains from Gough's Cave (Somerset, England)'. *Bull Natur Hist Mus (Geol)* **58** (suppl), 59–81

Andrews, P and Stringer, C 1999 'The palaeoecology of the faunas from Westbury Cave', *in* Andrews, P, *et al* (eds) *Westbury Cave: The Natural History Museum Excavations, 1976–1984*. Bristol: Western Academic & Specialist, 195–210

Anon 1936 'Tilly Manor'. *Proc Somerset Archaeol Natur Hist Soc* **82**, 45–6

ApSimon, A M 1951 'Gorsey Bigbury: The second report'. *Proc Univ Bristol Spelaeol Soc* **6** (2), 186–200

ApSimon, A M 1965 'The Roman temple on Brean Down, Somerset'. *Proc Univ Bristol Spelaeol Soc* **10** (3), 195–258

ApSimon, A M 1986 'Picken's Hole, Compton Bishop, Somerset: Early Devensian bear and wolf den, and Middle Devensian Hyaena Den and Palaeolithic site', *in* Collcutt, S N (ed) *The Palaeolithic of Britain and Its Nearest Neighbours: Recent Trends*. Sheffield: J R Collis, University of Sheffield, 55–6

ApSimon, A M 1997 'Bos Swallet, Burrington, Somerset: Boiling site and Beaker occupation site', *Proc Univ Bristol Spelaeol Soc* **21** (1), 43–82

ApSimon, A M, Donovan, D T and Taylor, H 1961 'The stratigraphy and archaeology of the late-glacial and post-glacial deposits at Brean Down, Somerset'. *Proc Univ Bristol Spelaeol Soc* **9** (2), 67–136

ApSimon, A M, *et al* 1976 'Gorsey Bigbury, Cheddar, Somerset: Radiocarbon dating, human and animal bones, charcoals, archaeological assessment'. *Proc Univ Bristol Spelaeol Soc* **14** (2), 155–83

Arnold, A and Howard, R 2011 *Warren Farm, Charterhouse, Priddy, Somerset: Scientific Dating Report*. English Heritage Research Department Report Series no. **25-2011**

Ashworth, H W 1970 'Report on Romano-British settlement and metallurgical site: Vespasian Farm, Green Ore, Wells, Somerset'. *Mendip Nature Res Comm J* **17**, 1–17

Ashworth, H W and Crampton, D M 1963 'Hole Ground, Wookey Hole'. *75–6th Annual Reports of the Wells Archaeological and Natural History Society for 1963–4*, 4–25

Aston, M 1988 'Land use and field systems', *in* Aston, M (ed) *Aspects of the Medieval Landscape of Somerset and Contributions to the Landscape History of the County*. Taunton: Somerset County Council, 82–97

Aston, M 1994 'Medieval settlement studies in Somerset', *in* Aston, M and Lewis, C (eds) *The Medieval Landscape of Wessex*. Oxford: Oxbow, 219–38

Aston, M 2003 'Early Monasteries in Somerset – Models and Agendas' *in* Ecclestone, M *et al* (eds) *The Land of the Dobunni*. King's Lynn, Norfolk: Heritage Marketing and Publications, 36–48

Aston, M and Bettey, J 1998 'The post-medieval rural landscape c 1540–1700: The drive for profit and the desire for status', *in* Everson, P and Williamson, T (eds) *The Archaeology of Landscape: Studies Presented to Christopher Taylor*. Manchester: Manchester University Press, 166–82

Aston, M and Burrow, I 1982 *The Archaeology of Somerset: A Review to 1500 AD*. Taunton: Somerset County Council

Aston, M and Costen, M 2008 'An early medieval secular and ecclesiastical estate: The origins of the parish of Winscombe in North Somerset'. *Proc Somerset Archaeol Natur Hist Soc* **151**, 139–57

Aston, M and Leech, P 1977 *Historic Towns in Somerset: Archaeology and Planning*. Committee for Rescue Archaeology in Avon, Gloucestershire and Somerset **2**. Bristol

Aston, M, Forbes, A and Hall, T 2011 'The Windscombe Project 2009'. *Proc Somerset Archaeol Natur Hist Soc* **153**, 167–9

Atthill, R 1976a 'Industry', *in* Atthill, R (ed) *Mendip: A New Study*. Newton Abbot: David & Charles, 145–79

Atthill, R 1976b 'Transport and communications', *in* Atthill, R (ed) *Mendip: A New Study*. Newton Abbot: David & Charles, 126–44

Atthill, R 1984 *Old Mendip*. Frome: Bran's Head

Audsley, A, *et al* 1988 'Charterhouse Warren Farm Swallet: Exploration, geomorphology, taphonomy and archaeology'. *Proc Univ Bristol Spelaeol Soc* **18** (2), 171–239

Bailey, M 2002 *The English Manor, c. 1200–c. 1500*. Manchester: Manchester University Press

Balch, H E 1914 *Wookey Hole and Its Caves and Cave Dwellers*. Oxford: Oxford University Press

Balch, H E 1926 'Excavations at Chelm's Combe, Cheddar'. *Proc Somerset Archaeol Natur Hist Soc* **72**, 97–124

Balch, H E 1928 'Excavations at Wookey Hole and other Mendip caves'. *Antiq J* **8** (2), 193–210

Balch, H E 1948 *Mendip: Its Swallet Caves and Rock Shelters*, 2 edn. Bristol: John Wright

Barber, M 2003 *Bronze and the Bronze Age: Metalwork and Society in Britain c 2500–800 BC*. Stroud: Tempus

Barker, H, Burleigh, R and Meeks, N 1971 'British Museum natural radiocarbon measurements VII'. *Radiocarbon* **13** (2), 157–88

Barlow, P 1967 'Interim report on a Romano-British site near Priddy', *77–8th Annual Reports of the Wells Archaeological and Natural History Society for 1965–6*, 7–11

Barrett, J C, Freeman, P W M, Woodward, A 2000 *Cadbury Castle Somerset: The Later Prehistoric and Early Historic Archaeology*. London: English Heritage

Barton, K J 1964 'Star Roman villa, Shipham, Somerset'. *Proc Somerset Archaeol Natur Hist Soc* **108**, 45–93

Barton, N 1997 *Book of Stone Age Britain*. London: B T Batsford

Barton, R N E, *et al* 1987 'Saye's Hole, Cheddar, Somerset: A new Late Iron Age site'. *Proc Univ Bristol Spelaeol Soc* **18** (1), 105–15

Batt, M 1975 'The Burghal Hidage, Axbridge'. *Proc Somerset Archaeol Natur Hist Soc* **119**, 22–5

Bax, S, *et al* 2010 *Stonehenge World Heritage Site Landscape Project: Winterbourne Stoke Crossroads*. English Heritage Research Department Report Series no. **107-2010**

Beachcroft, G and Sabin, A (eds) 1938 *Two Compotus Rolls of St Augustine's Abbey, Bristol, for 1491–2 and 1511–12*. Bristol Record Society **9**

Bell, M G 1990 *Brean Down Excavations, 1983–1987*. Archaeological Report **15**. London: English Heritage

Bello, S M, Parfitt, S A and Stringer, C B 2011 'Earliest directly-dated human skull-cups'. PLoS ONE **6** (2): e17026. doi:10.1371/journal.pone.0017026

Bettey, J H 1986 *Wessex from AD 1000*. London: Longman

Bettey, J 1988 'The church in the landscape, part 2: From the Norman Conquest to the Reformation', *in* M Aston, M (ed) *Aspects of the Medieval Landscape of Somerset and Contributions to the Landscape History of the County*. Taunton: Somerset County Council, 55–65

Billingsley, J 1797 *General View of the Agriculture in the County of Somerset*, 2 edn. Bath: R Cruttwell (printer)

Billingsley, J 1807 'An essay on waste lands'. *Letters of the Bath and West of England Agricultural Society* **11**, 2–93

Bishop, M J 1974 'A preliminary report on the Middle Pleistocene mammal bearing deposits of Westbury-sub-Mendip, Somerset'. *Proc Univ Bristol Spelaeol Soc* **13** (3), 301–18

Blair, J 1996 'Palaces or minsters? Northampton and Cheddar reconsidered'. *Anglo-Saxon Engl* **25**, 97–121

Blair, J 2005 *The Church in Anglo-Saxon Society*. Oxford: Oxford University Press

Bodman, M 1990 'Mills of the Upper Chew'. *Bristol Ind Archaeol Soc* **22**, 12–22

Bond, C J 1994 'Forests, chases, warrens and parks in medieval Wessex', *in* Aston, M and Lewis, C (eds) *The Medieval Landscape of Wessex*. Oxford: Oxbow, 115–56

Boon, G C 1950 'A Roman field-system at Charterhouse-upon-Mendip'. *Proc Univ Bristol Spelaeol Soc* **6**, 201–4

Bowden, M 2005 *The Malvern Hills: An Ancient Landscape*. Swindon: English Heritage

Bowden, M 2009 *Dolebury Hillfort, Churchill, North Somerset: Analytical Earthwork Survey*. English Heritage Research Department Report Series no. **59-2009**

Bowden, M and McOmish, D 1987 'The required barrier'. *Scott Archaeol Rev* **4**, 76–84

Bowden, M, Field, D and Soutar, S 2012 *Stonehenge World Heritage Site Landscape Project: Lake Barrows, The Diamond and Normanton Gorse*. English Heritage Research Department Report Series no. **29-2012**

Boycott, A and Wilson, L J 2010 'Contemporary accounts of the discovery of Aveline's Hole'. *Proc Univ Bristol Spelaeol Soc* **25** (1), 11–25

Boycott, A and Wilson, L J 2011 'In further pursuit of rabbits: Accounts of Aveline's Hole, 1799 to 1921'. *Proc Univ Bristol Spelaeol Soc* **25** (2), 187–232

Boyd Dawkins, W 1865 'On the caverns of Burrington Combe, explored in 1864, by Messers W Ashford Sandford, and W Boyd Dawkins'. *Proc Somerset Archaeol Natur Hist Soc for 1863–4* **12** (2), 161–76

Bradford, G (ed) 1911 *Proceedings in the Court of the Star Chamber in the Reigns of Henry VII and Henry VIII*. Somerset Record Society **27**. London

Bradley, R 1990 *The Passage of Arms: An Archaeological Analysis of Prehistoric Hoards and Votive Deposits*. Cambridge: Cambridge University Press

Bradley, R 1998 *The Significance of Monuments: On the Shaping of Human Experience in Neolithic and Bronze Age Europe*. London: Routledge

Bradley, R 2000 *An Archaeology of Natural Places*. London: Routledge

Bradley, R 2002 'The stone circles of north-east Scotland in the light of excavation'. *Antiquity* **76**, 840–8

Bradley, R 2007 *The Prehistory of Britain and Ireland*. Cambridge: Cambridge University Press

Branigan, K and Dearne, M J 1991 'Romano-British usage of the caves of Cheddar Gorge'. *Proc Univ Bristol Spelaeol Soc* **19** (1), 19–31

Brett, C 2007 *The Manors of Norton St Philip and Hinton Charterhouse, 1535–1691*. Somerset Record Society **93**. Taunton: Somerset Record Society

Bromwich, D 1971 'Axbridge mint'. *Axbridge Caving Group Archaeol Soc Newslet* June, 39

Brown, D 1999 *Somerset and Hitler: Secret Operations in the Mendips, 1939–1945*. Reading: Countryside

Brown, D 2011 'Mendip starfish', *in* Lewis, J (ed) *The Archaeology of Mendip*. Oxford: Heritage, 359–72

Brown, G 2008 *Dispersed Settlement on the Mendip Escarpment: The Earthwork Evidence*. English Heritage Research Department Report Series no. **72-2008**

Brown, G and Field, D 2007 'Training trenches on Salisbury Plain: Archaeological evidence for battle training in the Great War'. *Wiltshire Stud* **100**, 170–80

Brown, I 2008 *Beacons in the Landscape: The Hillforts of England and Wales*. Oxford: Windgather

Bryant, A 2011 'Iron Age cave use on Mendip: A re-evaluation', *in* Lewis, J (ed) *The Archaeology of Mendip: 500,000 Years of Continuity and Change*. Oxford: Heritage, 139–57

Buckland, W 1822 'Account of an assemblage of fossil teeth and bones of elephant, rhinoceros, hippopotamus, bear, tiger and hyaena, and sixteen other animals, discovered in a cave in Kirkdale, Yorkshire, in the year 1821: With a comparative view of five similar caverns in various parts of England, and others on the continent'. *Phil Trans Roy Soc* **225** (1), 171–236

Buckley, V 1990 (ed) *Burnt Offerings: International Contributions to Burnt Mound Archaeology*. Dublin: Wordwell

Budge, A R, Russell, J R and Boon, G C 1974 'Excavations and fieldwork at Charterhouse-on-Mendip, 1960–7'. *Proc Univ Bristol Spelaeol Soc* **13**, 327–47

Burgess, R L 1971 'Investigations in Ubley's rakes, Charterhouse-on-Mendip'. *Bristol Ind Archaeol Soc J*, 5–9

Burrow, I 1981 *Hillfort and Hill-Top Settlements in Somerset in the First to Eighth Centuries AD*. BAR Brit Ser **142**. Oxford: British Archaeological Reports

Cal Chart Rolls = Calendar of Charter Rolls, 6 vols. London: HMSO

Cal Close Rolls Hen III = Calendar of Close Rolls, Henry III, 15 vols. London: HMSO

Cal Close Rolls Ed 1 = Calendar of Close Rolls, Edward I, 4 vols. London: HMSO

Cal Pat Rolls Ed I = Calendar of Patent Rolls, Edward I, 4 vols. London: HMSO

Cal Wells MSS = Calendar of the Manuscripts of the Dean and Chapter of Wells, 2 vols. London: Historical Manuscripts Commission

Caley, J and Hunter, J (eds) 1814 *Valor Ecclesiasticus Temp. Henr. VIII Auctoritate Regia Institutus* vols **1** and **2**. London: Record Commission

Campbell, J B 1977 *The Upper Palaeolithic of Britain: A Study of Man and Nature in the Late Ice Age*. Oxford: Clarendon

Campbell, J, *et al* 1970 *The Mendip Hills in Prehistoric and Roman Times*. Bristol: Bristol Archaeological Research Group

Chadwyck Healey, C E H (ed) 1897 *Somersetshire Pleas, Rolls of the Itinerant Justices (Close of the 12th Century–41 Henry III)*. Somerset Record Society **11**

Chapman, E 1955 'Preliminary report on the excavation at Chapel Close, Winthill'. *J Axbridge Caving Group Archaeol Soc* **2** (4), 29–30

Charles, R 1989 'Incised ivory fragments and other late Upper Palaeolithic finds from Gough's Cave, Cheddar, Somerset'. *Proc Univ Bristol Spelaeol Soc* **18** (3), 400–8

Clarke, A G and Stanton, W I 1984 'Cornish miners at Charterhouse-on-Mendip'. *Proc Univ Bristol Spelaeol Soc* **17** (1), 29–54

Clarke, G T 1850 *Report to the General Board of Health on a Preliminary Inquiry into the Sewerage, Drainage, and Supply of Water, and the Sanitary Condition of the Inhabitants of the City and County of Bristol*. London: Her Majesty's Stationery Office

Clarke, R L 1969 'Christon'. *Search: J Banwell Soc Archaeol* **9**, 8–17

Clarke, R L 1970 'Christon'. *Search: J Banwell Soc Archaeol* **10**, 8–14

Clarke, R L 1973 'Christon'. *Search: J Banwell Soc Archaeol* **13**, 15–20

Cocroft, W and Thomas, J C 2003 *Cold War: Building for Nuclear Confrontation, 1946–1989*. Swindon: English Heritage

Coles, B and Coles, J 1986 *Sweet Track to Glastonbury: The Somerset Levels in Prehistory*. London: Thames and Hudson

Coles, J, Gestsdottir, H and Minnitt, S 2002 'A Bronze Age decorated cist from Pool Farm, West Harptree: New analyses'. *Proc Somerset Archaeol Natur Hist Soc* **144**, 25–30

Collinson, J 1791 *The History and Antiquities of the County of Somerset*. Vol **3**. Bath: Cruttwell (printer)

Conneller, C 2006 'Death', *in* Conneller, C and Warren, G (eds) *Mesolithic Britain and Ireland: New Approaches*. Stroud: Tempus, 139–64

Cook, J 1999 'Description and analysis of the flint finds from Westbury Cave', *in* Andrews, P, *et al* (eds) *Westbury Cave: The Natural History Museum Excavations, 1976–1984*. Bristol: Western Academic & Specialist, 211–74

Costen, M 1992 *The Origins of Somerset*. Manchester: Manchester University Press

Coward, H 1978 'The Manor of Hutton in 1309'. *Search: J Banwell Soc Archaeol* **14**, 33–50

Cox, E G H 1936 'Gourney Court'. *Proc Somerset Archaeol Natur Hist Soc* **82**, 40–5

Cox, J C and Greswell, W H P 1911 'Forestry', *in* Page, W (ed) *The Victoria History of the County of Somerset* **2**. London: Archibald Constable, 547–72

Crook, K M and Tratman, E K 1954 'Burledge Camp'. *Proc Univ Bristol Spelaeol Soc* **7** (1), 39–41

Cunliffe, B 1993 *Wessex to AD 1000*. London: Longman

Cunliffe, B 2003 *Danebury Hillfort*. Stroud: Tempus

Currant, A P, Jacobi, R M and Stringer, C B 1989 'Excavations at Gough's Cave, Somerset 1986–7'. *Antiquity* **63** (238), 131–6

Currant, A P, Jacobi, R M and Rhodes, E 2006 'A new look at the Pleistocene sequence at Brean Down, Somerset, and some observations on the earlier part of the last cold stage in western Mendip', *in* Hunt, C O and Haslett, S K (eds) *Quaternary of Somerset: Field Guide*. London: Quaternary Research Association, 25–30

Darvill, T 2010 'Neolithic round barrows on the Cotswolds', *in* Leary, J, Darvill, T and Field, D (eds) *Round Mounds and Monumentality in the British Neolithic and Beyond*. Oxford: Oxbow, 130–8

David, A, *et al* 2004 'A rival to Stonehenge? Geophysical survey at Stanton Drew, England'. *Antiquity* **78**, 341–58

Davies, J A 1921 'Aveline's Hole, Burrington Combe: An Upper Palaeolithic station'. *Proc Univ Bristol Spelaeol Soc* **1** (2), 61–72

Davies, J A 1922 'Second report on Aveline's Hole'. *Proc Univ Bristol Spelaeol Soc* **1** (3), 113–18

Davies, J A 1923 'Third report on Aveline's Hole'. *Proc Univ Bristol Spelaeol Soc* **2** (1), 5–15

Davies, J A 1925 'Fourth report on Aveline's Hole'. *Proc Univ Bristol Spelaeol Soc* **2** (2), 104–14

Dawkins, W B 1863 'Wookey Hole Hyena Den'. *Proc Somerset Archaeol Natur Hist Soc* **11** (2), 197–219

Dawkins, W B 1864 'On the caverns of Burrington Combe'. *Proc Somerset Archaeol Natur Hist Soc* **12**, 161–76

De Boise, A 2010 'Are bipartite cottages potential vestiges of twelfth-century buildings?' Unpublished research paper on findings from the Whittlewood Project on the Buckingham/Hampshire border

Defoe, D 1968 *A Tour thro' the Whole Island of Great Britain Divided into Circuits or Journies giving a Particular and Diverting Account of Whatever Is Curious and Worth Observation: Particular Fitted for the Reading of Such As Desire to Travel Over the Island*. London: Frank Cass (new impression of new edn)

Dennison, E and Russett, V 1989 'Duck decoys: Their function and management with reference to Nyland decoy, Cheddar'. *Proc Somerset Archaeol Natur Hist Soc* **133**, 141–56

Dickinson, F H 1889 *Kirby's Quest for Somerset*. Somerset Records Society **3**

Dobinson, C S 1996 *Twentieth Century Fortifications in England, Vol 3: Bombing Decoys of World War II: England's Passive Air Defences, 1939–45*. York: Council for British Archaeology

Dobinson, C 2000 *Fields of Deception: Britain's Bombing Decoys of World War II*. London: Methuen

Dobson, D P 1931 *The Archaeology of Somerset*. London: Methuen

Donovan, D T 1955 'The Pleistocene deposits at Gough's Cave, Cheddar, including an account of recent excavations'. *Proc Univ Bristol Spelaeol Soc* **7** (2), 76–104

Dowd, M A 2008 'The use of caves for funerary and ritual practices in Neolithic Ireland'. *Antiquity* **82**, 305–17

Dyer, C 1986 'English peasant buildings in the later Middle Ages (1200–1500)'. *Medieval Archaeol* **30**, 19–45

Dyer, C 1995 'Sheepcotes: Evidence for medieval sheep farming'. *Medieval Archaeol* **39**, 136–64

Dyer, C and Jones, R 2010 *Deserted Villages Revisited*. Hatfield: University of Hertfordshire Press

Dymond, C W 1883 'Dolebury and Cadbury'. *Proc Somerset Archaeol Natur Hist Soc* **29**, 104–16

Dymond, C W 1885 'Society excursion'. *Proc Somerset Archaeol Natur Hist Soc* **31**, 16–17

Dymond, C W 1902 *Worlebury: An Ancient Stronghold in the County of Somerset*. Bristol: W Crofton Hemmons

Ecclestone, M, *et al* (eds) 2003 *The Land of the Dobunni*. King's Lynn, Norfolk: Heritage Marketing

Eeles, F C 1929 'Church of Saint James, Windscombe'. *Proc Somerset Archaeol Natur Hist Soc* **75**, 41–5

Erskine, J 2007 'The West Wansdyke: An appraisal of the dating, dimensions and construction techniques in the light of excavated evidence'. *Archaeol J* **164**, 80–108

Evans, J 1980 'Banwell on show: Items at Woodspring Museum'. *Search: J Banwell Soc Archaeol* **16**, 47–52

Evans, J 1985 *Worlebury: The Story of the Iron Age Hill-Fort at Weston-super-Mare*. Woodspring: Woodspring Museum

Everton, A 1967 'Wookey, Ebbor Rocks'. *Archaeol Rev* **2**, Council for British Archaeology Group 13 (South-West), 23–4

Everton, A 1975 '23 West Street'. *Axbridge Caving Group Archaeol Soc Newslet* Dec

Everton, A 1978 'No. 26, High Street, Axbridge: The excavation'. *Axbridge Archaeol Local Hist Soc Newslet*, 6–18

Everton, A and Everton R 1972 'Hay Wood Cave burials, Mendip, Somerset'. *Proc Univ Bristol Spelaeol Soc* **13** (1), 5–29

Everton, A and Kirk, J 1982 'Notes on the excavations at 31 High Street Axbridge'. *Axbridge Archaeol Local Hist Soc Newslet* **64**, 4

Farrant, A 2008 *A Walker's Guide to the Geology and Landscape of Western Mendip*. Nottingham: British Geological Survey

Finberg, H P R 1964 *The Early Charters of Wessex*. Leicester: Leicester University Press

Findlay, D C 1965 *The Soils of the Mendip District of Somerset*. Harpenden: Agricultural Research Council

Firth, H and Faxon, K 2008 *Somerset Aggregates Lithics Assessment*. English Heritage Report **5285**

Fleming, A 1988 *The Dartmoor Reaves*. London: Batsford

Foyle, A and Pevsner, N 2011 *Somerset: North and Bristol*. Buildings of England. London: Yale University Press

Fradgley, N 1997 *Court Farmhouse, Wookey, Somerset*. NBR no. **45605**. English Heritage Archive

Fradley, M 2009 *Charterhouse, Somerset: The Development of a Romano-British Mining Settlement and Associated Landscape*. English Heritage Research Department Report Series no: **9-2009**

Garrod, D A E 1926 *The Upper Palaeolithic Age in Britain*. Oxford: Clarendon

Garwood, P 2007 'Before the hills in order stood: Chronology, time and history in the interpretation of Early Bronze Age round barrows', *in* Last, J (ed) *Beyond the Grave*. Oxford: Oxbow, 30–52

Gelling, M and Cole, A 2000 *The Landscape of Place-Names*. Stamford: Shaun Tyas

Gough, J W 1928 'The Witham Charterhouse on Mendip'. *Proc Somerset Archaeol Natur Hist Soc* **74**, 87–101

Gough, J W 1930 (repr 1967) *The Mines of Mendip*. Newton Abbot: David & Charles

Grant, R 1991 *The Royal Forests of England*. Stroud: Alan Sutton

Gray, H St G 1909 'Excavations at the "Amphitheatre", Charterhouse on Mendip, 1909'. *Proc Somerset Archaeol Natur Hist Soc* **55** (2), 118–37

Green, E 1892 *Feet of Fines for the County of Somerset, Richard I to Edward I*. Somerset Record Society **6**

Green, M 2000 *A Landscape Revealed: 10,000 Years on a Chalkland Farm*. Stroud: Tempus

Greswell, W H P 1905 *The Forests and Deer Parks of the County of Somerset*. Taunton: Barnicott & Pearce

Grinsell, L V 1957 'A decorated cist-slab from Mendip'. *Proc Prehist Soc*, **23**, 231–2

Grinsell, L V 1970 'The Mesolithic, Neolithic, and Bronze Age', *in* Campbell, J, *et al*, *The Mendip Hills in Prehistoric and Roman Times*. Bristol: Bristol Archaeological Research Group, 12–16

Grinsell, L V 1971 'Somerset barrows, part II: North and east'. *Proc Somerset Archaeol Natur Hist Soc* **115**, 44–132

Grundy, G B 1935 *The Saxon Charters and Field Names of Somerset*. Taunton: Somerset Archaeology and Natural History Society

Hack, B 1985 'Fieldwork notes of local interest: (1) sixteen stones above Cheddar Head'. *Search: J Banwell Soc Archaeol* **21**, 4–7

Hack, B 1987 'A Neolithic habitation site at Priddy Hill, Somerset'. *Search: J Banwell Soc Archaeol* **22**, 58–62

Haldane, J W 1969 'A gold bracelet from Hope Wood'. *Proc Somerset Archaeol Natur Hist Soc* **113**, 99–101

Hall, D 1995 *The Open Fields of Northamptonshire*. Northampton: Northampton Record Society

Hall, T 2003 'The reformation of the British church in the West Country in the 7th Century', *in* Ecclestone, M, *et al* (eds) *The Land of the Dobunni*. King's Lynn, Norfolk: Heritage Marketing, 49–55

Hansell, P and Hansell, J 1988 *Doves and Dovecotes*. Bath: Millstream

Hasler, J 1995 'Wookey Manor and parish, 1544–1841'. *Somerset Record Society* **83**. Taunton: Somerset Record Society

Hasler, J and Luker, B 1993 'The site of the bishop's palace, Wookey'. *Proc Somerset Archaeol Natur Hist Soc* **137**, 114

Hasler, J and Luker B 1997 *The Parish of Wookey: A New History*. Stroud: Wookey Local History Group

Haslett, S K, *et al* 2001 'The changing estuarine environment in relation to Holocene sea-level and the archaeological implications', *in* Rippon, S (ed) *Estuarine Archaeology: The Severn and Beyond*. Archaeology in the Severn Estuary **11**. Bristol: Severn Estuary Levels Research Committee, 35–54

Hassell, D and Wilson, Z 2005 *This Special Place: A History of St Michael's Home, Axbridge*. UK: White Space Design

Hawkes, C J 1968 *Archaeological Review* **3**. University of Bristol, Department of Extra Mural Studies, 20

Hawkes, C J and Jacobi, R M 1993 'Archaeological notes: Work at Hyaena Den, Wookey Hole'. *Proc Univ Bristol Spelaeol Soc* **19** (3), 369–71

Hawkes, C J, Tratman, E K and Powers, R 1970 'Decorated pieces of rib bone from the Palaeolithic levels at Gough's Cave, Cheddar, Somerset'. *Proc Univ Bristol Spelaeol Soc* **12** (2), 137–42

Hawkes, C J, Rogers, J M and Tratman, E K 1978 'Romano-British cemetery in the fourth chamber of Wookey Hole Cave, Somerset'. *Proc Univ Bristol Spelaeol Soc* **15** (1), 23–52

Hawkins, A B and Tratman, E K 1977 'The Quaternary deposits of the Mendip, Bath and Bristol areas, including a reprinting of Donovan's 1954 and 1964 bibliographies'. *Proc Univ Bristol Spelaeol Soc* **14** (3), 197–232

Hawtin, F 1970 'Industrial archaeology at Charterhouse-on-Mendip'. *Ind Archaeol: J Hist Ind Technol* **7**, 171–5

Helbaek, H. 1952 'Early crops in southern England'. *Proc Prehist Soc* **18**, 194–233

Herring, P 2003 'Cornish medieval deer parks', *in* Wilson-North, R (ed) *The Lie of the Land: Aspects of the Archaeology and History of the Designed Landscape in South West England*. Exeter: Mint

Hibbert, F A 1978 'The vegetational history of the Somerset Levels', *in* Limbrey, S and Evans, J G (eds) *The Effect of Man on the Landscape: The Lowland Zone*. Council for British Archaeology Research Report no. **21**, 90–5

Hirst, S M and Rahtz, P A 1973 'Cheddar vicarage, 1970'. *Proc Somerset Archaeol Natur Hist Soc* **117**, 65–96

Hoare, R C 1821 *The Ancient History of Wiltshire: Volume II (Part 2)*. London: William Miller

Hodder, M A and Barfield, L H (eds) 1991 *Burnt Mounds and Hot Stone Technology*. Sandwell: Sandwell Metropolitan Borough Council

Hollinrake, C and Hollinrake, N 1986 'Survey of Dolebury Hillfort and Dolebury Warren'. *Bristol & Avon Archaeol* **5**, 5–11

Hollinrake, C and Hollinrake, N 1997 'Old show ground evaluation'. Unpublished site report

Holmes, T S 1885 *The History of the Parish and Manor of Wookey, Being a Contribution Toward a Future History of the County of Somerset*. Bristol: T Jeffries

Hooke, D 2003 'Landscape studies', *in* Ecclestone, M, *et al* (eds) *The Land of the Dobunni*. King's Lynn, Norfolk: Heritage Marketing, 68–76

Horne, E 1931 'Excavation of Pool Farm barrow, West Harptree, Somerset'. *Proc Somerset Archaeol Natur Hist Soc* **76**, 85–90

Hoskins, W G 1953 'The rebuilding of rural England, 1570–1640', *Past & Present* **4** (1), 44–59

Humphrey, L T and Stringer, C B 2002 'The human cranial remains from Gough's Cave (Somerset, England)'. *Bull Natur Hist Mus (Geol)* **58** (2), 153–68

Hunt, J 1961a 'Banwell Camp: 1958 and 1959 excavation'. *Search: J Banwell Soc Archaeol* **1**, 9–23

Hunt, J 1961b 'Excavations at Winthill'. *Search: J Banwell Soc Archaeol* **1**, 26–34

Hunt, J 1962 'Banwell Camp: 1960 excavation of a possible hut site'. *Search: J Banwell Soc Archaeol* **2**, 11–19

Impey, E A 1999 'The seigneurial residence in Normandy, 1125–1225: An Anglo-Norman tradition?' *Medieval Archaeol* **43**, 45–73

Isles, R and Kidd, A 1987 'Avon archaeology, 1986–7'. *Bristol and Avon Archaeol* **6**, 44–56

Jacobi, R 2000 'The Late Pleistocene archaeology of Somerset', *in* Webster, C J (ed) *Somerset Archaeology: Papers to Mark 150 Years of the Somerset Archaeological and Natural History Society*. Taunton: Somerset County Council, 45–52

Jacobi, R M 2004 'The late Upper Palaeolithic lithic collection from Gough's Cave, Cheddar, Somerset, and human use of the cave'. *Proc Prehist Soc* **70**, 1–92

Jacobi, R M 2005 'Some observations on the lithic artefacts from Aveline's Hole, Burrington Combe, North Somerset'. *Proc Univ Bristol Spelaeol Soc* **23** (3), 267–95

Jacobi, R and Currant, A 2011 'The Late Pleistocene mammalian palaeontology and archaeology of Mendip', *in* Lewis, J (ed) *The Archaeology of Mendip: 500,000 Years of Continuity and Change*. Oxford: Heritage, 45–84

Jacobi, R M and Pettitt, P B 2000 'An Aurignacian point from Uphill Quarry (Somerset) and the earliest settlement of Britain by *Homo sapiens sapiens*'. *Antiquity* **74** (285), 513–18

Jacobi, R M, Higham, T F G and Ramsey, C 2006 'AMS radiocarbon dating of Middle and Upper Palaeolithic bone in the British Isles: Improved reliability using ultrafiltration'. *Journal of Quaternary Science* **21** (5), 557–73

Jamieson, E 2001 *Larkbarrow Farm, Exmoor, Somerset*. English Heritage Archaeological Investigation Report **AI/18/2001**

Jamieson, E 2006 *The Historic Environment of the Mendip Hills Area of Outstanding Natural Beauty: Project Design*. English Heritage Research Department

Jones, A 2005 *Cornish Bronze Age Ceremonial Landscapes, 2500–1500 BC*. BAR Brit Ser **394**. Oxford: British Archaeological Reports

Jones, F C 1946 *The Bristol Waterworks Company, 1846–1946*. Bristol: St Stephen's

Jones, J L 1972 'Farming under a Victorian roof: Eastwood Manor Farm, Somerset', *Country Life* 12 October, 919–20

Jones, S J 1935 'Note on excavations at Gorsey Bigbury, Charterhouse-on-Mendip, Somerset, 1931–1935'. *Proc Univ Bristol Spelaeol Soc* **4** (3), 174–8

Jones, S J 1938 'The excavation of Gorsey Bigbury'. *Proc Univ Bristol Spelaeol Soc* **5** (1), 3–56

Jordan, M 1994 *The Story of Compton Bishop and Cross*. Axbridge: privately published

Julleff, G 2000 'New radiocarbon dates for iron-working sites on Exmoor'. *HMS News: Newslet Hist Metall Soc* **44**, 3–4

Kelly, S E 2007 *Charters of Bath and Wells*. Oxford: Oxford University Press

Knight, F A 1902 *The Sea-Board of Mendip*. London: J M Dent

Knight, F A 1915 *The Heart of Mendip*. London: Dent

Last, J 2007 'Covering old ground: Barrows as closure', *in* Last, J (ed) *Beyond the Grave*. Oxford: Oxbow, 156–75

Lawton, R 1978 'Population and society, 1730–1900', *in* Dodgshon, R A and Butlin, R A (eds) *An Historical Geography of England and Wales*. London: Academic, 313–66

Leach, P 2001a *Excavation of a Romano-British Roadside Settlement in Somerset: Fosse Lane, Shepton Mallet, 1990*. London: Society for the Promotion of Roman Studies

Leach, P 2001b *Roman Somerset*. Wimborne: Dovecote

Leach, P 2007 'Archaeological Excavations in Beacon Wood'. Unpublished report

Leach, P 2009 'Prehistoric ritual landscapes and other remains at Field Farm, Shepton Mallet'. *Proc Somerset Archaeol Natur Hist Soc* **152**, 11–68

Leach, P and Watts, L 1996 *Henley Wood, Temples and Cemetery: Excavations 1962–1969 by the Late Ernest Greenfield and Others*. York: Council for British Archaeology

Leary, J and Pelling, R 2013 *Priddy Circle 1, Somerset: Archaeological Evaluation Report*. English Heritage

Leech, R 1986 'The excavation of a Romano-Celtic temple and a later cemetery on Lamyatt Beacon, Somerset'. *Britannia* **17**, 259–328

Levitan, B M and Smart, P L 1989 'Charterhouse Warren Farm Swallet, Mendip Somerset: Radiocarbon dating evidence'. *Proc Univ Bristol Spelaeol Soc* **18** (3), 390–4

Lewis, C, Mitchell-Fox, P and Dyer, C 2001 *Village, Hamlet and Field: Changing Medieval Settlements in Central England*. Macclesfield: Windgather

Lewis, J 1998 'The Everton flint collection in Wells Museum'. *Proc Univ Bristol Spelaeol Soc* **21** (2), 141–8

Lewis, J 2000 'Upwards at 45 degrees: The use of vertical caves during the Neolithic and Early Bronze Age on Mendip, Somerset'. *Capra* **2**

Lewis, J 2003 'Results of geophysical surveys at two barrow sites in Cheddar and Priddy parishes, Mendip'. *Proc Univ Bristol Spelaeol Soc* **23** (1), 9–15

Lewis, J 2005 *Monuments, Ritual and Regionality: The Neolithic of Northern Somerset*. BAR Brit Ser **401**. Oxford: Archaeopress

Lewis, J 2007 'The creation of round barrows on the Mendip Hills, Somerset', *in* Last, J (ed) *Beyond the Grave*. Oxford: Oxbow, 72–82

Lewis, J 2011 'On top of the world: Mesolithic and Neolithic use of the Mendip Hills', *in* Lewis, J (ed) *The Archaeology of Mendip: 500,000 Years of Continuity and Change*. Oxford: Heritage, 93–117

Lewis, J and Mullin, D 2001 'The Middle Down Drove Project: Fieldwalking, test pitting and excavation, Cheddar, Somerset, 1997–9'. *Proc Univ Bristol Spelaeol Soc* **22** (2), 203–23

Lewis, J and Mullin, D 2011 'New excavations at Priddy Circle 1, Mendip Hills, Somerset'. *Proc Univ Bristol Spelaeol Soc* **25** (2), 133–63

Linington, R E and Rogers, G B 1957 'The Locking Roman site'. *Locking Review*, 17–19

Macklin, M G, Bradley, S B and Hunt, C O 1985 'Early mining in Britain: The stratigraphic implications of heavy metals in alluvial sediments', *in* Fieller, N R J, Gilbertson, D D and Ralph, N G A (eds) *Palaeoenvironmental Investigations: Research Design. Methods and Interpretation*. BAR Int Ser **258**. Oxford: British Archaeological Reports, 40–54

Macphail, R I and Goldberg, P 1999 'The soil micromorphological investigation of Westbury Cave', *in* Andrews, P. *et al* (eds) *Westbury Cave: The Natural History Museum Excavations, 1976–1984*. Bristol: Western Academic & Specialist, 59–86

Marshall, S 2006 *Mendip Hospital: An Appreciation*. Ely: Melrose

Mason, E J 1953 'Romano-British smelting site at Priddy, Somerset'. *Belfry Bull, Bristol Explor Club* **70**, 1–4

McBurney, C B M 1961 'Two soundings in the Badger Hole near Wookey Hole, in 1958, and their bearing on the Palaeolithic finds of the late H.E. Balch'. *Seventy-First and Seventy-Second Annual Reports of the Wells Natural History and Archaeology Society for 1959–1960*, 19–27

McDermott, M 2006 'The Somerset Dendrochronology Project: Phases 5 and 6'. *Proc Somerset Archaeol Natur Hist Soc* **149**, 89–96

McDonnell, R R J 1984 'Duck decoys in Somerset: A gazetteer'. *Proc Somerset Archaeol Natur Hist Soc* **128**, 25–30

McOmish, D 2005 'Bronze Age land allotment on the Marlborough Downs', *in* Brown, G, Field, D and McOmish, D (eds) *The Avebury Landscape: Aspects of the Field Archaeology of the Marlborough Downs*. Oxford: Oxbow, 133–6

McOmish, D, Field, D and Brown, G 2002 *The Field Archaeology of the Salisbury Plain Training Area*. Swindon: English Heritage

Miles, D H and Worthington, M J 1999 'Somerset Dendrochronology Project phase three'. *Vernacular Architect* **30**, 111

Millet, M 1990 *The Romanisation of Britain: An Essay in Archaeological Interpretation*. Cambridge: Cambridge University Press

Mills, A D 1991 *A Dictionary of English Place Names*. Oxford: Oxford University Press

Minnitt, S 2008 'The Shepton Mallet amulet'. *Archaeol South West* **22**, 32

Minnitt, S and Payne, N 2012 'Hoard of Middle Bronze Age gold ornaments from Priddy, Somerset', *in* Trigg, JR (ed) *Of Things Gone But Not Forgotten*. British Archaeological Reports, International Series. Oxford: Archaeopress, 109–14

Morris, C 1947 *The Journeys of Celia Fiennes*. London: Cresset

Morris, E L 1988 'Iron Age occupation at Dibble's Farm'. *Proc Somerset Archaeol Natur Hist Soc* **132**, 23–81

Neal, F 1976 'Saxon and medieval landscapes', *in* Atthill, R (ed) *Mendip: A New Study*. Newton Abbot: David & Charles

Nott, A G W 1996 'The park of the Bishop of Bath and Wells at Westbury, Somerset'. Unpublished MA thesis, University of Bristol

Osborne, P 2008 'A Carthusian grange at Green Ore on Mendip'. *Proc Somerset Archaeol Natur Hist Soc* **151**, 181–2

Oswald, A 1997 'A doorway on the past: Practical and mystic concerns in the orientation of roundhouse doorways', *in* Gwilt, A and Haselgrove, C (eds) *Reconstructing Iron Age Societies: New Approaches to the British Iron Age*. Oxford: Oxbow, 87–95

Palmer, L S and Ashworth, H W W 1958 'Four Roman pigs of lead'. *Proc Somerset Archaeol Natur Hist Soc* **101**, 52–88

Parker Pearson, M 1993 *Bronze Age Britain*. London: B T Batsford

Parkin, R A, Rowley-Conwy, P and Serjeantson, D 1986 'Late Palaeolithic exploitation of horse and red deer at Gough's Cave, Cheddar, Somerset'. *Proc Univ Bristol Spelaeol Soc* **17** (3), 311–30

Parry, R F 1931 'Excavations at Cheddar'. *Proc Somerset Archaeol Natur Hist Soc* **76** (2), 46–62

Pattison, P 1991 'Settlement and landscape at Ramspits, Deer Leap, Westbury-sub-Mendip: A new survey by the Royal Commission on the Historical Monuments of England'. *Proc Somerset Archaeol Natur Hist Soc* **135**, 95–106

Payne, N 2003 'The medieval residences of the Bishop of Bath and Wells, and Salisbury'. Unpublished PhD thesis, University of Bristol

Penoyre, J 1998 'Medieval Somerset roofs'. *Proc Somerset Archaeol Natur Hist Soc* **141**, 76–89

Penoyre, J 2005 *Traditional Houses of Somerset*. Tiverton: Somerset

Penoyre, J and Penoyre, J 1999 'Somerset Dendrochronology Project, phase 3'. *Proc Somerset Archaeol Natur Hist Soc* **142**, 311–15

Pevsner, N 1958. *The Buildings of England: North Somerset and Bristol* (repr. Harmondsworth: Penguin 1990)

Phelps, W 1836 *The History and Antiquities of Somersetshire*. London: Nichols

Phillips, C W and Taylor, H 1972 'The Priddy Long Barrow, Mendip Hills, Somerset'. *Proc Univ Bristol Spelaeol Soc* **13** (1), 31–6

Pitts, M 1978 'Footprints on the sands of time'. *Antiquity* **52**, 60

Pollard, J 2005 'Memory, monuments and middens in the Neolithic landscape', *in* Brown, G, Field, D and McOmish, D (eds) *The Avebury Landscape: Aspects of the Field Archaeology of the Marlborough Downs*. Oxford: Oxbow, 103–14

Powlesland, I 2009 *The Later Prehistoric Landscape of the Bristol Avon Region*. Oxford: Archaeopress

Priest, R and Dickson, A 2009 *Archaeological Aerial Survey in the Northern Mendip Hills: A Highlight Report for the National Mapping Programme*. English Heritage Research Report

Proctor, C J, *et al* 1996 'A report on the excavations at Rhinoceros Hole, Wookey'. *Proc Univ Bristol Spelaeol Soc* **20** (3), 237–62

Rackham, O 1986 *The History of the Countryside*. London: Dent

Rackham, O 1988 'Woods, hedges and forests', *in* Aston, M (ed) *Aspects of the Medieval Landscape of Somerset and Contributions to the Landscape History of the County*. Taunton: Somerset County Council, 13–31

Rahtz, P A 1979 *The Saxon and Medieval Palaces at Cheddar*. BAR Brit Ser **65**. Oxford: British Archaeological Reports

Rahtz, P A and Greenfield, E 1977 *Excavations at Chew Valley Lake, Somerset*. London: Her Majesty's Stationery Office

Rahtz, P and Watts, L 1991 'Pagans Hill revisited'. *Archaeol J* **146**, 330–71

Rahtz, P, *et al* 1992 *Cadbury Congresbury, 1968–1973: A Late-Post-Roman Hilltop Settlement in Somerset*. Oxford: Tempus Reparatum

Rahtz, P, Hirst, S and Wright, S M 2000 *Cannington Cemetery: Excavations, 1962–3, of Prehistoric, Roman, Post-Roman, and Later Features at Cannington Park Quarry, near Bridgewater, Somerset.* London: Society for the Promotion of Roman Studies

Raistrick, A and Roberts, A 1990 *Life and Work of the Northern Lead Miner.* Stroud: Alan Sutton

Rattue, J 1995 *The Living Stream: Holy Wells in Historical Context.* Woodbridge: Boydell

Read, R F 1923 'Report on the excavation of Mendip barrows during 1923'. *Proc Univ Bristol Spelaeol Soc* **1** (2), 65–73

Read, R F 1924 'Second report on the excavation of Mendip barrows'. *Proc Univ Bristol Spelaeol Soc* **2** (2), 132–46

Reid, R D 1979 *Some Buildings of Mendip.* Bristol: Mendip Society

Reimer, P J, *et al* 2013 'IntCal13 and Marine13 radiocarbon age calibration curves 0–50,000 years cal BP', *Radiocarbon* **55**, 1869–87

Richardson, A 2007 '"The king's chief delights": A landscape approach to the royal parks of post-Conquest England', *in* Liddiard, R (ed) *The Medieval Park: New Perspectives.* Macclesfield: Windgather, 27–48

Richardson, M 1998 *An Archaeological Assessment of Axbridge.* English Heritage Extensive Urban Survey

Riley, H 2006 *The Historic Landscape of the Quantock Hills.* Swindon: English Heritage

Riley, H and Wilson-North, R 2001 *The Field Archaeology of Exmoor.* Swindon: English Heritage

Rippon, S 2006 *Landscape, Community and Colonisation: The North Somerset Levels during the 1st and 2nd Millennia AD.* York: Council for British Archaeology

Rodwell, W 2001 *Wells Cathedral: Excavations and Structural Studies, 1978–93* **1**. London: English Heritage

Ross, L (ed) 2004 *Before the Lake: Memories of the Chew Valley.* Harptree History Society

Russell, M and Williams, D 1998 'Petrological examination and comparison of Beaker pottery from Bos Swallet and Gorsey Bigbury'. *Proc Univ Bristol Spelaeol Soc* **21** (2), 133–40

Rutter, J 1829 *Delineations of the North Western Division of the County of Somerset and of Its Antediluvian Bone Caverns, with a Geological Sketch of the District.* Shaftesbury: privately printed

Rye, G P 1968 *Roman Villa at Banwell.* Weston-super-Mare: Weston-super-Mare Public Library and Museum

Savage, W G 1915 *Rural Housing.* London: T Fisher Unwin

Sawyer, P H 1968 *Anglo-Saxon Charters: An Annotated List and Bibliography.* Royal Historical Society Guides and Handbooks **8**. London: Offices of the Royal Hist Soc

Scarth, H M 1874 'Roman remains found in (Somerset)'. *Proc Soc Antiq London* 2nd ser **6**, 187–91

Schofield, A J, Webster, C J and Anderton, M J 1999 'Second World War remains on Black Down: A re-interpretation'. *Somerset Archaeol Natur Hist Soc* **142**, 271–86

Schulting, R J 2005 '"… Pursuing a rabbit in Burrington Combe": New research on the early Mesolithic burial cave of Aveline's Hole'. *Proc Univ Bristol Spelaeol Soc* **23** (3), 171–265

Schulting, R J, *et al* 2010 'The Mesolithic and Neolithic human bone assemblage from Totty Pot, Cheddar, Somerset'. *Proc Univ Bristol Spelaeol Soc* **25** (1), 75–95

Shackleton, N J and Opdyke, N D 1973 'Oxygen isotope and paleomagnetic stratigraphy of equatorial Pacific Core V28-238: Oxygen isotope temperatures and ice volume on a 105 year and 106 year scale'. *Quaternary Research* **3**, 39–55

Shaw, T R 1987 'Oluf Borch at Wookey Hole in 1663 and his ideas on speleothem formation'. *Proc Univ Bristol Spelaeol Soc* **18** (1), 65–71

Sheridan, A, *et al* 2010 'The Breamore jadeitite axehead and other Neolithic axeheads of Alpine rock from central southern England'. *Wiltshire Archaeol Natur Hist Mag* **103**, 16–34

Smith, H, Marshall, P and Parker Pearson, M 2001 'Reconstructing house activity areas', *in* Albarella, U (ed) *Environmental Archaeology: Meaning and Purpose.* Dordrecht: Kluwer Academic, 249–70

Smith, N 1999 'Burnt mounds of the New Forest'. *Northern Archaeol* **17/18**, 41–7

Smith, R M 1978 'Population and its geography in England, 1500–1730', *in* Dodgshon, R A and Butlin, R A (eds) *An Historical Geography of England and Wales.* London: Academic, 151–79

Somerset Vernacular Building Research Group 2008 *Somerset Villages: Combe Nicholas. An Examination of Fifty of the Traditional Houses and Farms in the Parish.* Somerset: Somerset Vernacular Building Research Group

Somerset Vernacular Building Research Group 2012 'Building recording in 2011'. *Proc Somerset Archaeol Natur Hist Soc* **155**, 221

Stanton, G R 1944 'A cinerary urn, found near Charterhouse on Mendip'. *Proc Univ Bristol Spelaeol Soc* **5** (2), 148

Stanton, W I 1981 'Archaeological notes: The Deer Leap Stones, Ebbor, Mendip'. *Proc Univ Bristol Spelaeol Soc* **16** (1), 63–70

Stanton, W I 1989 'Beaker Age deposits on Mendip at Charterhouse Warren Farm Swallet and Bos Swallet'. *Proc Univ Bristol Spelaeol Soc* **18** (3), 395–9

Stocker, D and Everson, P 2006 *Summoning St. Michael: Early Romanesque Towers in Lincolnshire.* Oxford: Oxbow

Stocker, D and Stocker, M 1996 'Sacred profanity: The theology of rabbit breeding and the symbolic landscape of the warren'. *World Archaeol* **28** (2), 265–72

Summerson, J 1977 *Architecture in Britain, 1530 to 1830.* Harmondsworth: Penguin

Sykes, N J 2007 'Animal bones and animal parks', *in* Liddiard, R (ed) *The Medieval Deer Park: New Perspectives.* Macclesfield: Windgather, 49–62

Sylverton, H 1956 'Preliminary report on the Shute Shelve excavations'. *Proc Axbridge Caving Archaeol Soc*, 5–7

Tabrett, I 1969 'Winthill excavation'. *Search: J Banwell Soc Archaeol* **9**, 21–6

Taylor, H 1923 'Third report on Rowberrow Cavern'. *Proc Univ Bristol Spelaeol Soc* **2** (1), 40–50

Taylor, H 1926 'Third report on the excavation of Mendip barrows'. *Proc Univ Bristol Spelaeol Soc* **3** (2), 211–15

Taylor, H 1933 'The Tynings barrow group: Second report'. *Proc Univ Bristol Spelaeol Soc* **2** (4), 67–127

Taylor, H 1951 'The Tynings Farm barrow group: Third report'. *Proc Univ Bristol Spelaeol Soc* **6** (2), 111–73

Taylor, J J 2001 'A burnt Mesolithic hunting camp on the Mendips: A preliminary report on structural traces excavated on Lower Pits Farm, Priddy, Somerset', *in* Milliken, S and Cook, J (eds) *A Very Remote Period Indeed: Papers on the Palaeolithic Presented to Derek Roe.* Oxford: Oxbow, 260–70

Taylor, J and Tratman, E K 1957 'The Priddy Circles preliminary report'. *Proc Univ Bristol Spelaeol Soc* **8** (1), 7–17

Thomas, R J C 2003 'Twentieth century military recording project: Prisoner of war camps (1939–1948)'. Unpublished report

Thompson, A 2010a 'Blacklands and adjacent fields, Priddy, Somerset: An archaeological geophysical survey by ALERT'. Report no. **11**

Thompson, A 2010b 'Underbarrow and Eastwater farms, Priddy, Somerset: An archaeological geophysical survey by ALERT'. Report no. **12**

Thompson, A 2011 'Praedium on Mendip?', *in* Lewis, J (ed) *The Archaeology of Mendip*. Oxford: Heritage, 201–56

Thompson, E M 1930 *The Carthusian Order in England*. London: Society for Promoting Christian Knowledge

Thorn, C and Thorn, F 1980 *Domesday Book: 8, Somerset*. Chichester: Philimore

Thurnam, R 1899 'The open-air treatment on the Mendips: First results of Nordrach treatment in England', *in* Morris, M (ed) *The Practitioner: A Journal of Practical Medicine and Surgery*, old series vol LXIII, new series vol X, July to December. London: Cassell

Todd, M 1993 'Charterhouse on Mendip: An interim report on survey and excavation in 1993'. *Proc Somerset Archaeol Natur Hist Soc* **137**, 59–68

Todd, M. 2003 'Roman pottery from the Charterhouse Valley'. *Proc Somerset Archaeol Natur Hist Soc* **147**, 185–6

Todd, M 2007 *Roman Mining in Somerset: Charterhouse-on-Mendip: Excavations, 1993–5*. Exeter: Mint

Tofts, S 2008 'Is this a deserted medieval village? Investigations of features in Lower Cowleaze, Charterhouse-on-Mendip'. Unpublished BA thesis, University of Bristol

Toulmin Smith, L 1964 *The Itinerary of John Leland on or about the Years 1535–1543, Parts I to III. Volume I*. London: Centaur

Tratman, E K 1926 'Fieldwork'. *Proc Univ Bristol Spelaeol Soc* **3** (1), 29–40

Tratman, E K 1927 'Field Work, 1926' [Somerset and Gloucestershire]. *Proc Univ Bristol Spelaeol Soc* **3** (1), 25–47

Tratman, E K 1935 'Field Work, 1933' [Somerset]. *Proc Univ Bristol Spelaeol Soc* **4** (3), 250–60

Tratman, E K 1958 'Archaeological notes: Another henge monument on Mendip'. *Proc Univ Bristol Spelaeol Soc* **8** (2), 124–5

Tratman, E K 1963 'Archaeological notes: Burrington Camp'. *Proc Univ Bristol Spelaeol Soc* **10** (1), 16–21

Tratman, E K 1964 'Picken's Hole, Crook Peak, Somerset: A Pleistocene site: Preliminary notes'. *Proc Univ Bristol Spelaeol Soc* **10** (2), 112–15

Tratman, E K 1966 'Gorsey Bigbury, Charterhouse-on-Mendip, Somerset: The third report'. *Proc Univ Bristol Spelaeol Soc* **11** (1), 25–30

Tratman, E K 1967 'The Priddy Circles, Mendip, Somerset: Henge monuments'. *Proc Univ Bristol Spelaeol Soc* **11** (2), 97–125

Tratman, E K 1968 'Archaeological notes: The Deer Leap Stones [Mendip]'. *Proc Univ Bristol Spelaeol Soc* **11** (3), 243–4

Tratman, E K and Henderson, G T D 1928 'First report on the excavations at Sun Hole, Cheddar: Levels from above the Pleistocene'. *Proc Univ Bristol Spelaeol Soc* **3** (2), 84–97

Tratman, E K, Donovan, D T and Campbell, J B 1971 'The Hyaena Den (Wookey Hole), Mendip Hills, Somerset'. *Proc Univ Bristol Spelaeol Soc* **12** (3), 369–71

Truscoe, K 2008 *The Aggregate Landscape of Somerset: Predicting the Archaeological Resource: Archaeological Aerial Survey in the Central Mendip Hills*. English Heritage Report

VCH 1906 *The Victoria History of the County of Somerset* **1**, ed. W Page. London: James Street

Waldron, C 1875 'Roman mining on the Mendip Hills'. *Trans Cardiff Natur Soc*, 1–5

Webster, C 2000 'The Dark Ages', *in* Webster, C J (ed) *Somerset Archaeology: Papers to Mark 150 Years of the Somerset Archaeological and Natural History Society*. Taunton: Somerset County Council, 45–52

Williams, D 1829 *Some Account of the Fissures and Caverns Hitherto Discovered in the Western District of the Mendip Range of Hills, Comprised in a Letter from the Rev. D Williams to the Rev. W Patterson*. Shaftsbury: John Rutter

Williams, E H D 1976 'Vernacular architecture', *in* Aston, M (ed) 'Somerset archaeology, 1974–75'. *Proc Somerset Archaeol Natur Hist Soc* **120**, 78

Williams, E H D 1991 'The building materials of Somerset's vernacular houses'. *Proc Somerset Archaeol Natur Hist Soc* **135**, 123–34

Williams, E H D 1992 'Church houses in Somerset'. *Vernacular Architect* **23**, 15

Williams, G 1988 *The Standing Stones of Wales and South-West England*. BAR Brit Ser **197**. Oxford: British Archaeological Reports

Williams, M 1970 *The Draining of the Somerset Levels*. London: Cambridge University Press

Williams, M 1971 'The Enclosure and Reclamation of the Mendip Hills, 1770–1870'. *Agr Hist Rev* **19** (1), 65–81

Williams, M 1972 'The enclosure of waste land in Somerset, 1700–1900'. *Trans Inst Brit Geogr* **57**, 99–123

Williams, M 1976 'Mendip farming: The last three centuries', *in* Atthill, R (ed) *Mendip: A New Study*. Newton Abbot: David & Charles, 102–25

Williams, R 1987 'Camps and caves at Dolebury, Burrington and Elm'. *Proc Univ Bristol Spelaeol Soc* **18** (1), 61

Williams, R G J 1999 'The St. Cuthbert's Roman mining settlement, Priddy, Somerset: Aerial photographic recognition'. *Proc Univ Bristol Spelaeol Soc* **21** (2), 123–32

Williamson, T 1997 'Fish, fur and feather: Man and nature in the post-medieval landscape', *in* Barker, K and Darvill, T (eds) *Making English Landscapes*. Oxbow Monograph **93**. Oxford: Oxbow, 92–177

Williamson, T 2007 *Rabbits, Warrens and Archaeology*. Stroud: Tempus

Winter, B 2007 'World War I and Blagdon'. *A History of Blagdon* **4**, 9–25

Woodland, W 2008 'Beacon Hill pollen assessment'. University of the West of England, Bristol. Unpublished report

Woof, P 2002 *Dorothy Wordsworth: The Grasmere and Alfoxden Journals*. Oxford: Oxford University Press

Wrightson, K 2002 *English Society, 1580–1680*. Abingdon: Routledge

Wroughton, J 1999 *An Unhappy Civil War*. Bath: Lansdown

Yates, D T 2007 *Land, Power and Prestige: Bronze Age Field Systems in Southern England*. Oxford: Oxbow

Yorke, B 1995 *Wessex in the Early Middle Ages*. Leicester: Leicester University Press

Young, D E Y 2008 'Iron Age, medieval and recent activity at Whitegate Farm, Bleadon, North Somerset'. *Proc Somerset Archaeol Natur Hist Soc* **151**, 31–81

INDEX

16th to 18th centuries 218–25,
219–24
18th and 19th centuries
226–32, **228–31**, 247, **250**
see also model farms
faunal remains
Palaeolithic **22**, 23, 24–6, **24**,
27, 30, 31
Iron Age 78–9
see also bone and antler objects
Fernhill Farm 34, 231–2, 258
field systems
later prehistoric 73, 79–84,
79–80, **82–3**, 270
Romano-British 109
medieval *see* common fields
Fiennes, Celia 1, 12
fire beacons 61
First World War 258, 259–62,
260–2, 271
fish ponds, later medieval 133–4,
134, 136, 141, 143, 145
FitzMartin family 131–2, 169
FitzWilliam, William 145
Flagstaff Hill 16
field system 80, 81, **83**, 270
see also Christon
flat axes, Early Bronze Age 57
Flaxley Abbey (Gloucestershire)
132
flint tools *see* stone and flint tools
forest law 132, 133
Forestry Commission 10, 258
forests *see* royal forest of Mendip;
woodland and forest
forts, Roman, Charterhouse-on-
Mendip 17, 90, 106–7, **106–7**,
109, 112, **116**, 270
Fosse Lane, Romano-British and
later settlement 113, 118,
120, 122, 123
Fosse Way 105, 107, 108
Four Barrows group 70
French Revolutionary and
Napoleonic Wars 193, 230
Frome, cloth production 237
fulling mills 237

G

geology 5–8, **5**
GHQ Green Stop Line 262
Gilling, Thomas 238
Glastonbury Abbey, estates 124,
126, 127
Gloucestershire County Council
Archaeological Service 21
Godwin, Thomas, Bishop of Bath
and Wells 194–5
Goldcliff Priory (Newport,
Monmouthshire) 132, 189
Golds Cross, Roman villa 109
Gorsey Bigbury, henge monument
46–7, **47**, 50, 51, **51**, **55**,
58, 270

excavations and finds from 15,
16, 51, 55–6, **56**, 57
Gough's Cave **28**, 29, 30–2, **30–2**,
34, 35, 270, **272**
Gough's Old Cave 108
Goundenham, John and
Agness 173
Gournay, de, family 135
Gournay Court *see* West Harptree
graves *see* burials and graves
Gray, Harold St George 14–15
'great rebuilding' 208
Green, Samuel 143
green-edge settlements 164
Green Hill, standing stone 53,
54, 270
Green Ore
estate of Hinton Charterhouse
126, 143–4, **144**, 164
sheepcote 190, 223
long barrow 41–2
mineral extraction
Romano-British 107, 112,
113, **113**, 114, 115
post-medieval 238, 248
place names 126
in Second World War 267
see also Hill Grove; Rookery
Farm
Greenfield, Ernest 16
Grinsell, Leslie 15–16
Gumm, Charles 238

H

Hack, B 17
haematite extraction, Romano-
British 115
Hale Combe, Romano-British
finds from near 108
halls
Cheddar royal palace 130
later medieval open halls 134,
134, 141, 178, 179, **180**,
181, 182
Bickfield (Moat Farm)
138–9, **138–9**
post-medieval 194, 196, **196**,
208–11, 212–13, 216
insertion of ceilings 162,
184–5, **185**, 194, 208, **209**
Ham Hill 94, 106
hamlets, settlement forms 164,
166–7
Harptree
place name 124
see also East Harptree; West
Harptree
Harptree, de, family 135, 169
Harptree Combe
aqueduct 251, **251**
calamine industry 241
natural environment 4
Harptree History Society 17
Harptree Minery 238

Haskins, Susan and Robert 247
Havyatt Farm, enclosure 85, **86**
Hawksley, T & C 252
Hay Wood Cave 41, 45–6, 270
Haydon Drove, long barrow
42, 44
Hazel Wood, place name 125
health, institutions devoted to
251, 253–7, **255–7**
henge monuments, Neolithic **41**,
46–51, **47–51**, **61**, 270
see also Gorsey Bigbury; Priddy
Circles
Henley Wood
Romano-British and later
cemetery 122, 123
Romano-Celtic temple 119
Herriott's Bridge
penknife points from 32
Romano-British site 108, 109,
115, 119, 126
Higher Pits Farm (near Ebbor
Rocks) 241–2, **242**, 271
Hill Grove (formerly Pen Hill
House), Mendip Hills
Sanatorium 257
hill-slope enclosures 86–7, 93, 95,
270
hillforts 73, 87, 94–104, **94**,
96–104, 270
reuse in post-Roman period
122–4
Hinton Blewett **3**
church 159
Church Cottage 161, 162, **162**,
184, 193
deer park 148
natural environment 12
settlement expansion 166
Hinton Charterhouse, estates
143–4, 173
see also Green Ore, estate of
Hinton Charterhouse
hoards
Middle and Late Bronze Age **74**,
75–6, **76**
Romano-British coin hoards
112, 113, 118
Hoare, Sir Richard Colt 13, 14
Hodgkinson, William Sampson
238
Home Guard 262, 266
Hope, abandoned farmsteads
168–9, **170**, 173, **177**, 178,
190, 271
Hope Wood, Easton, bracelet
from 75
Horrington
Anglo-Saxon estate 127
see also West Horrington
Horrington Hill, hoard from
75–6, **76**
horses
in First World War 260

in lead working industry, horse
whims and horse engines 244
hospitals *see* asylums; sanatoria
house plans
three-unit houses 182, 185,
208, 212–15, **213–14**, 220
two-unit houses **180–1**, 181–2,
185, 208–12, **212**, 216, 247
houses and housing
later medieval, village houses,
architectural evidence 166,
178–85, **179–85**
post-medieval, rural housing,
16th and 17th centuries
208–16, **209–15**, **217–18**
20th century 259
see also cottages; farmsteads;
halls; house plans;
longhouses; manor houses;
warreners' lodges
human remains
Palaeolithic 26, 31–2, **32**
Mesolithic 30, 35–6
Neolithic 40, 43, 45–6, 51–2, 55
see also burials and graves;
cemeteries; cremation
Hunters Lodge
disc/bell barrow **61**, 70, **70**, 270
henge monument 46–7, **47**, 50,
51, **61**, 270
natural environment 11
hunting
Anglo-Saxon 128
later medieval 145–9
see also parks; royal forest of
Mendip
Hurle, Gertrude 215
Hutton **3**
Anglo-Saxon estate 127
church 153, 159
enclosure 186, 225
Hutton Court 194, **194**
mining 241
natural environment 11, 12
see also Elborough Hill; Ludwell
Farm
Hyaena Den 13, 14, 15, **25–6**,
25–6, 27, 28–9, **28**
Hydon *see* Charterhouse-on-
Mendip
Hye, Isabelle ate 173
Hythe, port 162
Hythe Lane, duck decoy 202

I

Ilchester, Roman town and fort
106, 109, 120
improvement, agricultural
16th to early 18th centuries
207–8
18th and 19th centuries 193,
225–36, 249–50
see also limekilns; model farms
industrial activities